AF715591

Hans Abbing

The Changing Social Economy of Art

Are the Arts Becoming Less Exclusive?

palgrave
macmillan

Hans Abbing
Amsterdam, Noord-Holland, The Netherlands

ISBN 978-3-030-21667-2 ISBN 978-3-030-21668-9 (eBook)
https://doi.org/10.1007/978-3-030-21668-9

Cover illustration: GFC Collection / Alamy Stock Photo

This Palgrave Macmillan imprint is published by the registered company Springer Nature Switzerland AG.
The registered company address is: Gewerbestrasse 11, 6330 Cham, Switzerland

The Changing Social Economy of Art

"This valuable text evokes Howard Becker's "Art Worlds", and likewise it will have strong repercussions in the contemporary triangle of the production, distribution, and consumption of the arts. Whether you agree or disagree with Abbing's provocative statements, undoubtfully his thoughts about the contemporary power of the economy and sociology of the arts are worthy of discussion. This book is a treasure trove of issues such as consequences of the still ongoing polarity of 'serious' and 'popular arts', opportunities for innovation in the arts, the obsession with authenticity and aura, the double-edged sword of commercialism and enrichment, and alternative ways of art sharing and finding new career paths for artists."

—Volker Kirchberg, Professor Sociology of the Arts, *Leuphana University of Lüneburg, Germany*

"Just as 'Why are artists poor' changed our view on the arts economy, this study will change our view on the social context of the arts. In the 19th century the separation of 'serious art' and entertainment coincided with the exclusion of lower social groups. Now the cross-over between art and entertainment along with the claim of inclusion bewilders the cultural gatekeeping elite. Abbing explains why this happens in a book which will be a must-read for many years to come."

—Joost Heinsius, Art Theorist and Consultant, *Amsterdam*

"A must-read for any artist. So much that puzzled me in the arts becomes understandable. Belonging to a new generation of musicians, I especially like Abbing's treatment of technological changes affecting artistic developments. Being a music producer of electronic music, I contribute to these developments. But I do not earn much money. (I therefore also make commercial work.) The same applies to many of my colleagues. It is a relief to know about the underlying reasons."

—Hiroaki Oba, Music Producer, *Berlin and Tokyo*

Contents

Preface

(1) These are exciting times in the arts. The arts are in turmoil. After more than a century of relative safety, many established art institutions are now trying to survive, while some flourish. Are those the right ones? Maybe not. Different paths are proposed and taken. In part of the established arts exciting new art is established, which no longer relies on conventional forms of consumption and expensive nineteenth-century ways of producing art. Popular art blossoms. A small part of it now tries to connect with the established arts; a larger part does not belie its lower-class roots. But respect among art elites for popular art and especially lower-class popular art remains limited. To understand the present changes and consider possible choices, knowledge of what went before is helpful.

In this book, I examine long-term developments in the arts. I compare the social economy of art in the period from circa 1880 to 1980, which I call the period of serious art, with the social economy before and after this period. I am especially interested in the changes in the last two decades of the twentieth century and those in the first two of the twenty-first. Changes in art production and distribution occur earlier and are stronger in the USA, and to a lesser degree also in the UK, than in continental Europe. The eastern and southern countries of continental Europe are dragging behind, while a country like the Netherlands holds an intermediate position. (For this reason, I do not hesitate to present relatively many Dutch examples.) Most of the theses at the start of each section refer to the period before 1980. In many theses the last paragraphs refer to developments over the last decades.

I argue that the social economy of art fundamentally changes in the late nineteenth century. Even though there are many differences, some of the recent changes mirror the earlier changes. For instance, in the nineteenth century, serious art becomes established and is separated from popular art, while at present serious art becomes less serious and the boundary between established art and popular art is less important. Moreover, at that time a process of de-commercialization starts, while around 1980 a process of re-commercialization begins.

When I write about the period after 1880, I deliberately write the text in the present tense. Reading about art in the twentieth century in the present tense, I expect

H. Abbing, *The Changing Social Economy of Art*,
https://doi.org/10.1007/978-3-030-21668-9_1

that older and even younger readers will recognize much of what was typical for art production and consumption in that century. In spite of changes, what was typical is still very much part of our mindset.

A proper understanding of social economic developments in the established arts requires an understanding of those in the popular arts. This is why I examine both and make comparisons. This is unusual. Although in the social sciences there is now far more research on popular art than on established art, the two are seldom compared. But comparisons are, nevertheless, illuminating. And, wanting to survive, the established arts can learn from popular art.

In this book, I pay most attention to creative artists. I foremost treat the social economic position of the art-worlds of visual art and music. The visual art-world is particularly interesting because of its large number of creative artists. The serious music art-world is or rather was large and is powerful. Other performing art forms have much in common with this art-world. Because the art-worlds of serious-literature and serious film differ from the other art-worlds and are less typical, I pay less attention to them, but do not ignore them because the differences with the other established art-worlds are illuminating.

I expect the book to be read by students in various academic courses as well as by artists, art-lovers and art administrators. Because of the unusual interdisciplinary approach and the hopefully broad readership, I have attempted to make the text as accessible as possible. I, however, use typical economic terms like consumption, production, commerce and profit, while I sometimes could have used other terms, terms that sound less painful in the ears of readers who are "in love with art"—Sometimes, as in the case of consumer and consumption, alternative terms are confusing.—I also use the terms, because after some inurement, these terms may stop being annoying and help readers to take a step backward from their object of love and their conventional way of thinking about art and the social economy of art.

I have inserted illustrations in italics in which a female visual artist called Anna tells about her personal experiences since the 1950s, experiences that are related to the argument in the text. The illustrations, however, do not serve as empirical proof of the arguments! My main intention is to let readers think of own experiences that are or are not in line with those of Anna. (Often Anna is my alter ego, but not always.)

Each section starts with one or more theses in capital letters. Although in the present tense, most refer to the position of the arts before 1980, a position which may or may not have changed since that time. The theses and the overall text apply foremost to the Western world, especially Europe, Australia and Canada and, to a slightly lesser degree, to the USA. Many recent developments also occur in Asian countries. I pay some attention to differences between Europe and the USA.

The theses which precede a section can be read as a summary of the section, and all theses taken together can be read as a summary of the book. Not all theses are proven the way a scientist likes to prove a thesis, but I have attempted to show that they are, at least, plausible. Because the topic of the book is very broad and I aim to develop general theories that explain major developments in the social economy of art, I need such plausible theses. As far as possible, I base my findings on many conversations with experts, publications and empirical research by others and, last but not least, on own (participating) observation.

I want the book to be accessible for many kinds of readers. Therefore, I have added lines in the margin to mark paragraphs in which I define and explain concepts that may not be that important for general readers. Also, to keep the text manageable, I put some additional text—I call them web-texts—and a large number of notes—web-notes—on the website—*www.hansabbing.com*—which accompanies the book. The web-note numbers are preceded by a slash. Some may interest all readers; others mainly academics. Holding a pc, tablet or phone next to the book, it is easy to "scan" these notes. (Quantitative data I mostly present in web-notes.)[1]

The book is "work in progress". I still develop my thinking, and I hope that the reader will do the same. Some of the theses can be proven or rejected in a more scientific way. It would be great if master and PhD students would attempt to find empirical proof or disproof. I, moreover, am no art-historian, and therefore, the book is likely to contain mistakes. Readers may be able to correct them. Other findings can be mentioned on the website and, if ever a second revised and improved edition were to be created, lead to changes in the text.

My approach or method is deliberately eclectic. I do not adhere to one school. I think that a proper analysis of the topics in the book is best served with the application of theories of more than one school. The methodology used in the book is anyway unusual. I start with micro as well as macro observations and next explain them with existing theories or existing theories which I have adapted.

No scientist—or artist—starts with a clean sheet. I have a personal and emotional history, which has had an impact on the choice and the treatment of some topics. Part of my own history rests in my life-long participation in both higher- and lower-class milieus. This allows me to look at the established arts from a distance. But I do not look down on established art, also not on the most elite forms. I nevertheless will argue that the establishments in classical music, opera and ballet harm their "own" art and endanger its future.

All through my life I have participated in serious art events, the same as in popular art events. Moreover, I know the arts as consumer as well as producer. I played in a classical music youth orchestra, was soundman and manager of a pop group, went to art school and still work as visual artist. I hope that this unusual combination of experiences and activities has added to useful insights in this book.

Given my relativism some readers may get the impression that I do not care about quality in the arts and have no artistic standards, and that I think that society does not need such standards. It is true that I pay attention to all sorts of art, from great classic art, like that of Rembrandt and Bach, and, so-called, contemporary art to alternative and to mainstream popular art, like that of Justin Bieber. But personally, I have standards, and I think that a continuous discussion in society about quality in the various kinds of art is important. But I also think that all kinds of art, including the art of disadvantaged groups, deserve and benefit from respect and an occasional public pedestal.

Finally, I decided to go for "he" and not "she"; that is, by lack of well-established gender-neutral terms; and because there is already enough unusual in this book. To compensate a little for all this maleness, I constructed a female alter ego.

(2) ACKNOWLEDGMENTS. I want to thank for their help the many people in various countries—experts, academics and common people—with whom I

discussed topics in the book. I learned much from the students I taught in 2017, 2018 and 2019 in the master of Cultural Economics and Entrepreneurship of the Rotterdam Erasmus University. I also learned from the members of staff seminars which, for many years, I took part in, in this department and in the department of Cultural Sociology of the University of Amsterdam. For their help I thank the following experts who I talked with: Tije Adams, Maks Banens, Ton Bevers, Laura Braden, Marsha Bradfield, Julyan Davey, Erwin Dekker, Rick Everts, Thomas Franssen, Mathieu Güthschmidt, Marcel van den Haak, Joost Heinsius, Jo Houben, Sacha Kagan, Arjo Klamer, Benjamin Low, Robert Mears, Henk van Os, Pieter Van Os, Georgios Papadopulos, Barend Schuurman, Kuba Szreder, Thomas Vaessens, Daniël Vargas, Olav Velthuis, Filip Vermeylen, Alex van Venrooy, PW Zuidhof.

Finally, I prepared and wrote this text in the following 26 cities. I thank the cities and their inhabitants for having me, inspiring me and enabling me to take some distance from art and art-worlds. They are Amsterdam, Athens, Bangkok, Berlin, Bucharest, Bratislava, Brussels, Chicago, Cluj-Napoca, Edinburgh, Groningen, Istanbul, Kyoto, London, Montpellier, New York, Newcastle, Orleans, Porto, Prague, San Sebastián, Seoul, Taipei, Tokyo, Vienna and Warsaw.

(3) TERMS WHICH ARE REGULARLY USED IN THE BOOK. In this section I explain terms which I regularly use in the book. Often their meaning will show from the context. But because I use some of them in an unconventional way, a more precise description is called for. I therefore advise students to read this section. General readers can, if they wish, skip the section and, if necessary, later return to it.

Text in the chapter marked with lines on either side refers to definitions and description of recurring concepts. This chapter is accompanied by web-notes and web-texts, which are available on the website: *www.hansabbing.com*. Numbers between brackets refer to other sections, including web-texts. Numbers at the end of a sentence preceded by a forward slash refer to web-notes. Holding a pc, tablet or phone next to this text, it is easy to "scan" the web-notes and web-texts. (Quantitative data I most often present in web-notes.)

I explain, among others, various forms of boundaries and barriers, and my notion of art-buildings and art-worlds, and I discuss various forms of art, like serious art, popular art and inferior-art. I tell why I use a hyphen between certain word combinations, as in art-building.

First, I explain the notion of boundary.[2] *Symbolic boundaries* are distinctions that groups of people make to categorize objects, people, practices and so forth. A single boundary separates two domains, like artworks and non-artworks, or people who visit classical concerts and who do not, or—as practices—the use of electronic amplification in concerts or not.

For a proper understanding of the social economy of art, a study of symbolic boundaries is essential. Often, they matter because when they are widely agreed upon, they can lead to and are accompanied by social boundaries and social barriers.

Social boundaries separate people, things and practices depending on required resources. Depending on resources some people can cross a social boundary while others cannot. Or people can let things and practices cross a social boundary. For a working man it is hard to join the group of art-lovers; and it is only with effort that some Jazz could become art. It follows that *social barriers* may exist for certain people and things. They cannot be crossed. People can be *under-resourced*. They do not have enough money to go to the theatre performance. Or they miss the social skills to join the group of visitors./1

In this text, main *art-buildings*—with a hyphen between art and building—are the main art museums, theatres and halls in which serious art is shown and performed, as well as the main buildings used for official art education. They are prestigious. Any citizen in a city knows the most prestigious art-buildings. Next to main art-buildings there are less prestigious *secondary art-buildings* and *art-spaces*./2

Art-spaces are special spaces where artist work, sculpture gardens, commercial-galleries offering serious art as well as record shops offering only classical/serious music—After 1970 the latter gradually disappeared. Secondary art-buildings are less prestigious buildings in which solely serious art is offered. The many new cultural centers where also popular art is offered and non-art events take place are no art-buildings. The same applies to churches in which classical/serious music is performed. (I write commercial-gallery instead of commercial gallery as is commonly done. This is because commercial galleries do not need to be commercial in the sense that the term is used in this text [60].)

An *art-lover* is a person who regularly visits art-buildings and not only museums of old art. I define the group in an own way. This is why I put a hyphen between art and lover. ("Regularly" is an elastic concept. Adequate data could allow an operationalization of the concept, demanding, for instance, at least five visits. But such data do not exist./3)

I operationalize the concepts of art-world-recognized or *serious art* and *unrecognized art* or popular/inferior art by their absence or presence in prestigious art-buildings. *Popular/inferior art* is unrecognized and cannot be found in such buildings. Serious art can *in principle* be shown or performed in them. This is indeed "in principle". Much serious art, especially visual art, is not actually present in the prestigious art-buildings, but could be there if there were no comparable works that are thought to be artistically more important. This kind of art can be present in less prestigious art-buildings, and art-spaces./4

Other possible ways exist to distinguish art from no-art, but they are hard to properly explain and operationalize. For instance, a definition based on serious or real art being ambiguous and difficult, as is often argued, is impossible to operationalize. An additional advantage of drawing the boundary between real and not real art on the basis of buildings is, that it is easy to "visualize" by readers. Thinking of a specific artwork—an object or performance—readers can, in their imagination, put it in a typical art-building to see if it fits. A Metal concert and a landscape painting à la those of Bob Ross do not fit.

Because over the last decades the notion of art-world-recognized art and its operationalization becomes less adequate, talking about recent times, I regularly use the terms *established art* and not-established art.

Only part of *overall art* or *art-in-a-broad-sense* is accepted and recognized as art by art-worlds and can in principle be present in art-buildings.—I explain the concept art-world below.—This is *art*, that is, art without adjective. Until recently popular art is not judged to be real art; it is entertainment, or it needs an adjective, that is, popular. However, not to confuse readers I often also add an adjective to real art as in *serious art, true art, art-world-recognized art* and *real art.* (I do not use the terms legitimate art, fine art and high art./5)

For a proper understanding of the social economy of art, the boundary between art-world-recognized and unrecognized art and artists is important. *Popular art* is unrecognized art. It is unrecognized art because its genres and styles do not fall in a category of real art, that is, in a category that art-worlds judge to be true art. For instance, vaudeville, Rock music and jive fall in categories that are not art-world-recognized as art, while (serious) theatre, classical music and ballet do. Moreover, popular artists have no *art intention*; they do not have an intention to make real art.

Major forms of popular art are popular music (including folk music), operettas, musicals, cabaret, popular drama, popular dances, popular literature, popular poetry (including nowadays Raps), comics, popular film (including popular animations) and popular visual art (including graffiti). The same as in real art in each of the popular art forms many genres and subgenres or styles exist.

Inferior-art is unrecognized art but, unlike popular art, could have been recognized as real art if the quality had been better. Inferior-art resembles real art. The works fall in a specific category of art-world-recognized art or, often, in several categories at the same time. Sometimes it contains elements of older serious styles in diluted forms. They can also be straightforward imitations of old or recent serious art. An example is paintings in a cubist style sold in an open-air market. (Until some decades ago outsider art was also judged to be inferior-art.) To acknowledge that many people do not judge inferior art to be inferior, I put a hyphen between inferior and art, that is, *inferior-art*. Moreover, for ease sake, when I refer to the combination of popular and inferior-art, I regularly use the term *popular/inferior art.*

Aside: by lack of clear art-buildings and art-spaces, in the case of literature and film, it is hard to operationalize the distinction between real literature and film and popular/inferior literature and film. Libraries exist but no typical serious literature art-buildings. Already for some time arthouse cinemas exist, but until recently no film museums. That in the period of serious art no established art-buildings exist for serious literature and film is understandable. The fact that all literature and film is technically produced in large series causes a less strong symbolic boundary between art and no art, with the consequence that a considerable gray zone exists. If main art-buildings exist, it is hard to decide what can be admitted and what not. In most of the new film museums also older blockbusters and popular comedies are shown.

Aside: Most of the time I do not distinguish *genre* and *style.*/6 I also do not distinguish *content* and *form*. In this text, form is an aspect of content.

To prevent confusion, I write *modern-art* and *contemporary-art* with a hyphen, to refer to the serious or established version of modern art and contemporary art, and therefore not to *all* art that is modern and contemporary, that is, including popular/inferior art made by living artists.

Modern-art generally refers to styles that are developed or come first between 1880 and 1970. *Contemporary-art* (or *postmodern art)* takes root in the 1950s. (Its styles only become well-recognized after circa 1970. Most often the terms contemporary-art and postmodern art are used interchangeably, but the latter is also used for a subset of styles or movements within contemporary-art.)

In practice for most music lovers, the term classical music not only refers to music from the classical period, but also to ancient music, baroque music, modern-music and even contemporary-music. However, calling the latter classic music is strange. To prevent misunderstanding, I use the term *classical/serious music*.

I distinguish "live" art from "not-live" art, like recordings and reproductions. Paintings and other original visual art are the same as performances, the real thing; they are "live".

In the social sciences, institutions and collectives are often treated as if they are persons, who act. They are called "actors". It is therefore possible to say things like "an art-world defines art", or "the art-world protests against subsidy cuts, even though groups or factions or individuals within an art-world may not agree with the existing dominant definition or may agree with the cuts. It is, anyway, good to keep in mind that ultimately it is individuals, that is, flesh and blood people who act and whose actions have certain effects: this person in the art-world did this, another that.

In this book an *art-world* consists of all persons within an overall *world of art* connected with an artform, who have a say in the definition of art in that artform. Together they are *gatekeepers* and monopolize the definition of art and the access to the art-world. Within a larger world of art they directly or indirectly determine which categories of art-in-a-broad-sense are art (or real art or serious art), with the consequence that the artworks can, in principle, be present in art-buildings. They control the main art-buildings and the official, that is, accredited, art education institutes.

This definition differs from other definitions, in particular from the wider definition of art world of Howard Becker which is well known.[3]/7 To remind the reader that my definition deviates, I write "art-world"—with a hyphen between art and world—instead of "art world" as Becker does. (Mine also differs from Arthur Dante's "artworld".) /8/9

Over the last decades two poles have developed in the, on average, weakening art-worlds. This is, on the one hand, an extreme of very serious, studious and supposedly autonomous art directed at artists and expert-consumers, who discuss art using a specialist's discourse. On the other there is an extreme of very user-oriented and even entertaining art for a large audience. In terms of demand and supply the extreme positions are less interesting. Looking at two broader domains between the two poles is more useful; on the one hand, a relatively small *studious domain* and, on the other, an ever-larger domain in which art-companies are oriented on consumers, a domain which I call the *user-oriented domain*.

To structure the analysis, I distinguish five interrelated main groups or *parties of art-world participants*. Each party is involved in gatekeeping and has a say in the definition of art and other art-world affairs. These are *experts/critics*, *consumers*, *artists*, *art-companies and official art education organizations*. The parties are not independent or autonomous. There is *interdependence*.—This is important for the analysis of the social economy of art.—The parties have links with three main outsider groups which indirectly have a say in art-worlds affairs: *sponsors*, *governments* and *donors*. I, moreover distinguish two subgroups of art-companies: *non-profit art-companies* and *for-profit art-companies*.

Artists are persons or small ensembles who actually create or perform artworks. Many creative artists are (legal) for-profits. *Art-companies* are persons, enterprises and organizations who process art; they play a direct or indirect role in bringing the artwork to the consumer. Examples of people or organizations who are usually for-profit art-companies are managers of artists, dealers, impresarios, bookers, publishers, bookshops and so forth. Music halls, theatres, art museums and large ensembles as well as foundations and institutions that offer grants to artists, are usually, but not always, nonprofit art-companies. (Because I use the term "art-company" in an unusual broad sense, I put a hyphen between art and company.)

All parties have representatives in an *art-world elite* or *art-world establishment* which is particularly influential as far as gatekeeping and other art-world affairs are concerned, for instance, in contacts with government or the running of art-world education institutes.

Discussing the social economy of art over the last two centuries, it is necessary to classify people according to social classes. In the traditional approach of class, *high class*, that is, *nobility* and *aristocracy*, *higher bourgeois* and *lower bourgeois* (or petty bourgeois), or instead *upper or higher middle class* and *lower-middle class* as well as *lower class* and *low class* are distinguished. I use the categorizations, be it not in a very precise sense.—Anyway considerable gray zones exist.—

Presently, the traditional concept of class is not used that often anymore. Society has changed and the traditional concept may have become less relevant. I, nevertheless, use the notions also for the last decades, but usually in combination with references to education level and income.

Notes

[1]The website, the web-notes and the web-texts are the sole responsibility of the author and not of the publisher Palgrave Macmillan.

[2]The following paragraphs are inspired by Michèle Lamont and Molnár's (2002) discussion of boundaries.

[3](Becker, 1982). (Arthur C. Danto, 1964) and (Helguera, 2012) also interpret the term in their own different ways. See the website-note.

Literature

Becker, H. S. (1982). *Art Worlds*. Berkeley: University of California Press.
Danto, A. C. (1964). The Artworld. *The Journal of Philosophy, 61*, 571–584.
Helguera, P. (2012). *Art Scenes*. New York: Jorge Pinto Books.
Lamont, M., & Molnár, V. (2002). The Study of Boundaries in the Social Sciences. *Annual Review of Sociology, 28*, 167–195.

The Triumph of Serious Art

In the course of the nineteenth century art becomes serious; art is no entertainment. A period of serious art commences. In this period art is triumphant, and popular art is no art. Non-profits are established and "commerce" or "being commercial" is rejected. Major art-buildings are erected. People who do not consume serious art respect and look up to it. In the last decades of the twentieth century overall respect for serious art gradually goes down. Popular art becomes more important. There is a re-commercialization in the arts and at least part of art is allowed to be entertaining. The period of serious art gradually comes to an end.

In the nineteenth century art-worlds become established which, with financial and moral support of governments and donors, govern the production and distribution of serious art. They do so without a need of state enforcement, as was common in earlier centuries. Art-world establishments guard artistic progress. They create an art heritage and classic artists and artworks. They also put demands on serious artists, demands which over time are becoming more constraining.

Both in the arts and in popular art, avant-garde groups exist. The first resist the existing art favored by *the* art-world; the last the mainstream art promoted by *the* industry. In the arts, this leads to conflicts and occasional artistic and social revolutions. The diffusion of new genres is slow and limited. In the popular arts, many parallel avant-garde scenes exist. They do not last as long as in the arts. When successful they expand, the new (sub)genres are relatively quickly diffused, while influencing mainstream popular art. In the arts, mainstream art is taboo.

The different trajectories partly follow from a different orientation of artists. For income and reputation, avant-garde artists in the serious arts are foremost oriented on donors and governments, and those in popular art on markets.

Lines on either side of the text indicate that recurring concepts are defined or described. This chapter is accompanied by web-notes and web-texts, which are available on the website: *www.hansabbing.com*. Numbers between brackets refer to other sections, including web-texts. Numbers at the end of a sentence preceded by a forward slash refer to web-notes. Holding a pc, tablet or phone next

H. Abbing, *The Changing Social Economy of Art*,
https://doi.org/10.1007/978-3-030-21668-9_2

to this text, it is easy to "scan" the web-notes and web-texts. (Quantitative data I most often present in web-notes.)

A High Respect for Art

(4) OVER TIME, THE ARTS START TO STAND OUT. IN THE NINETEENTH CENTURY, A PERIOD OF SERIOUS ART COMMENCES. Art, as we understand the term, did not always exist. What the term art refers to, changes over time. In this section I briefly examine changes in the use of the term art and I explain related concepts. (Students should certainly pay attention to the marked paragraphs in this and following sections; others may only "scan" them.)

Before the seventeenth century *the* arts as a collective noun denoting all the later fine arts did not yet exist. There were only *arts in the form of crafts or skills* including such arts as medical arts, performing arts, military arts and visual arts./1 Moreover, within art, disciplines were broad. For instance, a woodcutter could be someone who carved wooden sculptures, decorated wooden boxes and created woodblocks for printing text. He may well have produced all three. Applied art was not yet a separate category. Also, the names of artists did not matter much. Artists or rather artisans often did not sign their works, and commissioners did not care much whether a work was made by one or another artist as long as the instructions had been followed. Moreover, buyers much appreciated not only hand-made replicas created by the artist, but also replicas created by other artists. (Their financial value was not much lower than that of the original.[1]) Artworks did not yet have the extreme goodness they have in the nineteenth and twentieth centuries. Only a very small group of artists was well known and well respected, but foremost because of their mastership and not their creativity.

Only in the seventeenth century did the *fine or creative arts* become a separate category, next to other categories within the arts or crafts. However, at first this categorization was still foremost practical and not a classification: the fine arts were not yet superior compared to the other arts. Also, a possible interrelationship between the various fine arts—the five main fine arts being painting, sculpture, architecture, music, creative writing and the performing arts of theatre and ballet/dance—was not a matter of much concern. It follows that when we say that works that were created before the seventeenth century are art we use a concept of art that is "constructed" later.

At the end of the eighteenth century, next to the terms fine and creative arts, the term *art* or *the arts* started to be used as a collective noun denoting the combination of all fine or creative arts. Moreover, art and *the* arts became synonyms. Art and *the* arts, that is, without adjective became an abbreviation for fine arts and did no longer refer to other arts, like the medical and military arts, which continued to require an adjective. That the fine arts and not any of the other arts became *art* or *the arts* could only happen because the fine arts had started to stand out among all arts; they had become the highest form of art. This is the first sign of the forthcoming triumph of art.

In the nineteenth century a further narrowing of the notion of art occurs. The distinction between art and applied art becomes important. Gradually, applied art is no longer real art; it needs an adjective. It has less goodness than art. In the course of that century a further narrowing of the notion of art occurs, which is important in the context of this book. The art that cultured bourgeois judge to be serious is separated from popular art and, what I call, inferior-art. The latter two are entertainment-art rather than real art. They are "no art". As such, they need adjectives, like popular, inferior, entertainment, commercial and so on. It is the art of the populace. The art-loving and cultured bourgeois monopolize the term art; only their serious art is art, that is, art without adjective. It is this kind of art that is triumphant.

The successive narrowing of the term art enables the convention of thinking of the arts and its many institutions as one world of art, a world that is of the same order as the worlds of religion and science, or even superior. The triumph of art also shows from the later annexation of the terms *modern art* and *contemporary art*. This is significant, because there is, of course, also much modern and contemporary popular/inferior art; in fact, there is far more of it than of serious art.

In this book I use the notion of *a period of serious art*, which could well be called the *golden age of serious art*. It is the period in the Western world in which art is serious and deep and the respect for art is extraordinarily high. Art and artists are much respected, art is not for everyone, popular art is no art, commercialism in the arts is rejected, art-worlds have much freedom (relative autonomy), artists are supposed to express themselves by creating authentic works. And artists hold a monopoly of creativity and authenticity. (I explain the term art-world in section 3.)

In the course of the book I mention and discuss more characteristics. Distinguishing the period is helpful for an investigation and proper understanding of the, over time, changing social economy of the arts.

The period has a gradual beginning and end. In a *prelude period* the typical later characteristics of art and its societal setting become more pronounced. In the *aftermath of the serious art period* they become less significant. I let the prelude period start around 1800; the *main period* around 1880 and the aftermath around 1980. The latter lasts to the present day. Around 1800 romanticism in the arts becomes important and art becomes more expressive. Around 1880 in most Western countries, art has become serious, and popular art altogether stops to be (real) art; in the arts nonprofits are established and the provision of art is less commercial, while respect for art increases much. Respect continues to be high well into the 1980s.

The beginning is not abrupt. There has been a run-up of centuries. And although in the aftermath many of the characteristics that art has in the main period are becoming less important, it is likely that some will continue to be significant for decades. The period of serious art has not come to an end.— Some developments at the start of the period correspond with developments in the aftermath, but differ in direction. In the early part of the period of serious art, there is a gradual *decommercialization* in the arts—art-companies become less entrepreneurial—while respect for serious art increases; and in the aftermath there is *re-commercialization,* while respect for serious arts goes down. This is not to say that there is no commercialism in the period of serious art. There is, but probably less than before and after. Commercialism is anyway more covered up, as we shall see in Chap. 5.—

In different countries, the phasing differs, as does the intensity of the typical characteristics. In the USA, the prelude period starts later than in most European countries, while the aftermath of the period of serious art starts earlier in the USA. Already for several decades in the USA, the symbolic boundary between art and popular art is less strong. Countries like England, France, Belgium and the Netherlands hold an intermediate position, while Spain and especially Germany, Austria and Italy are late, the same as countries further east. Much of what will be said about the art-period in this book applies strongest to countries like Germany, Austria and Italy. Arguable in the second half of the twentieth century, in several Asian, African and a few Arab countries an art period starts which is somewhat comparable with the period of serious art in the Western world as discussed in this text. (The Western world includes Australia.)

In the Western world the period of serious art corresponds with the later part of so-called Modernity. This is not accidental. The process of individualization which is important in Modernity affects the arts and promotes certain characteristics of art and of artists which are typical for this period, like the phenomenon of artists being expected to make authentic works.

During the period of serious art, a, what I call, *art ethos* exists. It is a *collection of moral convictions and norms,* which are shared by participants in art-worlds and to a lesser degree in society at large. They justify behavior./2 Convictions are, for instance, that art is sacred and has much goodness, and that commercialism in the arts is bad. Corresponding norms are: "one must respect art" and "artists must not make commercial work". To different degrees the participants in art-worlds have internalized the values, beliefs, convictions and norms in the art ethos./3

The art ethos develops and changes over time. It can be more or less forceful. Examples of developments are that in the course of the twentieth century the goodness of innovation in the arts is increasingly emphasized—artists and their works must be innovative—and that in the aftermath of the serious art period the moral conviction that commercialism in the arts is wrong becomes less intense.

(5) During the period of serious art: ART IS MUCH RESPECTED AND ART AND ARTISTS HAVE A HIGH STATUS. RESPECT FOR SPECIFIC ART EVOKES RESPECT FOR ALL ART. Before the period of serious art respect for art and artists was not particularly high. For a long time paying respect to art or *the* arts was not even an option because, as mentioned, the term art as a collective noun denoting all the later "fine arts" did not exist. But along with the unification of the fine arts the social status of each of the art forms increased./4

In the period of serious art along with the higher status of art forms and of art, the social status of artists increases, as does their relative autonomy. Before the Renaissance, "artists" were foremost anonymous craftsmen who did not sign their works, and this indicates that the social status of the items and activities of what we now call (true) art and of those who created it was not especially high. Also later on, the social status of most artists was not higher than that of other craftsmen. There were exceptions. Exceptionally good artists, like Leonardo Da Vinci, Albrecht Dürer, Johann Sebastian Bach and William Shakespeare, were sometimes admired—the same as before them Virgil and Homer. They could be celebrities and were regarded as masters in their craft, and sometimes their Patron or Maecenas gave them more freedom in making own artistic choices and in expressing themselves than their contemporaries./5

Nevertheless, up to the period of serious art, court painters and court musicians were predominantly a higher type of servant. Even the already well-known composer-performer Joseph Haydn (1732–1809) still had to sit with the other servants during dinner—something he did not like. This would have been unthinkable in the case of later composers, including, not much later, Ludwig von Beethoven (1770–1827). And in the nineteenth century a successful painter connected with one of the major Academies is somebody who mingles with other "learned men".[2]

Beethoven and many other successful artists are not rich, but they start to have a high social status. Gradually the position of artists, at least of the somewhat successful artists, is reversed. From being inferior in comparison with the art consumer, whether king, prince, bishop or merchant, they increasingly become superior. People look up to successful artists. They have authority and have more autonomous space than before. *The reversal shows well from Gustav Courbet's painting* The Meeting (Bonjour Monsieur Courbet) *(1854), in which he painted himself in the company of the important collector Alfred Bruyas. He depicts himself as equal to his benefactor, if not as superior. At that time the painting calls forward criticism from the traditional art elite, but he gets away with it, and for a new art elite the painting is altogether acceptable.*

A clear sign of a high respect is the growing relative autonomy of art-worlds and some artists. Unlike before, society allows and enables them to be relatively autonomous. The relative autonomy is made possible by expanding markets for art and by private and public support, and neither would have occurred without much respect for art.

Later in the nineteenth century there is no need any more for a somewhat provocative depiction of this reversal. The superiority of successful artists has become self-evident. *This shows, for instance, from the strong features of the busts of living and dead artists, like Bach and Beethoven, which start to be made.* These busts are interesting: they do not look at the viewer. The artists are in another world, a world beyond and above us; they are part of a superhuman realm: the realm of art. The use of the term "genius" in the case of such artists also suggests that something supernatural is at stake.

Beginning with the enlightenment a person who demonstrates exceptional intellectual or creative powers is called a genius; he is a uniquely gifted creative individual. In the case of artists, the talent of the genius is often thought to be the result of a supernatural intervention. It is not inherited or acquired through education or personal effort. It is extraordinary, and stems from God or a higher force. Artists "breathe life" in dead material and doing so are guided by God./6 The work of the genius is sublime. This explains that artists, the same as priests, are said to be "called" and to have a "calling". Moreover, great artists are often regarded as prophets and visionaries, who lead the way. In the perception of the art-lover they are ahead of their time. Works of the geniuses are all time masterpieces; they are immortal, and their creators should be immortal. Bach and Rembrandt were no geniuses in their own time, but with retro-active effect during the period of serious art they become geniuses.

In this period, art is thought to have much goodness and hence there is much respect for artworks, artists, art-worlds and above all for art. Respect for art is widely shared in society, also among those who do not consume art. Respect often comes "naturally". Not showing respect or showing disrespect is exceptional; a person makes a statement by not showing respect. Disrespect calls forward indignation. Moreover, respect for specific artists and for artworks in the various art forms evokes a simultaneous respect for *all* art or *the* arts. When talking about a certain artist or artwork or just thinking about them, there is always the association with art or *the* arts.

In the serious art period *art-lovers* belong to and are part of not only a specific art-world, like the music art-world, but also of what they perceive to be the *"world of art"*. They feel at home in the arts and can therefore be said to belong to a family, the *"family of art"*. They regularly participate in *art events* in *art-buildings* and *art-spaces*, that is, they regularly visit art museums, concert halls, theaters, art-spaces and so forth. The family symbolically "owns" art and it has appropriated the term art.

As noted, popular art is no art. Moreover, the "family members" or insiders tend to feel superior and are inclined to exclude outsiders. Outsiders look up to them. In the period of serious art, being an art-lover brings membership and distinction. Art is "sacred" for the family of art, and therefore worthy of much respect. They share art, venerate it, and, if necessary, protect it against outsiders, who are disrespectful./7

Art is a *sacred object* as sociologist say. Many more things can be sacred objects and as such worthy of respect: from a just born baby surrounded by adults, a manager addressing his personnel to an ideology to which a group of people adhere. It follows that the communities who share the object can have different sizes. Moreover, it can also be an *imagined community* whose "members" do not meet in person. An inclination to feel superior and to exclude others who could bring down the shared object is normal.[3]

A significant difference between art and popular art is that in popular art no imagined community of popular art-lovers exists which venerate these arts. Whereas, respect for specific art easily evokes respect for all art, respect for specific popular art evokes no respect for all popular art. During, before and after a performance of a Bach piece a visitor may feel a member of the family of art and his respect for the music extends to all art. At a Rolling Stones concert, nobody imagines a family of lovers of popular art or has feelings of respect for popular art in general.

Nineteenth- and early twentieth-century examples of an outspoken association of artworks and artists with art-in-general can be found in descriptions, like those of Marcel Proust, of the gatherings in the saloons of the rich. In the presence of a musician, poet or painter not only their artworks and the corresponding art form but also art-in-general is praised. Up to the present day, the same applies to countless conversations in the foyers of theaters and concert halls. The goodness of art is emphasized. It raises the spirit in meetings.

People associate art with good "things. "Art creates profound human emotions". "Art possesses inner beauty and depth". "Art enriches and civilizes". "Through art people become better people". Such stereotypical knowledge and moral convictions are widely shared and continuously reproduced within the family of art. They are part of the art ethos. And if art is good or has goodness, those who create art, the artists, must have goodness as well. In art events, the goodness of art shines on artists and it shines from them. "Artists are creative, sensitive, vulnerable". "Artists are authentic and free; they do not compromise". "Artists are true to themselves and show this in their works". "Artists are passionate and selfless, and not interested in money".

I use the term goodness deliberately. Art being good has a moral dimension. For instance, during the break, the visitor of a serious music concert may well say to his companion, "I wish people would realize how good art could be for them". No visitor of a popular music concert would say, "I wish people would realize how good popular art could be for them". Art is far more emotionally charged than popular art. The moral dimension also shows from expressions like: "I ought to go more often" —that is, to the art museum or art performances. The speaker implicitly condemns himself for not choosing what is good, and what is good for him.

During the period of serious art, showing respect for art is not only self-evident, it often comes naturally. People have internalized the knowledge that art is good and requires respect. An example is that of the tone of a conversation becoming more serious when the conversation moves to art, without people being aware of this.

As we shall see below, *over the last decades,* respect for art and artists go down.

(6) During the period of serious art: CELEBRATIONS AND MAGNIFICENT BUILDINGS MARK THE GREATNESS OF ART. Various, intangible as well tangible, symbolic "pedestals" testify of the greatness of art.

The ceremonial character of art performances and the stillness of audiences in concert halls, theaters and art museums befit the seriousness of art and testify of much respect for art. Moreover, the fact that art is used during certain private and public events marks the importance of the event as well as the high status of art. Serious-music is, for instance, used in funerals and other important live events. During important receptions of corporations, serious-music is performed, and during the reception of heads of state and meetings in the context of diplomatic- and business-missions, art is live performed. Sometimes whole orchestras and ballet/ dance companies travel along with the dignitaries.

Public festivities surrounding the recurring jubilee celebrations of the birth or death of important classic artists clearly testify of the widely shared respect for art and artists. Outstanding examples are those of Bach, Da Vinci, El Greco, Handel, Mozart, Rembrandt, Schiller, Shakespeare and Van Gogh. In the twentieth century, their celebrations have far more grandeur than those of famous politicians, scientists or theologians, like Cromwell, Newton and Luther.

In this period other symbolic "pedestals" are also erected for major classic works and classic artists which testify of the high respect for art and artists. These are pedestals in the form of prestigious art-buildings with a luxurious or noticeable expensive interior. From the 1800s onward, magnificent freestanding buildings are an essential part of, what I call, art-setting, a setting which is serious [24]. Within the buildings, prestigious rooms are called after important artists. In the Concertgebouw in Amsterdam just below the first balcony, the names of the major classic composers are engraved in stone. Art museums sometimes carry the name of an important artist, like the Turner Gallery in London, various Picasso museums in Europe and the prestigious Van Gogh museum in Amsterdam. The Rijksmuseum in Amsterdam does not carry Rembrandt's name, but it basically is a majestic palace built around Rembrandt's Night Watch—a painting that still has the most prominent place in the museum.

The magnificent buildings are showpieces and major symbols of the world of art-and-culture, if not civilization. The fact that such buildings, the same as churches, are freestanding matters. This way they do not only draw more attention, they also enable "a spatially separate zone" and "a realm apart from ordinary life", in which art can be "treated with respect, as a "sacred thing".[4] They are spaces that enthuse art-lovers.

Before the early period of serious art, theaters were made of wood and did not have a roof. Municipal theaters were incorporated in a continuous street façade, while most other theaters and concert halls were part of palaces.[5] But since the beginning of the nineteenth century, concert halls, theaters and art museums are not only freestanding buildings, they belong to the most opulent and prestigious buildings constructed. They not only compete with churches, universities, town halls, law courts, stock exchanges and the headquarters of multinationals, they increasingly surpass them in grandeur./8

In the twentieth century, they become comparable with the cathedrals of old and surpass the buildings of prestigious and globally operating corporations. Early examples are The Guggenheim in New York (1937), Sydney Opera House (1958) and Centre Georges Pompidou (1971) in Paris.[6]

Over the last decades the respect of populations and politicians for established art goes down as shows from cuts in subsidies for the production and offering of art. But, at least up to 2000, this does not stop the erection of new prestigious art-building in cities in Europe and the USA. They serve the cultural competition of cities, regions—and states in the USA—and of countries. From Metz in France, New Castle in England to Bergen in Norway, Graz in Austria, and Kansas City and Durham in the USA, eye-catching new concert halls, theaters and museums for modern-art have been built. They befit a new user-oriented direction in the arts. In comparison, most of the venues that host popular music concerts and are built before 2000 are functional rather than prestigious. They contain little unused space, whereas a striking characteristic of most of the newer prestigious art-buildings is the percentage of unused cubic meters of space.

In the new more user-oriented domain in the visual arts, some buildings are now exuberant. They serve a large clientele of middle-class people and not only the much smaller groups of typical art-lovers who visit the traditional art-buildings. People go there for the exhibited art, but not only: they go for an overall pleasant experience. The events are part of an "experience economy".[7]Outstanding examples are The Guggenheim in Bilbao (1997), and the recent *Louvre* and *Guggenheim* in Abu Dhabi. They are beyond comparison. But now many buildings in the more user-oriented domain are less prestigious. They may even be multifunctional: both serious music and theatre may be performed in the same building and sometimes even popular art, like musicals and pop music. The new and growing number of for-profit museums is usually—but not always—also relatively simple.

Aside: *Over the last decades,* new prestigious museums have been constructed for film and applied art.[8] As we shall see, on a small scale also impressive popular music buildings are erected, more so in the USA than in Europe. This is clearly a sign of changing times. It signifies that the hierarchical symbolic boundary between art and not really art is becoming less important. Buildings are never neutral. The architects of the buildings are aware of this. This shows from the exterior as well as interior of buildings. Significant in this respect are the new buildings that, in principal, offer only contemporary-art to groups of expert-consumers. They befit the, still to be discussed, new more studious domain in the arts. Some are simple, others prestigious. But the architecture anyway differs from that of the just mentioned prestigious art-buildings. Exterior and interior are often impressive, but the appearance is solid and serious rather than pompous. The interior of the rooms is simple in order to promote an intense focus on "art itself"./9

(7) During the period of serious art: RESPECT FOR ART IS HIGH AND DISRESPECT IS PUNISHED. THIS HAS CHANGED. CUTS IN SUBSIDIES ARE STILL CRITICIZED BUT NO LONGER STOPPED. In the course of the period of serious art, the general associations with art and the stereotypical beliefs about art become widely shared. They also become part of the imagery of not art loving bourgeois and of lower-class people.

This is not to say that more specific stereotypes do not differ among social groups and in different countries. For instance, high class, higher bourgeois (or upper middle class) people are likely to associate art with civilization and the superiority of the own group, while lower-class people may well associate it foremost with civilized manners, education, opulent art-buildings and the riches of the other group. But artists are anyway special and this brings benefits.

The fact that workers within the labor movement of the early twentieth century demand access to art and the world-of-art, and believe to have a moral right to art, demonstrates that respect for art is indeed widely shared. For them, art is evidently important. And when in the nineteenth and twentieth centuries people start to publicly celebrate the death of famous artists, such celebrations are also popular among lower-class people and many participate in the festivities. In 1906 in Amsterdam, tens of thousands of common *Amsterdammers* were present at the first open air celebration of Rembrandt's birthday. Moreover, according to research done by economists, shortly after the Second World War in Europe and Australia, a large part of the population was in favor of public support for art.[9]

In her contact with working-class people Anna also noticed that respect for art is widely shared./10 It is not accidental that up to the present day artists sometimes wear easily recognizable symbols of being an artist in order to profit from the respect for artists./11

A high respect for sacred art can contribute to disrespect for specific artworks and styles; not only among non-art-lovers, but also art-lovers. Average art-lovers can disagree with art experts and critics. For them certain artworks are inferior-art. And because art is sacred, protests can be violent. *In 1913 in France, during the first performance of Igor Stravinsky's Rites of Spring (Sacre du Printemps) there were major disturbances. Protests were also intense when during the early and later culture wars groups of art-lovers in the USA judged certain works to be immoral and of low quality. An example is the 1975 Mandy Havers' Pink Crucifixion. This is a sculpture of a hanging, anatomically detailed leather straitjacket, complete with genitals.*

An important sign of the sacredness of art is the phenomenon that people who in the eyes of art-lovers disrespect or insufficiently respect art are shamed. They are outsiders, who threaten the sacred object. *In the 1970s, shaming and expulsion was the fate of a Dutch economist and Member of Parliament: Drees junior. (He was the leader of a center-left political party, which for a while was part of the government.) This showed when he pleaded for lower government expenditures and did not make an exception for the arts. One of his arguments was that well-to-do people profited most from the subsidies. He was immediately and successfully put down as a cultural philistine and barbarian by the art establishment. (Being an art-lover, he never fully recovered from this particular accusation. It contributed to his decision to leave politics.)*

Nowadays, shaming a politician who proposes cuts is much harder, and this is a sign of diminishing respect for art. This shows, among others from the changed behavior of members of parliaments and governments from centre-right parties. They had always been in favor of (more) subsidies for the arts, and in particular for the prestigious art institutions frequented by an elite which they were part of—several were member of the boards. But in the twenty-first century in many countries such politicians no longer resist cuts and often promote them. For instance, in the Netherlands, the Secretary of State responsible for the 2011 cuts in art subsidies is a centre-right politician./12 He even dared to tell on television that for the occasion he had visited an art museum with his children and they had found the visit boring. Shaming by the art-world people was intense, but unsuccessful./13

Among common people as well, respect for serious art is going down. Fifty years ago, people who never visited an opera performance were still in favor of opera subsidies, while now they are not. And long ago, purchases of very expensive art by governments was not resisted, while now the decision to purchase or much subsidize them are taken secretly. (This was recently the case when the Dutch government decided to subsidize with €80 million the purchase of two Rembrandt paintings by the Dutch Rijksmuseum together with the French Louvre.)

Significant, as well, is the gradual change in the title and content of the pages in quality journals in which art events are discussed. "Art" changed in "Art and Culture" and now it is just "Culture". If earlier popular art was reviewed at all this happened on other pages than where serious art was reviewed. Moreover, on the web editions of the *New York Times* and the *Guardian* the sport section now precedes the art/culture section.

It, moreover, is significant that nowadays intense protests can arise in the case of very prestigious and costly art-buildings that can only be erected thanks to much public money, that is, taxpayers' money. This happened among others during the very costly construction of the Elbphilharmonie in Hamburg./14 It testifies to a decreasing respect for art. Respect is certainly no longer self-evident.

A diminishing respect for art also shows from the phenomenon that the term "art" now can have a negative connotation, especially among younger people. It is associated with little interesting and boring art events. Probably the most important sign of less respect is the gradual re-commercialization in the arts. Art becomes less sacred and trade no longer has to be restrained or covered up.

Nevertheless, among smaller groups of art-lovers, the veneration of art continuous. Not only politicians have experienced this. *After an earlier publication, I was pilloried as "a stranger in the world of art". I did not belong to the family of art, which, being a visual artist, I found a bit strange.*/15

Separation of Art and Entertainment

(8) During the period of serious art: PROSPERITY AND AN EXPANDING MARKET ECONOMY IN THE ARTS CONTRIBUTE TO THE TRIUMPH OF ART.

Before the period of serious art, what we now call art stood out because it was consumed by a small group of very rich people: sovereigns, bishops, nobles and rich merchants. Part of art was well noticeable for others, as in the case of the facades of castles, churches and mansions. Art formed an integral part of a wide collection of luxuries—goods and services—that demonstrated the power of the rich and brought respect and distinction. But the arts were not yet triumphant.

Up to 1800 sovereigns, princes, bishops and rich merchants and powerful and rich "organizations", like the church and the city councils in prosperous towns, spent a considerable part of their wealth on art. This group of art consumers formed only a very small part of the overall population. The incomes of the by far largest part of the population is so low that apart from free art and very cheap art they cannot buy art. The group of not that poor people, however, bought relatively cheap art. For instance in the seventeenth century in the Netherlands, a considerable group of not very poor people bought cheap paintings. Moreover, poor people paid for theatre—morality plays—and music performances or gave money, like we do, to buskers. Moreover, in many churches people had free access to paintings, sculptures and music. Nevertheless, the average person had very limited luxury consumption space and even less art consumption space.

The overall, what I call, *luxury consumption space* is the space in terms of time and money people have for luxury consumption, that is, after all basic needs have been met. It is always limited and can be zero. Given persistent preferences for other luxury goods, the *art consumption space* is smaller./16 Time and money are related *means*: people with money can often buy time and people with time can sometimes earn more money.[10]

Aside: I count paid-for art—including art visits—as luxury goods or luxuries. This is because people must earn more than is necessary to sustain themselves and to be able to buy art. This does not imply that art for society at large is dispensable.

Even as late as 1800 the large majority of the population is still very poor./17 Up to that time the overall luxury consumption space in society was anyway small when compared with our time and the art consumption space was even smaller. The markets for what we now call art were small—because several of the paintings, sculptures and musical compositions that were created before the nineteenth century continue to fascinate us and are regarded as cornerstones of civilization, presently people are little aware this.

It is only in the eighteenth and nineteenth centuries that median (average) incomes start to rise a little. More important is that a bourgeois group develops with far more free time and money. The luxury consumption space of the growing and more prosperous bourgeoisie is considerable. They tend to use a considerable part of it on the consumption of art and applied art. Urbanization also contributes to art consumption by the higher bourgeois. It enables the establishment of art societies, larger orchestras and prestigious venues, which in turn stimulate the consumption of, what by then can be called, serious art. Art markets, including "markets" for commissions, expand due to a somewhat higher average income, a slightly less skewed income distribution and an increase in the size of the population. In the nineteenth century, markets for popular/inferior art continue to grow. But because an increasing part of the well-to-do bourgeois is foremost interested in relatively expensive serious art, the new markets for serious art grow as well. (This does not imply that they do not at all consume popular/inferior art [83].)

In the course of the nineteenth century, artworks and applied artworks start to have a prominent place in the life of the bourgeois. Their world becomes aestheticized.[11] In their homes, artworks are all around. There are pianos, and family members and guests regularly gather to listen to a family member or an invited musician. As mentioned, artists are welcome guests in the households of the rich. Frequent visits to concerts, operas and theatre performances, and somewhat later, also to ballet performances and art museums become standard practice. It is attractive to be an art-lover, that is, a cultured person with a feel for aesthetics.

Aside: It is foremost thanks to a *market economy* that art flourishes during the serious art period and after. This is not to say that, unlike in earlier times, art markets are altogether free. New style art-worlds govern, at least part of, art production. This is a topic further down in this chapter.

Over the last decades, the luxury consumption space of most people in Western countries continues to increase, be it far less than before. Part of it is spent on the consumption of art. But in spite of high expenditure at the top end of serious art markets, it is popular art that profits most from the increased prosperity. Most money, however, goes to well-designed non-art consumer goods.

(9) BEFORE THE PERIOD OF SERIOUS ART, ART WAS ENTERTAINING, CONTEMPORARY AND FASHIONABLE. BEHAVIOR IN HALLS AND THEATERS WAS DISORDERLY. As we shall see, during the period of serious art,

in both the USA and Europe, a clear symbolic and social boundary between art and not-really-art, that is, popular/inferior and applied-art exists. Art is serious. It is no entertainment. Before this period, this is not the case.

In Europe, already in aristocratic times, a symbolic and social boundary had been established that separated high and low culture, but much of the high culture at the courts, like the court of Louis XIV, and in aristocratic and merchant homes contained a much wider variety of art and art-like products, some of which were clearly entertaining. Moreover, even after a symbolic boundary has been established, there is no social boundary. Art had to be entertaining. As late as 1850, in London, a Beethoven symphony was performed between sessions of dance-music or the performance of the latest Meyerbeer opera was offered together with a performance by the real "Scotch Quadrilles, introducing the Highland pipes"—as well as with experiments with the "Colossal Magnifying Lens".[12]

In Europe before 1800 and in the USA well into the nineteenth century, in many art events low- and high-class people participated together. This applied to the Elizabethan theatre in England. And in the nineteenth century in the USA, parts of Shakespeare's plays and Verdi operas were performed along-side cabaret and circus; and paintings and sculptures were exhibited together with curiosities, like bearded women and mutant animals.[13] American circuses employed Shakespearian clowns who recited his verses in full clown make up. In the streets, lower-class people could be heard reciting the texts of Shakespeare plays. And in the USA and Europe, they sang the arias of Verdi operas.[14] (In Italy they still do.)

In the early nineteenth century sharing in the USA has becomes less common. Moreover, in both the USA and Europe, gradually a separation of popular culture and civilized culture emerges, the same as between serious art and popular art./18 But for the bourgeois both in the USA and Europe much art was still a form of entertainment. This showed, for instance, from the popular panorama paintings and dioramas. Many bourgeois visit the special buildings, each of which showed a very large panorama painting—paintings that sometimes crossed the Atlantic. Later they also visit buildings in, so called, pleasure gardens where dioramas were shown.[15] In most art events consumption practices were hardly serious: there was seldom undivided attention, and behavior was not subdued.

For a long time moving one's body along with the music or occasionally singing along during a concert or laughing in an unrestrained way during a theatre performance was normal. People would dance on some baroque music while courting others. And later, people would sing along with certain arias in Verdi operas. While Liszt played the piano, people often talked, while every now and then they would burst out in loud applause. And as late as the last decades of the nineteenth century, in some halls and theaters audiences could still be unruly and noisy. While the orchestra was playing, people smoked and talked; there were tables and chairs, waiters served wine and lemonade and people came and left while the orchestra played.[16] There was much turmoil in the well-lit halls in which operas were performed.[17] The opera was a meeting ground for "genteel prostitution"./19 And in the corridors of the new museums, people could still be found parading through the corridors of the museums with paintings on either side, engaged in loud conversation not at all related to art.

Moreover, the same as music, paintings and sculpture served as background decoration for meetings, from a rendezvous with a mistress at the court to the reception of guests in mercantile homes.

In the centuries preceding the period of serious art, art is contemporary art. *Contemporaneity* was important. In the eighteenth century, a succession of contemporary fashions in art contributed much to the entertaining character of art. For members of the aristocracy and a mercantile class of bourgeois going for fashions and fads was exciting. They bought or listened to contemporary artworks, that is, artworks created by living artists. Music was written by living composers. The heydays of the Renaissance were long passed and the elite was interested in contemporary art.

Musical works including operas had short life spans, the same as verses (poems) and theatre plays. Some five to twenty years after the death of a composer his work was no longer performed. An Italian opera rarely survived more than a decade after its premiere.[18] Moreover, it was common that works were created with a onetime event in mind and not with the intention to last. When works served recurring events like carnival or the name day of a dignitary, each time new pieces would be created./20

Before the period of serious art, most composers were also performers. And as performers, they were "personalities". An example is Liszt, who displayed not only his music, but also his personality, the same as many pop stars do now. This contributed to the phenomenon of fads and fashions, the same as in present day popular music. Art markets existed. And an orientation on the markets stimulated commercialism and fashions. A good example is the market in which Italian opera is offered.[19] Already earlier there were markets in literature with advanced marketing techniques. People did not criticize commercialism in the arts.

The situation of visual art is not altogether comparable with that of performance art./21 But it is significant that, unlike during the period of serious art, the majority of painters and visual art consumers were not that interested in the durability of works. The immortality of art and hence the preservation and restoration of works only becomes important in the course of the period of serious art. In the seventeenth century large numbers of cheap Dutch watercolor paintings on linen were shipped to the Americas. Both artists and consumers knew that the paintings would perish before too long as the linen would not last. In contrast, nowadays even amateurs go for paints and varnishes that last hundreds of years.

Over the last decades in most art-worlds contemporaneity becomes more important again—be it least in serious music. During his lifetime Matisse was successful, but he was only known in small circles of art-lovers, while at present many people know the name of Damien Hirst and have seen pictures of his work. It is also significant that a growing group of visual artists is now less interested in the durability of their works and sometimes make, again, easily disposable works, like installations, performance art, Instagram works or create temporary interventions in public space. (The phenomenon that many postmodern artworks are apparently unrelated, casual, accidental and fleeting, contributes to inner-art-world contemporaneity.)

Contemporaneity is best noticeable in the new more user-oriented and more entrepreneurial domain in the arts. New fashions are labeled and much advertised by for-profits as well as non-profits. Commercialization contributes to contemporaneity. Presently, in the higher regions of the visual art market and in many modern art museums fashions come and go, comparable with the same phenomenon in the fashion industry.[20] (Some people worry about this development.)

Although still resisted by many art-lovers, sometimes serious and popular music are again offered in the same events [89]. This applies, for instance, to the, so-called, popera performances in which famous classically schooled singers alternatively perform traditional areas and popular songs. In his recent concerts André Rieu goes a step further: he combines serious music with entertainment acts, like popular sing-along music and an old-fashioned coach moving over the stage. Such performances resemble performances which existed before the period of serious art.

Finally, by now serious art is allowed to be entertaining. At least, this appears to be the case if one reads reviews of certain serious performances, exhibitions and books. The term also occurs in advertising of some serious theatre and on the covers of certain serious literature. The term is only missing in the case of classical/serious music—*and as Anna noticed, this is not only caused by composers composing very serious music.*/22

(10) During the period of serious art: ART AND ENTERTAINMENT ARE SEPARATED. ART CONSUMPTION IS INSULATED. A PROPER CLASSIFICATION, ETIQUETTE AND SETTING ARE ESTABLISHED. NON-PROFITS ENABLE THE SEPARATION OF ART AND ENTERTAINMENT. In the late nineteenth century, a very clear symbolic boundary and, to a lesser degree, also a social boundary between on the one hand serious art and on the other popular/inferior and applied art, or in other words between art and entertainment, has been established. It is widely advertised by art-worlds.

The actual process of part of art becoming serious has been prepared for over centuries. Early on, art theorists in the visual arts and literature had become interested in successions of styles. But unlike other scientists at universities, they had little authority. Their interest in artworks of old was not shared by art consumers. The findings were of little use for the "practical arts".[21] But in the course of the nineteenth century, art theorists and other experts, also in music, start to have authority. A new cultural elite who wants to get away from frivolous contemporary art, asks for guidance. What new art is good, and what bad? Which old art is worth watching or hearing? An art heritage is created. The discourse changes and a process of intellectualization in the arts commences [55].

In the nineteenth century, experts and critics and the better educated cultural elite start to persuade the upper bourgeois to break away from the dominant contemporaneity in the consumption of artworks. The art they promote is serious and includes many works from the past. The new belief in progress, which is also typical for Modernity, raises an interest in artworks of old. Authenticity is important [52]. One example of the changed attitude is the removal of opera in English translation. It is not serious enough.[22]

A condition for art being and remaining serious is the presence of a well-known *classification*, a typical *art-setting* and *insulation*. In the major part of the nineteenth century the *classification* of art and no-art is not yet self-evident. It is advertised by the new cultural elite; not only among the bourgeois, but also among the population at large. By the end of the nineteenth century there is a clear understanding of what is and what is not art. Serious art is separated from entertainment by insulation in art-buildings.[23] In the buildings there is an art-setting. Part of the setting is a serious etiquette and consumption practice. The people in the halls and theaters know how to behave.

The serious consumption practice also shows from the undivided attention for performances in the halls and the art objects in the newly erected museums. At times also at home there can be undivided attention for artworks. This is not to say that before this period there were no social events in which people focus relatively much and for some time on art. But they are rare.[24]/23

At the end of the nineteenth century a serious setting has become normal. Its promotion by the new cultural elite has been successful. But earlier there certainly was resistance. Aristocrats and some bourgeois still felt entitled to amusing art.[25] They do not easily give up their privileges. *When in 1888, the board of directors of the Amsterdam Concertgebouw decides to ban the smoking of cigars during performances, several dignitaries protested. They rejected the new austere etiquette. Their formulation in their letter to the editor of a quality journal is significant: "Music should serve the visitor and the visitor should not have to serve music".*[26]

I return to etiquette and classification in the next chapter. Here I say more about insulation. A well-noticeable material expression of the classification and the separation of art and entertainment follow from the insulation of art and art events in art-buildings (in a broad sense), buildings in which there is no room for popular/inferior-art. The insulation of serious and sacred art is further emphasized by the fact that the buildings are free-standing—the same as churches. (This is not to say that there is no serious art, like sculpture, in public space. Moreover, as we shall see [83], in the privacy of homes and in semi-public space, both serious- and non-serious art are consumed.)

A further spatial separation shows from the common location of the venues. Art-buildings can usually be found in the city centers or otherwise in well-to-do neighborhoods. Most of the spaces and shops for inferior-art are located further away from the city center. (Also, most of the newly erected large and somewhat prestigious venues for the consumption of not-really-art are located further away from the center of the city. Most of them are multi-purpose venues.)

Most buildings are run by non-profit art organizations or, as I call them, non-profit art-companies [3]. The establishment in the nineteenth century of non-profits represents a vital step in the process of art becoming serious. Without them separating art and no-art or recognized and unrecognized art would not have been possible. They offer only recognized art and no combinations. The non-profit character of the institutions moreover sends various messages. The most important message is: what we do is not for money, it is for art; the art we offer is serious and pure, and not contaminated by the simultaneous presence of popular art and other entertainment products./24 This way non-profits indirectly contribute to the establishment of a proper and widely shared classification. In the serious art period and up to the present day the majority of larger art ensembles and organizations running art-buildings, including art education institutes, are non-profits.

In Europe for many centuries, part of what we now call art had been commissioned, and sold and bought in markets. But most art markets were regulated [13]. It is only in an intermediate period in the eighteenth and nineteenth centuries that markets for serious art are relatively free and there is much commercialism. In this period serious art and popular/inferior-art are usually offered in the same events. In the USA, most art provision is from the start commercial. There as well offerings are mixed. But after this intermediary period in both Europe and the USA, a-commercial non-profits are established which offer only serious art.

Aside: in Europe, the origin of most late nineteenth-century non-profits is different. Already at the courts of monarchs, bishops and noblemen, and in the early nineteenth century also in the saloons of rich upper bourgeois, music and theatre performances were performed for somewhat larger groups of invited people. Over time this practice was complemented and largely replaced by performances for larger audiences in societies and associations with members and guests—in the associations the performers were often talented amateurs— later, performances started to be offered for paying audiences, but to cover cost rather than making profit. Many of such institutions develop into non-profits.

In the USA and in some European countries, at first the entrepreneurs of for-profits were sometimes "subsidized" by rich bourgeois if they were willing to offer also events with only serious arts. Simultaneously, subscription systems were developed that would stimulate demand for serious art. (In non-profits subscription systems last to the present day.) There is, however, much demand for combinations and little demand for only serious art. Providing events with only serious art is often loss making. Also, good willing entrepreneurs draw a line and drop out. And because subsidies for entrepreneurs who are after profit can end up in their pockets instead of serving art, the final step in the USA as well as in Europe is the establishment of non-profits receiving donations as well as subsidies, next to income from the market. In the boards, there are members of the new cultural elites, many of whom are local dignitaries. They have a large say in the choice of art products offered and so help establish and advertise the classification of art and no art./25

By the end of the nineteenth century there are very prestigious non-profits all over Europe and the USA, from the *Rijksmuseum* in Amsterdam to the *Philadelphia Orchestra*. By the middle of the twentieth century many more have been established in opera, theatre and ballet/dance, like the *Royal Opera and Royal Ballet Covent Garden* and the *Goodman Theatre in Chicago*. Numerous non-profits with high, but more local reputations in large, middle and small size cities add to the high prestige of true art and high culture. The boundary and barrier between the worlds of art-and-culture and entertainment is a fact.

Other serious-art-companies continue to be for-profits in a legal sense. This applies to many impresarios, publishers, some record labels, so-called, commercial-galleries and so forth. But they as well adopt an art ethos which opposes a commercial or entrepreneurial logic. The same does not apply to most providers of popular art; they are for-profits which are thought to maximize profits. Aside: Many of the non-profits in the arts are actually state owned and not-for-profit. For ease sake, I call them non-profits. Most creative artists, on the other hand, are legal for-profits. (More about the difference between for- and non-profit organizations in the web-note./26)

The emergence of non-profits is part of a longer-term process of de-commercialization in the arts. With some exceptions, like that of free museums, they operate in markets, but it appears that an orientation on income does not to come first./27 "Commerce" and commercialism are therefore not absent but limited. (In Chap. 5, I show that in the period of serious art and after, there is more commercialism in the arts, also among non-profits, than people think, but it is true that in this period the shared attitude is anti-commercial.)

As mentioned, the markets of serious art are not free. The production and distribution of a large part of art—that of popular/inferior art—continue to take place in more or less free markets, but that of true art is not. Through financial support of donors and governments and thanks to non-profits and other activities of the art-world, still to be discussed, an effective gatekeeping is developed which indirectly and without legal enforcement by states regulates the markets of serious art.

The separation and establishment of a symbolic boundary between, on the one hand, serious art and, on the other, popular/inferior-art results in three markets of art. One is a relatively small market of serious art. The two others are much larger: one of popular art and one of inferior-art. The same applies to the number of artists offering art in these markets; especially the markets of serious art and inferior-art overlap. The social boundary of artists and works is less strong than the symbolic boundary.

Over the last decades in the more user-oriented domain the setting of much serious art is now less serious. People may well agree that "Music should serve the visitor and the visitor should not have to serve music". The social and symbolic boundary separating serious art and popular art has become less strong. There is a process of re-commercialization. Many non-profits have become more openly commercial. They differ little from certain for-profits in the arts [75].

(11) During the period of serious art: ART CONTINUES TO BE USED FOR "DECORATION", DISTINCTION AND THE REALIZATION OF POLITICAL AND ECONOMIC GOALS. In spite of a separation of art and popular art and an increasingly serious art-setting, art remains useful. Art is useful for private consumers, companies and sponsors, and it is directly or indirectly useful for donors and governments. Art (or fine art) is useful because it *also* serves non-artistic goals. It is useful without being applied art, that is, utilitarian objects in everyday use to which artistic design has been applied. (Several of the uses mentioned below I discuss in more detail in later chapters.)

It is true that in the late nineteenth century and increasingly in the twentieth century there are many artists and art-lovers who disapprove of art being useful. An "art for the sake of art" becomes the dominant tune in art circles. Nevertheless, without a continuous use of art for other purposes, art could not have become triumphant. Moreover, not all art-lovers reject certain instrumental uses of art. They think that some underscore the greatness of art.

It is also true that in earlier times the use of art was often more openly instrumental by serving non-artistic goals. Art served in religious events: religious music, oil paintings, stained-glass paintings and so forth promote devotion. Secular paintings like commissioned portraits of family members, kings and groups of officials—a good example is Rembrandt's *The Sampling Officials* (*The Staalmeesters*)—also tell stories to the viewer about the portraited people and intend to call forward certain responses like devotion, respect, submissiveness. Often music is performed and paintings and sculpture exhibited to impress various groups, and show them how powerful the monarch, prince, merchant or bourgeois family is. They serve distinction. (All such uses continue to the present day but are more "covered up".) During the period of serious art, art is important because it is art. Other uses are secondary. But they are not absent. They may well represent the main reason why art is used.

All through the period of serious art the use of art by state institutions, companies and major donors is important. This largely explains their purchases and commissions of artworks as well as their subsidies and donations. It is beneficial to associate the own institution and its political, social or market cause with art, with art organizations, art ensembles and individual artists. In celebrations and other public events, art often serves to emphasize the seriousness, importance and/or merriness of the event. Art is used to entertain and impress larger groups; from groups present in receptions of captains of industry and heads of state to very large groups in national celebrations.

In the nineteenth century, in a joint effort of institutions and art-worlds, a widely experienced association of art and the new nation states is established. The already much respected arts give extra legitimization, grandeur and an "invented tradition" to the still feeble nation states.[27] Art assists in their consolidation, while state institutions assist in the establishment of classic art and classic artists.

As mentioned, magnificent art-buildings and festivities celebrating the birth or death of classic artists serve to show the superiority of the country which produced these artists and of the prosperous towns which largely finance the art-buildings. Generously subsidized art ensembles, like major orchestras and opera companies also serve the enhancement of international prestige.

Also, during proper art events, that is, during visits to museums and to performances in art-buildings, art hardly ever only serves artistic purposes. It is true that visitors in the concert hall and theatre focus much on the music and the play, but this is not the sole reason why they go to the events. The events enable them to socialize, have a good time and/or to engage in networking activity. In spite of rather formal behavior, for the insiders, the atmosphere in the halls is cozy, they are among them and this is satisfying. (Consumers do not always have a good time. Occasionally, while watching, listening and reading, art experiences can well be distressing.)

Some uses of art are well noticeable; others are not. The latter, for instance, applies to the very important use of art consumption for the "purchase" of symbolic and social memberships in real and imagined art communities. Such memberships, as well, can be very satisfying. Moreover, in the case of both individuals and groups, art consumption often serves social distinction as well.

In the twentieth century and up to the 1980s state institutions subsidize the use of art by lower-class people in order to prevent social unrest and to promote social cohesion and social welfare. Even though terms like "elevation" and civilization are used, politicians are open about these instrumental uses of art. The same applies to the use of art for the realization of economic goals. Whether effective or not, attempts to "help" the economy are common all through the period of serious art, and up to the present day.

As we shall see [25], a very important use of art in the main period of serious art is that expressive art allows individuals to develop own imagined artworks with personal meanings and messages and have own "deep" art experiences. They have private "needs" for art that are related to the process of individualization in Modernity. More than anything else it is this use that contributes to art's triumph in the main art period.

By now, economic benefits of art in the form of tourism, the attraction of foreign investors, gentrification of poor neighborhoods and so forth are much emphasized. Economic values appear to crowd out cultural values. Moreover, so-called instrumental rationality has become important.

(12) Intermezzo. MORAL VALUES AND MEASURED VALUES DIFFER. ARTWORKS HAVE NO UNIVERSAL AND TIMELESS CORE. ARTWORKS HAVE INTRINSIC AND EXTRINSIC VALUE. ART IS ALWAYS USEFUL. AN "ART FOR ART'S SAKE" MAKES NO SENSE. PURPOSELESS ART DOES NOT EXIST. MANY ARTISTS ATTEMPT TO ONLY PURSUE ARTISTIC GOALS. As noted, without being applied art, art can be useful because it *also* serves non-artistic goals. Having looked at the many, instrumental uses of art which are not "for the sake of art", the question arises if art is *always* useful. To answer this question, by way of excurse, in this section, I discuss the notion of artistic value and the belief that art has *universal value.* Next, I discuss interpretations of the notions of "art for art's sake" and art being "purposeful purposeless". I also discuss the notion of art, artists and art organizations being relatively artistically autonomous. (In this web-note, I first present a brief discussion of different interpretations of the term value and the (im)possibility to measure them./28) Readers with little time—but not university students—can skip this section, and, if needed, read parts later.

An essentialist notion and the conviction that art has a *universal artistic core* are widely shared during the period of serious art. Also today, there are many people who are convinced of its existence. The core is thought to be artistically important, independent from what specific people in different situations perceive and value. It is also independent from human interaction. The judgments of the importance of the artistic core may change over time, but the "real" (artistic) value of the artwork is thought to be permanent and cannot be changed other than by changing or destroying the artwork./29 Nevertheless, as we shall see, judgments of experts and art-lovers on artistic importance of artworks change all the time [17].

In the period of serious art, the notion of immortal artistic masterpieces or classics is thoroughly colored by this *essentialist notion of art*. For instance, because of a timeless valuable core, people take for granted that the artistic value of Western masterpieces, like *King Lear, Don Giovanni, Guernica* and works by Homer and Rembrandt, can, in principal, be acknowledged and appreciated by any generation in any part of the world. Thinking in terms of a universal core also much encourages the belief that there are many artists who make great art, but are never discovered, or only after their death. (In practice the art that in the period of serious art is thought to be immortal, is solely Western art. It, moreover, is only the serious art of higher social groups in the Western Countries. This ethnocentrism indicates that the core is a constructed core and that the artistic value of art is indeed a social value.)/30

Aside: When questioned, most present-day art historians and art-lovers will admit that the notion of an essential and universal artistic value makes no sense, but in their day-to-day encounters with artworks they are nevertheless inclined to see universal value: and they cannot stop themselves from believing that, given universal properties, anybody who opens himself up to a famous work—from a Venus figurine, a self-portrait of Rembrandt, the well-tempered Clavier of Bach to a Balloon Dog by Koons—cannot but have an intense artistic experience.

Speaking of *intrinsic value* of artworks, art theorists and social scientists refer to the phenomenon that the valuable qualities of an artwork serve a very personal art experience. In this respect, the artwork is irreplaceable. In the case of *extrinsic value,* they refer to the phenomenon that qualities of artworks serve non-art goals. Artworks are replaceable. Often non-art works can also serve the same goals.[28] (Aside: The way many non-scientists use the expression "intrinsic value of art", intrinsic value stands for valued universal qualities of artworks.)

It follows that if artworks have intrinsic value this does not imply that they are useless. Given the intrinsic and extrinsic value of artworks, all art is useful. All art is valued by at least some people for its usefulness in realizing one or more of their values. When art would not have uses, it would not exist. It follows that art is always useful or functional. In the previous section we came across many extrinsic uses of art.

Most art-lovers much resent the notion that art is useful. This is the reason why in this intermezzo, I say more about art's usefulness. The *usefulness of artworks* for individuals and groups depends on actual uses and interests. They change over time. Only in use, individuals experience art and construct in their mind meaningful artworks on the basis of what they see, hear or read, and so have a valuable art experience. The literary theorist Barbara Hernnstein Smith eloquently argues: "The recurrent impulse and effort to define aesthetic value by contradistinction to all forms of utility or as the negation of all other nameable sources of interest or forms of value—hedonic, practical, sentimental, ornamental, historical, ideological, and so forth—is, in effect, to define it out of existence; for when all such utilities, interests, and particular sources of value have been subtracted, nothing remains. Or, to put this in other terms: the 'essential' value of a work of art consists of everything from which it is usually distinguished".[29]

Friedrich Nietzsche rhetorically asks: "…what does all art do? does it not praise? glorify? select? highlight? ….how could one understand it as purposeless, as aimless, as *l'art pour l'art?*"[30] His answer is that this is not possible.

Art is always useful and therefore *functional.* Part of art's usefulness follows from the *instrumental use of art.* In this kind of use, the goals of the use are not or hardly related to art being art. An example is art serving diplomacy. But the goals can also be predominantly artistic goals, goals that are strongly related to art. This kind of enjoyment appears to follow from a "consumption of art for the sake of art", that is of art that is "produced for the sake of art". The well-known expression "art for art's sake ("l'art pour l'art") refers to either or both of them. But art being an inhuman thing, a notion of art being valuable for art ultimately makes no sense. (Moreover, if art for the sake of art would be used in a metaphorical sense implying that certain *art is divorced from any utilitarian function for humans*—including didactic and moral functions—art for the sake of art would not exist.)

However, listening to artists and art-lovers, *art for the sake of art* is sometimes also used in another metaphoric sense: it is then a shortcut for saying that artists pursue only *artistic goals.* Only then do they "serve art". Although it would be better to speak of "art for the sake of the art-world", I occasionally use the phrase in this metaphoric sense, and emphasize the somewhat strange metaphoric by continuing to put the expression within inverted commas: "art for art's sake".

Even though Immanuel Kant, and many others, demand that art is *purposeful purposeless*, purposeless art does not exist—and Nietzsche evidently agrees. But if *purposeful purposeless* would be interpreted as a demand to *ignore* as much as possible any possible social functions of art, the expression can make sense.

In practice, artworks are useful and often serve clearly distinguishable purposes. Art like muzak in shopping centers can serve as "background" to shopping—in this case the term background art or *utility art* applies. Or it can serve other art, like film music. In that case it falls in a category which may be called art-serving-art. Moreover, art can also be *tendentious art*—art with a message—like art that is used for political propaganda. (But note that none of these is applied art.)

Art-world people do not deny that such uses exist, but many of them, including artists, demand that when artists create works, they do not take such possible uses into account. "Art for art's sake" means "art for art's sake *only*": the artist should only have artistic goals in mind while creating his work. And during the period of serious art an ever-larger group of artists become aware of this demand and start to adhere to it.

Art-Worlds with Authority

(13) During the period of serious art: ART-WORLDS GOVERN THE PRODUCTION OF SERIOUS ART AND CONTROL THE NUMBER OF SERIOUS ARTISTS. EARLIER, GUILDS, RULERS AND ACADEMIES GOVERNED ART PRODUCTION. IN AN INTERMEDIARY PERIOD, MARKETS ARE RELATIVELY FREE AND COMMERCIALISM IS NOT TABOO. Before the

period of serious art, various institutions with authority—guilds, bishops, sovereigns, town councils and so forth—governed art production and distribution by regulating art education and art markets. A market economy existed, but without much freedom. Next, markets became freer and there is considerable commercialism. In the nineteenth century, art-worlds start to restore some of the governance of the earlier art institutions. But control is indirect and does not cover all professional artists. (In this web-note, I explain forms of "governance" that existed in the centuries up to circa 1900 in more detail than in the following text./31)

From the thirteenth century onwards, guilds were backed up by local and central governments; they also governed training and sales. The governance was formal. In the sixteenth and seventeenth centuries, artists' guilds mainly controlled training and sales leaving artists more negative freedom with respect to artistic choices.

In the eighteenth century, depending on the country, various forms of formal and informal control continued in the visual and performing arts. This showed when visual art academies started to replace the guilds. At the time, education became organized and controlled by academies. Clear quality standards existed and were taught: standards that de facto limited the kinds of art that artists could produce. Even when there was no system of "professional disqualification" (or "berufsverbot"), supply as well as number of artists were controlled. Artists had little autonomy.

Although in the performing arts there always has been censorship, no guilds of any importance existed. Most often, local and central governments straightforwardly issued privileges and permissions to ensembles and later to academies. The result was largely the same as in the visual arts.

In the publishing industry, which printed literature/poetry, scores and scripts, similar guilds as in the visual arts had existed, but they either collapsed or were abolished. Instead, publishers were granted not only privileges and permissions, but also patents by one or another authority. In spite of regulations, which served the prevention of libel, already in the seventeenth and eighteenth centuries, considerable series of printed artworks were offered for relatively low prices in large markets, while sophisticated merchandizing and retailing techniques were developed and applied. Other than by censorship, trade was therefore hard to control by authorities. This is why the control of markets collapsed already in the eighteenth century./32 It affected the music business. Because much music was played at home, not only literature—and journals with graphics—but also printed scores of, among others, so-called hausmusik to be played at home, were important consumer goods. Therefore, after the removal of regulations, music publishers indirectly contributed much to the growth in demand and supply of music performances.[31]

In the course of the eighteenth and nineteenth centuries, in both visual art and live performing art, it is the expansion of markets that indirectly promotes the transition from the formal governance of art production by guilds and academies to new not formal forms of governance by art-worlds. As noted [8], this expansion foremost follows from increased prosperity and a larger diversity in tastes. Due to market pressure, formal governance in the form of control of the overall volume of art production and the number of artists is no longer possible and no longer befits the changing spirit of the times.

The authorities and art institutions do not give up power easily. For instance, in France, for a long time, innovative realist painters are refused access to the all-important annual and bi-annual Salons of the Parisian Academy. But in the nineteenth century, unofficial free markets for real paintings have emerged and when dissident artists created an own salon, the *Salon des Refusés*, next to the existing bi-annual Salons of the Parisian Academy, they can no longer be stopped.[32]/33 The unofficial markets for art that earlier was unrecognized and excluded, that is, art that was judged to be inferior, have become too important, in size as well as in variety of content/form. (That the visual art market expanded much is largely due to the pressure of, at first, unmet or unsated demand for certain art, art that is attractive for the bourgeois. This, for instance, applies to the works of impressionist painters./34)

The expansion of relatively free markets brings along commercialism. Commercialism in the provision of literature and visual artworks comes first.[33]/35 It is followed by commercialism in the provision of performances and exhibitions: among others, in those in which serious and light art are offered in the same events [9]. In the early nineteenth century this becomes important in all art forms.

Prosperity and free markets lead to larger numbers of artists and frivolous art with relatively little prestige. It also calls forward a detestation of commercialism among part of the bourgeois. Therefore, after this intermediate period of commercialism, in the course of the nineteenth century, art-worlds emerge which reject commercialism. Art-worlds, moreover, gradually develop an effective system of gatekeeping of recognized art as well as recognized artists. Only part of artists and art is art-world-recognized. Art becomes serious and the number of serious artists is controlled and reduced. A monopoly on real art has been created.

By claiming that only serious art is true art, and that only recognized artists make real art, the prestige of art and artists is increased. Through financial support of governments, and by "accreditation" of certain art education by the latter, the system of gatekeeping and monopolization is indirectly supported by states, but unlike in the past, gatekeeping itself is indirect.

In Europe this could only happen after the new bourgeois elite overthrew or made peace with the earlier aristocracy, and the old art organizations and establishments started to lose their official powers. In the USA, it happens within a broader process of upper-class formation by urban elites, elites that are familiar with the European classic artists and artworks.[34] The outcome is the same: in less-formal and less noticeable ways, art-worlds start to govern the production, distribution as well as the proper consumption practices of part of art, the serious part. But the supply of serious art and the number of serious artists is no longer straightforwardly controlled.

The new governance requires government and donor support; not in the form of regulations but in the form of subsidies, gifts (non-market income) and accreditation of part of art education, the "official" part. For art-worlds to be powerful and have authority, a subsidized material infrastructure in the form of prestigious art and education buildings is essential. It enables the final stage of gatekeeping and monopolization. The works of only a selection of artists enters these buildings.

The support also enables the new art-worlds and their recognized artists to be relatively autonomous. The artists can afford to care less about income from consumers. They can make real art and do not need to compromise much [70]. And their art-worlds can afford to impose own norms on both the production and the use of its products.[35] In this respect in the serious art period, the realm of serious art has become somewhat comparable with those of religion and science. But market income still matters.

That market income and market forces matter shows from the phenomenon that *over the last decades*, not only lower subsidies but also, even more, lower demand (per inhabitant) has contributed to art-worlds having less authority. Their governance has become less effective. Popular art has become more important and, though art-worlds still manage to keep up a symbolic and social boundary, the boundary is less clear and less strong than before.

(14) ART-WORLDS HAVE VARIOUS MEANS OF GATEKEEPING. BEING ADMITTED TO STATE ACCREDITED ART EDUCATION AND RECEIVING SUBSIDIES HELPS TO BECOME AN ART-WORLD-RECOGNIZED ARTIST. BEING A RECOGNIZED ARTIST IS IMPORTANT FOR ARTISTS. Before the period of serious art, control of numbers of artists is formal. During the period of serious art and after, the new art-worlds recognize artists and so indirectly control the number of recognized artists. They do so in a variety of ways of which official schooling is only one. Many artists without "official" schooling also become recognized within art-worlds.

In the period of serious art and after, being a professional artist is *a self-declared state*. Aspiring artists will usually only declare themselves artist after some confirmation. Confirmation can have many forms. It can, for instance, come from family members, friends, artists who the aspiring artist knows, teachers at primary and secondary school, teachers in unofficial and official art schools, and so forth. Other confirmation can come from having graduated from such schools. The same applies to being able to sell one's work, including manuscripts, performances and commissioned art, or to be able to make a living from art.[36] In the popular arts, being able to make a living is more important as confirmation of being an artist than in the arts.

During this period and up to the present-day the social boundary between amateur and professional artist is weak, but this does not apply to the symbolic boundary. Moreover, the number of professional (or self-declared) artists can potentially become very large, which, indeed happens in the second half of the twentieth century. Gatekeeping by art-worlds serves, among others, to keeping the number of "true" artists down.

Before the period of serious art, being an artist was seldom a self-declared state. Gatekeeping was relatively simple. From the thirteenth century onwards, education one way or another is organized and gives access to the profession. The common form of education was the apprenticeship. Under supervision of one or more well-established professional artists, the aspiring artist learned the "trade", could become a professional artist and stop being an amateur. Strong conventions and/or control by an authority with power made it impossible to make a living as an artist without "official" education. Thanks to the existing systems of education, there are not too many and also not too few artists, with the consequence that most of the time artists earn enough to make a decent living. (There are exceptions to the rule of needing to be educated, but, other than in literature, these are unimportant.)

This changes in the serious art period. Gatekeeping now takes the form of art-worlds recognizing certain artists and not others. As mentioned, popular/inferior-art is no longer art, and the people who make such art need to be excluded from the realm of serious art. Art education by official art institutions remains an important means of gatekeeping, but not the sole means. Not all artists without a degree are excluded. Becoming recognized as a serious artist no longer can be simply a matter of having been educated and also not of having graduated from a recognized school. Too many good artists would remain unrecognized and too many "bad" artists who after all make inferior-art would be recognized.

Therefore, the means to recognize artists become more varied. Artists can also become recognized later in life or they can lose recognition later in life. The notion of the artist being called and possibly be an artistic genius is incompatible with demanding a degree. At the same time the notion makes the art profession extra attractive with the consequence that there are many artists and excess supply [41]. This increases the need for more and other forms of gatekeeping./36

In the period of serious art as well as today, many professional artists have been taught by peers or teachers, who themselves are practicing professional artists. This is the same as earlier. Many artists receive their first education in classes for amateurs, amateurs of whom some aspire to become artists. Or they are taught privately in the homes and studios of professional artists. (Also, teachers in not accredited and accredited art education institutes are often practicing artists. Writers are often almost altogether self-taught, but the same as others need forms of confirmation to declare oneself a professional artist.)

At present the number of professional artists or "working artists" that have followed official art education is very low. In the USA, only 16% of them have a bachelor degree in the arts; they are "arts graduates".[37] In the major part of the twentieth century, when the number of artists (in relation to the size of the population and the demand of art) was lower, the corresponding percentage was probably higher, but not that much./37 ("Working artists" or professional artists are those who in surveys indicate that art is their primary occupation, i.e. they perceive themselves as professional artists. They "declare" that they are artists.)

This is not to say that since circa 1980 for art-worlds official art education has become an altogether unimportant means of gatekeeping. At present the percentage of officially educated artists among serious recognized artists is probably much higher than in the overall group of artists. Official art education does help in crossing the social barrier around serious or art-world-recognized art. It helps in developing a network and it allows, so-called, screening by art-producers.[38] The chances to become art-world-recognized and a bit successful increase. (In web-text wt-14 I say more about the (un)importance of art education for a career in the arts.)

Over the last two decades official art education still can make a difference for success, but as a mechanism of gatekeeping, it has become far less important. This is because during this period rapidly new and parallel, what I call channels of scouting and gatekeeping with corresponding new career paths have emerged. This is the topic of section 92.

(15) During the period of serious art: ART-WORLDS DIFFER IN FLEXIBILITY AND STRENGTH. THE CLASSICAL/SERIOUS MUSIC ART-WORLD IS STRONG AND INFLEXIBLE. VESTED INTERESTS ARE IMPORTANT. THERE IS PATH-DEPENDENCY. THE NATURE OF ART-BUILDINGS MATTERS. Several factors influence the strength and flexibility of art-worlds and their development over time. In the performing arts the nature and history of the art-buildings are particularly important. Their main products require different buildings. Next the buildings, to different degrees, limit the development of new products.

The usefulness of the nineteenth-century concert halls is most limited. Given its acoustics—much reverberation (echo)—and the size of the halls—not too small—they almost exclusively suit performances by large symphony orchestras. Opera houses with their pit can host both opera and ballet performances. In opera houses, a compromise is sought between more reverberation to make the sound of the orchestra attractive and less reverberation to make the sung or spoken text understandable. With or without a pit, traditional theatres with little reverberation can host theatre, opera and ballet. They are multi-functional./38

Aside: Some degree of inflexibility is typical for all art-worlds, but it is strongest in the art-world of classical/serious music. Understanding the causes in this art-world helps in understanding the less extreme inflexibility in other art-worlds. In this art-world one important cause indeed rests in the nature of the art-buildings for music performance. They serve the performance of orchestral music. Sometimes there is a small extra room for performances by small ensembles, but this is secondary.

In the course of the nineteenth century the core business of the classical/serious music art-world has become music produced by large symphony orchestras. This promotes the erection of the new halls and vice versa. There would be no Mahler without halls with much reverberation allowing a subtle sound balance. (The strong echo in the churches in which Bach's cantatas had been performed did not allow a subtle balance.)

In this art-world, much time and money has been invested in a specific set up. It has been invested in large orchestras and in expensive buildings of which the main room with the largest number of seats is only altogether suitable for the production and consumption of music by large orchestras or, otherwise, soloists with a loud voice or instruments like the grand piano. There has also been much time and money invested in the education of musicians who perform in large orchestras, as well as in the buildings that serve official music education. Alternative creation and production, for instance by small ensembles, is not impossible and occurs, but the art-world as a whole is both inflexible and strong because of the halls and the large orchestra. It depends on them, and this brings along so-called path dependency. It also brings along ever higher cost per visiting hour, as we shall see in section 34.

Social scientists speak of path dependency. *Path dependency* refers to the phenomenon that, even though past circumstances no longer exist, present choices are limited by decisions taken in the past.[39] They are not really limited. In theory new and different paths are possible but they require new investments and appear to be unattractive.

In the classical/serious music world the nineteenth-century material and mental investment has indeed been large. It is therefore understandable that when in the twentieth century some musicians propose and later demand that baroque music is performed by smaller ensembles, this demand is at first rejected. The same applies when later electronic amplification becomes available, allowing performances in larger halls. Also, when more electronic instruments become available allowing the composition and performance of new and attractive music this is rejected. The outcome is that also today in most areas of classical/serious music production a "tired, old technology", a nineteenth century technology, continues to be used.

Art-worlds are more or less flexible. This is related to the mentioned difference of art-buildings. But apart from the freedom that the opera art-world allows itself in the choice of stage setting and acting, the world is as inflexible as the classical/serious music art-world. The ballet art-world is slightly more flexible. The modern- and contemporary-dance sub-art-world is again more flexible. The fact that the latter does not rely on large orchestras but usually on small ensembles or (increasingly) on recorded music makes a difference. Of the performing arts the serious theatre art-world is most flexible.

Most flexible is the art-world of the visual arts. "Live" visual art is offered in very flexible or "multipurpose" art-buildings. They can host flat and 3D works, large and small works, projections, visual art performances, soundscapes and so on. They can, if they want, host popular art.

Aside: Flexibility in this art-world is so great that already for a considerable time major art academies, like Goldsmith in London, have departments in which popular music is taught—some major pop musicians, among them James Blake, graduated at the Goldsmith department. Some 50 years ago no popular music skills—let alone the ability to compose—were taught in the conservatoires controlled by the inflexible classical/serious music art-world. And at present in Europe, it still is mainly technical skills which future pop musicians learn.

In the performing art-worlds there is anyway more fear for popular art being so successful that it endangers the own art-world by pinching its audience, which, indeed, has already happened and may continue to happen. But in dance and theatre fear is diminishing. One realizes that the old days will not return and accept that the consumer has found attractive alternatives. Moreover, in the case of theatre there are ties in the personal sphere. Ever more established theatre actors also act in movies while the opposite also occurs. Moreover, sometimes movies are based on plays—and of course literature. (This affects copyright income.)

In the long run, little flexible art-worlds are strong, but in the very long run, more flexible art-worlds are stronger. The inflexible art-world of classical/serious music and opera is, given its control over the music halls and the education institutes, still powerful—it is supported by many subsidies. But over the last 50 years the more flexible visual art-world is rapidly becoming as strong. And looking at the development of demand for "live" art—performances as well as originals in museums—the first is bound to lose much of its power, while the latter is likely to remain relatively powerful.

The overall art-world of ballet/dance and the art-world of theatre hold intermediate positions. But their size in terms of numbers of artists and consumption hours is much smaller and this makes them less powerful. (As I will argue, over the last decade along with fading boundaries in the arts all art-worlds are losing strength.)

Art-worlds which do not offer "live" art but only (re)productions are least strong and most flexible. The strength of the literature art-world and the later film art-world is indeed limited. They are not able to develop and maintain a strong symbolic boundary between art and no art. Too many consumers are involved. There are few non-profits while most production and distribution are done by for-profit companies which usually have an interest in flexibility and not in a strong boundary.

Given path dependency, it is understandable that not only in the twentieth century but even in the twenty-first century, halls, like recently the very costly Elbphilharmonie in Hamburg, are designed to best serve performances by large symphony orchestras, including operas and ballets. Even if one wanted to, breaking such a logical chain of buildings, events and attitudes is very difficult. But such buildings will not stop the decline of classical music. As we shall see, the decline has several causes, but they are enhanced and they remain active due to inflexibility.

Given the arguments presented in these sections, the question arises if the establishment in the classical music art-world can be blamed for the present decline in demand. It can be blamed for not attempting more to lower cost per visiting hour [54]. It can be blamed for feeling threatened by popular music, putting down popular music and so enhancing its success and not seeking to connect to it by producing and promoting real crossover music. (The opposite happened in the visual arts.) But given the mentioned inevitable path dependency connected with the existence of outdated concert halls, defensive behavior is understandable but not wise—it leads to expressions of superiority which are contra-productive. Among major players, a notion of "it will last my time" may well be present. Going for change is anyway risky, and more so because it is not very clear which course(s) will bring a lasting revival of heritage music and new music in the classical tradition. Less protocol and a more informal atmosphere in the halls will not be appreciated by the graying audiences, but is bound to be attractive for groups who have lost interest [92]. But choosing to let orchestras more often accompany well-known pop musicians and DJ-producers, as presently happens, is almost certainly unwise in the long run. In the longer run, both parties are bound to lose interest. *(Anna visited several of such concerts and thought the artistic quality to be low. Playing with large orchestras brings popular musicians temporarily prestige, but their work without orchestra is much better.)*

(16) During the period of serious art: ART-WORLDS GUARD PROGRESS. SUCCESSFUL INNOVATIONS ARE THOUGHT TO HAVE BEEN NECESSARY. NEW ART MUST REPRESENT A NEXT STEP IN A LONGER-TERM DEVELOPMENT. Before the period of serious art, there was no strong sense of progress in the arts, but in the period of serious art, the notion of progress and continuity in art is important. An art heritage is constructed and maintained.

In the eighteenth century and even more in the nineteenth century, when Modernity has gained momentum, a belief in a linear sense of time with an open future becomes important. Eyes are increasingly directed at the future; people observe and expect progress. In the new art-worlds a historical conscience develops. Art-worlds become guardians of tradition as well as of progress. They create an art heritage and judge the artistic quality of new art, while keeping in mind what went before. By putting new work in a historical context, they "enrich" the work and make it more interesting. Classics and other consecrated and preserved artworks serve as points of reference. The works form a canon of exemplary works.

New kinds of work are supposed to go in new directions but must be properly rooted in what went before. Innovations in the arts are described and understood in terms of progress. When they become successful, they are presented as understandable, good and necessary. The new is good and better than what went before./39 (Not all artists adhere to the idea of progress in the sense of "being better". For instance, the radical avant-garde often denied and mocked progress in art.)[40]

In the first half of the twentieth century prominent innovative artists regularly start to justify their major innovations by proclaiming that the till then dominant art genre can no longer be further developed; it has fully developed, has matured and is exhausted. The new art is necessary and better. For instance, in the 1920s Arnold Schoenberg and colleagues, who at the time developed the twelve-tone technique—later called serial music—argue that their music not only represents a logical but also a necessary progression of what went before. (It is thought to be the music of the future—which it, however, never became./40) Others, however, think that already an earlier stage in the development of art is final. In the same way that the nineteenth century nation state is thought to be natural, necessary and final, so is the art of the nineteenth century.[41]

Aside: In the arts, major innovations (or a new paradigm) are often attributed to a single artist. He is the author and a highly respected lonely genius—Sometimes, in exalted terms, he is said to be a prophet who envisions the future and shows the way. But when the new is inevitable, it is likely that a "necessary" innovation is "in the air" and that one or more groups of cooperating artists, critics, experts and users together take the next step. From a distant view, the notion of "being ahead" is anyway strange. Art "mirrors society".[42] Societal developments always influence the form and content of artworks.

In the second half of the twentieth century, many "ordinary" artists present their works as innovative and most experts/critics as well as groups of consumers expect artists to be innovative, while art-companies start to select artists whose work they judge to be innovative and forget about others. Together they make the new works more special and "enrich" the works by adding a new narrative: "This is innovative".

(17) During the period of serious art: WITHIN ART-WORLDS, A QUALITY HIERARCHY OF ARTWORKS, GENRES AND ARTISTS EXIST. QUALITY JUDGMENTS CHANGE WITH TIME. ART-WORLD UNITY MUST BE MAINTAINED. Quality judgments in art are subjective. They depend on the ways people understand art. Lower- and higher-class people may well "understand" a Vivaldi piece in a different way and judge its quality to be higher or lower. And both "understand" and appreciate Vivaldi's music differently when compared with a seventeenth-century listener.

A common way of understanding and judging can indeed change over time. The people who in churches cried while looking at the Stations of the Cross understood the paintings differently than the people who now look at them silently in museums, or see them on postcards. And the crowds that in the time that Baroque music was created listened in churches, or listened while dancing in the room of a palace, must have understood and judged the quality of the music differently than the people who now motionless, sitting on chairs with straight backs, listen to Baroque music in the concert hall.

The question arises if superior ways of understanding exist. Is the present propagated way of understanding and appreciating works by Bach or seventeenth-century genre paintings superior when compared to the most common way that people understood them at the time of their creation? Given the very different circumstances and mindsets the answer is no./41 But in spite of necessarily different understanding, art-world experts compare works which are created in the same period, "measure" their quality and order them according to their supposed artistic value./42 Often also works created in different periods are compared and ordered. The same applies to their creators. The one work or artist is better than the other. For centuries art scholars have produced rankings of artists and artworks based on various forms of expert knowledge.

The orderings in the visual arts of artistic quality do not change much over time.[43]/43 In the nineteenth century in the new serious art-worlds in the various art forms, art-lovers as well become interested in the created artistic quality hierarchies, and experts become authorities—works in the overall art heritage that they classify as classics are sometimes thought to have stood the test of time. Later more recent classics are constructed and added. The classics are immortal and certainly no ephemera [10]. The overall result of classification is a quality hierarchy—a hierarchy of aesthetic value—that appears to be of all time./44

Looking more carefully, with time the orderings of experts in the arts change considerably, also during the last decades. But in as far as art historians are aware of changes, they tend to argue that the previous hierarchy (and canon) was wrong, and not that quality judgments are subjective and related to the needs of the own time and own social group./45 (In this long web-note I present and discuss various examples of changes over time in widely shared quality judgments and the possible impact of social factors.)/46

Within art-worlds experts influence the judgments and choices of art-lovers. Supposed artistic merit in the arts determines success or *must* determine success. A belief in a *meritocracy of artworks and artists* exists. In their consumption art-lovers go along. Due to expert judgments people now go for and pay for the performances of the works of Johann Sebastian Bach and not for those of his son Johann Christian, whose works at the time were more popular. Also, the willingness to pay for certain kinds of paintings changes due to changing expert judgments.

The fact that groups of experts sometimes disagree, does not necessarily imply that their judgments do not influence success. Different groups of experts may influence different groups of art-lovers. Therefore, parallel art quality meritocracies exist. For instance, during a large part of the twentieth century a dominant meritocracy of artworks existed in the domain of traditional art and a parallel other meritocracy in the, at first much smaller, domain of modern-art.

It is significant that in popular art, groups of experts/critics are more modest. They seldom construct general artistic quality hierarchies of works. Instead they emphasize the relativity and subjectivity of their judgments. Moreover, they tend to look at far more than artistic quality, but also at other qualities, like works being more or less soothing, exciting, well produced, danceable and so forth.

How come in art-worlds the inclination of art-world participants, including experts, to make overall quality judgments is so strong? They are believed to be of all times, or at least valid for a specific period. The inclination is usually strongest in the case of art of the own period. Why must artistic quality determine success? What is at stake is the strength and authority of art-worlds. To maintain them, shared judgments and thus art-world unity is required. Deviating opinions go at the cost of unity. Every now and then the activities of dissenting factions within art-worlds—usually factions that promote new art—go at the cost of overall unity, but each time unity is restored [21].

This is not to say that after the restoration of unity what is new has ample chances. In inflexible and strong art-worlds, like the classical/serious art-world, to remain united the new must remain unimportant. In comparison in the flexible worlds of art in the popular arts what is new has ample chances.

A contemporary example of a well-noticeable and undeniable changing judgment—and also of disagreement—is that of artworks by certain women artists. Now, among certain groups of art-world participants and experts they and their works are judged to be higher than earlier was commonly the case. This also applies to older works by female artists. The works did not change but along with changes in society, their artistic value has. Visual artworks created by women (and non-whites) are dug up and added to the selection that is shown in the prominent rooms of museums. It is certain that also in the future certain groups of works whose artistic quality is now judged to be low by experts will be judged to have much artistic value by future experts. Artistic quality is very relative.

Over the last decades art-worlds lose strength and unity has become less important. Along with this development, parallel channels of gatekeeping become established in an art form, that is, channels which correspond with different ways to reach higher levels of success [92]. It leads to more relativism and the acknowledgment that experts are not independent [88]. They were never independent, but their dependence increases.

(18) During the period of serious art: ART-WORLDS MAINTAIN A PUBLIC ART HERITAGE. ART CLASSICS ARE CREATED WHICH ARE EXTREME WINNERS. IN THE ART-WORLD OF SERIOUS MUSIC, THEY CONTRIBUTE TO FOSSILIZATION. Guarding progress is only possible with knowledge of what went before. It requires a preserved and accessible art heritage.

A *public art heritage* refers to the combination of two kinds of heritage: an *accessible public art heritage* and a *hidden or stored public art heritage*. A heritage is partly material and partly intangible. A *material public art heritage* exists of old visual artwork, manuscripts, photos and recordings, video tapes and their modern digital equivalents. An *intangible public art heritage* is performances of works of old. Next to a public heritage, a *private art heritage* exists. Owners can refuse access.

Some collectors of visual art make works accessible by loaning works to museums, while major collectors, including companies, regularly or permanently exhibit works from their collection. Sometimes and increasingly, they do so in own museums. In the long run, one way or another, a large part of important visual artworks ends up in the public domain.

In all art-worlds, including the new film art-world, the maintenance of a public art heritage is judged to be important. And, whether or not one thinks in terms of progress, the presence of an accessible public art heritage undoubtedly has an impact on the development of new art.

The establishment of a heritage of classics starts in the early nineteenth century, at a time when there still is much contemporaneity in the arts, also in the art consumed by higher bourgeois—the latter applies most strongly to music. In the prelude to the serious art period in the early nineteenth century, certain works in music, opera and theatre are selected and regularly performed. The works become classics within the overall public art heritage—from Haydn and Monteverdi to Shakespeare. The interest in the works of older visual artists, like Jacques-Louis David also increases, but the creation of an accessible tangible public heritage of visual art in museums starts later.[44]/47 Performances are supported by governments and donors, but audiences are also willing to pay. In the case of museums, sometimes all cost is paid for by donors and governments.

Somewhat later also serious contemporary art is created which gradually become classics. In music, these are works in romantic style, as in the work of Hector Berlioz. But it is the romantic works of Tchaikovsky and Mahler which become the major new classics in music. The new cultural elite has a need for romantic music [25]. In the visual arts painters like Manet and Matisse become major classics.

It is not only a detestation of frivolous art and new needs that explain the construction of an art heritage of classic works in the nineteenth century. It also follows from the successful joint effort of state institutions and the new art-worlds to let artworks and artists stand for the goodness of the new, little unified and still feeble nation state. Much respected art of old gives the states legitimacy and grandeur. The suggestion that the states have a cultural build-up of centuries is created; a "tradition is invented" and great artists and artworks play an important role.[45]

Regular re-evaluations of classics would go at the cost of the tradition and the power of nation states. This partly explains why, in spite of major societal changes in the nineteenth and twentieth centuries, the heritage and certainly the top of the heritage become largely fixed. The importance or artistic value of the main classics from before the period of serious art, continues to be judged to be very high. This applies to artists like Shakespeare, Bach and Rembrandt. For audiences they remain in the top of a hierarchy of classics. And up to the present also for many experts and expert-consumers the relative ranking at the top is fixed.

Also, the collection of new major classics which are created in the second half of the nineteenth and the first half of the twentieth century becomes, to a slightly lesser degree, fixed. A significant example showing that later on as well national interests are important is that for a while there was strife between France and the Netherlands about the status of Van Gogh. Was he a French or a Dutch artist? The Dutch won. In this respect "enrichment activities", like celebrations and intense marketing by—subsidized—museums, can make a difference. (I explain the notion of enrichment in section 77. Here it suffices to say that in enrichment extras are added to artworks. This can be information, but also such things as celebrations, presence in the most prestigious art-buildings and so forth.)

In the period of serious art, in art-worlds the importance of classics is so much emphasized, that the major interest in the fixed heritage and its classics starts to go at the cost of contemporary art. This contributes to major conflicts, conflicts between a large conservative part of an art-world and small factions which promote innovative contemporary art [20].

A heritage can only be maintained when it is meaningful for people. It therefore needs to be alive and on the move. This, moreover, requires that the present production is also alive and successful, and people can link it with what went before. No old without new. A lively heritage may seem a contradiction in terms, but it is not. It is not accidental that for intangible cultural heritage to become recognized as important heritage and to be put on the heritage list of the UNESCO, the latter demands that the heritage is alive and not static. This certainly does not apply to the intangible heritage of classical music.

With time, a static art heritage becomes more and more meaningless for people, that is, other than artists and scholars. A continuous promotion and enrichment of classics of old or even just a few classics—the top of the top—can go at the cost of the appreciation by larger audiences of new work. It can also go at the cost of the appreciation of the classics of old. This is what clearly happens in the serious music art-world, and until some decades ago also in the visual art art-world. (In this web-note I say more about the phenomenon.)/48

That a lively heritage is not a contradiction in terms is shown by the visual art-world and its museums of old art. All through the twentieth century they have been accessible to broader audiences than the concert halls and theaters. For a long time, managements were aware of an educational role. And *over the last decades* they find ever new ways to keep the heritage alive and "on the move". It happens that old and new art are shown together in the same rooms. Sometimes this is used to illustrate changes in society. Without paternalism a "healthy" relationship between old and new is created. (In this web-note I say more about the treatment of the intangible and tangible heritage in other art forms.)/49

All in all, *over the last decades* in the more user-oriented domain in the arts, due to a livelier presence of new work, consumer demand for a lively art heritage is probably increasing. Museums of old art which go along with the user-oriented trend in the arts attract more visitors. A limiting factor is that the lively heritage must also be accessible, that is, tickets must be affordable. Rising ticket prices may again endanger the art heritage./50

What also shows ever clearer is that a limit exists to what new and more varied audiences appreciate when it comes to a heritage that is little alive. Continuing enrichment of older classics can start to go at the cost of the attraction of the older classics in general. *Over the last decades* in classical music the "over-enrichment" of a few winning classics within the overall heritage starts to endanger the whole heritage. *When Anna hears or reads well-known composers and classical musicians state on television or in popular blogs that Bach is the greatest, it puts her off.* This, nevertheless, is what many classical music lovers want to hear.

In certain domains of popular music an awareness of a heritage develops and the maintenance of a heritage become a matter of interest. But so far, few argue that the maintenance of an intangible heritage requires government funding.

(19) In the period of serious art: ART-WORLDS CAN ONLY EXIST AND BE STRONG THANKS TO MUCH GOVERNMENT AND DONOR SUPPORT. VARIOUS JUSTIFICATIONS ARE GIVEN. In the previous sections we have already seen that for various reasons art-worlds much depend on support of donors and direct and indirect support of governments. In this section, which is a summary of web-text wt-19, in this web-text I look at the amount of support, and the justifications that are given for support. I explain concepts from welfare economics, like public good, merit good and externalities, which especially in the 1970s play an important role in attempts to justify support. Because some art policy makers still refer to and base recommendations on welfare economic findings, students in cultural economics are advised to read the web-text.

Especially in the twentieth century there is much financial government support. The same applies already earlier to overall private support. That public support is considerable is not true in an absolute sense, or as percentage of GDP or as part of overall government expenditure. Other sectors of production, like at some time agriculture, receive more. It is exceptionally high in relation to the overall cost of production of serious art./51

Governments subsidize the cost of art-buildings, the activities of art-companies and those of ensembles and artists. Much government support serves the maintenance of an art heritage. Over time, the justifications of government support changes.

In data on government support of art and artists and thus on the amount of subsidy that indirectly flows to consumers, the subsidies for the maintenance of art-buildings are often not included. Overall subsidies per visitor or more precisely per visiting hour are higher. (In data on overall subsidization of the arts sometimes also the direct and indirect subsidization of movies is not included. The latter is largest in Europe.)

Forgetting about tax redemptions looking at ticket prices in Europe in the performing arts, usually the largest part of overall cost is covered by market income. But between 1950 and 1980, in many countries an almost as large part of what consumers pay for tickets is financed by governments and sometimes much more, up to 90%. Presently in the case of the opera performances by the most important opera companies, subsidies are even higher: By now, it is "excellent art", like high-end opera, theatre and classical music that receives most subsidies per visiting hour. If museums are free an even larger part of the overall cost is covered by governments. In some countries purchases of (certain) visual art by individuals is also subsidized.

Government support of art in the USA is not lower than in Europe, but a considerable part is indirect.[46] Government money is, de facto, distributed by rich individuals, foundations and corporations. Tax redemption rules make this possible. (In practice it is counted as private support and this leads to much confusion.) Worth noting is that in the USA, universities also support art—mainly new and experimental art. The percentage of cost of the latter that is covered by subsidies is substantial both in the USA and in Europe.

Support strengthens art-worlds and the authority of art-world establishments. Without support, much serious art could not exist, given the high cost of production of, assumedly high-quality, serious art, especially performing art. As noted [14], support also enables gatekeeping by art-worlds and thus the establishment of a symbolic and social boundary between serious art and inferior-art as well as popular art. It, moreover, enables the maintenance of an art heritage.

Public support and art policies must be justified and agreed on by parliaments and indirectly by populations. The maintenance of an art heritage is only one goal. In the course of the book and in the web-text I mention others. Justification requires arguments related to goals. Goals are, among others, accessibility, raising the income of (poor) artists, promoting art because it is good for groups of people who are little aware of this, promoting high-quality art and maintaining an art heritage because art is good for society at large, and promoting art because it brings economic benefits. Arguments are used to justify the goals I discuss in several chapters. Most arguments are related to the welfare economic concepts discussed in the web-text.

Various distinctions matter. Goals and arguments can differ in the case of central government and local governments. It is good to distinguish proclaimed goals and real intentions. Opportunism is possible. But also without opportunism it is good to distinguish between intentions and outcomes. Certain outcomes may not have been intended. Finally, periods can be distinguished. In the 1970s, social welfare often comes first in policy documents. In the 1980s, economic benefits are stressed; in the 1990s, the need for excellent art is emphasized, while at present, at the level of local government accessibility and participation (of others) appears to come first.

Some possible unintended negative effects of (much) public support have already been mentioned and more will follow. It is important that many subsidies can make art-worlds and their art-companies "lazy". It allows them to persist in a once chosen course. There is little incentive to lower cost [54]. In music sticking to the existing course, also goes at the cost of a lively heritage and the development of a new attractive repertoire. A negative effect I much stressed in an earlier publication is that ample subsidies for individual artists can lead to more artists and more poor artists.[47]

Over the last decades in the USA, the amount of direct government subsidies remains more or less the same. In most European countries the amount of overall government support goes down, but it remains large. (Considerable differences exist between European countries. In most of them direct support goes down, while in some indirect government support increases a little.) Income from donations increases in Europe. As noted, goals and justifications of subsidization change with time. *Over the last decades* everywhere economic benefits of supported art are more often emphasized. Especially the disproportionally high subsidies of high-end performances are motivated for their contribution to international prestige and their indirect contribution to national economies.

Innovative Art and Mainstream Art

(20) During the period of serious art: IN SUCCESSIVE STAGES, ART-WORLDS PUT MORE RESTRAINING DEMANDS ON ARTISTS. IN THE TWENTIETH CENTURY, NEW ART MUST BE INNOVATIVE. TENDENTIOUS ART IS REJECTED. IN THE ARTS, A DOMAIN OF RESTRICTED PRODUCTION EXISTS. To govern production and to guard progress, art-worlds put demands on art-world-recognized artists. The demands limit their negative freedom and autonomous space. For the artists who agree with the demands this is no problem, but others feel restrained or go their own way, that is, a way that deviates from the one promoted by the art-world. (The concept autonomy and related concepts I discussed in Section 26.)

Four stages or overlapping phases, can be distinguished which bring along different demands on artists. Before the period of serious art, artists can pursue any self-chosen goals. Expressing oneself is a rare goal. Instead, pleasing an audience with one's artworks is a common goal. Earlier, in the period of serious art, in a second stage, artists are expected to independently and truthfully express themselves. They and their works must be expressively authentic [31]. Non-artistic goals may supplement artistic goals and do not need to be subservient. An artist may, for instance, next to artistic goals pursue political goals or religious goals. It follows that tendentious art—art with a message—is not taboo.

In a third stage artists must *only* pursue artistic goals. The demand is an "art for art's sake and *only* for art's sake". The "art for art's sake" can, in principal, lead to a separation of art and society. In the course of the twentieth century the demand becomes more important. Many artists and art movements do not agree. Movements like Dadaism, Bauhaus and Fluxus, incorporate political messages in part of their works.

Artists making art with a political message are usually not unrecognized, but they and their work are little appreciated within art-worlds or by their establishments. This of course does not apply to famous artists, who *occasionally* make political art. Examples are the twentieth-century composers Hans Eisler and Peter Schat, and the painter Pablo Picasso, who painted the *Guernica.* Also, several twentieth-century choreographers, playwrights and writers occasionally create political works.

But artists who make social realist art and praise communism and other artists whose oeuvre largely consists of political works (without irony) and whose works are popular, are much criticized, and they and their work are unrecognized instead of little-recognized. Usually their artworks are judged to be inferior-art. In the 1970s, the criticism of popular tendentious literature is particularly strong./52 In the previous century, Charles Dickens' successful oeuvre with a very critical societal message was not at all put down in the literary world of his time; and it is significant that it is still regarded as a highpoint in the history of literature. It is also significant that in *popular art* and especially in popular music, "art with a message", including a political message, reaching large audiences is not and never has been taboo. Unlike in the arts there is no separation of art and society.

In the fourth stage the demand of "art only for art's sake" gets a new dimension. Art for the sake of art turns into an "art for the sake of art as defined by the art-world". Art must be "art-world art". The artworks must fall in a category of art that is defined as true art by an art-world or rather, by the art-world establishment and those in the establishment who feel responsible for the category. For instance, in the late twentieth century a dance performance must be a genuine instance of contemporary-dance as defined by those in the establishment who feel responsible for this category of dance. Due to effective attunement most art-world-recognized artists make *art-world art.* Without being aware of this their own artistic goals and those of their art-world coincide. Their *own art* is art-world art. But the art-world demands restrain artists who decide to give in to art-world demands but actually prefer to make own art [70].

Artists may also pursue artistic goals which deviate from the dominant artistic goals in an art-world. First, some artists who make inferior-art, which could never enter art-buildings and art-spaces, honestly believe that they pursue their own artistic goals. *Anna met Dutch artists painting works depicting tulips who do so.* But because the works usually sell well, they are, unjustly, accused of compromising [70]. The same often applies to outsider artists and mavericks. Their work may well be very creative, if not groundbreaking. But it is unrecognized. (Unlike the outsider artist, the maverick attempts to work within the boundary of an art-world, but his work is, indeed, unrecognized and he may well be expelled from his art-world.)[48]

Second, groups of artists exist who within the boundary of art-worlds deliberately pursue own artistic goals and develop new styles. They do so in opposition to the existing well-approved art-world styles. At the start their work may be altogether unrecognized—it does not fall in a category of recognized art, but if they are successful in their opposition, their kind of work first becomes a little recognized and later altogether recognized. In the intermediate period the groups represent disagreeing factions within art-worlds, who later join the establishment and change the definition of true art [20]. After having "taken over" the art-world, they are the ones who put demands on artists. An example is that of groups making modern-art who first represented oppositional factions, but after their victory demand that all artists are innovative.

The innovation demand does not so much represent a new stage. It is part of a later sub-stage of the stage of artists being demanded to only pursue art-world goals. In the course of the twentieth century, there is demand on artists to pursue exclusively artistic goals which implies that their work must be innovative. Art-world art is innovative art. Progress in art demands innovation. Every artist is supposed to be an avant-gardist. This puts much pressure on artists and art students [20]. The creation of work in the previous and "outdated" styles, that is, *old-style artworks* or *old-school artworks*, becomes taboo. Art-worlds condemn artists who continue to produce such art and cling to the old rules, norms or codes. Their works regress and hinder progress.[49] (Recently, however, some, so called, *neo-styles,* are becoming acceptable. An example is neoclassical serious music: a previously conservative elite enjoys listening to it.)

Aside: dead artists are not affected and certainly not if in their time their work was innovative. Famous older artists who made innovative art when they were younger are also not criticized—some may, however, be criticized for only "repeating themselves". Such old-school older artists do not or do hardly lose art-world recognition. Examples in the visual arts are Frank Auerbach and Lucian Freud before he died in 2011.

But the unjustified belief that younger artists who continue to make old-school art can never be innovative is strong. They are blamed for this. It can cause considerable distress. If due to the art-world's judgment, they do not receive subsidies or donations, and they earn little money in the market, their autonomous space or positive freedom is reduced and this causes further distress. (This is a case of discordance: the relative autonomy of the art-world goes at the cost of the relative autonomy of certain artists [26].)

Going from one to the next of the four phases or stages, production of serious art becomes more restricted. This can be explained in various ways. One explanation, among others, is that with an ever-growing number of prospective and professional creative artists, who attempt to make recognized art [42], controlling and limiting the number of recognized artists is important. At the end of a stage their number has grown again, while in the beginning of a new stage numbers are reduced. This is part of long-term governance. As noted [14], overall effect of gatekeeping on numbers goes up and down, but the long-term effect is a restriction of production.

A new wave of reduction in numbers is sometimes preceded by a wave of factions or avant-garde circles opposing existing production while restricting production in the own ranks. In the 1960s and 70s, preceding the victory of modern-art this leads to, what Bourdieu calls, a field of restricted production.[50] Instead I speak of one or more *domains of restricted production*, which exist all through the twentieth century, in the arts as well as the popular arts. In the period which Bourdieu studied, in the arts these areas are very important and interconnected; together they form a field or domain. In all cases the goal of restriction is not a control of numbers of artists. Artistic goals and the goal of protecting what is new from becoming diluted or mainstream come first. But resistance against longer existing areas which have become successful, in which artists sometimes earn high incomes and which offer more employment to growing groups of recognized artists, is important. (Much more can be said and has been said about Bourdieu's field of restricted production.)/53

Over the last decades, a fifth stage is developing. Along with the acceptance of contemporary-art, in order to conform to the demands of the art-world, the artist creating contemporary-art must produce artworks that *noticeably* differ from what went before. They no longer need to follow from what went before. A logical succession of styles (or genres) have become unimportant. Moreover, sometimes artists are demanded *not* to conform to any existing artistic standard.[51] The interpretation of "innovative" has changed.

In this last stage, artists have more choice. Serious art becomes more diverse—the same as occurred already much earlier in popular music. Second, art with characteristics that are typical for older genres, in particular pastiche works and works with quotations of earlier works and styles have become acceptable, that is, acceptable as long as the surrounding discourse is a contemporary-art discourse.

New art is now apparently unrelated, casual, accidental and floating. This increases the separation of art and society. When art comments on society, as it does in some newly created operas and plays or in free interpretations of older pieces, it is in a distant and harmless way. However, *over the last decades*, social critical art in the form of visual art installations in public space is no longer taboo and it draws attention of far more people than social critical operas. Finally, some recognized artists relatively autonomously decide to give up some of their artistic autonomy by choosing to make market-oriented art, while they are not forced to do so given their little means [43]. Significant as well is that a genuine interest in outsider art develops. Nevertheless, so far, the production of new old-school art is still taboo, unless it is in the form of a pastiche or with an ironic undercurrent.

(21) During the period of serious art: AFTER THE DEVELOPMENT OF A SUCCESSION OF NEW GENRES, MAJOR CONFLICTS ARISE, BUT UNITY IS RESTORED. In spite of the mentioned attunement, sometimes fundamentally different opinions exist in an art-world on the right course. In a first major social revolution art became serious. Next in intermediate periods minor conflicts connected with the introduction of new (sub)genres (or styles) add up and lead to three

other artistic as well as social revolutions. In each of the three cases "progressives" win and take over the establishment and the governance of the art-world. However, usually a majority of art-lovers is conservative and only follows much later. (Along with the successive revolutions different and more constraining demands start to be made on artists as mentioned in the previous section.)

That art establishments tend to be conservative is what can be expected. The members have vested interests. They do not only love longer existing art; they also have a reputational and financial interest in the status quo. The conservatism explains that activities of groups of artists and other participants, who develop or renew art genres, are not promoted and sometimes openly put down. But with time the changes accumulate and lead to a revolt and social revolution which affects the whole art-world. The revolution is successful when an art-world establishment agrees with the new styles. This usually only happens when a larger part of consumers—though usually still a minority—go for works in the new styles, implying that the *diffusion of the innovations* has become successful.

After a social as well as artistic revolution the new or converted members of the establishments are inclined to proclaim a new era in art production.[52] Arguable, the result of an artistic revolution is a paradigm shift. Another result of a successful revolution is that art-world unity is restored, at least for a while. This is important because some degree of unity is required to maintain trust in art-worlds. Also, the shared belief in the goodness of art needs to be maintained.

The first revolution appears in all art forms. A new art elite wants art to be serious and civilized [10]. This was resisted by older conservative elite with major vested interests, among others in venues and the management of events. After the revolution has become successful, artists who continue to make frivolous art as well as "not-serious" consumers are "expelled" from the world of art. As noted, another outcome is the creation of an art heritage with retro-active effect.

The gradual emergence of modern-art in the last decades of the nineteenth century leads to a second and third revolution. These revolutions are best noticeable in the visual arts. Between the first and the second revolution, realist and impressionist styles are developed. They start to replace the dominant classic and romantic styles favored by the official art institutions. In France, the vested interests of those involved in the before-mentioned Parisian Academy organizing important annual and bi-annual Salons are large. The innovative painters are refused access. They revolt and, as mentioned, organize an own salon: the Salon des Refugés. Thanks to the growing success of the new styles among groups of consumers, the Academy and its education institutes gradually start to also educate the new styles. Though classic art remains popular, ever more consumers buy realist and impressionist works. The revolution is successful. The transition in the establishment and its institutes takes time and there is little "bloodshed".

The third revolution is the outcome of a succession of new modern-art styles and sub-styles; "isms", like primitivism, expressionism, neoclassicism, futurism, surrealism, Orphism, serialism and so forth. Often, movements are involved. There is criticism of preceding styles. Around 1960, successive relatively small revolts connected with developments in modern-art, result in a clearly noticeable general revolt and the start of a revolution.

The role of professional art education is pivotal. Vested interests of the establishment in education institutes are large. This explains that in spite of an ever-growing attraction of the new styles among artists, groups of well-to-do buyers and of visitors of art museums, the social revolution only becomes successful in the 1980s, when the orientation in the art academies changes dramatically. At the time, most consumers still prefer and buy works in pre-modern styles, but the group that goes for the modern styles is rapidly growing. But by then the diffusion of the innovative styles can be said to be successful and irreversible.

Long after the appearance of the first modern-art styles, around 1880, these styles including the abstract art styles start to be taught in art academies. At that time, the education of the previous realist figurative styles becomes taboo. Vested interests in museums are less large. Already earlier some art museums start to also show modern-art and a few museums exhibiting only modern-art are established./54 Because the transition in the art schools is a matter of a few years only, there is much bloodshed: within a few years, teachers who are able and eager to teach the competences needed for the production of modern (including abstract) art take over.

Anna remembers the transition well. In 1985, life drawing was removed from the curriculum of the Rietveld Academy, which at the time was the leading visual art academy in the Netherlands—not only as an obligatory course but also as elective./55 Not much later all but one of the art academies in the Netherlands did the same. As a consequence, an older friend of Anna and a wonderful life drawing teacher at the academy, who had taught her earlier when she studied at the academy, was fired. He never got over it.

The reduction in numbers of visual artists in a new phase, and in this case at the start of the phase in which modern art has become victorious, is reflected in the expulsion of Anna's teacher and many other teachers from art schools. The nature of the gatekeeping by new teachers in the course of the successive years of teaching and in their contacts with scouting dealers and museums has changed. Control of numbers of recognized artists has become again tighter.

The acceptance of so-called contemporary-art or post-modern art by the art education institutes and by the establishment connected with them coincides or almost immediately follows the acceptance of modern-art. The institutes start to teach competences needed to create conceptual art and other forms of contemporary-art. It marks the success of the fourth revolution. This transition also occurs many decades later than the first creation of conceptual works, which goes back to at least 1917, when Marcel Duchamp shows his *Fountain*. Since then a minority but growing number of artists start to make works that can be said to be conceptual works. Because existing vested interests had already been given up with the teaching of modern-art, the further transition did not pose problems. Most teachers who are into modern-art manage to go along with the last transition and there is little additional bloodshed. Since that time, academies are interested in new developments in the arts, respond faster and sometimes initiate developments. Students are taught to develop a "project" and do "research".

The revolutions in the visual arts occur as well in the other art forms and their art-worlds. Only the revolution of contemporary-art is sometimes less successful. From the first decades of the twentieth century onwards, modern-art artworks are also created in music, theatre, ballet/dance, literature and in film. Again, after a succession of new styles between 1960 and 1980, major revolts occur. In the performing arts, they become successful as far as acceptance by art-worlds is concerned, but only in theatre and dance, the establishments also start to promote the modern- and postmodern art genres and styles. In theatre and ballet/dance the revolts are in every respect successful, because with time new and younger audiences become interested in the modern and postmodern pieces and in "re-compositions" of old work. Diffusion is successful.

In theatre, new theatre pieces and re-composed works replace the traditional repertoire theatre. (*Anna remembers that more than one altogether gory re-composition of Shakespeare's Macbeth was performed. She was shocked and liked them.*) The development in ballet/dance is remarkable: two sub-art-worlds come into existence: one of ballet which continues to offer traditional performances to part of the consumers and one of (modern) dance which serves another part./56 (Later on, in the latter (sub)art-world also, interesting crossovers of the new and the old art are developed.)

Even though the establishment in serious music recognizes the importance of modern-art styles and postmodern styles and their composers, they are not promoted and there is no changing of the guard. Most of all in Europe, up to the present day the so-called war horse repertoire rules.[53] As noted, the vested interests in the large symphony orchestra are too large [15]. The serious music establishment is successful in maintaining the status quo, but at high cost.

Vested interests in all performing arts are large, especially when the average ensemble size is high. Establishments resist changes that could bring along smaller ensembles. The consequence is that "revolutionaries" sometimes feel they have no choice but use drastic means, sometimes causing temporary bloodshed. *In 1969 in Amsterdam, Anna was present in the prestigious Amsterdam* Concertgebouw *when among the audience young composers started to shout during the performance of* Mahler's Symphony Nr. 7 *conducted by the world-famous conductor* Bernard Haitink, *demanding, among others, more performances of works for small ensembles composed by living composers. Haitink had to terminate the performance. Even more vicious was earlier in the same year the throwing of tomatoes at the well-known actors on the stage by rebel actors and directors sitting in the front rows during a performance of Shakespeare's* Tempest *in the prestigious Amsterdam* Schouwburg./57 *They also argued that too few plays of living artists—usually plays with fewer actors on the stage— were performed.* Unlike in serious music the revolution in theatre is successful. (But the number of visitors goes down.)/58

Aside: First, successful revolutions or not, because in all art-worlds the importance of modern and contemporary-art has been recognized, in conservatories, the education of future creative artists and many future performing artists is modified and continues to change. Second, by lack of strong art-world establishments and a strong boundary between serious and popular art, the developments in literature (including poetry) and film cannot be compared with those in other art-worlds. Temporary subsidies for modern- and postmodern literature and film, however, indicate changes in the orientation of the art-world establishments. But though promoted, never a considerable readership or audience develops for the rather esoteric modern- and postmodern styles./59

Finally, in the first half of the twentieth century in the art-world of serious music another major and remarkable conflict arises. It is remarkable because it does not concern new, but instead old styles. It is a conflict about the proper performance of baroque and old music. Smaller ensembles and other instruments are required. The in section 15 discussed dominance of large orchestras and the related path dependency explain why this is at first much rejected in this little flexible art-world. The rebels largely have their way while sometimes a compromise is established—performances by ensembles of different sizes. But looking at resources, the victory is not that large. The government subsidy per listening hour is much smaller than in the case of large orchestras and the art-world promotes the performances far less than those of the large orchestras.

Whereas in most art forms successive revolutions lead to an, at least temporary, reduction of recognized creative artists, in the performing arts a resistance against revolutions, which in music is successful, can also be explained from a wish to maintain the employment of performing musicians. It follows that differences exist between the developments of the various art forms. These are not accidental. Art-worlds have different economies.

Over the last decades no longer major conflicts occur in the established art-worlds. On the one hand, art-worlds have lost strength. On the other, along with post-postmodernism no longer clearly distinguishable new styles are developed that could threaten people with vested interests. Not everything new goes, but, the same as in popular art, there is more tolerance, and developments are now more organic. The open commercialization in the new more entrepreneurial part of art-worlds and a consequent stronger orientation on audiences with more varied tastes has contributed to this development.

(22) EXCURSE. THERE IS MUCH ARTISTIC INNOVATION IN POPULAR MUSIC. APPLICATION OF COST-SAVING TECHNIQUES PROMOTES INNOVATION. This section is as web-text wt-22 available on the website. It may interest all readers. In it, I discuss technological, social and artistic innovations in the popular arts.

Some older, ill-informed art-lovers may still think that in popular art there are no artistic innovations, let alone artistic revolutions. In as far as there are artistic innovations they are thought to be derived from innovations in the arts. As far as music and dance are concerned, younger readers will almost certainly not agree. In the second half of the twentieth century there are many profound innovations in music, and at least one major artistic revolution, that of Dance music (electronic music). In contrast to what some people think, its origin does not lie in the innovative work of Philip Glass and Steve Reich.

Usually an initial development and application of cost-saving techniques, from amplification to the replacement of acoustic by electronic instruments, leads soon after to important artistic innovations. In the serious art period with its emphasis on authentic techniques, this phenomenon is missing in the arts [33 and 34].

(23) IN POPULAR ART AND THE SERIOUS ARTS, INNOVATIONS DIFFUSE IN DIFFERENT WAYS. MAINSTREAM IS TABOO IN THE ARTS. RECYCLING OF STYLES AND IMITATION ART STIMULATE THE DIFFUSION OF INNOVATIONS IN POPULAR ART. For a proper understanding of the social economy of art, a further comparison of art and popular art is useful. In the arts as well as in popular art avant-garde circles of artists exist which develop new (sub) genres. But the process of the diffusion of their innovations follows different trajectories.

Before explaining the theses, it is important to acknowledge that the innovations created by avant-garde circles in the serious arts tend to be more profound than in popular art. This corresponds with fewer created parallel subgenres as exist in popular art and in particular in popular music. In popular music ever new avant-garde circles create many new subgenres, which do not differ much from other subgenres. In other words, inventions are more superficial. But they add up and taken together innovations can be as profound as in the serious arts. Rock music and later Dance music are good examples. In many parallel endeavors, new musical paradigms have been developed, which are comparable with those in the serious arts, but are developed in a more organic process and are less disruptive. For various reasons explained in this section, this is understandable.

Artists in the avant-garde circles usually meet in person in cafés and studios and together develop new art. They reject existing successful art or, in popular art, they reject mainstream art. Their disapproval of what is popular and successful energizes them. It stimulates their innovative activities. But the trajectory innovative new art follows while becoming diffused in the serious arts and popular art differs. The diffusion is much slower in the arts, while innovations are more profound.[54]

The first stage is not yet very different in the serious arts and popular art. In both, the avant-garde circles consist of a few creative artists who regularly meet in person, for instance in a studio or café. (Nowadays they may instead be in contact through the internet, but occasional meeting in person remains important.)[55] Before long a small group of "fans" joins the group, which so develops in a small scene. The fans are: some enthusiastic consumers, a few experts, a few sympathizing artists and a few producers, like supportive owners of cafés and small venues, minor and unimportant agencies, labels, commercial-galleries and publishers, and so forth, as well as shops selling things like materials, records, equipment and books. One may well argue that in this early scene-phase, participants, including the small group of consumers, collectively develop, produce and protect the new (sub)genre. Bourdieu calls all these participants, including the small group of consumers, "producers".[56] In both serious and popular art, this first phase usually does not last long. Many circles dissolve because the artistic innovation is unsuccessful and innovators lose interest.[57]

So far diffusion of innovations is very limited, a matter of at most a few hundred people. In the early stages of a second phase—a scene phase—the initial community grows. Usually the shared attitude is still one of staying among themselves. The new (sub)genre is vulnerable and must be protected against a possibly malicious outside world. For the participants the new is a "sacred object" and they are afraid of dilution, imitation, absorption in other (sub)genres and a premature success that is temporary only.[58] In the arts the outside world may well be thought to be "*the* art-world" and complacent consumers, and in the popular arts "*the* industry" and complacent consumers. An aversion to them is an important driving force for the innovation and its further development.

Nevertheless, already at this stage two differences start to stand out. Most importantly, probably because innovations are more profound, the protective attitude among artists and fans is stronger in the arts. In the popular arts, fans do not hold back and enthusiastically start to "spread the gospel". The community continues to grow and sometimes exponentially. The second difference is related to the first. Popular artists start to orient themselves on income from the market while serious artists often, not always, also turn to supporters, in particular governments, as well as a small group of supporting buyers of works and tickets, who offer them a more or less stable income. There is less competition and less need for larger markets. They operate in the earlier mentioned domain of restricted production. There small venues, minor and unimportant agencies, labels, commercial-galleries and publishers, consumers and in the case of visual art also a few rich buyers continue to support them.

The combination of both factors leads to a more rapid diffusion in popular art than in the arts. If a new (sub)genre is a bit successful, sometimes already within years, in a more or less diluted form it enters the phase of industrial production. It may even become mainstream. Naturally, not all artists who are at the heart of the innovation are happy with this process. But usually they do not attempt to stop it. They need income to survive as artists. In music, at first they are happy with gigs, later with a contract with a minor record label. Whether they like it or not they rely on the market. Sometimes it is other artists who start to dilute the innovation, but they may well go along.

In the serious arts in a scene, there is enthusiasm, but it is not outward directed. There is an orientation on market income, but most innovators do not rely on markets. This partly explains the slow diffusion of innovations. The belief that scene participants share is that the new genre needs protection. The members of an avant-garde scene feel connected with members in other innovative scenes including scenes in other art forms. They distrust "ordinary" consumers and art-world establishments, and they believe they are misunderstood and this brings solidarity. Together they are part of the domain of restricted production—or as Bourdieu calls it: a field of restricted production, a field in which artists are thought to have more autonomy.[59]/60

Keeping things for the own group makes innovation disruptive rather than organic. Unlike in the popular arts it appears to be an all or nothing affair. Most art-lovers are confronted with a new art which for them is daunting, and not something to try out. It nevertheless, indirectly puts innovators on a footstall, which is of course much appreciated in their avant-garde circles. It also enhances the notion of the misunderstood genius. And it offers the opportunity to blame anything and anybody but oneself. That is, blaming art-lovers unwilling to buy what is new, progressive and innovative, and a serious art industry which offers attractive but outdated alternatives.

In popular art there is no overall domain of restricted production.[60] Sometimes underground artists feel connected and the term alternative art is used, but within alternative art (sub)genres come and go. Many subgenres move upward; they become more successful and end up as mainstream within an overall genre. I call it genre-specific mainstream.

In this context a definition of general and genre-specific mainstream is helpful. I present and discuss these in the short web-text 23.

The upward movement often leads to a feedback loop, in a financial as well as artistic sense. First genres moving up offer more income to those innovators who go along. With the help of other artists, the subgenre in diluted form turns into genre-specific mainstream and may even influence the general mainstream. Now some consumers—with sufficient luxury consumption time [8]—become intrigued and want to find out about the subgenre in earlier, less diluted stages. Their consumption raises the income of old and new innovators. It enables and stimulates a further development of the subgenre and/or the development of new subgenres.

In popular art, expert-consumers may look down on “easy” mainstream art. But they do not stop its creation. They judge mainstream art to be (too) easy. It usually is diluted art. Sometimes it is imitation art or retro art. But it is not stopped. Market forces are too powerful. The overall recycling much enhances innovation. (When questioned, the critics may well admit that they also listen to mainstream popular music and watch broadcasts of mainstream performances and enjoy them.)

In the established arts, art-lovers believe or want to believe that mainstream serious art does not exist. Its creation is taboo. And to a degree, it indeed does not exist. Imitation art and retro art are judged to be inferior and banned: it is not serious art. The taboo is so powerful because it is also propagated in the large less restricted domain in the arts, even though in that domain market forces are stronger. (Upon closer examination, serious mainstream art of old exists but it does not contribute to a contemporary feedback loop, as I show in the web-text.)

The absence of a feedback loop and recycling as well as the absence of many parallel and expanding enthusiastic scenes in the restricted domain in the arts not only slows down diffusion. It also promotes more profound and disruptive innovations and therefore conflicts. It does not stop innovation but it prevents much diversity and contemporancity as exists in popular art. And as we shall see in later chapters, more diversity is a sine qua non for the arts becoming less exclusive.

Notes

[1](De Marchi & Van Miegroet, 1996) 50.

[2](White & White, 1995) 18.

[3]Among others (Durkheim, 1965) and (Collins, 2005) use the term "sacred object" and (Anderson, 1991) the term, imagined community.

[4](Collins, 2005).

[5](Blanning, 1969) 131.

[6]The Centre Pompidou clearly surpasses its counterpart, the Lloyd's building in London, which was designed by the same architect.

[7]Cf. (Pine & Gilmore, 2011).

[8]An example is the Design Museum in London.

[9](Throsby & Withers, 1983).

[10]Cf. (Frey & Pommerehne, 1989).

[11](Campbell, 1987).

[12](Blanning, 1969) 135.

[13]Dimaggio (1982).

[14](Levine, 1988) presents many other examples.

[15](Oettermann, 1980) (in German). One of the few remaining panoramas is the well-known *Panorama Mesdag* in The Hague.

[16]Smithuijsen, C. (2001) (in Dutch).

[17]Gay (1995), 14.

[18](Weber, 1984) 175.

[19]Cf. (Weber, 1984) 176.

[20](Velthuis, 2016).

[21](Weber, 1984) 182.

[22]For the USA: (Levine, 1988).

[23]Cf. (Dimaggio, 1982).

[24]See website.

[25](Weber, 1984) 192.

[26](Gay, 1995).

[27]Cf. Hobsbawn and Ranger (1983). *The Invention of Tradition* is the title of their book.

[28]Cf. (Hernstein Smith, 1988) 34 and (Klamer, 2016) 84.

[29](Hernstein Smith, 1988) 32. Speaking about the role of interpretation, the philosopher Arthur (Danto, 1986) 26–43 comes to a similar conclusion.

[30](Nietzsche, 1990) 24.

[31](Finkelstein & MacCleery, 2005).

[32]Cf. (White & White, 1995).

[33]For visual art: (White & White, 1995) and (Arora & Vermeylen, 2013).

[34](DiMaggio, 1991) 135.

[35]Cf. (Bourdieu, 1984) 3.

[36]For a visual artist having a first exhibition certainly is important, also for becoming a more successful artist. Cf. (Fraiberger, Sinatra, Resch, Riedl, & Barabási, 2018).

[37](Susan Jahoda & a.o., 2014).

[38]Cf. (Towse, 2006).

[39]This is a broad definition of path dependency. (Mahoney, 2000) presents a detailed treatment of the concept.

[40](Doorman, 2003) in Dutch.

[41](Doorman, 2003) 12 (in Dutch).

[42]For an exposition of the various forms of the so-called *Reflection Approaches* in art sociology, see (Alexander, 2003) 21–40.

[43](Vermeylen & Van Dijck, 2013).

[44]Cf. (Bennett, 1995).

[45]Tradition can be said to have been invented in the nineteenth century. Cf. (Hobsbawn and Ranger, 1983). *The Invention of Tradition* is the title of their book.

[46]Cf. (O'Hagan, 1998).

[47](Abbing, 2002).

[48]Cf. (Becker, 1982).

[49](Doorman, 2003) 22 and 73 (in Dutch).

[50](Bourdieu, 1993). To prevent confusion, I use the more general term "area"; in order to not get involved in the specifics of what Bourdieu calls a "field".

[51](Laermans, 2009) 133.

[52]Cf. (Gielen, 2010) 282.

[53]Over time, in the USA, the share of the war-horse repertoire of music (only music of European composers) is going down but still high. For the period 1842 to 1969, see (Dowd, Liddle, Lupo, & Borden, 2002).

[54]The text in this paragraph is inspired by (Lena & Peterson, 2008) and (Lena, 2014) who did research on trajectories in the popular arts.

[55]Nevertheless, most artists also travel and meet in person. On the importance of meeting in person, see (Collins, 2005).

[56](Bourdieu, 1977).

[57]Cf. (Lena & Peterson, 2008) and (Lena, 2014).

[58]On smaller group being protective of a "sacred object", see (Collins, 2005).

[59](Bourdieu, 1977).

[60]This does not apply to seperate (sub)genres. For instance, in the case of underground Rap music (Oware, 2014) speaks of restricted production.

Literature

Abbing, H. (2002). *Why Are Artists Poor? The Exceptional Economy of the Arts*. Amsterdam: Amsterdam University Press.

Alexander, V. D. (2003). *Sociology of the Arts. Exploring Fine and Popular Forms*. Malden: Blackwell Publishing.

Anderson, B. (1991). *Imagined Communities: Reflections on the Origin and Spread of Nationalism*. London: Verso.

Arora, P., & Vermeylen, F. (2013). The End of the Art Connoisseur? Experts and Knowledge Production in the Visual Arts in the Digital Age. *Information, Communication & Society, 16*(2), 194–214. https://doi.org/10.1080/1369118X.2012.687392.

Becker, H. S. (1982). *Art Worlds*. Berkeley: University of California Press.

Bennett, T. (1995). *The Birth of the Museum: History, Theory, Politics*. London/New York: Routledge.

Bille, T., & Jensen, S. (2016). Artistic Education Matters: Survival in the Arts Occupations. *Journal of Cultural Economics, 42*(1), 23–43.

Blanning, T. C. W. (1969). The Commercialization and Sacralization of European Culture in the Nineteenth Century. In T. C. W. Blanning (Ed.), *The Oxford Illustrated History of Modern Europe*. Oxford: Oxford University Press.

Boltanski, L., & Esquerre, A. (2016). The Economic Life of Things. *New Left Review, 98*, 31–54.

Boltanski, L., & Thévenot, L. (1991). *On Justification. Economies of Worth*. Princeton/Oxford: Princeton University Press.

Bourdieu, P. (1977). The Production of Belief: Contribution to an Economy of Symbolic Goods. In R. Johnson (Ed.), *The Field of Cultural Production. Essays on Art and Literature*. Oxford: Polity Press, 1992.

Bourdieu, P. (1984). *Distinction. A Social Critique of the Judgement of Taste*. London: Routledge and Kegan Paul.

Bourdieu, P. (1993). *The Field of Cultural Production: Essays on Art and Literature*. Cambridge: Polity Press.

Campbell, C. (1987). *The Romantic Ethic and the Spirit of Modern Consumerism*. Oxford: Blackwell.

Collins, R. (2005). *Interaction Ritual Chains*. Princeton/Oxford: Princeton University Press.

Cowen, T. (2002). *Creative Destruction: How Globalization Is Changing the World's Cultures*. Princeton: Princeton University Press.

Danto, A. C. (1986). *The Philosophical Disenfranchisement of Works of Art*. New York: Colombia University Press.

De Marchi, N., & Van Miegroet, H. J. (1996). *Mapping Markets for Paintings in Europe 1450–1750* (Neil De Marchi & Hans J. Van Miegroet, Eds.). Turnhout: Brepols.

Dimaggio, P. (1982). Cultural Entrepreneurship in Nineteenth Century Boston: The Creation of an Organizational Base for High Culture in America. *Media, Culture and Society, 4*, 33–50.

DiMaggio, P. (1991). Social Structure, Institutions, and Cultural Goods: The Case of the U.S. In P. Bourdieu & J. Coleman (Eds.), *Social Theory for a Changing Society* (pp. 133–166). Boulder: Westview Press.

Doorman, M. (2003). *Art in Progress: A Philosophical Response to the End of the Avant-Garde*. Amsterdam: Amsterdam University Press.

Dowd, T. J., Liddle, K., Lupo, K., & Borden, A. (2002). Organizing the Musical Canon: The Repertoires of Major U.S. Symphony Orchestras, 1842 to 1969. *Poetics, 30*(1), 35–61. https://doi.org/10.1016/S0304-422X(02)00007-4.

Durkheim, E. (1965). *The Elementary Forms of Religious Life*. New York: Free Press.

Finkelstein, D., & MacCleery, A. (2005). *An Introduction to Book History*. New York: Routledge.

Fraiberger, S. P., Sinatra, R., Resch, M., Riedl, C., & Barabási, A.-L. (2018). Quantifying Reputation and Success in Art. *Science*. https://doi.org/10.1126/science.aau7224.

Frey, B. S., & Pommerehne, W. (1989). *Muses and Markets. Explorations in the Economics of the Arts*. Oxford: Basil Blackwell.

Gay, P. (1995). *The Naked Heart*. New York: Norton.

Gielen, P. (2010). The Art Institution in a Globalizing World. *The Journal of Arts Management, Law, and Society, 40*, 279–296.

Heinich, N. (2005). *L'Élite Artiste, Excellence et Singularité en Régime Démocratique*. Paris: Gallimard.

Hernstein Smith, B. (1988). *Contingencies of Value. Alternative Perspectives for Critical Theory*. Cambridge: Cambridge University Press.

Klamer, A. (2016). *Doing the Right Thing. A Value Based Economy*. London: Ubiquity Press.

Laermans, R. (2009). Artistic Autonomy as Value and Practice. In P. Gielen & P. de Bruyne (Eds.), *Being an Artist in Post-Fordist Times* (pp. 125–137). Rotterdam: NAi Publishers.

Lena, J. C. (2014). *Banding Together: How Communities Create Genres in Popular Music*. Princeton: Princeton University Press.

Lena, J. C., & Peterson, R. A. (2008). Classification as Culture: Types and Trajectories of Music Genres. *American Sociological Review, 73*, 697–718.

Levine, L. W. (1988). *Highbrow/Lowbrow: The Emergence of Cultural Hierarchy in America*. Cambridge, MA: Harvard University Press.

Mahoney, J. (2000). Path Dependence in Historical Sociology. *Theory and Society, 29*(4), 507–548.

McCloskey, D. N. (2010). *Bourgeois Dignity: Why Economics Can't Explain the Modern World*. Chicago/London: The University of Chicago Press.

Nietzsche, F. (1990). *Twilight of the Idols (Götzen-Dämmerung)*. London: Penguin Classics.

O'Hagan, J. (1998). *The State and the Arts. An Analysis of Key Economic Policy Issues in Europe and the United States*. Cheltenham: Edward Elgar.

Oettermann, S. (1980). *Das Panorama; Die Geschichte eines Massenmediums*. Frankfurt am Main: Syndikat.

Oware, M. (2014). (Un)conscious (Popular) Underground: Restricted Cultural Production and Underground Rap Music. *Poetics, 42*, 60–81. https://doi.org/10.1016/j.poetic.2013.12.001.

Pine, B. J., & Gilmore, J. H. (2011). *The Experience Economy*. Boston: Harvard Business Press.

Smithuijsen, C. (2001). *Een Verbazende Stilte. Klassieke Muziek Gedragsregels en Sociale Controle in de Concertzaal*. Amsterdam: Boekmanstudies.

Susan Jahoda, & a.o. (2014). *Artists Report Back, A National Study on the Lives of Arts Graduates and Working Artists*. Retrieved from BFAMFAPhD website: http://bfamfaphd.com/

Thornton, P. H., & Ocasio, W. (2008). Institutional Logics. In C. O. R. Greenwood, R. Suddaby, & K. Sahlin-Andersson (Eds.), *The Sage Publications of Organizational Institutionalism* (pp. 99–129).

Throsby, C. D., & Withers, G. A. (1983). Measuring the Demand for the Arts as a Public Good: Theory and Empirical Results. In J. L. Shanahan a.o. (Ed.), *Economic Support for the Arts*. Akron: Association for Cultural Economics.

Towse, R. (2006). Human Capital and Artists' Labour Markets. In V. A. Ginsburgh & D. Throsby (Eds.), *Handbook of the Economics of Art and Culture* (pp. 865–894). Amsterdam a.o: North-Holland.

Velthuis, O. (2016). Are We in a New Era of the Art Market? In *Art in the Periphery of the Center* (pp. 456–465). Berlin: Sternberg Press.

Vermeylen, F., & Van Dijck, M. (2013). The Test of Time: Art Encyclopedias and the Formation of the Canon of 17th-Century Painters in the Low Countries. *Empirical Studies of the Arts, 31*(1), 81–105.

Weber, W. (1984). The Contemporaneity of Eighteenth-Century Musical Taste. *The Musical Quarterly, 70*(2), 175–194.

White, H. C., & White, C. A. (1995). *Canvases and Careers*. New York: Wiley.

Authentic Art and Artists

In various ways, an expectation and demand of authenticity in the arts affects the social economy of art. Two related forms of authenticity can be distinguished: expressive authenticity and nominal authenticity. Artists are expected to be authentic in expressing themselves and be true to themselves. Ordinary bourgeois are not in a position to do so. They envy artists and put art and artists on a pedestal. This partly explains THE almost religious ambience and atmosphere in art-buildings. Along with informalization, for many people the atmosphere has become unattractive.

Moreover, people increasingly believe that they as well can and must be authentic. This often does not work out. This is one reason why the art's professions remain very attractive, with as a consequence precarity among artists.

Second, nominal authenticity is demanded. Artworks must be genuine. And performances must conform to the artist's instructions or intentions, or they must conform to the dominant artistic tradition. The latter demands have major consequences for the art's economy. It prevents the application of cost-saving techniques. Instead costs rise much faster than elsewhere in the economy. Ever-more subsidies and donations are required, while, more recently, ticket prices have been raised much. These demands make the arts more exclusive.

Lines on either side of the text indicate that recurring concepts are defined or described. This chapter is accompanied by web-notes and web-texts, which are available on the website: *www.hansabbing.com*. Numbers between brackets refer to other sections, including web-texts. Numbers at the end of a sentence preceded by a forward slash refer to web-notes. Holding a pc, tablet or phone next to this text, it is easy to "scan" the web-notes and web-texts. (Quantitative data I most often present in web-notes.)

H. Abbing, *The Changing Social Economy of Art*,
https://doi.org/10.1007/978-3-030-21668-9_3

In Search of an "Authentic Self"

(24) Introduction. THE ART-SETTING AFFECTS THE ART EXPERIENCE. CONSUMERS DEVELOP OWN "ARTWORKS" WITH OWN "NARRATIVES" AND MEANINGS. THE "WORK ITSELF" DOES NOT EXIST. In the previous part of the book I emphasized the importance of art-buildings and art-spaces. In such buildings a specific *art-setting* exists. It is a setting that makes art serious, or, in other words, it turns art into serious art. In combination with its setting, art is meaningful. Meanings for an individual depend on the context, on personal histories and on the social group he belongs to.

A universalist and essentialist view of art promotes the belief that certain things and performances are art irrespective of their setting, but this is incorrect [12]. An extreme example of something turned into art thanks to an art-setting is that of the ordinary urinal that Marcel Duchamp exhibited in an art-building between other artworks. The urinal needs a room in an art-building to be an artwork, an artwork with a title, that is, *Fountain*, and not a nameless urinal. It follows that the urinal and the setting cannot be separated. The artwork is in the room and the room is "in" the artwork, that is, in the artwork that well-informed consumers construct. They properly understand the artwork: urinal in art-setting. A not well-informed consumer is unable to see an artwork.

An art-setting refers to more than a room. An *art-setting* is anything that accompanies the consumption of artworks and may influence the perception of the works. Examples of components of a setting in a narrow sense are the interior of the location, the tuxedos of musicians. The silence of the audience, the color of the walls in the museum—presently mostly white—the frame of the painting at home and so forth. Examples of those of an art-setting in a broad sense are also the exterior of the building, the behavior of attendants, the behavior in the foyers, the serious tone of a conversation about a work, its advertisement and the frame of a painting at home.

Many artists (not all) want people to understand their artwork the way they intended [39]. A physical art-setting can help. A sculpture in a museum may sooner be "properly" understood by average viewers than the same sculpture in public space. Sometimes certain kinds of art have different rules for "properly" understanding the works. Nevertheless, whether or not they know the rules, when people perceive a certain artwork and have an *art experience*, they will not always discern intended meanings or apply the "proper" rules for understanding an artwork. Perceiving a work they always (also) "understand" the work in own ways. In their imagination they construct own artworks which are bound to differ from the artworks of other consumers.

Duchamp says that the observer makes the painting.[1] Earlier Voltaire wrote: "The most useful books are those where the readers themselves do half the work".[2] And art historians say: "the work is in the eye of the beholder". In other words, people develop and create own meaningful artworks on the basis of a perceived actual artwork which is created by a visual artist, composer, playwright, choreographer and writer as well as by a conductor and director, and which is presented in an art-setting. Developing and producing own narratives and own "artworks" is an active process. What one develops is a "film". The work is, the same as a performance, created in real time. While looking at a painting, which is usually a matter of scanning the surface, the film develops and "frames" change. There is a narrative. Meanings can change along with the changing frames and episodes. The self-constructed film, however, usually has one dominant meaning or message.

To refer to the "artwork" that is created and imagined by consumers when experiencing art, I use the terms *artwork in a broad sense, user-constructed artwork, self-constructed artwork* and *imagined artwork or film*. Even though art consumers can be said to produce artworks, to prevent confusion I only call the artist's creation an *artwork*, that is, artwork without adjective. The latter work is a product that the same as other products can, in principle, be *bought and sold*./1 Moreover, even though *a ticket for a performance or art museum* is in itself no artwork, in this text buying an artwork can also be the purchase of a ticket./2 The art-setting affects the imagined works.

It follows that ultimately there is no "*work itself*". Both settings and people change and so do imagined works. Different occasions, like listening to music alone at home or with a partner, or with many others in a music hall, bring different art-settings and art experiences along. The other people may be noisy or still. People may talk in loud voices or whisper in the room of a museum. People are sitting on chairs with straight backs—as is common in music halls—or are sitting in more comfortable chairs—as is common in theaters—or stand—as is often the case in popular music concerts. The concert is given in a large or in a small hall. The paintings hang close together or further apart. And so forth. Such components affect the work of art that people perceive and construct. All the different constituents of the art-setting are "in the work"; and so is the beholder, or listener, or reader and his peculiarities. The "work itself" that he constructs is special and experienced as singular. Both objective components and private components affect the meaning(s) of somebody's self-constructed artwork.

Not all components are tied to a hall, theater or room. Many other components exist, of which several have little to do with the artwork. It is, for instance, not uncommon that prices can make a difference. In front of a painting of which the viewer knows that for its purchase the museum has spent tens of millions of dollars, the viewer may well foremost see a dollar sign and forget about other self-constructed meanings. But, of course (or hopefully) not all the time. Self-constructed artworks can indeed change over time, during a single viewing or listening occasion or from one session to another. When a person regularly listens to a musical piece which he likes, or when he rereads a book, he may well each time have a different art experience and construct a different artwork.

Art experiences can be more or less intuitive or controlled. At the one extreme, when perceiving the artist's artwork, a consumer develops a self-constructed artwork by letting himself go. He does not attempt to steer the experience. At the other extreme the consumer consciously and deliberately constructs his own artwork. In the latter case he may well consider the assumed intentions of the artist. (In a museum he may have read a text on the wall mentioning intentions of the artist.) (In spite of personal histories, not all private inputs in user-constructed artworks are unique. As we shall see [85], due to shared histories people in the same social group may well develop similar own artworks. In this chapter I, however, focus on very private art experiences.)

The sociologist Howard Becker—the author of the well-known book Art Worlds—as well argues that the work itself does not exist. He says that the common choice of a "work itself" depends on shared conventions, conventions which differ and change over time. This led Howard Becker to the formulation of what he calls the *principle of the fundamental indeterminacy of the art work*. He writes: "That is, it is impossible, in principle, for sociologists or anyone else to speak of the "work itself" because there is no such thing. There are only the many occasions on which a work appears or is performed or is viewed, each of which can be different from all the others".[3]

(25) During the period of serious art: ART BRINGS ENCHANTMENT IN A DIS-ENCHANTED WORLD. BOURGEOIS ENVY ARTISTS FOR THEIR FREEDOM. AN IDEAL OF AUTHENTICITY AND AUTONOMY IS IMPORTANT IN MODERNITY. In the period of serious art, art has several interdependent new functions, which much contribute to the triumph of art: imagination, enchantment, compensation, escape and assistance in a search for an "authentic self". Earlier religion offered similar possibilities, but it brought people to a shared God and not to an individual self.

In the formal society of the nineteenth and the major part of the twentieth century, artists with a relatively free live style are well-noticed, certainly when their number starts to increase. Bourgeois reject their free lifestyle, but also envy them. The latter is understandable. The bourgeois believe in the goodness of much self-control but at the same time suffer because of it. Deep down they wish that they could live the same free and authentic lives as that of (part of) artists.

To properly explain this phenomenon and to explore the concept of authenticity and the related notion of an "authentic self"/3, I first briefly discuss the romantic ideal of authenticity, which, together with an ideal of freedom (or as much autonomy as possible) and the primacy of the individual, is important in Modernity and most of all after 1800 when Modernity has gathered much momentum. Up to the present day, a romantic ideal of autonomy and of authenticity exists in society. (Several different notions of authenticity exist.[4] Further down I treat another notion of authenticity, that of nominal authenticity.)

Expressive authenticity refers to a being true to oneself while expressing a personal emotional state and/or a personal view in one's work and life.[5] *Autonomy* refers to the condition of *self-government* [26]. What the philosopher Charles Taylor calls, a *self-determining freedom* can exist.[6] Sufficient autonomy or freedom enables forms of *self-realization* or *self-fulfillment*.[7]

Gradually in the nineteenth century both ideals become important among the bourgeois. And in the second part of the twentieth century they also become important among ever larger groups of, first, lower middle-class people and *over the last decades* also lower-class people.

The strife for personal autonomy and authenticity in the nineteenth and twentieth centuries is part of a longer-term *process of individualization*. In pre-capitalist society being different from others is not something people are very aware of or strive for. They are not individuals in the sense we use the term. At birth a child's career is predictable. Most likely it will not differ from that of the parents. The son of the merchant will be a merchant and the son of the medical practitioner a medical practitioner. What stood out was the collective, not the individual. A person felt part of a collective, which defines him. There was more attention for sameness than for difference.[8]

But with increasing competition, specialization and rationalization of production in industry and administration, a person's place in society is no longer given. He becomes an individual and is expected to be an individual, but not a free individual who can realize himself. He must be an impersonal individual and not a "personality". Having to perform activities in industry and administration as part of a production chain, a person becomes a specific but also an accidental collection of functions instead of an integrated person./4 He is an individual who is expected to function as a cog in a machine; a de-humanized and alienated individual. His work and life is "compartmentalized". Bourgeois have more freedom but still have to follow rules. They have internalized the rules of their society including the demand to conform. This further contributes to a long-term process of formalization. They want to but cannot be authentic individuals in their formal and imposing society. They have to control themselves and hold back personal inclinations. It follows that in the main period of serious art there is a strife for an authenticity and degree of autonomy which cannot be realized.

Bourgeois yearn for an *enchantment* of their increasingly disenchanted world, that is, the, compartmentalized, rational, bureaucratic and hierarchical world that is typical for the main period of serious art. And they find it, among others, in art. Art offers enchantment./5 This way it also offers *compensation* for the disciplined and self-controlled life of the bourgeois and a possibility to temporarily *escape* from this life.

Aside: Even though in the perception of the bourgeois and of the later middle classes the arts represent an important source of imagination and enchantment, it is not the only source. Especially in the nineteenth century there are forms of learning and of entertainment which stimulate the imagination and bring enchantment. There are for instance journals with much attention for exotic countries, the mysteries of nature and technological innovations. Or learning and entertainment are combined as in the visits to the dioramas and panoramas, which are enjoyable and feed the imagination. But along with an increasingly strong separation of art and entertainment, for the nineteenth-century bourgeois and for the middle classes of the first half of the twentieth century, art becomes *the* source of inspiration and imagination.

(26) Intermezzo. FREEDOM, AUTONOMY AND AUTONOMOUS SPACE. In preparation of later sections and chapters in this short section, I say more about these concepts.

As said, *autonomy* refers to the condition of self-government. In other words, it refers to the ability to select and pursue own goals independent of others.[9] Complete independence is impossible. Therefore autonomy is relative.

Relative autonomy implies two forms of freedom. First, it implies *negative freedom or liberty*, that is, freedom *from* external control or influence when selecting goals. This ability implies that inclinations and desires are not influenced by others. Second, it implies *positive freedom or liberty*: that is, *having the means* and thus freedom to realize own goals.

I use the term *autonomous space* to denote the overall freedom and thus the combination of the negative and positive freedom of an artist or art organization. Autonomous space can be described in terms of time, other means and negative freedom. In the case of commissions and most performing art, the *negative freedom* of an artist is limited. The artist has to follow the instructions. Censorship and inevitable self-censorship also limit negative freedom. An autonomous space can be very large, but autonomy remains relative. A person can never be altogether autonomous. This also applies to so-called autonomous artists.

Available means in terms of *time* and *other means* (or *capital*) always limit the possibilities of artists. An artist has only a maximum of hours per day that he can make art, and limited capital in the sense of money, skills, a network and so forth. Because, from one situation to another, it is foremost financial means or money whose availability differs, without explication; in a discussion of degrees of autonomous space I usually only consider money and no other forms of capital./6 (Forgetting about other means, readers can picture autonomous space in the form of a two-dimensional space with money on one axis and time on the other.)

Expressive autonomy is a special case of relative autonomy. It refers to the relative freedom and ability to independently express oneself. People and not only artists have more or less expressive autonomy. *Artistic expressive autonomy* or, shorter, *artistic autonomy* is a specific form of expressive autonomy. It refers to the relative freedom and ability to select own *artistic goals* independent of others and to pursue them while creating art.

In this text *artistically autonomous art* is art that is created by an artist who creates works while *only* pursuing own artistic goals—At least that is what he thinks. Artists are often supposed to make such art. But many artists relatively autonomously chose to pursue *also* non-artistic goals. They make own art that is relatively autonomous from an own perspective, and not just artistically relatively autonomous art. This, for instance, applies to artists creating political art or "art with a message" (or tendentious art).

Aside: First, when people talk about art and the artist, the terms autonomy and autonomous almost always stand for expressive artistic autonomy and expressive artistic autonomous. Therefore, in the following text, when there is no chance of misunderstanding, I follow this practice and leave out the adjectives. Second, also when only (supposedly) own artistic goals are pursued, these may not be in line with the artistic goals that are promoted by the artist's art-world. If the goals are not or little art-world-recognized goals, their art-world may judge the works not to be real art.

It must be emphasized that artistic autonomy is relative. It does not imply that artists are not influenced. They may for instance be influenced by a partner. Moreover major societal developments always influence the content and topics of artworks.

Art "mirrors" society. But artists may think or want their goals to be purely artistic. (I do not follow this line of reasoning, but in theory these outside forces could be said to limit their artistic autonomous space.)

Autonomy is not only relative: it is also *relational* and often *discordant*. In the case of a commission the artist may negotiate the conditions of the commission. And autonomy can be discordant, because the autonomy of one can go at the cost of the autonomy of another. The autonomy of a commissioner can go at the cost of the autonomous space of the artist, while a successful and therefore relatively powerful artist can change the terms of the commission and so increase his autonomous space at the cost of that of the commissioner.

Finally, the assumption that a maximum of autonomy and a maximum of creativity correspond is ungrounded. Constraints often promote creativity.

Over the last decades artists probably become less autonomous; their autonomous space becomes smaller. Many artists have no choice but pursue also or only other goals than their own artistic goals. However, as we shall see [70], there are now also artists—hybrid artists—who relatively autonomously chose to give up some artistic autonomy.

(27) ARTWORKS ARE EXPRESSIVE AND PERSONAL. THE ARTIST IS "IN THE WORK". Ultimately all artworks are expressive and *expressively authentic*. All art, one way or another, tells about the person who has created the work. When this is well noticeable, it allows the viewer, listener and reader to relate to him as a person and to project own personal feelings on him and his work when creating his self-constructed artwork. Before the period of serious art, self-expression in art is less important for artists and consumers. And in the aftermath, it is also less important for many artists. But for most consumers the possible self-expression of dead and living artists remains important.

Longer ago most often artists did not intend to tell a personal story but they nevertheless, willingly or not, left a personal mark. Contemporaries were not interested in their personal expressions and marks. In the period of serious art, however, ever more people become interested in the personal expression in earlier art. They like those works best in which the personal expression is best noticeable. They can relate to artists—who may have been dead for centuries—and this makes it easier for them to have a personal art experience when seeing, hearing and reading their apparently authentic works, works in which the artist is thought to have been "true to his self".

It is therefore understandable that art-historians and musicologists select the works of artists who appear to also express themselves. Bach and Rembrandt are examples. They carefully store their works. Next, a smaller selection is regularly reprinted, performed and exhibited, while some works and their artists are put on a pedestal. Selections change over time. People look for works with other narratives and other meanings to construct works that befit their contemporary needs. (I say more about this in the web-note and in later sections, sections that, among others, treat an art heritage./7)

In the nineteenth century more expressive artistic styles develop. Many works in these styles are noticeably self-expressive; and often it is the intention of the artists to express themselves. The artist can be said to be "in the work". This makes the works unique and experienced as particularly singular [37]. As the group of artists who openly express themselves grows, so does the group of consumers who is interested in their works. The artist is thought to express his innermost feelings, his self in his work and this is appreciated by consumers. Work and artist are inseparable. The work is the artist and the artist the work. This is an important reason why for consumers artworks have an aura [37].

In this century it is the intention of many artists to express themselves. In literature there is far more reflection on personal experiences. Following Goethe, writers like Dostoevsky and Proust regard their entire oeuvres as being "confessional". Unlike before, accounts of an inner spiritual life are thought to be important. The number of autobiographies increases. *Confessions* of Rousseau is a good early example. Even musicians—among them Wagner—write long autobiographies. Many musical pieces, like some of Berlioz, Tchaikovsky and Mahler, have an autobiographical streak.[10] In painting ever more, expressive self-portraits are created, while in portraits of others artists attempt to tell more about the inner feelings of the sitter.

In the period of serious art and after, people are not only interested in the "artist in the work"; also the personal lives of the artists of old are interesting./8 When they are a bit adventurous this is highlighted in biographies and biographical films (biopics), as in the case of Rembrandt and Mozart, and if the lives are (too) ordinary, like that of Vermeer, they are made exciting, as in the movie about Vermeer, *Girl with a pearl earring*.

The widely shared conviction in the nineteenth century is, that artists, unlike others, are honest, they are themselves: they make authentic works and live authentic lives. And it is true that many artists are in a different position than most bourgeois. Because they do not have demanding jobs in industry or administration, they have more (negative) freedom. (If their income is low this does not apply to their positive freedom.) Not only are their working conditions less demanding, supposedly they also care less about the imposing and restraining demands inherent in the existing widely shared moral convictions; they "do their own thing" and apparently have some "self-determining freedom".

This certainly does not apply to all artists. In the nineteenth century and the first half of the twentieth century, the majority of artists continue to be (almost) as conformist as the bourgeois. Nevertheless, in the course of the twentieth century, the part of artists who noticeably care little about the widely shared imposing moral convictions grows. It is also significant that in the second half of the twentieth century, the large majority of artists present themselves as if they are true bohemians, the same as the few bohemians of the nineteenth century.

Even though in the nineteenth century many bourgeois admire the apparently free artists and envy them, at the same time they may well look down on them because of their supposedly free lifestyle and low incomes. There is rejection as well as attraction. The arts and the art's profession are attractive as well as dangerous. *Thomas Mann's famous novel* Buddenbrooks *offers a wonderful account of this. Since the merchant family of Buddenbrooks has become successful, the first-generation merchant is not interested in the arts. The second-generation son is somewhat interested. He marries a woman, who is dedicated to art. But he still fears the arts and his suspicion is well-founded. Much to his regret the third-generation son is no longer interested in commerce but only in art. He is artistic and weak and his father looks at him with contempt. At the end of the novel, before adulthood the son dies of typhus. Mann suggests that otherwise he would have become artist.*

In the course of the twentieth century, art styles are developed that are less expressive and less self-expressive, but this does not imply that artists do not leave a personal mark.[11] Also in the case of some typical contemporary-art, it is sometimes impossible not to see the artist-in-the-work. *(In the i–Note I present an illustration of a situation in which a colleague of Anna rejected an interpretation of her work related to her personal history while Anna thought the relationship was very clear./9)*

In the twentieth century and up to the present day, much popular art and especially music is expressive. It is also confessional and increasingly so *over the last decades*. This certainly explains part of the success of popular music.

A lack of personal expression, as well as intellectualization, may well explain the decline of serious art, most of all performed art. Going from modern-art, via conceptual art to contemporary-art, art appears to become less expressive and less self-expressive. The ongoing process of intellectualization in the arts, which I discuss in section 55, contributes to this development. But the overall interest in society—also of higher educated people—in romantic or otherwise very personal popular music is large. (The romantic period is long past, but romantic thoughts and preferences are more important than in that period. They are omnipresent and not only among an elite.)

Serious artists did not really get rid of a long history of much appreciated authentic work. It is significant that *over the last decades*, authenticity starts to fascinate groups of serious artists. First, after 2000 there are groups of visual artists who try to make works that are clearly inauthentic. Or in an exaggerated way they ironically fake authenticity. But some of the recent works appear to be more authentic (and romantic). It is significant that there is now much research by artists and art theorists on authenticity in the arts. This suggests that the taboo on (expressive) authenticity is becoming less strong in post post-modern art or post art. (In popular art theory authenticity has always been and still is an important topic.[12])

Especially when consuming art by dead artists, many art-lovers continue to look for the artist-in-the-work and have a personal relationship with him. The small busts with the very expressive faces of the much-admired composers Bach, Beethoven and Mozart have disappeared from the pianos in the living rooms, but books and films telling about their personal lives are very popular. Examples of films about famous serious artists of old are films about Mozart, Van Gogh and recently *The Girl with the Pearl Earring* about Vermeer. We identify with popular art stars and with serious art stars of all times. It appears that if you can be like them you can be yourself. "Be your-self" is *the* slogan of the last decades, and not only in commercials.

Aside: Not all conceptual artists go along with the idea that their art is not or must not be authentic. Damien Hirst, for instance, promotes the idea of the artist being in-the-work. Talking about his spot paintings he says in an interview in 2012: *"Every single spot painting contains my eye, my hand, and my heart".*[13] (The example is interesting, because of the 1400 spot paintings all but 25 were painted by assistants.)

(28) During the period of serious art: ART SERVES INTROSPECTION. PEOPLE SEARCH FOR AN "AUTHENTIC SELF". As said, given social economic constraints and related conventions of proper behavior, in the main period of serious art, living authentic lives is no option for ordinary art-lovers. But being in contact with one's self is not impossible and artworks can facilitate this. Finding the artist's true expression of his self in an artwork and thus finding the artist-in-the-work can bring along intense art experiences and help the development of own very personal artworks. This way the art-lover can explore an own inner-self.

A lack of freedom caused by their economic circumstances, the impossibility to realize oneself and the consequent alienation are is painful. It is therefore understandable that bourgeois increasingly search for an indivisible whole, a "self". They assume there is an own inner world. Compared with earlier centuries this is new. Referring to the late eighteenth and early nineteenth centuries, Taylor writes: *"The source we have to connect with is deep in us. This is part a massive subjective turn of modern culture, a new form of inwardness in which we come to think of ourselves as beings with inner depths"*. For him finding oneself is a very private affair. *"Being true to my self means being true to my own originality, and that is something only I can articulate and discover. In articulating it, I am also defining myself. I am realizing a potentiality that is properly my own. This is the background understanding to the modern ideal of authenticity, and to the goals of self-fulfillment or self-realization in which it is usually couched".*[14]

It is indeed a potentiality. During the main art period most art-lovers cannot "find" their selves, and they are aware of this. Or their imagined self is elevated and has little to do with real life. It is not accidental that in 1894 the Dutch poet Willem Kloos writes: "Deep in my mind I am a God". (Often transcendental and cosmic experiences and individualistic experiences enhance each other. Nietsche's and Wagner's penetration in the *Weltgrund* and Schopenhauer's idea of music serving the penetration in the depth of the own psyche do not exclude each other./10)

Most adults—also today—believe in the existence of "the real me", a finalized self. Earlier many people think in terms of a pre-existing self that needs to be uncovered and can possibly be developed, leading to self-realization. Now it is more common to think that a self only develops after birth in relation with others. Both notions of self have adherents, as shows from the contents of modern self-help books and, presently, podcasts and video lectures and video essays.

Whether it is a matter of finding one's self or developing a self: art can be helpful. When focusing on a visual artwork or a performance or when reading a book or watching a movie, while constructing own work, it is almost impossible not to embark on minor and sometimes major journeys of introspection and self-discovery. (As said, self-constructed works are like films.) This applies to abstract artworks as well as figurative artworks and to performances, books and films. Moreover, one may argue that ultimately any art experience has the form of an internal conversation. (For instance, with internalized "others" like a father, friend and enemy.[15]) It is a conversation in which the viewer, listener or reader explores his inner-self.

Because art performances, books and movies are consumed over time in a largely prescribed fashion, they are somewhat comparable with guided tours. This certainly applies to the eighteenth and nineteenth century symphonies with their meta-narrative. The common meta-narrative of "order overcoming chaos" connects well with secret individual fears as well as possible strength. (In the long web-note I discuss and provide examples of personal narratives.)[16]/11

In Freudian terms the internalization of rules of behavior and the resulting strong self-control in the daily interaction with others generally implies the repression of feelings as well as escapism. In the period of serious art this applies to many bourgeois and middle-class people. But unlike the Freudians in the nineteenth century, the bourgeois think that repression of hardly conscious inner drives or impulses and self-control is good. By listening to music, reading poems and books or watching paintings, the self can be explored and controlled while dangerous feelings can be sublimated. A mental "letting go" in an altogether safe setting, as, for instance, exist in a still concert hall among hundreds of other still people, is a possibility. This possibility explains part of the success of art during the main period of serious art. Story-telling and romantic art, including non-figurative abstract art, promote introspection and an exploration of one's self./12

But people seek "something" that they cannot have given their social and economic situation in society. Many early romantic philosophers and poets refer to failure to find oneself or realize oneself. Friedrich von Schelling speaks of "the infinite lack in being" and Novalis points to the person failing to find what he seeks. Novalis therefore advices to instead enter the "world of art". Or in the terms of this chapter: to escape and find compensation for "an infinite lack".

Up to the present day people search for an inner world and an "authentic self". Art of all times continues to help in the search. This now applies foremost to popular art, and, as said, less to the serious contemporary or post-modern art of the last decades. The nature of the search has changed. Most people now believe that it is possible to find one's self, to express oneself and to realize oneself. But next, many also find out that self-realization is still beyond reach. These are topics I discuss in the last sections of this chapter.

(29) During the period of serious art and after: THE ATMOSPHERE IN ART-BUILDINGS IS SERIOUS AND SUBDUED. PROTOCOLS EXIST. OUTSIDE THE BUILDINGS, ART-SETTINGS ARE LESS IMPOSING. As noted [9], before the period of serious art behavior was not very respectful in the venues in which art was offered. But in this period behavior is respectful, and the overall art-setting in the art-buildings expresses the importance and the seriousness of the artworks that are present or performed.

The art-setting—in a broad sense—matters [24]. The impressive interior and the subdued and respectful behavior of the audience tell that in the building something very important is happening or going to happen. When people enter the building and later watch the paintings or enjoy the performance, they bring along with them the earlier perception of the exterior and the position of the free-standing building in the very center of the town; it affects the experiences they have inside the building. The impact of the tangible setting, including the spatial arrangements, on the nature of the art experience of the art consumers is large. Buildings are never neutral. The architects of the exterior and interior of the buildings are well aware of this./13

Aside: As said, before the period of serious art in most art events consumption practices were little serious: there was seldom undivided attention, and behavior was not subdued. Over time the dominant ways, in which art is consumed, changed considerably. In the middle ages it was common to show emotions; sometimes people wept in front of religious paintings. And not long before the period of serious art in the encounter with art self-control was still limited, not only among low-class people but also among the aristocracy and bourgeois.

The rich decorations of the facades and the general opulence within the buildings—from carpets in the corridors and chandeliers in the foyers to a beautiful large painting on the ceiling of the theaters—express grandeur. They symbolize the victory of the bourgeois—among others a victory over the aristocracy. But they symbolize even more the triumph of serous art; art that no longer has to be shared with common people. They evoke in the visitor a combination of feelings. On the one hand there are feelings of superiority—"we have been and are victorious". On the other, more modest and respectful feelings: "…our art is immortal and more important than we are". The bourgeois visitors take such feelings along with them to the actual performance; and in this way as well, the art-setting colors their art experience.

Even though behavior in the art-buildings is controlled and restrained, there may well be a festive mood in the hall and a cozy atmosphere in the foyers. The bourgeois are among similar-minded people, several of whom are local dignitaries. They are "among themselves" and this is comforting. It adds to the attraction of the event. A civilized and a cozy atmosphere go well together. It differs altogether from the atmosphere and rumbustious behavior as existed in the earlier for-profit halls, as well as the contemporary dance halls and popular music venues.

Most bourgeois also behave elsewhere in a civilized, controlled and formal way. Self-control comes effortlessly; it is second nature. But in art-buildings behavior is often more formal, civilized and restrained than elsewhere. More than elsewhere, exceptions are taboo. In the halls and theaters where the concert, play, opera or ballet takes place, people speak in low voices. They certainly do not shout to somebody at a distance that they happen to know. Also the behavior of service personnel and in particular of attendants is formal, civilized and subdued—be it often in a somewhat stiff way, because for them behaving this way is no second nature. Evidently the vicinity of great art invites and requires from everybody a behavior that is very controlled and respectful./14

Much audience behavior in the foyers is formal and scripted. Etiquette is important—*To give an example: Anna remembers that her parents taught her that in the hall moving to one's chair, one must not turn one's back to the people one passes.*—Etiquette extends to a dress code. Dresses are an important part of the tangible art-setting. Men wear similar suits. Art may stand out; audience members must not.

Women have more choice, but (other than in opera performances) their clothes must not be eye-catching. In the case of concerts, the dress code of the performers is altogether fixed. The men wear tuxedos; and women wear only black-and-white clothes. It is all about the music and not about individuals. (In popular art event people have much more choice, both in the hall and on the stage. In the early 1960s The Beatles and other pop bands still wore uniform costumes, but not much later, along with a general informalization in society [38], they were replaced with personal clothing. Clothing is used to express one's identity.)

In the case of classical concerts, for performers, scripted behavior takes the form of a *protocol*, turning the art event in a *ceremony*. The ceremonial character testifies of a high respect for art. It also enhances the festive mood. The protocol is precise. These are some details: the musicians wear tuxedos. The conductor comes down the stairs, and with one accord, the musicians rise from their seats. The conductor raises his baton and within seconds thousands of people are still. The audience applauds after the final part of the piece (but not after the earlier parts). The conductor bows. He shakes the hand of the first violinist. And so forth. The ceremonial character of art events can clearly intensify the art experience. Randall Collins writes: "Ceremonies that are alive make people focus and bring about a strong common mood, feelings of solidarity and excitement. They give energy. Not sticking to its prescriptions is experienced as disrespectful".[17] (But he also warns that ceremonies of old can become "dead letters".) *When she was young and visited concerts together with her parents, Anna loved the ceremony. It made her think of a fairy tale.*

In various ways art-settings are also created outside art-buildings and art-spaces, that is, in public and semi-public spaces, in work spaces and at home. An example of a simple setting is that of people having paintings on their walls which are framed, or that of sculpture in public space positioned on pedestals. The pictures and sculpture stand out both literally and figuratively. People rightly guess: this is art and it is important. But the setting is usually less imposing than in an art-building. Often people ignore the artworks; or they perceive them in a casual way. Even when they focus on them, they construct other "artworks" than they would have done in the forceful art-building situation.

This is not to say that art-lovers at home never treat artworks with respect. They do so when they decide to watch works or listen to works in a concentrated, still and respectful way. This often happens in the presence of guests. Respectful conversations may develop about the artworks that are watched or listened to together. Such behavior is part of a locally created art-setting. Moreover, in Victorian times, family members would sit together and read. This was a significant event. An art-setting was created. Occasional conversations about the contents of the books were part of it.

When Anna's father listened to serious music—most often with Elisabeth Schwarzkopf singing—he sometimes created an art-setting by not only sending Anna and other children away but also by drawing the curtains and closing his eyes. Anna on the other hand developed as a young adult the habit of listening to, among others, Vivaldi's The Four Seasons*—while showering on Sunday mornings. And her* *brother regularly directed an imagined orchestra playing with wide arm gestures while listening to Rachmaninov's* Symphony no 2. *They as well created a personal art-setting—a setting their father disapproved of. (It was only when very old, that Anna's father told her that when he listened to Schwarzkopf, he was not only into the music; he also had erotic feelings.)*

Finally, an art-setting can be created not only by the words and sentences people speak but also by their tone. *Over almost 50 years while working in her studio, Anna has been listening to radio stations which play serious music and to other stations playing popular music. She noticed that on the classical radio-stations the voices of the presenters were low, restrained, somewhat solemn and certainly not playful, while on the popular music stations they were normal and sometimes excited.*

Sometimes a typical art-setting is missing. Certain important artworks are not present because they are too large.—This applies among others to many sculptures by Henry Moore and the temporary installations of Christo and Jean-Claude.—But documentation is present. This even applies to the works of groups who want their work only be present outside art-buildings, like artists in the Fluxus movement./15

Over the last decades the number of contemporary sculptures (and installations) without pedestals in public space is increasing. Often the works are located close to an art-building. Or they are so large and expensive looking that there is no misunderstanding: they must be art.—Think of Amish Kapoor's *Cloud Gate* (the "Chicago bean").—At the same time the group of artists who seek to present their art—often critical art—outside art-buildings is growing again.

Over the last two decades the tone of the serious music presenters is less subdued. It is significant that the same often does not apply to presenters who do not belong to the art-world. They may still show an extra-ordinary respect. *Occasionally Anna watches a certain talk show on television.*/16 *The presenter's tone is informal. He treats his guests as equals. However, occasionally his guest is a well-known serious music conductor or soloist, and suddenly the presenter's tone becomes more formal and he treats the musician very respectfully. When a fragment of the musician's new CD is played, he folds his hands, closes his eyes and listens motionless to the music. However, in 2015 something remarkable happened. Suddenly the presenter's behavior changed: his tone and wordings in the conversations started to be just as informal as in the other conversations, and he listened to the music in the same way as he listened to popular music. Anna thinks that the editor of the program had told him to do so, because his serious behavior had become rather strange. Very likely, the serious musicians had complained.*

The ceremonial character of the larger serious music events has not or hardly changed. At the same time since the 1960s, the group that does not appreciate the atmosphere, the stillness and the traditional protocols and ceremonies and stays away has grown much. *Over the last decades* this phenomenon has only increased. Research shows that this is indeed an important reason to stay away or, for younger people, not to start visiting concerts.[18] For many people the protocol and ceremony are now merely "an empty going through of forms", which bores rather than excites: in other words: "dead letters". They, moreover, remind people of an earlier far more hierarchical society and this is unpleasant./17 Ever since the 1960s among an increasing part of art-lovers also the preference for very subdued behavior has gone down. All these changes demand an explanation. The main explanation rests in an informalization of society [38].

(Finally, now folkloristic art performances exist in which ambiences and protocols of old are recreated. They are exceptional and as a form of folklore they are attractive for groups of rich consumers./18)

(30) During the period of serious art and after: DISTRACTIONS ARE THOUGHT TO GO AT THE COST OF AN INTENSE ART EXPERIENCE. MUCH SELF-CONTROL IS DEMANDED FROM AUDIENCES. During the period of serious art, for people to have a deep art experience, an art-setting is required which is not distracting. Visitors—who themselves represent an important part of the overall setting—are relatively still in the rooms of the museum and still during the performance of music, opera, ballet and theater. This is common, and it is demanded. Distractions and disturbances are taboo. This is not just a matter of civilized behavior. Referring to music, Peter Gay writes: "…serious listeners' irritation with distractions is more than a snobbish sense of their superiority over the uncouth. It almost literally takes them away from themselves". It takes them away from inner explorations.

As noted, earlier behavior in the rooms, halls and theaters could be noisy. But, as said, at the end of the nineteenth century, a serious setting has become normal and stillness is part of it. Stillness has become a "sacred object", as sociologists say.

A ban on such things as talking and the smoking of cigars is not that strange: these are activities that are not related to the performance, and they disturb the twentieth-century art-lovers. This also applies to unrelated bodily expressions which are hard to prevent, like coughing. Whispering is also taboo, even though the conversation may be about the performance; it disturbs.

Clapping between movements is related to the artwork but is nevertheless judged to be distracting. During concerts, not only tapping one's feet but even noticeably moving one's body along with the music is taboo. Listeners must be able to exclusively focus on the artwork and possibly embark on private journeys. Often the mentioned inwardness comes naturally. Otherwise it is hard to explain why on television registration of concerts almost all faces show no emotion.

In the twentieth century, conductors, directors and knowledgeable art-lovers know that the composers and playwrights of old were aware that most of the time their works would be performed for audiences that were not still. But to justify the present very still consumption practice, they assume that these artists would have had a still and focused audience in mind when they created their works. Given this supposed intention, they sometimes argue that a still consumption practice is *the* authentic practice.

Creating their works, the composers and playwrights of old cannot but have had a far from still and often responsive audience in mind. Composing dance music, they saw a lively and gay audience, and certainly not the motionless and stiff audiences who are now listening to minuets and many other forms of baroque dance music, seated on chairs with straight backs. And artists, like Mozart and Shakespeare would certainly not have wanted their audience to be unresponsive. (Straight chairs keep people focused and prevent much movement.)

Richard Wagner was the first composer who publicly started to emphasize the importance of stillness. Nevertheless, even in the first half of the nineteenth century, audiences were not altogether still and unresponsive. *Berlioz remarks in his diary that next to him somebody was humming along with the music. He evidently did not find this disturbing.*[19] But not much later humming or tapping of feet or whispering is altogether taboo.

Aside: It is significant that in the course of the twentieth century along with the acceptance of Jazz—a kind of music which certainly calls forward an inclination to move along with the music—the audiences of serious Jazz performances start to listen in a still way. It may well be that stillness has been one, among other, condition for (part of) Jazz becoming art.

Already earlier in the halls and theaters much self-control is demanded of the bourgeois, but given their socialization the control is automatic; after a certain age it does not take an effort anymore. (*Anna was early in being able to be still in the concert hall.*/19) And if some outsiders have a hard time to control themselves, they are called to order—sometimes made to feel guilty—and so controlled. In the concert hall control is anyway in the air.

Aside: First, an over-attention for people who may "disturb" can turn into a permanent form of distraction. This also shows from distorted perceptions as Anna experienced./20 Second, due to a different history during opera performances not all disturbances and interventions are or were taboo. This applies not only to women's closing, but also to the "bravos". Over the last decades, in many countries they as well have become taboo as have the large women's hats.

Not only audience members must not disturb one another; the material setting as well must not distract them. Therefore, unlike before the period of serious art, during the performance, lights in the halls and theaters are dimmed. And in museums visual distractions are minimized by painting the walls white and mounting artworks not close to one another.

Aside: First, whereas most art-lovers need stillness to have an intense art experience; this need is clearly not of all times, and not all social groups need stillness. Most social groups are responsive during popular music, popular theater and popular dance performances. The very noticeable collective effervescence in the halls enhances the artistic experience. (It can also enhance a shared focus on the performance. *This is what Anna recently noticed during a Rap/Hip-hop concert. Unlike in some pop concerts few people were doing little music-related things, like texting and taking photographs of the performers.*) Second: In theory moving along with music, including serious, music, may not only increase focus, but also enhance the "learning" and understanding of music [84]. Third, also during still performances there can be collective effervescence.[20]/21

In the concert halls not only audience members but also performers can cause distractions which are thought to go at the cost of an intense art experience. Therefore faces as well usually show little emotions, even when the music is very emotional. Moreover, it is not accidental that since large video screens have become available they are used in popular music events and not in serious music events. The faces and facial expressions of the musicians must be largely invisible for the visitors in the halls.

They are, indeed, hard to see, not only for people further away from the stage—the large majority—but, due to the high stage in the traditional halls, also for those in the front rows. (Maybe not only a possible distraction is at stake. It is possible that in the symphony orchestras—a nineteenth-century invention—for the sake of art and the artwork, musicians must be instruments rather than human beings.)

Over the last decades the facial expression of the average musician has become less restrained. This shows when one compares video registrations. The facial expression of conductors has probably never been restrained, but unlike in the registrations it remains invisible during regular concerts. (In the case of the, so-called big bands, the conductor stood on the side, half way turned to the audience. He shows himself and communicates with the band as well as the audience. Now, some unrecognized classical/serious music conductors, like André Rieu, do the same.)

As also shows from television and new media broadcasts, *over the last decades* otherwise still audience members more often show emotions on their faces during music, theater and dance performances. Moreover, as we shall see below, during certain concerts audiences have now more freedom to move and do not have to feel guilty when they cause minor disturbances.

Nevertheless, as late as 2010 in the Concertgebouw in Amsterdam, there are posters on the walls with the text: Coughing Disturbs. The person who cannot stop himself from coughing is bound to feel guilty. (This is extra unfair, because the graying of audiences—and along with it an increased coughing—is not caused by the individual who coughs, but by the serious music establishment who wants to stick to the status quo.)

Large video-screens showing the emotional faces of conductors and musicians are still absent in almost all halls, even though such screens may well be attractive and the opposite of disturbing for non-traditional audiences. That in the registrations all the time close-ups of the musicians' faces are shown is not accidental. People appreciate it and it probably enhances their artistic experience. (*Over the last decades* in opera performances, there are now subtitles in the own language, but no video-screens. One wonders what would be more distracting.)

In theater the introduction of large video screens is amazingly late, but by now they are regularly used. They not only bring visual amplification but also contribute to artistic innovation [34]. What at first may have been experienced as distracting has become a new and powerful creative mean.

An Obsession with Authenticity, Authorship and Aura

(31) First introduction. EXPRESSIVE AUTHENTICITY, NOMINAL AUTHENTICITY, AUTHENTIC WORK AND GENUINE WORK. As said, the term authenticity is used in several different senses.[21] Authenticity is judged to be important in the arts (as well as in the popular arts), but it is often not clear what kind of authenticity people have in mind. Is it the expressive authenticity that has been discussed in the previous section? Or is it the authenticity of a so-called authentic performance? Or something in between? To prevent confusion some precision is called

for. The notion of the authentic performance also matters because in the serious music art-world much value is attached to it which, as we shall see below, causes rapidly rising cost.

In the context of this book, two notions of authenticity are particularly useful. The first has been discussed in the previous section.

An artwork is *expressive authentic* if when creating the work the artist has been true to himself and has expressed a personal emotional state and/or a personal view. An artwork can also be nominal authentic. *Nominal authenticity* can refer to different things.[22] First, an art object, visual artwork, manuscript and so forth, can be nominal authentic because it is *genuine*; it is not *fake* or *an unauthorized replica,* or it is not *incorrectly attributed.*/22 Second, a performance can be nominal authentic because it *conforms to the artist's instructions or intentions. Third, a performance can be "historically informed"*, implying that it is as much as possible the same as at the time of the creation of the artwork that is performed. The performance practice is authentic. Third, it can also be nominal authentic because it *conforms to the dominant artistic tradition.*—The last two forms of nominal authenticity usually come together but not always.—Finally, the term authenticity may refer to *a mix of expressive and nominal authenticity.*

Inauthenticity can be undeliberate, as in the case of a false note, or a line which an actor did not remember. More interesting is the phenomenon of deliberate inauthenticity. For instance, in a play, lines could have been skipped and changed, or there could be more or less musicians or actors on the stage than prescribed by the author. Sometimes, authors do not include instructions because they are self-evident. Therefore, using a grand piano instead of a harpsichord to perform a Bach piece can be said to be a deliberate "mistake", because at the time of Bach, the former did not exist and Bach could not have intended its use. (Degrees of inauthenticity exist, but ultimately all such performances are nominally inauthentic and "counterfeits".)

Especially in serious music, the performances must conform to the composer's intentions. Given the less detailed scores and plays of authors from before the period of serious art, their intentions are seldom clear. As we shall see, the various ways in which this "problem" is solved matters for the social economy of art. Moreover, a work that is judged to be authentic because it conforms to the dominant artistic tradition does not have to be authentic in the sense of conforming to the instructions or intentions of the author.

For instance, in the twentieth century, a group of musicians pleaded for performances of baroque and early music to be performed according to the instructions and intentions of the composers which implied fewer musicians on the stage and the use of, sometimes reconstructed, musical instruments as existed at the time of the first performances. Others rejected this and wanted to stick to the traditional performance practice involving the use of more musicians and the use of later developed instruments. This led to a major conflict in the world of serious music with consequences for the social economy of serious music. [33 and 34]

Finally, a mix of expressive and nominal authenticity is usually deliberate. A performance may well be called authentic because both the instructions of the author are followed and the conductor or director honestly expresses himself. The one enhances the other. But more often they go at the cost of one another. The score or script or choreography leaves the conductor or director less autonomous space than he would need to make a truly expressively authentic work, a work in which he is true to himself.

Aside: Art objects can also be inauthentic. An assistant may not have correctly executed the instructions of a visual artist. Or a publisher may have left out paragraphs in the manuscript, that is, without the consent of the writer. (When authors are dead, it is always without their consent. In this case the works are not only not according to the assumed wishes of the author; they are also not genuine.) Ultimately such works are "counterfeits".

(Usually the meaning of the term authenticity will show from the context. However, to prevent misunderstanding I every now and then add the adjectives nominal and expressive. In this and the following sections, this is foremost "nominal" in the sense of being genuine or conforming to the artist's instructions or intentions.)

In daily speech, as well as by some scholars, the term authenticity is now being used more and more loosely. For instance, authentic, natural and artisan are terms that are used interchangeable. Even food, holidays, solid wood and lotions can be "authentic". Other scholars, however, emphasize that these are commodities produced in series and therefore "inauthentic" par excellence.[23] People have in mind all sorts of unclear mixtures of nominal authenticity, expressive authenticity and other qualities. The products are said to be genuine, honest, traditional and so forth. Also, when the term authenticity foremost appears to refer to a "being true to oneself", it can be used loosely; for instance, in advertisement, self-help books and the media. All sorts of references or intended associations can apply, from spontaneous and non-conformist to natural and pure.

Other references are more closely related to the two notions of authenticity used in this book: as-it-was-in-the-past, sincere, uncompromising, honest, self-realizing, self-fulfilling and self-determining. All such references show that in practice the concept of authenticity has parallel and floating meanings.

(32) Second introduction. ORIGINAL, MULTIPLE, RE-COMPOSITION, ART-IN-THE-STYLE-OF, REPLICA, REPRODUCTION, PRODUCTION AND RELATED TERMS. Correspondences and differences between these concepts matter for a study of the social economy of art in this and the following chapters. I define and explain them in web-text wt-32. Students are advised to read this section. Others may scan or skip the web-text and, if necessary, return to it.

Here I just mention that in the book I distinguish reproductions and productions. Reproductions are also called technical or mechanical reproductions. Without explication they can be recordings as well as visual reproductions. Productions are originals in series. This can be be a small series of etchings or a very large series as in the case of a popular book or a studio produced piece of music—like Dance music, which is streamed all over the world. I usually use the term production to refer to large series.

(33) PERFORMANCES *MUST* BE AUTHENTIC. "During the period of serious art, people increasingly care about the nominal authenticity of performances. This applies strongest to classical/serious music including the music in ballet and opera.

Most lovers of serious music still care much about authenticity. Saying that an obsession with authenticity exists is no exaggeration. Consequences for the social economy of serious music are profound. It leads, among others, to ever higher cost, and therefore to more exclusion of people with little money. This is the topic of the section 54. (In a more voluminous book, I should and would have said more about several of the topics that are now briefly discussed in this section. I therefore present additional text in the web-notes accompanying this section which may well interest general readers.)

Before explaining the thesis that performances are demanded to be authentic, it is good to know that even when instructions are very precise, authors cannot but leave room to conductors and directors to "improvise". Therefore the latter are creative artists—and not mere performers of instructions—who create own originals and as such authentic works based on the original works of the authors, the composers, choreographers and playwrights.—As said in web-section wt-32 the performances are both instances of the original works and new originals.—But during the period of serious art in the case of works of old, and especially music works, the authenticity of the new derived original works created by conductors and directors as well as soloists do not figure high in the mind of art-lovers. Arguments about the authenticity of a music performance are arguments about performances as genuine instances of the original as created by the author or as conforms to a traditional performance practice.

In the course of the twentieth century, the same no longer applies to theater directors. They are often praised for their personal, creative and very free interpretation of the works of old. (*The bloody performances of Shakespeare's Macbeth, which Anna saw in the 1970s, differed much from one another and certainly differed from those in Shakespeare's time or from the performances in the nineteenth and first half of the twentieth century. In this respect they were very inauthentic.*)

Aside: The strictness of the demand for nominal authenticity does not only follow from the nature of instructions but also from the flexibility of art-worlds. As noted, the classical/serous music art-world is little flexible [15]. Artworks and their execution must be well-controlled [35].

The expressive authenticity of the author and of the creative performing artist can easily collide. Although a nominal authentic performance is never a mere execution of the instructions in a score, script or choreography, the freedom of the authors restrains the freedom of conductors, directors, choreographers and soloists, that is, their freedom to make a new original in which they can truly express themselves. Or in other words, in the case of the latter, nominal authenticity can go at the cost of expressive authenticity. This applies strongest to music with its detailed instructions in scores. (I present more examples, also of other art forms in this lengthy web-note.)/23

In the course of the twentieth century in the serious music art-world, the respect for the classic composers and their works has increased much. Nominal authenticity is very important, sometimes in terms of genuineness and sometimes of conforming to a longer existing tradition. It is not accidental that major conductors emphasize their subservient role: they serve the sublime works of composers of genius who made excellent or sublime works and they underplay their own creative role./24

Aside: Respect was not always so high. Mendelssohn made specific cuts in Bach's *Matthew Passion*, without being clear about this.—Whether he created a re-composition or counterfeit is a matter of opinion.—And Mahler said: "Of course the works of Beethoven need some editing". But when in 1900 in some performances he actually did so, he was violently attacked for this sacrilege.

In the twentieth century in the serious music art-world, artistically interesting "inauthentic" performances are taboo and rare. The composers of old are geniuses who make sublime works, and intervening with their work is perceived as presumptuous if not a form of sacrilege.—Before the period of serious art, the creation of adaptations and more drastic re-compositions of an original composition and performance was common. This is comparable with the production of many covers in popular music, covers, which are almost always re-compositions./25—

Twentieth-century composers create artistically interesting re-compositions, but they are seldom performed. An example is Hans Eisler's re-arrangement for a chamber orchestra and re-composition of Anton Bruckner's *Symphony No. 7*. Earlier it was put down as just an exercise./26 Only recently this work has started to be performed.

Although it is always "the authenticity of sound" that is demanded, it appears that "visual authenticity" is just as important. Given that differences in musical quality are small while visual differences tend to be large, it is well possible that music lovers expect and much appreciate visual authenticity. Performances must not only sound the same as 100 years ago but also look the same. Both forms of authenticity contribute to the focus and artistic experience of classical/serious music lovers.

Recently indirect proof of this could be given. For a while now virtual players and partly or altogether virtual orchestras can be employed in performances. (Their use leads to much lower cost per visitor. This is a topic in the next section.) In an altogether virtual orchestra 75 players are replaced by two who play a special kind of keyboard as is commonly used by pop musicians in live performances. Technical quality is so high that since 2005 virtual players already have been used by orchestras accompanying ballet and opera performances in order to bring the number of live players down. In 2006 in performances of the Nutcracker Ballet by the Los Angeles Ballet, there are 22 live players and 32 virtual players. A large orchestra was performing in a pit space which was too small to let 54 musicians play./27 By now the technique is so advanced and the results are so good that also famous opera companies consider the use of a virtual orchestra. Cost savings are large.

But also at present no existing symphony orchestra (not accompanying ballet or opera) considers the use of a large number of virtual players or a virtual orchestra, and they almost certainly will not in the decade to come. The difference with ballet and opera cannot be explained from the fact that audiences put lower demands on the technical quality of symphony orchestras accompanying opera and ballet. It can only be explained from the fact that orchestras are hidden from view in the case of ballet and opera. The visuals in the traditional set up have to remain the same. They must be authentic.

Aside: In many respects, authenticity is fabricated.[24] For instance, musicians fabricate authenticity by arguing that their interpretations are authentic. Their interpretations are authentic and conform to the intentions of the composer or to the tradition, while those of certain colleagues are not. But from a more distant point of view or in hindsight, the successful interpretations are foremost in line with the "spirit" of its own time. The "authentic" bombastic performances of Bach's music by Mengelberg befitted dramatic times. And when in the course of the second half of the twentieth century Bach performances become "cool" and precise, they are thought to have been so at the time Bach composed the works. It befitted the spirit of the time in which a new intellectual cultural elite dominates the art-worlds. We will never know what the "right" interpretation is. Given the fact that much of Bach's music was religious and performed in churches, a term pragmatic may be more adequate than bombastic or cool. (In Section 78 below, I discuss economic interests in the "fabrication" of authenticity and of other imagined qualities of artworks.)

Aside: In *popular art* a strife for nominal authenticity in the sense of "according to tradition" is not altogether absent. In well-established new musical genres that are passed their zenith, there is disdain for the deviant mainstream version of the genre. Subgroups of musicians and consumers want to go back to the basis and perform the music as it was at the time of its first creation.

Over the last decade the rejection in the classical/serious music art-world of artistically interesting rearrangements, adaptations and more drastic re-compositions of earlier works appears to become somewhat less intense. This shows among others from the mentioned recent performances of Eisler's re-composed Bruckner's symphony. It shows even more from the success of the mentioned artistically interesting thoroughly re-composed Vivaldi's *The Four Seasons* by Max Richter./28 (The re-composition is criticized, but probably most because he adds electronic instruments and includes much digitally produced sound.) It is also significant that presently there is more attention again for improvisation and the artistic use of the space the composers of old left for various forms of improvisation.

Nevertheless, the emphasis on authenticity is still very intense and not much less than it was 50 years ago. As a consequence, a public art heritage is artificially maintained, but without being alive in society [18]. This partly explains why by now only a limited social group still visits live concerts of old works and, even fewer, visit performances of contemporary works. A lively heritage is, moreover, a condition for real innovation and for enthusiasm for new work. The fact that the classical/serious music due to its focus on authenticity has done little to counter the so-called cost disease adds to its decline. This is the topic of the next section.

(34) THE OBSESSION WITH AUTHENTICITY AND THE CONSEQUENT AVERSION OF THE APPLICATION OF NEW TECHNOLOGIES CAUSE EVER HIGHER COST OF PRODUCTION IN THE PERFORMING ARTS. IN MUSIC THIS "COST DISEASE" CONTRIBUTES TO THE DECLINE OF CLASSICAL/ SERIOUS MUSIC. Since the middle of the nineteenth century, the cost of live performances of existing works (per visitor-hour) increases disproportionally. The increase is particularly large in the course of the twentieth century. Also cost of newly composed and performed work is usually high. There is an aversion of the application of new production techniques. This hinders innovation. The phenomenon of rising cost becomes life-threatening for the heritage of classical/serious music.

The term *cost disease* refers to the phenomenon that over time the cost of production of certain goods and services inevitably rises more than that of the cost of consumer goods in general./29 This is the case when labor productivity does not increase or increases less than in other sectors of production.

It is a situation that clearly applies to the performing arts in the period of serious art. The authenticity demand is a demand for unchanged quality or "constant quality" of live performances of longer existing pieces. To maintain constant quality, labor productivity can (almost) not be increased.—At least this is the common belief, also of economists.—This inevitably causes ever-rising costs.

A symphony that in the nineteenth century was performed by 75 musicians and a work for string quartet by four musicians is now performed by the same number of musicians and not 20 or two. Only this way quality and authenticity is maintained. Labor productivity could have increased if audience size had further increased than the halls allow. But this is thought to go at the cost of authenticity and therefore not regarded as a realistic option. It follows, that quality can only be kept constant and the disease contained by ever higher prices, lower incomes of musicians, more public and private support, and nowadays also from side-line activities.

It is significant that in the twentieth century the necessity of authenticity and constant quality is not only self-evident for art-lovers but also for economists. And for some well-known economists, higher subsidies are the obvious means for limiting the negative effects of the cost disease. As late as 1997 the famous economist William Baumol publicly blames the US government for having insufficiently subsidized theater with the consequence that between 1965 and 1995 in the USA, the average cast size had fallen from 16.8 to 9 actors.[25] It had not countered the cost disease by more generous subsidies. He therefore pleads for more subsidies. Aside: In music the average number of musicians on the stage also went down during this period and after. But this is solely due to different programming. More often pieces require fewer musicians, like a single pianist or a soloist singing with a small ensemble are programmed. But unlike in theater the authenticity of the works is maintained.

The more flexible serious theater world is interesting. In the twentieth century playwrights start to write pieces for fewer actors. Deliberately or not, cost is lowered and the cost disease made less severe. The new pieces are also innovative and therefore not always appreciated by older audiences. But before too long, younger audiences appreciate the new plays. Several twentieth-century composers also write pieces for smaller ensembles, but given the vested interest in large orchestras and traditional halls, only the works of these composers for large orchestras are promoted.

Next in theater older pieces start to be re-composed by directors and fewer actors are used than before. Older audiences protest but younger audiences soon appreciate this change as well. This is understandable. The new and the re-composed works are artistically innovative. Earlier only star actors could show the subtle personal characteristics of the person they were enacting, while others were just extras. Now all of the few actors express noticeable individual characteristics. This way the works become richer. Along with a rise in labor productivity and the countering of the cost disease, innovative and attractive performances have been developed.

Over the last two decades in most performances, actors' voices are electronically amplified allowing a far more subtle and personal way of speaking. With the by now common use of visual amplification by means of video screens, showing, among others, close-ups of the actors, not only a new artistic instrument is added but also larger audiences can be offered attractive plays. Both techniques enrich performances while lowering cost per visitor. A need or wish to lower cost leads to innovation, including artistic innovation.

During the major part of the period of serious art, this mechanism does not or does hardly exist in the world of music with its emphasis on authenticity. Before the period of serious art, this was very different. In the preceding two centuries the, partly unsated, demand of the bourgeois for live music increased much and entrepreneurs sought for ways to serve larger audiences. This much stimulated the development of louder instruments which could be used in larger halls. Cost per visitor could be reduced and ever larger audiences could be served. Not always immediately but soon composers became aware of the new artistic possibilities which the new instrument offered.—Sometimes this led to further adaptations in the new instruments.—Well known is the succession of harpsichord, fortepiano, grand piano and the again louder grand piano. Examples of such successions of other instruments can be given. The lowering of cost through louder instruments was important.—The Steinway family was clear about their intention of making grand pianos that would sell well because they were louder.—

Aside: In this period in all artforms new production techniques were developed with the goal of lowering cost and serving larger groups of consumers. This, for instance, applies in the visual arts, among others, to various new graphic techniques for multiplication, like lithography. There are important, what economist call, *economies of scale*.

In the nineteenth century a major invention in the world of music allowing less cost per visitor is the development of the new and by now traditional music hall. Productivity increases much thanks to acoustic amplification brought about by reverberation and a long reverberation time. In this case the artistic possibilities of the larger halls are particularly important. The halls contribute to the development of the romantic repertoire in classical/serious music.

However, after the construction of the new, for the time large halls, there no longer is unsated demand for classical/serious music and authenticity becomes important. It is therefore understandable that no more new and louder instruments are developed or applied, nor are different kinds of halls developed. This is a situation that lasts to the present day. As noted [15] the halls contribute to the inflexibility of the serious/classical music art-world. An inflexibility which in turn causes a purist interpretation of authenticity and the refusal of the application of modern techniques. Because productivity no longer increases, with time the cost disease starts to take its toll: higher cost, little artistic innovation that is attractive for larger audiences and an overall decline in the public interest in live classical/serious music, also a decline in the heritage part of the music.

In theory various remedies exist that can at least partly, "heal" the cost disease. They reduce or stop the disproportional growth in cost. One that has added to productivity is improved or changed skills of musicians. Musicians are now able to perform a much larger variety of genres and styles than they did only 50 years ago. Most important could have been the use of electronic amplification and the renewed development and use of louder instruments. (So far the only electronic instrument that since circa 2010 is sometimes used by classical/serious music ensembles is the electronic cello.) Another remedy is the lowering of the salaries of ordinary musicians. In the twentieth and twenty-first centuries, this medicine is used. The salaries of musicians were never high, but over time, they have become lower, that is, they increased less than in professions that require a similar level of previous education. Even in world-famous orchestras, ordinary musicians have amazingly low salaries. Recently a related medicine that is increasingly applied is no longer offering musicians employment contracts. Instead they work as free-lancer who must be available on demand. This is less remarkable in our present gig-economy. (The same happens in the other performing arts.)

Other possible remedies exist that can lead to lower cost per visitor-hour. This applies to less costly stage settings in, especially, opera. Presently the opposite is the case. It also applies to the offering of the same performance on several successive days or weeks. The cost of rehearsals and in opera of the stage setting per visitor is lower. But, unlike in musicals, the runs tend to be short. In the offering of symphony music a long run is also uncommon. However, by now in the case of not just a few top-ensembles but many ensembles, the overall number of a specific performance has increased because they are touring and visiting various halls in different countries./30

Aside: First, longer runs bring along additional cost for extra repetitions, for stand ins and for the occasional replacement of musicians and actors. But given larger sales these costs are easily covered. Second, in popular music the phenomenon that many ensembles regularly tour and visit several countries started much earlier. Third, in popular music venues are more flexible. If a forthcoming performance is quickly sold out, sometimes a second performance for the following night is organized. More common is, however, that when a performance turns out to be successful in one country larger halls can be and are still chosen in successive countries. As noted, thanks to amplification these can be very large halls. Finally, when runs are longer or there is more touring, overall cost of advertisement per visitor can be lower. It is significant that tours in pop music have names that are widely advertised, like at present the No Filter tour of the Stones.

Until circa 1980 subsidies and donations still allow many orchestras to cover costs and stay in business. The subsidies enable the classical/serious music art-world to remain conservative. They so indirectly contribute to the cost disease. But with less subsidy, diminishing demand and ever rising cost, especially after 1980 the overall number of orchestras goes down. Only the famous orchestras survive thanks to donations, sponsorship and subsidies which in their case remain high.

Nevertheless, *over the last decades* the ongoing cost disease starts to induce changes, changes that are medicines for the disease. Various electronic techniques allowing lower cost, which earlier were taboo because of assumedly less authenticity, have started to be used; foremost amplification. Less noticeable, but important are also changes in the choice of repertoire of the managements of halls. Each year there are fewer large orchestra performances programmed and more performances requiring fewer musicians on the stage, like piano recitals and soloists accompanied by small ensembles. Cost per visitor is much lower.

But changes are limited. In the classical music world, authenticity in the sense of remaining true to the composers of old and/or the existing tradition is also important today. Performing existing pieces for large orchestras with a smaller ensemble than intended by the composer, is still altogether taboo, and re-compositions of the pieces for smaller ensembles are still rare. There still is no visual amplification by means of video-screens showing the expressive faces of conductors and musicians. And there is no or little awareness that changes may lead to attractive artistic innovations. But it is predictable that re-compositions will become more important in the years to come.

What is also predictable is that the number of already existing symphony performances produced by orchestras of very talented and sometimes trained amateur performers and a paid conductor will increase much. Because they only receive a small financial compensation, cost per visitor are much lower. For non-expert-consumers, the quality loss is small.

(35) VISUAL ARTWORKS MUST BE AUTHENTIC. AUTHORSHIP IS IMPORTANT. A CORRECT ATTRIBUTION HAS AN IMPACT ON THE FINANCIAL VALUE OF WORKS. So far, I discussed the obsession with the form of nominal authenticity that implies a "conforming to the authors instructions and intention" and/or a "conforming to an artistic tradition". In this section I treat the demand that artworks must be nominal authentic in the sense of "being correctly attributed" or "genuine": the work's origin, authorship and/or provenance must have been correctly identified. In the period of serious art and up to the present day, art-lovers and the buyers and sellers of artworks want to know that a certain well-recognized artist has created a work and not somebody else. Authorship is very important.

The obsession within art-worlds and among their experts with authorship and correct attribution can, at least partly, be explained from the mentioned necessity of having one immutable hierarchy of works and artists which everybody in the art-world agrees on [17]. Such a hierarchy is only acceptable if works can be attributed to specific artists with specific positions in the hierarchy. If interesting but unattributed works could have been made by multiple artists with different positions, the ordering loses its foundation. However, once a hierarchy has been established on the basis of assumedly correctly attributed works and, later on, they are shown to have been created by lesser artists, this also runs down the hierarchy. But until recently, the latter is hardly acknowledged. In the visual arts, wrong attribution of works which were attributed to great artists affects their prices but not the position of the great artists in the quality hierarchy.

By now it has become clear that whole plays or large parts of plays attributed to Shakespeare have been written by other playwrights or in cooperation with them. Before the eighteenth century, there was also much cooperation in the workshops of visual artists. A single artist may have received the commission and could be held responsible for a failure to deliver, but rather for being a bad employer than as artist./31

That authorship and attribution matter for the social economy of art also shows from much attention for plagiary and fraud./32 Especially wrong attribution can have major financial consequences. *For a long time, Rembrandt's painting* Man with the Golden Helmet *was regarded as one of his best paintings. But when it turned out that not he, but a former pupil had painted it, the painting was moved to another far less prestigious room in the Gemäldegalerie in Berlin and its estimated financial value dropped to one tenth of what it had been before. As a curiosity it still draws attention but the auratic experience has changed and the authority of the work has gone down. It has become less meaningful.* Because the painting itself did not change and is artistically as good or bad as before, this signifies that also for experts it is not only artistic quality that counts [17].

The opposite also occurs: For instance, a painting or sketch bought in a thrift store for a few dollars can turn out to have been painted by an important artist and its financial value becomes many times higher. An example is that of the truck driver Teri Horton, who for eight dollars bought a painting—that she did not like much but thought to be funny—in a thrift store, which at the time experts judged to have been painted by Jackson Pollock. Its financial value had risen from $8 to some $50 million. (Later on, the attribution was disputed again.)

Aside: Art historians and art-lovers also find it important to know who is the "author" of an artistic breakthrough. They want to be able to attribute them to single individuals rather than to groups of artists. But findings may well be incorrect. Innovations almost always stem from groups—or scenes. Pablo Picasso is not the sole inventor of cubism, nor is George Braque—for a while they were part of a small scene of artists in Paris. They, nevertheless, both claimed authorship. Also the visual art-world wanted a winner. Picasso won./33

Moreover, unlike before the period of serious art, imitation art is experienced as a form of infringement of the symbolic authorship of artists. Imitation art is not illegal, but it is taboo in the arts. In inferior-art circles and in popular art circles it is not taboo [23].

For art consumers right attribution is also important for other reasons. They want to relate to a specific artist and not any artist. Well before the period of serious art, there was little attention for the identity of an artist. In Medieval artworks, signatures were often absent or not judged to be important. Later a stipulation in contracts for commissions that the artist must have painted at least certain parts—usually the heads—suggests that authorship becomes more important.[26] But it is only in the period of serious art that attention has turned into an obsession. Signature and correct attribution of works are important for art-lovers, with the consequence that the financial value of a signature can be very high. People want to know if a painting attributed to Rembrandt really has been painted by him and not by another artist, or if the Vermeer painting is not a fake? For the appreciation of the works and for the nature of the self-constructed works that are based on the perceived works, the knowledge makes much difference. It also matters for the financial value of the works.

The two are related. The high financial value of a rightly attributed Pollock painting, makes people look more carefully. Right attribution to famous artists affects the self-constructed works (or films) of viewers. And, as said [24], the viewer may well foremost see a dollar sign and forget about other self-constructed meanings. A visual artist who is well aware of the relationship between a signature and financial value is, again, Damien Hirst. This shows from what he tells the writer of a book about his work, when the talk about his spot paintings. (I present a (funny) citation in the web-note.)/34

When a work is attributed to a specific artist, people can, in their imagination, have a personal relationship with the artist, and this much affects their artistic experience. Usually relating to a genius brings along more attentiveness and stronger emotions. People spend more time standing in front of the painting. Or they listen more carefully to a musical piece. It is easier to imagine an artist with not only a name but also personal characteristics. People can, for instance, imagine a real person in the act of putting paint on the canvas or sitting behind a table writing and correcting the score, script, choreography or manuscript. This adds much to their auratic experience [37]. They can imagine a human being putting his soul in the work, a person who is possibly a genius and yet as human as they are. (In section 27 I discussed the importance of the artist-in-the-work and I will say more about this in section 40.)

Aside: After a work has been correctly attributed to a specific artist, art historians almost always produce additional knowledge: the artist lived in this town, was a friend of a better-known artist, he died early, and so forth. Such knowledge makes it easier to develop a relationship with the artist in-the-work.

Over the last decades not only artists but also certain other workers in art-worlds claim authorship and nowadays claim the title artist. This signifies the obsession with authorship, but indirectly also of less respect for the (traditional) artist. For instance, curators increasingly claim symbolic authorship: they are authors of exhibitions, which as a collage can well be said to be an original and authentic artwork.—If DJs are (popular) artists, then curators must be (serious) artists.—In the *reputational economy* of the arts, curators now, often successfully, strive for and attain higher reputational positions than the traditional artists. This often goes at the cost of the latter.[27] (Aside: Recently social scientists have argued that the collections of artworks of collectors are also original artworks. The collectors do not just add works to their overall "work"; they make deliberately choices to create a coherent and important work.[28])

Authorship and correct attribution continue to fascinate us. The same as before, knowing that more than one author is "in" certain works of old, this may be disappointing, but now this knowledge can also be somewhat exciting. Expert research has become ever more extensive and viewers are in various ways informed about research results. In program notes and notes on the walls of museums, the fact that there are not one but two or more authors in-the-work is made known. People like to know this, and be educated. It is interesting that by now also several movies have appeared in which the authorship of Shakespeare is questioned.

The obsession with single authorship rather than a cooperative of artists remains intense. It is significant that part of film could only become serious art after the authorship of the director had become more acknowledged.

In the course of the period of serious art not giving credits has become ever more common in the visual arts. Andy Warhol still gave his assistants credits. He acknowledged their creative input, and their names are well known. This does no longer apply to the assistants of Hirst. The names of the assistants of the extremely successful Japanese artist Takashi Murakami are hardly known even though the creative input of some may well be more important than that of Warhol's assistants.

The reasons for the continuing importance of authorship have become more varied. In a more superficial celebrity culture not only authenticity but also authorship and an experience of aura and singularity matter for audiences, even when the importance of works and artists foremost rests on fame. Moreover, the financial aspect of authorship and attribution has probably become more important. Legal authorship is a form of property and property matters much in a capitalist society.[29] But whereas earlier in the serious arts the importance of the financial aspects of authorship has been largely ignored, now the very high prices of artworks have raised the interest in the financial aspect of authorship. This applies to successful artists who earn a lot and can earn even more if they exploit their intellectual property rights; but it also applies to the large majority of creative artists who have a hard time making a living and cannot afford to let their works be used for free.

I expect that in the coming decade somewhat successful visual artists will more often employ other trained artists to execute works and that before too long these artists will no longer get away with not giving them public credits for their artistic input—and not paying them properly.

(36) BEING SOLE AUTHOR IS ATTRACTIVE. CONTRIBUTIONS BY OTHERS ARE OFTEN NOT ACKNOWLEDGED. CREATIVE ARTISTS FIND IT HARD TO COLLABORATE. For most creative artists it is unattractive to create artworks in teams, that is, in teams that as team take responsibility for the final artwork. They much prefer to be the sole author of a work, an author who is responsible for the artwork and takes responsibility for it.

Typical for the period of serious art is that the contribution of *the* author, including the director and conductor as author of specific performances or films is singled out and glorified, while the input of other people is taken for granted, played down, covered up or ignored. The artist gets all the praise and others, especially when they are alive, get little or no credits. Art-lovers together with artists continuously reproduce the notion of a "peerless" artist. In the popular imagery the successful author is a lonely, altogether independent genius who on his own creates something wonderful. And if the works of an artist are evidently strongly influenced by that of a colleague, the artist may well be blamed for this. There is little prestige for teams of creative artists or artists' collectives—who make collaborative work and together take responsibility for them.

Aside: An exception in the visual arts is that of couples working together; they together take responsibility for their works. It is an exception that is not really an exception: the couples often present themselves as one person, and in the imagination of the art-lover, they fuse.—A good example is *Gilbert and George.*—Another exception is many small serious music ensembles, like quartets which are known for their name and not for the name of an individual musician within the quartet. They form a collaborating artistic team and often there is no single member who has the final say in the creative process.

Given little prestige, lower income and a strong belief in the importance of own individual expressions, it is not amazing that those creative artists who take responsibility for works seldom acknowledge, let alone emphasize, the creative input of others. But, although the inputs of assistants of visual artists and members of an orchestra are, in different degrees, creative inputs, they are often not credited at all, or not credited for their artistic input. They are treated as "support personnel".[30] And being treated as just an assistant can be frustrating. *(Anna had a friend who after a long time stopped working as camera man for a well-known visual artist, who made foremost film and video art. Over time Anna's friend started to feel increasingly frustrated, because he never received credits or public thanks, while many vital ideas had come from him. His contribution had beyond any doubt been very creative and irreplaceable: after he quitted, the artist's work clearly changed.)*

Up to the present day, composers of classical/serious, playwrights and choreographers seldom cooperate with one another. But conductors and directors are, of course, well aware of working together with a team of performers. At the end of a performance, when present, all take a bow. And on record and CD sleeves conductor, the whole orchestra as well as possible soloists are all more or less equally credited.

Aside: In popular music composer/performers, soloists and so-called producers often artistically cooperate. They are all creative artists. But crediting is often unequal. However, at present, composer/performers often work together and feature one another on a project basis, and are both credited—for instance on platforms like Spotify. In the case of duos, both take responsibility for the artwork. A more openly market ethos in mainstream popular music production evidently does not stand in the way of this kind of cooperation. It rather promotes it./35/36

The serious arts tend to drag behind, but over the last two decades, the number of critical and other collaborative projects in and outside art-buildings that draw much attention has increased much./37 Often artists willingly give up sole authorship. A small but increasing number of creative artists are involved in the projects. It, nevertheless, is too early to tell if this development is part of a temporary wave, as there have been several before, or that collaborative projects by artists' collectives are now turning into a permanent feature of art-worlds.—So far, for most of the involved artists, the collaborative activities or so-called social practices are temporary activities or something they do next to making truly own art.—When teams of artists succeed in making critical art that is effective, they have "voice", and for a while this can be rewarding for the participants. Financial rewards which often come from local governments are, however, limited. For governments there is more prestige in the subsidization of traditional art.

Aside: Some symbolic benefits for critical artists come from being the topic of many texts, including several books with appealing pictures, about collaborative practices, as well as from museum exhibitions about their works—exhibitions that at present are somewhat popular. But this as well could well be a temporary affair. Moreover, the texts may well serve a cultural re-appropriation and hence lead to a neutralization of new forms of critical art.

An important development—important in terms of working hours and thus in employment—is that of visual artists, musicians, writers and so forth cooperating with non-artists in teams that realize projects, that are no artworks and not applied artworks. Their activity is, nevertheless, artistic. Participation in the projects brings income to the participating artists. The result of the projects is, for instance, a game, a website, an overall design for signposting in a building, and so forth. Some hybrid artists emphasize that such cooperation is not a second choice; they chose this way of working. At present only a few of these cooperating artists gain much institutional art-world recognition, but in the more user-oriented direction in the arts, this is likely to change [70]./38

Finally, assistants of visual artists are increasingly unhappy about not being credited and let this know. This may, also in the visual arts, lead to more crediting.

(37) CONSUMERS EXPERIENCE AURA, SINGULARITY AND EXCLUSIVITY. ARTISTS, EXPERTS AND ART-COMPANIES MAKE THE EXPERIENCE MORE INTENSE. THIS CAN BE PROFITABLE. That artworks have unique properties is much appreciated by consumers. It explains an obsession with singularity. Aura and singularity are related. Knowledge about the history of works increases the experience of aura and makes them appear more singular. Experts and both for- and non-profit art-companies, like museums, halls, dealers, impresarios and large ensembles, can enrich works and increase the experience of aura and singularity, and so increase their reputation and/or profit. I start by explaining the concepts singularity and aura—concepts I use all through the book.

Aura refers to unique "presences" or "testimonies" in a work.[31] An *experience of aura* or *auratic experience* exists thanks to what a person knows about the history of a work. Usually the more interesting the history is, the more intense will be the experience of aura. The work appears to have a halo. Both aura and an auratic experience are a matter of degree. Some experts know more things or other things in the history of a work than do others. And not everybody knows as much about a work or cares as much about what he knows. They judge aura to be higher or lower. Knowledgeable art-lovers may have a more intense auratic experience than less knowledgeable art-lovers, but not necessarily.

As noted, the artist-in-the-work is very important for art consumers. This largely explains an obsession with aura. But not only the artist and knowledge of his life's events but in the case of older works also knowledge of what happened to the work after the author's death are presences in the work and can bring along a more intense auratic experience. Knowing that part of Rembrandt's "Night watch" has later been cut off, because it was too large to store adds to the auratic experience of some. Also knowing that Leonardo DiCaprio owns a specific Picasso drawing may for consumers, who know about this, increase the aura of the specific drawing, and to a lesser degree also of Picasso drawings in general, and even of all Picasso's works. For them not only Picasso is in-the-work but also DiCaprio. Because the work being owned by DiCaprio is a unique quality, it also increases an experience of singularity. That Picasso in some of his works used a kind of indigo paint which is seldom used by painters makes these works more singular for experts but does not increase their aura for others.

Singularity refers to the phenomenon that things have properties that experts and critics judge to be unique and think are appreciated by users.[32]/39 Singularity as well as *an experience of singularity* are a matter of degree.

Certain experts can judge the singularity of a thing to be higher than other experts. And certain consumers can have a more intense experience of singularity than other consumers. An original artwork as well as a copy of a series of technical (re)produced artworks can be judged to be relatively singular, or can be experienced as relatively singular. The same can apply to an oeuvre or a collection—for instance, a specific collection of paintings—and to a style, genre or kind of art, like ancient music. Each can have relevant unique properties, which others do not have, and which for users bring along an intense experience of singularity. Expert-consumers may have stronger experiences of singularity than average art-lovers, but not necessarily./40/41

Aside: The realization that judgments on singularity depend on the person, and that experts often have different opinions matters. In 2010 the sociologist Lucien Karpik in a well-known book he wrote said that the degree of singularity in popular music in general is lower than in serious music, and in the case of US popular music also lower than in the case of French popular music.[33] He evidently believes that experts agree with him, but many experts certainly do not agree. His conclusion is subjective.

An obsession with singularity is for more than one reason understandable. First, an awareness of unique properties can be very satisfying. When Simon Rattle conducts Tchaikovsky's first piano concert, an expert listener is likely to hear differences in comparison with performances of the same work by other conductors. Second, art-lovers resent "more of the same" in art. "This artist just repeats himself; all his work is the same". They especially resent this in popular art, art that is associated with "standardization" and impoverished work. And third, artworks that are judged or experienced to be particularly singular are often—but not always—relatively exclusive and art-lovers love exclusivity.

Aside: That expert-consumers are aware of more and other unique characteristics than most consumers, does not imply that they necessarily have more intense art experiences. Too much knowledge and analysis of interesting unique characteristics can stand in the way of an intense experience. Moreover, expert-consumers often appreciate the presence of many unique characteristics which taken together bring along an experience of complexity which is appreciated./42

In the arts an obsession with the aura of originals or works that are produced in very small numbers, like etchings, exists. It makes people look down on much popular art and the consumers who buy posters or only listen to best-selling mainstream recorded music. The question is, what is more important for them: the aura of originals or their exclusivity? I will argue in Chap. 4 of the book that exclusivity is very important for art-lovers.

In my approach copies of originals and of art (re)produced in possibly large series can have aura and bring along a, sometimes intense, experience of aura. The art theorist Walter Benjamin suggests in a famous text, that technical (re)productions always have little or no aura; and he thinks that this is caused by the fact that they can be indefinitely (re)produced.[34] It is, indeed likely that an experience of aura is more intense in the case of, for instance, paintings, live performances and etchings than in the case of films, photos and recordings. Looking at Leonardo's *Mona Lisa* in the Paris Louvre, it is easier to imagine Leonardo putting paint on the canvas than at home looking at a sizeable reproduction of the painting. (That is, even though in the Louvre the painting is exhibited behind 3 cm thick glass giving the painting a greenish glow.) But Benjamin's view is colored by the time he wrote his text. In 1935 some (re)produced works start to be mass produced and are distributed and consumed in large numbers and art theorists must have been puzzled by the new phenomenon and its possible consequences.

Can technical (re)productions, indeed, have a considerable aura, even though they can, in theory, be produced (re)produced indefinitely? The question matters. Because art-lovers tend to look down on visual art reproductions, and earlier also on music recordings, and on the people, who go for these inferior works, and emphasize the lack of aura. Compared with unique originals they are thought to have no aura and are inferior-art. This has an impact on the social economy of art [53].

Anna is an art-lover who loves literature. When she holds a (heavy) copy of James Joyce's Ulysses in her hand, she has a strong auratic experience, an experience that at the same time is an experience of singularity. She reads it for the second time and tells her friends about it, and she is aware that she does so also to impress them—in which she succeeds. She also likes that she belongs to a small circle of readers and an even smaller circle of second-time readers. Even though the copy she holds in her hand is no unique work of art, holding the book in her hand makes her envisage Joyce sitting behind a desk writing the book. She, moreover, remembers that after Carl Jung wrote a rather negative review and that Joyce said "Hang it low". For her these are presences in the book.

Experts and art-companies continuously attempt to increase an experience of aura, singularity and exclusivity of artworks. They "enrich" works; make them more special. Museums and experts, for instance, may call attention to the fact that Van Gogh was very poor and killed himself and so add to the aura of his oeuvre. Or the manager of a famous orchestra or hall may much emphasize that their orchestra performs for the first time with the world-famous guest-conductor Simon Rattle, making the concert more singular.

For financial reasons or not, art-companies, experts and critics have always stimulated the obsession with singularity and aura. By "enriching" works they not only fabricate (an experience of) authenticity, but also fabricate and increase (an experience of) aura and singularity [77]./43 The fabrication can well be just a matter of make believe.

By now most consumers do not care about the phenomenon that photos, films and media products can be produced indefinitely. It is self-evident. They can have an intense experience of aura and singularity.

Informalization

(38) GRADUALLY INFORMALIZATION REPLACES FORMALIZATION. THIS PARTLY EXPLAINS THE SUCCESS OF POPULAR ART AND THE DECLINE OF THE SERIOUS ARTS. The phenomena so far discussed in this chapter, and in particular the subdued, civilized and formal behavior, do not only exist in art-buildings. In less extreme fashion, they are typical for all behavior of bourgeois, for instance, at work, and even at home. Everywhere behavior is far more controlled and formal than it is today. However, since around 1960, society becomes more informal. This has important consequences for the social economy of the arts.

Earlier people hold back immediate impulses and control themselves. They are also demanded to do so. There are formal rules and etiquette—the etiquette in the Victorian age is detailed and strict. Most "rules" are internalized. In the case of adults, self-control is automatic; it is "second nature". In an art-building a person does not shout to somebody further away, not in the hall and also not in the foyer. The possibility does not occur. Higher bourgeois are ahead of the lower classes, but with time self-control among workers also increases much, and they demand it from one another. In the notoriously oppressive 1950s also the behavior of the lower middle class is restrained and formal, be it sometimes in an artificial rather than natural way. The phenomenon is part of a long-term, so-called, *civilization process,* which commenced many centuries ago. Until circa 1960, it is accompanied by a dominant process of formalization.[35]

Self-control, natural or artificial, and holding back impulses have a price./44 One price bourgeois become ever more aware of, is that they are not an integrated person; in the bureaucracy and in industry, they have (to play) roles that are functional. It is therefore understandable that bourgeois search for an own "uncontrolled" self. Finding and expressing and showing it would be attractive, but is impossible; hence, the envy of artists who can and are allowed to express their selves.

During the major part of the period of serious art, all workers are "demanded" to control themselves. Economy and culture are not independent and influences are never unidirectional. But the industrial capitalist mode of production of the nineteenth and the larger part of the twentieth century does require discipline—not unlike the discipline in the symphony orchestra—and self-control is welcome. Around the 1960/1970s, however, the capitalist mode of production is entering a new phase, a phase in which there is more demand for flexible workers and sometimes also creative workers. This partly explains that a process of informalization starts to surpass the process of formalization and with time largely replaces it.

Aside: Over time the capitalist mode of production changes. Phases exist which, among others, differ in spirit, ethos and legitimation.[36] It can be argued that after *merchant capitalism* and *industrial capitalism*, around the 1950/1960s, capitalism enters a new phase, that of *network capitalism*—also called *post-industrial* or *post-manufacturing capitalism, post-Fordism, cognitive capitalism* and *late capitalism.* Phases and "eras" overlap and subdivisions are possible. Since the times of Reagan and Thatcher, we now live in a neo-liberal era, or *neo-liberal capitalism*, which can be regarded as part of the *post-manufacturing era* or as a new major stage. The spirit is certainly different. Depending on the aspect of capitalism that is studied, also other terms are used for the next (and present) stage of capitalism; foremost *finance* or *financialized capitalism* and *aesthetic capitalism.* As we shall see [79], the last is a useful term in the context of this book, but it certainly refers only to part of the ongoing story of capitalism.

Formalization remains the dominant trend till around 1950, but a contrary trend of informalization is already noticeable in the nineteenth century. The bohemians care less about formal rules and, although still a very small group, they and their art draw attention and show that a freer lifestyle is possible. From the late nineteenth century onward, there are waves of informalization involving ever larger groups. Usually artists are involved. This happens, for instance, during the Fin de Siècle and the Roaring Twenties. (It is not accidental that at the time new, more free dance styles develop, but later become more formalized again.)

The waves are part of a new phase in the continuing civilization process: a process of informalization. Shortly after the 1960s' counter revolution—in a coming together of a cultural and economic "revolution"—its effects start to exceed those of the earlier formalization process.[37] (In the 1980s and 1990s, there is some re-formalization, but the effects are limited. The long-term trend is one of informalization.) Gradually a more informal, a less openly undemocratic and hierarchical society develops; a society in which there is also less room for paternalism. It, partly, explains the decline of the established arts with their hierarchical organization and paternalistic attitudes.

Whereas increasing self-control is typical for the process of formalization, increasing controlled-decontrolling is typical for that of informalization. Controlled-decontrolling refers to less restrained behavior and a "letting go in a controlled fashion". An example is that of behavior on the dance floor during a popular music concert. People sometimes dance in an expressive little controlled style which takes much space. But when more people enter the floor and they may hinder others, they change their style and use less space. This is not just a matter of conventions. They automatically control their impulse to let go and dance expressively or "negotiate" with others./45

Given a succession of generations, with time, socialization changes and controlled decontrolled behavior starts to come naturally. (The 1960s' youngsters still had to show off their new ways; their successors do not.) With informalization a "third nature" replaces the earlier "second nature".—Now a formal etiquette as exists in art-buildings is unpleasant. It goes against the nature of the new generations. But the art-worlds and their establishments are conservative. It contributes to the decline of serious art after the 1960s.

From an outsider perspective, it can be argued that the younger generation which dances during a popular music concert is now more civilized than the older generation in the concert hall who needs much self-control not to disturb one another.

Civilized or not, the behavior itself cannot and is not always called civilized. According to the press, they were not. *After the import of American Jazz in Europe, educated youngsters visited concerts and went crazy. In The Hague in the 1950s, they stand on chairs during a concert of Herbie Hancock and the press cries shame over it. But the frenzy and consequent collective effervescence may well have been such, that they did not disturb one another.*

Aside: Even though behavior may be said to have become more civilized, this does not imply that it is more "natural", or that the third nature is more natural than is the second. One may be inclined to say—the same as earlier Peter Gay did—that the twentieth century's still consumption practice in art-buildings is "unnatural", because it goes against human nature. Gay wrote: "Undivided silent attention to a musical performance does violence to basic human impulses… Just as many visitors to an art museum cannot resist the itch to run their fingers over paintings and sculptures even educated listeners, are tempted to hum along with the tune or sway to the beat, tap their feet or drum their fingers, shake their head or conduct the orchestra from their seat, to say nothing of gratifying the itch to explain their ineffable responses to whoever sits next to them".[38] But there is no imminent "natural" way: humming along is not more natural than listening in silence and vice versa.

Typical for popular art and (re)produced serious and popular art, from reproductions and recordings in one's home to pop concerts, is that, it allows little attention and occasional intense focus. In the new society, disturbances become less disturbing. Gradually people have become ever better in multitasking and filtering information. *Presently when Anna is in a pop concert and during the performance the people standing next to her are talking, are texting or taking pictures of the performers, or of one another, this does not disturb her and does not keep her from having an intense art experience.*

Informalization has far reaching consequence for the social economy of art. It affects lifestyle choices and along with this the consumer demand for serious and popular art.

Art-settings always change, but only slowly, and during the period of serious art, they change very little. Compared with the popular arts with much more variety in atmospheres in their events, a term like monoculture still largely applies to art events. Nevertheless, *over the last decades* the common atmosphere is less formal than earlier and, within limits, there is more variety in the atmosphere. That is, indeed, within limits, because also today art-lovers agree that "unruly" settings must be taboo; settings as can, for instance¸ be found in Metal concerts with a mosh pit, in Breakdance and Hip-hop dance battles, and in poetry slams. In the arts also, less de-hierarchization and a continuing paternalism keep events unattractive for large groups. But especially in the art museums and to a lesser degree in theaters, already for some time the atmosphere is more informal, and people are returning.

In the concert halls behavior is now also somewhat more informal, but in most classical concerts the overall setting remains old fashioned and imposing, and many people who like serious music still feel uncomfortable or stay away. This explains the graying of audiences.[39] The implicit dress code continues to be unattractive for youngsters who like much variety and use their clothing (and hairstyles) to express themselves. (The code is less strict and imposing than earlier, but choices are still limited. There are now two clear alternatives: visitors can choose between suits and casual clothing, but the latter is far more codified than the term casual suggests.)

Nevertheless, even in the halls where ceremony persists around the actual performance, the overall setting is somewhat more informal. This shows, among others, from the phenomenon that the behavior of service personnel is now far less subdued and artificially civilized than 30 years ago.—It is significant because it is a deliberate decision of managements to hire a different kind of personnel.—

The main development toward events with a more informal setting takes place outside art-building. This applies, for instance, to open-air theater festivals, serious music performances in stadiums and in clubs. The consumption practice is less still in these situations.

I say a bit more about recent developments in the serious music world, because this is the art-world that has been and still is slowest in readjusting to our new more informal society. That they are slow has many reasons and one is that given the nature of live music—unamplified and regular soft passages or overall silences—stillness is thought to be necessary. The same, of course does not apply to behavior before and after the actual performance; or between movements. Since 2010 in the Proms in the Royal Albert Hall in London, the audience applauds between movements, and musicians say that they much appreciate this. The audience more often can let go in bodily activity. Nevertheless, a survey shows that the majority of the present audience goes along but judges it to be wrong: *"Clapping between movements is barbarous"*.[40] (By now the average age of the musicians in most orchestras is considerably lower than that of their audience.)

Significant are the new open-air serious music festivals with a more informal atmosphere.[41] Compared with pop music and theater, serious music was late with the provision of open-air festivals but they are emerging. During the actual performance, audiences are relatively still but the same does not apply before and after. Then the atmosphere is informal, be it usually not elated as is common during pop festivals.

Also significant are changes in broadcasts of classical music. A new type of serious music programs on television have emerged. In these programs, performances of around five minutes alternate with very informal interviews with the performers. In the discussions there are jokes and the heavy veneration of the composers of old and their music is absent. Only ten years ago the serious music establishment would have cried shame over such practice while now leading lights participate and evidently not only opportunistically but with pleasure. They as well appear to be relieved. Groups of musicians and music students certainly are, as shows from the successful Amazon's television series *Mozart in the Jungle*.[42]

Over the last two decades, small initiatives have emerged that result in live performance outside the music halls with a more informal overall atmosphere and less stillness during the performance.—An early example are the Yellow Lounge concerts.—In terms of listening hours, the initiatives are still unimportant, but they signify a longing among both young audiences and musicians for change. For instance, at the moment alternative concert series are offered in a club setting. Audience members can keep their drinks and move in and out during the actual performance. There are disturbances, but participants do not mind. They are good in filtering. A more drastic new formula is that of the, so-called, classical music raves. DJs play mixes of serious music pieces for a large audience that dances on the music, the same as in Dance music parties./46 Disturbances are considerable, but it does not stop people having intense art experiences. *When Anna took part in a rave, she noticed that moving her body with the music made her hear more details than if she had been still.*

In the context of this book, the Yellow Lounge concert series are interesting. They started off in the early 2000s in Berlin's trendy Techno Clubs and now have become available in all major cities, from New York to Singapore. They are interesting, because they were initiated by a large for-profit company: Deutsche Grammophon./47 It appears that at the time the famous and prestigious label worried more about the future of serious music than the serious music establishment. (It probably also worried about its income/profits and its own future, but such worries can well have positive effects.)

The conservative classical music art-world is slow. But it is predictable, that given a decreasing demand and thus also due to market forces, new kinds of accessible and attractive serious music will be developed and more concerts will start to be offered with different atmospheres, giving consumers more choice in programs as well as settings, including more informal settings. The serious music art establishment will start to openly promote alternative and far more informal live concert series. It is, however, questionable if, in the long run, such series will be successful when they are situated in the existing concert halls with their serious and elitist imago, an imago that has been build up for a century and a half. Maybe organizing them in other buildings will be more effective [80]. (In popular music, the concert organizers of one main venue now increasingly organize parallel concerts in several venues in the same city under the name of their main venue.)

(39) LITTLE CHOICE AND PATERNALISM DO NOT BEFIT AN INFORMAL SOCIETY. THE DICHOTOMY OF ARTIST AND SPECTATOR CONTINUES TO BE IMPORTANT. ARTISTS MUST BE IN CHARGE. ACTIVE AUDIENCE PARTICIPATION IS NOT APPRECIATED. In the informal society, along with increasing prosperity, a very diverse supply of products has developed. There is much choice. There is also more freedom of choice. Fewer institutions, like earlier the church and governments, tell people what they must choose and what they must

not choose. Much paternalism does not befit the informal society. But, at least until recently, a limited choice and paternalism are typical for the serious arts.

In the second half of the twentieth century, average luxury consumption space grows rapidly and the number of goods that people can buy and choose from increases much. This also applies to art and especially popular art. (As said, paid-for art is a luxury good.) The popular arts offer a rich variety of live art products, that is, many different kinds of art in many different art-settings. The average price is such that also people with lower incomes can afford to visit them, be it not every week. Often different social (sub)groups prefer different kinds of art and different art-settings, and popular art event organizers provide them.

Also *over the last decades* the established arts drag behind. In serious/classical music, the variety in the artworks of our time is limited. More than one kind of "contemporary-music" exists, but they only appeal to small groups of expert-consumers. To a lesser degree, the same applies to conceptual visual art and visual contemporary-art. What is most striking is that in the period of serious art, there is no choice in art-settings. Only one kind of setting is offered: this is the serious setting that was described and discussed in section 50. This is now changing a bit, but the large majority of events still have the same setting. Aside: Giving people no choice in art-settings, groups are excluded who otherwise may have been interested in the artworks that are offered. Exclusion of groups in the arts is a topic I treat in Chap. 4.

During most serious music performances, works of more than one composer are performed by the same ensemble. Programmers attempt to make combinations that are attractive for the kind of audience they expect. But not always: in the 1970s and 1980s, many serious music concerts were offered to audiences interested in traditional music that consisted of a traditional piece followed by a short contemporary-music piece before the intermission and after the intermission another traditional piece. The goal was to educate audiences, while the means was paternalistic. People had no choice. Few got educated, many went along without enthusiasm but also many stopped coming to these concerts. After some years the practice was discontinued. (There was no enthusiasm in the hall and often also not on the stage, while contagious enthusiasm is essential for "learning art" [40].)

Not only are the behavioral possibilities of visitors in art-building very limited, audience participation during performances is also constrained. In the performing arts, most artists are unhappy with participating audiences, because participation implies interference with the author's and their own artwork. In the arts the dichotomy of artist and spectator (or listener or reader) is much emphasized. The artist is active; his audience is passive, and must be passive. In their mind audiences may co-produce but they must not have a creative input in an artwork and so creatively interfere with the artwork and change it, that is, make it less authentic. The artist must be in charge and be the only author.

Aside: To control the artwork the audience must be controlled. This usually implies that it must be still. In some serious art performances and in the case of interactive visual art audiences are sometimes allowed to respond, but only within set limits. In a few, rare, serious music concerts audience members are asked to participate but in an altogether prescribed fashion. In theater comedies audiences have slightly more freedom and can occasionally laugh aloud. But if they laugh at the wrong moment directors will change the piece. Unlike in the popular arts, in the arts control by artists does not allow or hardly allows a "letting go" by audience members; controlled de-controlling is hardly an option. (This is not to say that still audiences are really passive.)/48

In popular art events, and especially concerts, audiences have more space to move, and motor activity contributes much to effervescence.[43] There is collective effervescence, and the same as in serious events, there is little noticed interaction between performers and audiences, but there is also much noticeable interaction and this enhances effervescence. By responding audiences participate and co-create the artwork. This certainly applies to life-sets of DJ-producers (or turntablists) in which in interaction with his audience the artist adapts his work.

In popular music enthusiasm is openly expressed and communicated in many different ways. Some responses come from individuals. Some responses are subtle, others more extrovert and deliberate. During the performance of certain songs, audiences become more still. Or an audience starts to applaud after a band has started playing a song that the audience knows. Or in order to raise spirits a singer or MC, in an improvised way, verbally communicates with the audience, also during the actual performance of the music. (After shouting "Hello Montpellier, how are you." the Montpellier audience responds enthusiastically.) Collaboration is continuous and altogether essential in the case of the rapper and his audience.

Aside: In this context concerts of 100% "not-real" music are interesting. The music has been altogether produced in a studio (or at home) and can be played but not performed in the traditional sense. There is live manipulation by DJs but the material has been produced earlier. Given that the music is not "real", one may expect that there is less collective effervescence following from a shared focus on the music. And it is true that in some Dance parties the focus on the music is not intense. It is better to say that focus comes and goes. The DJ with manipulations—among others of the volume—arm movements and so forth every now and then increases focus and collective effervescence.

That noticeable interaction or communication is not appreciated in the arts is understandable, given the high value of authenticity and authorship. The conductor and director take responsibility for the performance of which they are the author, and they are held responsible for it by their audiences—as well as critics. They, moreover, feel responsible for the preliminary artwork as created by the author of the score, play or choreography. The audience must in no way interfere with these artworks. (An exception is the mentioned disturbing "bravos" during opera performances—a leftover from less serious times in opera consumption. But by now also these interferences have become taboo and no longer occur.)

In the formal society people usually went along with being patronized. The result is that their behavior is officially or de facto controlled by others; for instance, by superiors in companies and government bodies which employ people. The organizational form is very hierarchical. Self-control and control by superiors enhance one another. In the new informal society in the arts, this organizational model still exists. It continues to apply to the organization of performers and especially the musicians in orchestras. The same as audiences, non-creative performers must be and are controlled by conductors and directors. During performances their input is altogether controlled. They have no autonomous space. Whereas the composers of old, often deliberately, left room for improvisation, in the period of serious art, conductors must be in control and prefer to just follow tradition rather than creatively fill in the room for improvisation.

In directing the musicians, serious music conductors usually stick to the very precise instructions in the score. And whereas it is already difficult to instruct and control a small ensemble, it is very difficult to let 75 musicians follow precise instructions and perform in a coordinated fashion. One may well argue that this is not of our time. The large symphony orchestra is indeed an early nineteenth-century invention; that is, a time in which disciplined behavior in offices and factories is normal and not that hard to work up. Now this is different. It is no accident that since the 1960s sickness absence among the musicians in large symphony orchestras is increasing and that there are now more musicians from East-European and Asian countries, countries where the process of informalization is or was less advanced./49

Aside: First, the control in the large orchestra goes further back than the art period. It partly stems from a world of pyramid-shaped structures of absolute authority, of aristocracy and monarchy, a hierarchy reflected in the structure of the orchestra. (The military is known for its hierarchy, but the continuous discipline demanded of the members of a large orchestra was and is larger.) Second, in the nineteenth century, wages are low and the bourgeois can afford to have 75 players on the stage. Third, in theater during rehearsals actors sometimes have some space and can co-produce the later performance. The same applies to the players in small music ensembles.

Above I presented examples of the offering of parallel more informal performances in the arts. I will not repeat them. Here I say more about festivals. Already for several decades in the popular arts the wish of audiences to have a choice of artistically different acts is answered, among others, by offering parallel acts during a festival. People are free to come and go during a performance, and if they wish, they can get a taste of something new and innovative without being obliged to stay for the whole performance.

Over the last decades, an increasing number of festivals exist in the serious arts, but they differ. It is rare that there are parallel performances. it is anyway impossible to move during performances from one performance to another. Generally, people pay for separate performances. (Sometimes also a pass can be bought giving access to all performances.)

In theater for some time open-air festivals with tents exist with parallel acts. Usually people pay for the festival as well as for separate acts. Parts of the acts are very entertaining and are judged not to be real theater by the theater establishment. Nevertheless, people in the establishment sometimes like the existence of such "cross-border" festivals because the visits can serve as a necessary step to the real thing, that is, theater performances in established theaters. This attitude is paternalistic.

Over the last two decades, the presence of and interest in so-called *participatory art* has increased. Different overlapping forms exist, like interactive, relational, cooperative art as well as activist, dialogical and community-based art. Many socially relevant or critical art projects outside museums can be qualified as participatory art. Both in the realization of such projects and in theorizing, the visual arts come first. Sometimes the nature of the participation is such that the non-artist participants can be said to not only co-produce but also co-create and thus symbolically co-author the works. Interesting is present social media use in co-creation of artworks. The projects are often initiated by art-companies. They have the means to organize them and also see them as promotional tools. The say that artists give individual "digital participants" is not large, but groups have freedom and the artist cannot fully control the artwork. (Sometimes the created artwork does not just exist virtually, but also in real space and sometimes in public space, and can be observed by participants and others.)

Recently, even "shopping" has become possible in certain serious music events. They are rare but interesting. An example is that of different serious music ensembles playing at the same time in various rooms and/or in different corners of the large main room of a venue. During the performances people are free to move from one ensemble to another. Though many serious music lovers disapprove, such new forms are no longer resisted, also because they take place outside the own art-buildings. (It is indeed significant that they take place in popular art venues.)

(40) IN THE SECOND HALF OF THE TWENTIETH CENTURY, PEOPLE APPEAR TO BE ABLE TO FIND THEIR "SELVES" AND EXPRESS IT. A PERSONAL CHOICE OF ART AND POPULAR ART HELPS THE DEVELOPMENT AND CONFIRMATION OF AN OWN IDENTITY. IN POPULAR MUSIC, PERFORMERS SHOW THEIR PERSONALITY. Thanks to controlled-decontrolling, expressing one's self and showing an own identity has become easier. Along with informalization people cannot only *search for* a self; they increasingly believe that they can *find* their selves.

The latter is largely a "made-belief". It is anyway questionable if people's possibility to realize themselves and have self-determining freedom has really increased. Freedom has also been reduced: people now *must* realize themselves and be "true individuals". The result is anyway that the consumption of personal, expressive and meaningful art is more important than before. Also, the "personality" of artists matters more than before.

As said, in a controlled fashion, people can let go. For instance, looking at people dancing during a popular music concert, one notices that they express themselves and show something of themselves that may well be called true or authentic. In many other situations as well, people can express their selves more than before. The transition affects the social economy of art. It contributes much to the increasing success of the popular arts after 1960 and the difficulties of the established arts.

Choosing a specific product or a specific selection from a wide collection of goods, from paintings and furniture to music, is thought to be a means to be an "authentic" person. A very diverse supply of products—think of, for instance, the t-shirts with numerous different texts and pictures—befits this society, that is, a society in which increasingly an "I-culture" exists. Belonging to a group with a certain identity is attractive as well. A choice of a certain kind of sneaker tells about the group one belongs to.

Most (popular) artworks and collections of these works have more characteristics that make them personal and experienced as more singular than other products. As such they are particularly useful for developing an own individual or group identity. Art allows detailed comparisons. And comparing one's art choices with friends is enjoyable. For various reasons a certain choice of popular music is particularly attractive.—Due to the omnipresence of certain popular music, everybody, also a lover of serious music, is now familiar with a huge collection of pop songs and loves some more than others or, instead, hates some more than others; and communicates this with people in the own circle.—Within different groups certain kinds of art are popular. It gives them an identity. The groups have "own art", like a certain kind of hip-hop music, and sometimes they—usually temporarily—do not want to share it with other groups [85].

What nowadays makes popular art, from popular music, musicals, dance and street art, so attractive is that intended meanings expressed by texts, personal voices or (moving) images, are not hard to perceive and understand. It helps the construction of own meaningful narratives. In popular music personalities are important. (When Ringo Starr of the Beatles sings, "With a little help from my friend" in the Beatle's song of the same name, most listeners will hear an altogether different story than in the case of Joe Cocker singing the same song./50)

Meaningful (popular) art does not require text but text is helpful, and contemporary texts, as in pop songs, are more helpful than the texts and narratives of old, like those of the librettos of traditional operas. Visual art also "tells stories", but other than in older visual art and in contemporary street art in the case of contemporary-art even expert-consumers find it often hard to grasp or develop meaning [55].

Also because of its omnipresence in daily life, popular music is more suitable for developing and expressing an own identity than serious music. As far as mainstream popular music is concerned, somebody from San Paulo can discuss personal preferences as well as of related identities with somebody from Berlin. (Also at the top of the mainstream level there is diversity and preferences can be telling.)

In mainstream popular music with vocals, as well as in, so-called, alternative popular music with vocals, it is differences in the voices of singers that make works different in ways that matter much for the meanings of works, the self-constructed artworks, and thus for the choice of people. Personal voices much "enrich" popular music. They become special, and there is a strong experience of unicity and singularity. This applies also to non-expert listeners. Whereas in part of the song-texts there is considerable sameness, the voices of the numerous singers always differ much. —Unlike in serious music, the listener does not have to be an expert-consumer to notice even subtle differences.—A different voice singing the same or almost the same text brings along a different meaning. It is the combination of a personal voice with a specific text that adds many relevant qualities to works./51

Since the 1960s the texts increasingly befit the mentioned modern "I-culture".—It is no accident that after the 1960s in pop songs not only the word "I" but also "you" are ever more used. In a lesser degree, this also applies to "we".—In this culture people are relatively ego-centric. But ego-centrism can only exist in relation to others. Difference as well as correspondence with people close to oneself is important. The classically schooled voice used in classical music and opera is far less personal. (More about this in the web-note./52)

Especially young audiences want to be able to identify with their heroes on the stage and learn from them. Since the 1960s, in both appearance and behavior, popular performing artists are expected to be personalities. The break away from the common standardized appearance took some time. At first the Beatles still wore uniform clothing, but in the 1960s, they and other bands started to wear different and personal clothing. Ever since, on the stage in their communication with the audience, popular music performers clearly show their personality. Well-known performers are examples for art consumers. They help them develop or confirm an own identity.

Some behavioral and dressing constraints in serious art events follow from the fact that expressing one's personality is unwanted, also after the 1960s. It is distracting. People must not show off differences also not in the way they dress. Creative artists, like conductors and directors, can express themselves and their personality in their artworks, but not on the stage. The same applies to other performers, like ensemble musicians, actors and dancers. Being a clearly identifiable personality does not befit the seriousness of the event and is disrespectful toward the author. This is in line with the already discussed phenomenon of formal, conventional and subdued behavior and the relative uniform clothing of audience members as well as performers. The tuxedos and/or black clothing make the performers interchangeable.

When behavior is extraordinary personal, this draws attention and is disapproved of by critics. *An example is the violinist Nigel Kennedy who in the 1980s behaved "like a popstar", also on the stage. Though a very good and successful musician—his CD sales were unprecedented—he was criticized to such degree that he withdrew from the public stage.*

In the context of a changing social economy of art, it is good to note that for-profit companies make use of people's wish to find and express oneself and to differ from others. They make people believe that "being oneself" is possible, that is, if one buys the right identity-making products. Already for a long time, "be yourself" is a commonly used advertisement slogan. People are expected to not only express themselves but also be their self. Because realizing oneself continues to be difficult, companies, de facto, create an insatiable demand for identity-making products. They promise authenticity but do not "deliver". (In practice they rather appeal to an also continuing wish of people to belong and thus conform.)

With time companies increasingly "sell" expressive authenticity, that is, they sell authentic or "honest" commodities—from "authentic" lotions, bread and furniture to holidays [31]. They also sell by more straightforward means from—financially very successful—self-help books to yoga lessons.

Disappointment is built into the new situation. Even the people who are now best in expressing their selves are aware that self-determination and much personal autonomy remain beyond reach. This explains the continuing attraction of the art profession.

Whereas in the 1980s Nigel Kennedy was still much criticized for showing his personality on the stage, *over the last decades* conductors, and to a much lesser degree also the musicians in an orchestra, are allowed to show more of their personality, also during the actual performance. People at home, but not in the hall, can notice this when watching their faces during television broadcasts. Moreover, in the hall conductors and soloists—but not ordinary musicians—sometimes wear unusual clothes and haircuts, and this tells a bit about their personality and even more of the fact that they are creative artists with a bohemian streak. Talk between pieces is still rare. In interviews conductors and soloists show more of themselves and more so than 50 years ago. Moreover, nowadays television programs exist in which only very short pieces by small ensembles and soloists are performed with personal conversations with the musicians in between the pieces.

Creative performers now also have a bit more freedom. On the stage well-known artists like conductors—with sometimes exorbitant haircuts—and soloists can express their personality, be it in appearance—clothing, hairstyle—rather than behavior. But hierarchy remains important. The freedom of ordinary orchestra members is still very limited.

In popular art performances, there are limits to what popular performers, singers and dancers can show of themselves. Therefore, in live performances and performances on television, singers and dancers often tell about how they feel about their dance or song. And in very popular television series, like the Canadian dance television series *The Next Step*, there are many short intermissions in which the young performers, facing the viewer, talk about their personal feelings.[44] (By now for youngsters the internet is probably the main source for identity building. It offers a rich choice of material, including popular art—visual art, art videos and poetry—which youngsters use to develop their self and build/construct their identity.)

An Attractive Low-Income Profession

(41) ARTISTS' INCOMES ARE LOW. AFTER 1960 THEY BECOME LOWER WHILE THE RELATIVE NUMBER OF ARTISTS INCREASES. ECONOMISTS ARGUE THAT THERE IS EXCESS-SUPPLY OF ART. In preparation of the next section and later chapters, in this section I look at developments in the income and number of artists. In the next section I explain why after 1960 the arts profession is still very attractive even though artists' incomes become ever lower. This is not what one would expect.

Incomes, numbers and other characteristics of artists are measured in more than one way. In web-text wt-41 I explain the notion of average or median values, as in "median income", and I discuss various aspects one must keep in mind when examining data on artists. I also mention that economists speak of an income penalty. And I mention that the level of education of artists' parents is higher than that of other higher educated professionals, making the art profession somewhat less risky and I discuss at some length the possibility of an over- or excess-supply of art. Opinions differ. I advise readers with sufficient time to first read the web-text.

For the time before circa 1970, no carefully measured data exists. Nevertheless, on the basis of the far more general research of art historians, certain plausible conclusions can be presented. In the old days the average income of the craftsman, who we now would call artist, was probably not lower than that of comparable professionals. But during the period of serious art, the average income of creative artists almost certainly goes down and increasingly so in the twentieth century. This suggests that in this period the art's profession becomes more attractive. This is in line with the reasoning in section 25: living authentic lives have become a goal for bourgeois, but an unattainable goal; artists form the exception.

Even though the nineteenth-century artist Van Gogh has become the prototype of the twentieth-century poor artist, at the time the typical artist may have earned less than other professionals, but not that much. It is only in the course of the first half of the twentieth century that the typical artist starts to earn little from his work as artist. This is also suggested by the phenomenon that many creative artists, some of whom are relatively well-known, have second jobs from necessity, or are supported by partners or intermediary producers like publishers. They cannot make a decent living from art. An example is Virginia Woolf.

Around 1970 the first results of systematic empirical research appear. They show that at that time incomes of *creative artists* are already very low. A large percentage is poor, or, as is presently said: they have an income at or below the "*poverty threshold*". This suggests that in the preceding two decades, median incomes must already have decreased much. Data shows that overall incomes and incomes from art work continue to decrease, at least till circa 1995./53

Dutch research shows that between circa 1980 and 2002, 40% of visual arts have a negative income from their work as artist—they cannot cover their cost—72% have an income lower than corresponds with the poverty threshold, and 94% earns less than the income of the average worker. The top 1%, however, earns many times more; the income distribution is therefore very unequal or, as economist say, skewed. Overall income is higher, but the income of almost 40% is still below the poverty threshold. Almost 40% can be said to be poor.[45] (Subsidies are included in the income from art work. Social benefits, income from second jobs and from partners and other similar sources are included in overall income./54)

Other research shows that over the last ten years, only 0.7% of Dutch writers of literature, that is, 1 of 140 writers—writers, of whom one or more works have been published—can make a living from their art job.[46]

In all arts the distribution of income of creative artists is not only very skewed; there also is a very long "tail" in the area of low incomes. The number of artists with very low incomes is much and much larger than those with very high incomes and also much higher than those with low but not very low incomes.

Performing artists earn considerably more than do creative artists. Part of them are employed by nonprofits. Collective agreements exist or minimum wages are paid. Incomes are nevertheless very low. Many work freelance or part time. Since ever more contracts become temporary contracts, while some serious performers are now flex workers, the difference with creative artists is becoming smaller. This leads to precarity. According to a recent study of incomes of dancers in Berlin, in 2016 their median income is circa €800 per month including income from art-related and non-art jobs. This is well below the poverty threshold.[47]

When data on the incomes of musicians of popular music are published, never a distinction is made between creative artists and performers and this is understandable, because in popular music most composers are also performers. But although part of the musicians are no creative artists, income is nevertheless very low./55

Data on artists' incomes from some countries shows that, taking into account inflation, after circa 1995, that is, *over the last decades*, average (median) incomes stabilize. Others show that incomes become even lower than before./56 The arts profession becomes even more risky, that is, precarity increases. The changes in income are small. Given the necessary arbitrariness of findings they could be absent or larger than reported./57 After much growth in the number of accredited art education institutes in some countries, the number of applicants of visual art academies now goes down. The same applies to conservatories, but not to accredited popular music institutes. Given the very large number of professional artists ("working artists") without a bachelor's degree—in the USA, 84%—it is doubtful if this development will lead to less excess supply and higher incomes. Whether the increasing and justified actions of artists against underpayment may contribute to a higher average income remains to be seen [45].

So far, the attraction of the art profession continues to increase. In all countries multiple jobholding increases. Interesting is the development that more artists with a bachelor's degree end up in non-art or art-related professions. In the USA, this applies to 90% of art graduates. (This percentage is much larger in the case of those with non-art degrees.) Finally, ever more artists have a degree or simultaneously develop skills in non-art professions. They evidently have a plan B and many of them execute this plan and choose an amateur status. (As I noticed: getting an MA degree in art management is popular.)

In this section and its web-text I did not discuss high incomes in the arts. As we shall see in section 77, *over the last decades*, top incomes in the arts have risen much, and more than in earlier decades.

(42) ARTISTS ARE ABLE TO GIVE PROOF OF THEIR ABILITY TO EXPRESS THEMSELVES AND BE AUTHENTIC. IN THE SECOND HALF OF THE TWENTIETH CENTURY, BECOMING AN ARTIST IS VERY ATTRACTIVE AND RELATIVELY EASY. THIS CONTRIBUTES TO LOW INCOMES. As noted, in spite of low incomes and no growth in consumer demand for established art, the number of artists has increased much since 1960; far more than in the decades before. It has grown very much in the popular arts, and much in the established arts; and anyway, more than corresponds with the growth in demand. This explains incomes that have become (even) lower. At first sight, this is not what one may have expected. (When in this and the following sections I use the term authentic, it is expressive authentic—a being true to oneself in one's expressions—and not nominal authentic [31].)

It is significant that since the 1960s, the term artistic and related terms are used in new and sometimes confusing ways. In 1972 the visual artist Josef Beuys said: "Everyone is an artist". (He probably uses the term in a metaphoric sense.) Foucault writes "we have to create ourselves as a work of art" and speaks of the democratization of the artistic and creativity. Boltanski and Chiapello speak of artistic capital and artistic capitalism.[48] Also the notion of *the* aesthetic has broadened much.

Since the 1960s along with informalization, artists have gradually lost their monopoly on self-expression and creativity. People no longer have to hold back. They are allowed and sometimes encouraged to express themselves and, in different degrees, many people do. The difference with the earlier controlled behavior is large. When everybody has more freedom and can express himself, the advantage of becoming and being artist disappears in this respect. Also the belief in artists being called and the art profession being a vocation becomes less strong. And yet: the art profession becomes more attractive. There are three explanations which supplement one another.

First, unlike others, artists can give a well-noticeable proof, of having expressed themselves in the form of their (expressively) authentic artworks. They can do so in their professional activity. In this they have a relative monopoly. But it is a monopoly that is somewhat threatened by a new and rapidly growing group of so-called creatives. I say more about this in the following section.

Second, expressing oneself is not the same as realizing oneself. People may believe or are made to believe that they can now realize themselves, but, on average, this is not the case. They can, more or less successfully, search for a self or own identity, but self-determination remains beyond reach. And, in spite of a superficial belief in the opposite, people are aware of this. Artists, on the other hand, realize themselves in their work. In this respect they continue to hold a relative monopoly. The profession is attractive and popular because of, as Julian Stallabrass argues, a prospect of work without a narrow specialization which allows artists to endow work and life with own meanings.[49]

Third, paradoxically, the new and widely shared possibility of expressing oneself and being creative contributes to a larger number of people becoming artist, exactly because, unlike before, now everybody can, in principle, be creative and become artist. Earlier in the period of serious art, the art profession was a vocation; one had to be called and be naturally talented. Quality was not always noticed, but the high quality of one's art work could be discovered, be it in the worst case only after one's death.

As said [14], in the period of serious art, being an artist is a self-declared state. After the middle of the twentieth century, declaring oneself to be artist has become easy, and given the "democratization'" of creativity, an increasing number of people declare that they are artists while fewer people contradict them. Nevertheless, before or after a self-declaration the person concerned will seek some form of confirmation, or people surrounding him will look for confirmation and let the artist or aspiring artist know what they think. Feedback can come from parents, other family members, friends, artists which the (aspiring) artists knows, teachers at primary and secondary school, teachers in unofficial as well as official art schools, from degrees and so forth. The one may supplement the other but no single one is required. For some people—but certainly not all—also actual events, like being able to sell work or perform for payment, receive a subsidy or donation, find a commercial-gallery, impresario or publisher, being able to make a living from art and so forth also represent confirmation that matters. The absence of one or more of these confirmations may also lead an artist to the decision to declare that he is no artist anymore or, even, that after all he has never been a proper artist.

Important differences exist between types of artists, like creative and performing artist, or an artist making serious art and inferior-art and popular art. For instance—as can be expected—being able to make a living from art is more often a source of confirmation in popular art than in the serious arts. Many popular musicians decide to stop declaring themselves artists, when after around five years they still cannot make a living from art. This corresponds with many at first having declared themselves artists.

All in all, youngsters in the second half of the twentieth century more easily declare themselves as an artist than before and are less often corrected by others. It follows that although artists no longer hold a monopoly on creativity, they have one important advantage: through their expressive works, they can give proof of being authentic. Moreover, it is easier than before to declare oneself artist—and not be corrected by others—.

Aside: There probably are stages in declaring oneself an artist as well as in a later declaration of being no artist anymore. (This complicates the mentioned counting numbers of artists on the basis of self-perception.)

Over the last decades and most of all over the very last decade, prospective artists are probably better informed about the disadvantages of being an artist, which leads them to wanting more confirmation. The consequence is that they, after all, do not declare themselves as an artist or sooner declare the opposite. Listening to my students I have the impression that this is indeed the case, be it more so in the established arts than the popular arts. In the popular arts now more youngsters appear to find and declare in between positions: They are neither artists nor non-artists. Being an artist anyway has less goodness and prestige than before.

(43) *Over the last decades*: THE RELATIVE MONOPOLY OF ARTISTS ON SELF-EXPRESSION AND SELF-REALIZATION BECOMES LESS STRONG. ARTISTS NOW COMPETE WITH OTHER CREATIVES. In the second half of the twentieth century, artists still hold a relative monopoly of self-expression and self-realization in their professional activities. They have more expressive autonomous space than other professionals including the many new creatives, but the difference becomes smaller.

As said, along with informalization and developments in capitalism, in this period in many companies, small groups of more creative workers are needed and welcomed. So called creative or cultural industries emerge and the number of creative workers—who now are often called "creatives"—grows. Over the last decades also the attention for creativity and professionals working in the creative industries has much increased. Books and articles are written about creative industries, creative cities and a creative class, of which the new creatives are part.[50] Artists as well, are increasingly categorized and called creatives, even though most (still) do not like to be called so. (They want to remain special.) Government reports treat and show the economic importance of creatives. Often artists are no longer acknowledged as a distinctive subset. And if there is attention for art and artists, the economic importance of art and artists turns out to be less than that of other creative sectors and workers.

It appears that becoming a non-art creative (an "almost artist") can have clear benefits compared with becoming artist. Within limits the new creatives can not only be creative but also have more possibilities than others to sometimes express themselves in their work. They, moreover, have an, on average, higher income and more job-security than artists. Nevertheless, in spite of low incomes, so far, the art's profession has remained very attractive. (Presently in the lower echelons of work in the creative industries job-security is going down as are incomes, but the relative difference with average artists still exists.)

That the art's profession remains attractive can largely be explained from a relative difference with other creatives and other professionals. Also without a monopoly, artists continue to have a relative advantage. Artists can not only make authentic works, they can also give proof of making them; a proof that is noticed in larger groups; from a local community or scene to a group all over the world. The advantage is, indeed, that they can show to larger groups that their work is authentic and creative. Most work of people in the creative industries is not authentic. It can be very creative, but outside a larger firm, few people attribute the creative work to a specific employee. In as far as the creative input is appreciated, recognition comes from colleagues and superiors.

Aside: Nevertheless, in the higher echelons, of companies and organizations, and not only companies in the creative industries, the creative work of some individuals now sometimes become well-known, also outside the walls of the company or organization. They may even be somewhat expressively authentic. An example is Steve Jobs./58 But in as far as they create irreplaceable and somewhat authentic works they do not do so with an art intention, that is, an intention to make real art. The works are not presented in an art-setting; and their works do not fall in a category of art-world-recognized art. (This may change in the decades to come.) Therefore, up to the present-day these people cannot call themselves artists and do not enjoy all of the benefits artists enjoy.

Workers at all levels in industry may be creative and create unique "works", but their creative works are not or hardly expressively authentic. (This is "creative" in a broad sense. For instance, solutions that managers find for a problem, can be very creative also when it does not straightforwardly affect a product.) This shows from the phenomenon that the creators are replaceable, while ultimately artists and their artworks are not. Any other creative (or, broader, any knowledge worker) is indeed replaceable—even a "genius" like Steve Jobs is replaceable. Within a week after a CEO's departure, another has taken his place. However, when an artist dies, no further works will appear in which he has expressed himself and which he usually underlines with his signature. After Mark Rothko and George Antheil died no longer new, expressively as well as nominally authentic, Rothko paintings or Antheil compositions have been produced.

Over the last decades the attention for creativity continues to grow. There is more praise for people doing creative work. In aesthetic capitalism they increasingly can also give proof of being creative and be acknowledged for that in larger circles of peers and consumers. In this respect the difference with successful artists becomes smaller and that with little- or not-recognized artists serving small markets disappears. Choosing for a creative non-art profession becomes a real alternative. One consequence is that the precarious situation of many artists continues while that of many other creatives increases.

It is understandable that there is now a growing group of "hybrid" artists, who start to regard work in collaboration with non-art creatives in employment situations not as a second job but as proper art work. Given their various forms of schooling, they believe that they can have an artistic input that differs from and supplements the input of non-art creatives. They may be right. The boundary between the two kinds of input is anyway unclear. They de facto broaden the selection of activities which could be counted as art work.

The fact that prospective artists now tend to have plan Bs and seek supplementary education allowing work in art-related areas, also signifies a change in the status of being an artist. They can be said to have developed an attractive *portfolio of jobs*.[51]/59 (I expect that quite a few readers of this book are students of cultural entrepreneurship who have followed some official art education or do so simultaneously.)

Also, the gray area between professional and amateur artists is likely to increase. It is likely that "artistic professions" and artistic activities will remain attractive, but becoming a traditional artist less attractive. Therefore, although not everybody is an artist, the question who is a professional artist or just a professional creative, becomes harder to answer or may with time even become meaningless. Finally, it is significant that now in daily speech the term authentic sometimes stands for creative and creative stands for authentic.

(44) Excurse. LOW INCOMES, LITTLE "VOICE" AND LITTLE RECOGNITION CAUSE DISTRESS. THE NOTION THAT ARTISTS ARE "COMPENSATED" BY AN UNUSUAL HIGH JOB SATISFACTION IS OFTEN NOT VALID. That the arts are extraordinary attractive implies that *expectations* are high and not necessarily that the benefits of being artist are high and come up to expectations. For some it does, for others it does not. It does not for most of the many artists who after having become artists are and remain poor.

It has been argued that low incomes are, at least partly, "compensated" by non-monetary benefits and in particular by an unusual high work satisfaction. But, unlike economists may be inclined to think: the fact that it takes a long time before poor artists decide to stop being a professional artist does not prove that they are compensated for hardship.

Recent scientific research on the motivation and work satisfaction of artists and "creatives" showing that they enjoy a far more than average work satisfaction has major flaws. This is still what people want to hear, but the reality is often different. This is not to say that there are no artists who very much enjoy creating art, but there are also many who experience distress even though they may not easily admit this.

An extended version of this section is as web-text wt-44 available on the website. It may interest all readers. In the web-text I stress that it is not only low income but also or even more a lack of recognition and voice that cause distress.

(45) *Over the last decades*: PRECARITY AMONG ARTISTS INCREASES. THE ATTRACTION OF BEING AN ARTIST LEADS TO INCREASING EXPLOITATION OF SERIOUS ARTISTS BY NON-PROFITS AND EXPLOITATION OF POPULAR ARTISTS BY FOR-PROFITS. Further commercialization, in the arts as well as popular art, probably has added to exploitation. Now groups of "entrepreneurial" artists protest against inner-art-world exploitation. And increasingly with success. To limit the number of pages and because these theses are less essential within this book, I discuss them in web-text wt-45, which may interest all readers and especially artists.[52]

Notes

[1](Martin, 1991).

[2]Preface of Voltaire *Dictionnaire Philosophique* (1764).

[3](Becker, 2006) 23.

[4]Cf. (Williams, 2009).

[5]Cf. (Laermans, 2009) 132. For an explanation of the romantic notion of expressive authenticity see (Vannini & Franzese, 2008).

[6](Taylor, 1989).

[7]Cf. (Taylor, 1991) emphasizes and explains the ideal of authenticity in Modernity.

[8](Taylor, 1991) 47.

[9]More nuanced interpretations of the term autonomy exist. See, for instance, (Blokland, 1997).

[10](Blanning, 1969) 127

[11]Cf. (Laermans, 2009) 132

[12]For instance, (Peterson, 1997) and (van Poecke, 2017).

[13]http://www.reuters.com/article/2012/01/11/us-damienhirst-spot-idUSTRE80A0W120120111.

[14]Cf. (Taylor, 1991).

[15]Cf. (Mead, 1934).

[16](Small, 1998) 164.

[17](Collins, 2005).

[18]Among others (Kolb, 2001).

[19]Berlioz later published his diary under the title *Mémoires*.

[20](Durkheim, 1965). (Collins, 2005).

[21]Cf. (Williams, 2009). In the book the earlier nuanced discussion of various forms of authenticity by (Peterson, 1997) is put in a broader perspective.

[22]I derive the distinction of nominal and expressive authenticity from (Dutton, 2003) 258.

[23](Gilmore & Pine II, 2007) speak of everyday life becoming saturated with "toxic levels of inauthenticity".

Lena, J. C. (2014). *Banding Together: How Communities Create Genres in Popular Music*. Princeton: Princeton University Press.

Martin, A. (1991). *Writings = Schriften / Agnes Martin; ed. by Dieter Schwarz*. Ostfildern: Cantz.

Mead, G. H. (1934). *Mind, Self and Society*. Chicago: University of Chicago Press.

Menger, P.-M. (2001). Artists as Workers: Theoretical and Methodological Challenges. *Poetics, 28*(4), 241–254. https://doi.org/10.1016/S0304-422X(01)80002-4.

Miller, D. (2005). *Materiality / ed. by Daniel Miller*. Durham: Duke University Press.

Peacock, A. (1968). Performing Arts: The Economic Dilemma: Review. *Economica, 35*, 100–101.

Pearson, M. P., & Richards, C. (2003). *Architecture and Order: Approaches to Social Space*. London: Routledge.

Peterson, R. A. (1997). *Creating Country Music. Fabricating Authenticity*. Chicago: The University of Chicago Press.

Rapoport, A. (1982). *The Meaning of the Built Environment: A Nonverbal Communication Approach*. Tucson: University of Arizona Press.

Shukaitis, S., & Figiel, J. (2019). Knows No Weekend: The Psychological Contract of Cultural Work in Precarious Times. *Journal of Cultural Economy*, 1–13. https://doi.org/10.1080/17530350.2019.1574863.

Small, C. (1998). *Musicking. The Meanings of Performing and Listening*. Middletown/Connecticut: Wesleyan University Press.

Stallabras, J. (2004). *Art Incorporated: The Story of Contemporary Art*. Oxford: Oxford University Press.

Szreder, K. (2013). Cruel Economy of Authorshop. In M. Lewandoskwa & L. Ptak (Eds.), *Undoing Property*. Berlin: Sternberg Press.

Taylor, C. (1989). *Sources of the Self, The Making of the Modern Identity*. Cambridge: Cambridge University Press.

Taylor, C. (1991). *The Malaise of Modernity*. Cambridge: Harvard University Press. In 1192 the book was reprinted under the title The Ethics of Authenticity.

van Poecke, N. (2017). *Authenticity Revisited: The Production, Distribution, and Consumption of Independent Folk Music in the Netherlands (1993–Present)*. Retrieved from Dissertation. https://repub.eur.nl/pub/102670

Vannini, P., & Franzese, A. (2008). The Authenticity of Self: Conceptualization, Personal Experience, and Practice. *Sociology Compass, 2*(5), 1621–1637. https://doi.org/10.1111/j.1751-9020.2008.00151.x.

Williams, J. P. (2009). *Authenticity in Culture, Self, and Society* (1st ed., P. Vannini, Ed.). Farnham/Burlington: Routledge.

Wouters, C. (2007). *Informalization, Manners and Emotions Since 1890*. London: Sage.

Exclusion

During the period of serious art, several social groups are excluded from art consumption and production. There are attempts by groups of art-lovers aimed at the inclusion of low-class consumers—rather than producers—but they are unsuccessful.

Exclusivity is a condition for art being serious and prestigious. Well-to-do art-lovers pay for exclusivity. This explains the high prices of some visual artworks and certain performances. A love of exclusivity is an important motor behind exclusion. Not all art-lovers have access to all serious art. In the course of the twentieth century, the intellectualization of the art discourse as well has led to inner-art-world exclusion.

Outside art-buildings and art-spaces, exclusion is less extreme. More serious art is consumed by lower social groups than art-lovers often think. Art-lovers, on the other hand, consume much popular art, and increasingly so after the middle of the twentieth century. The symbolic boundary between serious and popular art nevertheless remains important. But looking at the different ways people "learn" and next understand art, it is rare that serious art is necessarily too difficult for others.

Social groups create and consume "own art", which they are proud of. If they, willingly or not, share their own art, they sometimes attempt to control the use of it. Art-worlds judge the control of the use of the own art of recognized artists by others to be important. They have more means and more effective means to control the use by others. This goes at the cost of sharing.

Lines on either side of the text indicate that recurring concepts are defined or described. This chapter is accompanied by web-notes and web-texts, which are available on the website: *www.hansabbing.com*. Numbers between brackets refer to other sections, including web-texts. Numbers at the end of a sentence in superscript preceded by a forward slash refer to web-notes. Holding a pc, tablet or phone next to this text, it is easy to "scan" the web-notes and web-texts. (Quantitative data I most often present in web-notes.)

H. Abbing, *The Changing Social Economy of Art*,
https://doi.org/10.1007/978-3-030-21668-9_4

Art Not for Everybody and Not by Everybody

(46) During the period of serious art: THE FAMILY-OF-ART IS PREDOMINANTLY WELL-TO-DO, WELL-EDUCATED AND WHITE. THIS APPLIES TO CONSUMERS AS WELL AS PRODUCERS. AMONG PRODUCERS WOMEN ARE ALSO UNDERREPRESENTED. THE DIFFERENCE WITH POPULAR ART IS CONSIDERABLE. I first look at art consumers and next to art-producers, that is, artists.

A social boundary with a gray zone exists between art-lovers, as defined in this text [3], and non-art-lovers, in particular lower-middle-class and low-class people. I first look at art consumers and next at artists. During the period of serious art some lower-middle-class people occasionally visit art-buildings. In as far as they visit them regularly and not only museums for old art, they are art-lovers. Visits by lower-class people to museums for old art are not that exceptional, but in the concert halls and theaters lower-class people are virtually absent. In the "family of art" (the group of art-lovers) they are altogether underrepresented./1

For the last 50 years numerical data exists that confirms most of the statements in this and following sections on the sizes of social groups, who in various degrees consume art and create art. I mention such data in this web-note./2 For the serious art period, data on underrepresentation of groups primarily follows from descriptions, graphics and later on also on photographs in journals and magazines. Older readers will have own observations from the 1950s and 1960s. Younger readers will have own observations for recent decades; they matter because numerical data seldom tells the whole story.

It is safe to assume that the underrepresentation of lower-class people before 1970 is even stronger than after 1970. What is, however, new is that from circa 1960 onward, higher educated young people—the age group of between 18 and 30 becomes—underrepresented. In other words, until recently, audiences of higher educated people have been gradually "graying", and most of all in the case of live classical/serious music [82].

Little numerical data exists on the consumption by lower-class people and other social groups of serious art in technically (re)produced forms—radio and television broadcasts, records, reproductions and downloads. It is likely that in this case the underrepresentation of the lower middle class and low class is considerably less than in the case of serious live art [83].

Data shows that higher-class non-white people are underrepresented among the overall group of higher-class participants, while lower-class non-white people are even more underrepresented than lower-class people in general./3 "Whiteness" is a quality that matters in many areas of consumption, and not only in the serious arts. But among art audiences the underrepresentation of non-white people is exceptionally high and much higher than in popular art. (We shall come across several explanations for the latter, but one is that venues as well as the recording industry are interested in "street culture"; the area where art production is particularly innovative.)

As said, observations of readers matter even though they do not offer proof. This also applies to Anna's observation when in 2005 she watched the Peter Brook play Tierno Bokar *in the prestigious* Holland Festival. *Among the around 1000 visitors there was only one* non-white *person, a Surinam woman accompanied by a white man. Anna found this shocking. She found it extra embarrassing, because on the stage there were 30 black actors and only one white actor. Afterward she mentioned the absence of non-white people among the audience to the friends who accompanied her. They said she was right but admitted that, when in the hall, this had not struck them as anything special.* (The latter is an example of so-called "color-blindness".)

Data shows that lower-middle-class and low-class people are also underrepresented in paid-for live popular art events, but less than in serious art events. (This is *overall* underrepresentation. Preferences of various social groups with respect to styles and genres differ. For instance, a decade ago in the USA, the underrepresentation of non-white people in Rap/Hip-hop was less than in most other genres—Since then audiences have become more White.—)

During the period of serious art and up to the present day, lower-class people and non-white people are not only underrepresented among art consumers but also among artists, both creative and performing artists. And among creative artists women are underrepresented and underpaid. In the arts these groups are more underrepresented than in popular art. With time the underrepresentation becomes less extreme, but it is still large. Because some of these artists become very famous and draw much attention, underrepresentation is easily overlooked. Their being non-white or female is emphasized and advertised. (Among prospective creative artists in art schools and conservatories, they are also more underrepresented than in comparable non-art education institutes.)

The typical artist is well-educated and white—be it not well-to-do. His parents are also higher educated and earn more than the average higher educated person. *(Other than one may expect, lower-class people are probably also underrepresented among artists producing inferior-art. Scouting open air markets and talking with the artists, I notice again and again that many of them are well-educated. Some also have been officially educated, sometimes even at well-established art education institutes.)*

Underrepresentation does not imply that there are no lower-class artists or artists with lower class parents. Looking at creative artists there are, and some of them become famous. In the visual arts examples run from George Bellows to Damien Hirst. In music the only from origin working-class composer I can think of is Havergal Brian. More examples exist of performing artists with a lower-class background. In popular music there are (and still are) many very well-known composers and composer-performers, as well as performers with a lower-class background.

Exceptions confirm the rule. Exceptions among performers are especially exciting. For instance, the contralto Marian Anderson who, between 1925 and 1965, performed in major music venues with famous orchestras throughout the USA and Europe was much celebrated; that is in a period that race discrimination in the USA among artists—and in art education—was still very extensive. Also among creative artists a "being different" draws attention, as in the case of black visual artists, from Robert Scott Duncanson to Jean-Michel Basquiat. (During the period of serious art, there are a few black composers, but they are never advertised. It is only now that some are being "rediscovered".)

That women are underrepresented and that their chances of becoming successful are lower than those of male artists indirectly shows from the phenomenon that female visual artists and writers sometimes use male (pen) names. Nevertheless, since the middle of the twentieth century in most art-worlds, the underrepresentation of women artists gradually decreases. But not only numbers, also earnings differ. Women art is less valuable also when the quality is exactly the same. This applies to other professions as well but probably more so in the arts. Indirect proof of discrimination shows from research. At auctions between 1970 and 2014, the works of women sell for almost half the price of those of male artists, and this cannot be explained from different artistic characteristics.[1] (In a test in which buyers did not know the sex of the artist, there was no difference in prices.)

Over the last decades underrepresentation of lower-educated and non-white people in art consumption and art production continues. (Data is rare, but in the webnote I present some data./4)

Among artists in small areas of art production among professional artists (or "working artists") underrepresentation of non-white people is now comparable with underrepresentation in other areas of production. But in general, it is stronger than elsewhere. In the USA the underrepresentation of Blacks and Hispanics among all artists is considerable. ("Among all artists" is: artists making serious art, popular art as well as inferior-art. It is also creative artists as well as performing artists.) Their number is circa one third of what it should have been, given their presence in the overall population.[2]/5 In Europe the underrepresentation of migrants is probably stronger.

Little-educated people are almost certainly mostly underrepresented. Part of the underrepresentation of Blacks, Hispanics and migrants corresponds with an on average lower level of education among these groups.

There are now more attempts and less paternalistic attempts in the established arts to include "others". It is, however, doubtful if the various attempts will lead to the inclusion of more little-educated people in the production and consumption of established art [56 and 85]. Their chances are much higher in some areas of popular art production.

With some exceptions in the USA, and almost certainly also in Europe, underrepresentation of women has disappeared in all of the main artists groups. Exceptions can be found in subgroups. Foremost the group of conductors—a supposedly physically too demanding profession—and, in a lesser degree, also DJ-producers—a profession that is still thought to be too technical.

(47) During the period of serious art: ART-LOVERS FEEL SUPERIOR. THEY DETEST THE POPULAR/INFERIOR ART OF COMMON PEOPLE. IT IS BAD ART AND IT IS ALSO BAD FOR COMMON PEOPLE. In the serious art period feelings of superiority as well as a general dislike of lower-class people and their art are intense among art-lovers. At the same time common people look up to people

visiting theaters and concert halls and their art. Evidently two strong symbolic boundaries exist.

Aside: Before anything else it must again be noted that high-class and higher middle-class people also deliberately consume and enjoy consuming popular/inferior art. They also do not dislike all art of others in the same degree. Generally, they dislike the art of low-class groups who are also otherwise discriminated most. An example is that of the art of Hispanic Americans.[3]

Art-lovers often have clear opinions about the reasons for the absence of "the others" in the museums, concert halls and theaters and the necessity to exclude them, and they are not afraid to express them. Art-lovers may for instance say: "Art is too difficult for working-class people—they would be restless and disturb performances". Others may say: "They must know that art is not for them". There, nevertheless, are also art-lovers who say: "Art is good for everybody and especially for common people. We must educate them and next make them feel welcome". But up to the middle of the twentieth century not many say so, and this is understandable.

Common people are thought to be inferior by nature. The symbolic boundary rests on a natural boundary, and nothing can be done about it. The belief among the higher-class bourgeois in an inborn inferiority of working-class people (or the proletariat) is not limited to art-lovers. The same as in aristocratic times in the nineteenth and early twentieth centuries, a general belief in inborn superiority is still widely spread and hardly disputed. There is doubt among some scholars, but they are exceptional. Well into the twentieth century, human races and even different types of subgroups of the Caucasian race continue to be classified by scholars: there are higher and lower kinds of humans.

In the nineteenth century, in a much-used educational illustration, which serves to demonstrate the superiority of the Caucasian race, the skull is depicted of a primitive with a low brow next to that of a civilized person, an artist, with a high brow. The latter is a picture of the face of William Shakespeare. It is not accidental that an artist is chosen, as it is not accidental that the terms high-brow and low-brow become substitutes for cultured and uncultured. This tells of the racist base of the notion of inborn superiority of civilized people and art-lovers. (I present the illustration in this web-note./6).

Along with new scholarly insights, in the second half of the twentieth century most art-lovers no longer believe in a natural boundary between high and low people. But the symbolic boundary between the two groups and between the corresponding two kinds of art, that is, serious art and popular and unacceptable art, continues to be important. Moreover, in a metaphoric sense, the notion of inborn qualities remains attractive. Pierre Bourdieu speaks of a charismatic ideology: good taste is "in" a person, and as such, it appears to be "a gift of nature".[4] (The association of popular with inferior people is not accidental. Earlier the term "popular" refers not only to successful among many people but also to "of the populace". When certain art-lovers talk about popular art one can still come across the association, be it less outspoken.)

Bourdieu much emphasizes that taste and competences are not "a gift of nature" but foremost the result of upbringing and education, that is, a *socialization* whose outcome is largely fixed later in life; it can never be altogether undone. The socialization of uncultured bourgeois and above all lower-class people differs fundamentally from that of cultured people. The consequence is that the former can somewhat develop or change their taste and competences, but they will never become the same as those of the art-lovers with a proper taste.

In practice the kind of conviction, nature or nurture does not have to make much difference. A belief in "incurability" in the case of grownups applies in either case and up to the present day it is expressed in many conversations of art-lovers, conversations that can for instance be overheard in the foyers of the concert halls and theaters. Even well-educated, but still not-cultured bourgeois, nouveau riche and other social risers are thought to be unable to ever become altogether cultured. And given their implicit definition of "cultured", art-lovers are right. Therefore, the existence of a social boundary between art-lovers and others is what can be expected. (Aside: A belief in "incurability" cannot but imply the superiority of the own group: the others are ill. From a more distant point of view, a belief in little "changeability" would have been more justified. After all, if the art-lover would be required to become like the people he looks down on, this would be just as impossible or hard.)

In the serious art period for art-lovers art has goodness, while popular art and many other entertainment products have badness. This is true in the beginning of the period, when the aristocrats and bourgeois are criticized for going for fashionable, frivolous, superficial, shallow, sentimental and commercial art; it merely serves entertainment. Later on the main attention of the bourgeois shifts to the lower classes, who consume similar wrong "art"; art that is bad for them. Now additional terms like ugly, vulgar, stultifying, dumbing, as well as standardized, uniform and more of the same are used for the popular art of the lower classes.

Convictions about the badness of popular/inferior art are communicated in minor as well as major events. *After he and his wife visited a vaudeville show, the American critic Henry Finck indignantly told his wife: "That's my idea of hell". He wrote about it in his memoirs. The same applies to Theodore Thomas, who wrote in his biography that for him symphony music is divine, and that light music has "more or less devil in it".*[5] *And when in the 1970s collector De Bruin regularly visited Anna's studio, he not only incessantly praised art and her art; he even more complained about the low quality of the visual art that one sees in many people's homes, about the popular music people listen to and about mass culture in general. Especially popular music was blamed for anything that is wrong in society.* This way the notion of the badness of popular/inferior art circulates and is reproduced.

The belief in "incurability" or rather unchangeability of "others" persists, and given the different socialization of the "others", the belief is, at least, partly correct. But *over the last decades* a belief in inborn inferiority has become exceptional. Moreover, also among the group of fanatic art-lovers the inclination to publicly put down popular art and those who consume it, has *over the last decades* become less common or rather less intense. On the basis of their implicit definitions of cultured and uncultured, certain groups of art-lovers still experience a social boundary between them and others, and between their art and the art of others, and the experience can still bring along feelings of superiority, but the boundary is not that robust anymore. (In the informal and less hierarchical society, open expressions of superiority have anyway become less acceptable.[6] The others" are also less inclined to view their own popular/inferior art as really inferior.)

Mechanisms of Exclusion

(48) INTERMEZZO: DEEP-POCKET MARKETS, MEDIUM-POCKET MARKETS, LOW-BUDGET MARKETS, NICHE MARKETS AND MASS MARKETS. PURCHASING POWER OF GROUPS. SYMBOLIC MEANINGS OF PRICES. In this section I explain concepts related to prices and markets that are important for understanding the text in this and the next part of the book. I advise all readers to, at least, scan the text. Prices matter for access to art. They also have meanings. Prices also have meanings. For instance, for a group for whom prices are low, a low price may stand for low quality of art, while for a group for whom prices are high, it may well tell "art is not for us".

Most people cannot afford a visual artwork that costs a thousand dollars. And at least until 1950 the majority of people could not afford records and a record player to listen to music at home. Till the present day, a majority cannot afford to regularly buy tickets for art performances in art-buildings.

Prices imply the presence of a *financial barrier*, which for some is easy to cross and for others hard or impossible to cross. If the latter cannot afford the price of a good, they are de facto excluded. For others their *willingness to pay* and not their ability to pay determines if they buy works or tickets. There is, what economists call, *price exclusion.*

Price exclusion usually does not serve the goal of making it impossible for others to acquire the good or service. But sometimes high prices are *deliberate*, or "half-deliberate". Those who determine the price want to make it impossible or unattractive for less well-to-do people to participate or buy works.

Given that art-lovers are often relatively well-to-do, while lower-class people are not, the result of relatively high art prices and a price barrier is that for the latter the barrier is hard or impossible to cross. As a consequence, the symbolic and social boundary between art and no-art corresponds with the symbolic and social boundary between higher-class people and lower-class people.

Price exclusion is one form of *formal exclusion.* Just stopping certain and not other people at the door of a building where a service, like a concert, is offered, is a more straightforward form of exclusion. This is *personal exclusion.* Thanks to one or another form of power, people can be prevented from entering. Longer ago certain powerful private owners had the means to stop unwanted people.—The owner of a palace had an armed guard keeping unwanted people out. Later there are legal property rights.—If necessary, the owner can call a law enforcement agency. This is possible thanks to the presence of a powerful authority, like a sovereign or government. In our modern societies most formal exclusion, and in particular price exclusion, as well as markets and a market mechanism can only exist thanks to legal *property rights*, which are protected and monitored by more and less democratically chosen governments.[7]

Sometimes price exclusion and personal exclusion come together. Not letting in non-white people and asking a price from white people is an example. When, however, economists use the term price exclusion, they tend to have only *price-exclusion-irrespective-of-persons* in mind: anybody who is able and willing to pay the price of a ticket or artwork is allowed to enter the art-building or purchase the work. During the period of serious art provision of art for a price altogether irrespective of persons gradually becomes the common way of provision./7

In markets, depending on their price, different groups can or cannot buy the goods and services. Some art markets are only accessible for extremely rich people, some for almost anybody. A contemporary example of the former is the market for visual artworks that cost more than a million dollars, and of the latter the market of music streams of serious music and popular music.

I distinguish three groups with different income and wealth with corresponding markets: *deep-pocket markets, medium-pocket markets* and *low-budget (or shallow-pocket) markets.*/8 In *deep-pocket art markets*, only well-to-do people can buy art.—They have deep and sometimes very deep-pockets containing much money.—Tickets for unique visual art works, graphics produced in small editions and expensive serious live-performances are sold in deep-pocket markets. Most other serious art is offered in medium-pocket markets, while low-budget markets for art (in a broad sense) are mostly markets of kinds of popular/inferior art./9

Due to the phenomenon that over time new art production technologies cause that certain art is produced at lower cost, there often is a trajectory that runs from deep-pocket markets to mass markets. For instance, the market equipment for playing sound media—from the early phonograph to recent earplugs in combination with a mobile phone—has moved from a deep-pocket market to a low-budget market. The same applies to the sound media themselves—from early records via cassettes and CDs to downloads and streams. Therefore, over time, the purchasing power in the overall market of technically produced music of not-rich people has increased as well as their say in the kinds of music which are produced most. (Suppose that in the near future soloists would increasingly perform with (partly or altogether) virtual orchestras, this may also lower prices and affect the choice of pieces performed.)

At present, in the super deep-pocket market of modern-art paintings that cost more than 100 million dollars, only a very small group of people determine that Picasso paintings are more or instead less expensive than Lichtenstein paintings. Many people, however, together determine that the sales of Mozart records are higher or lower than of Bach records or that Michael Jackson records sell better or worse than Bruce Springsteen records. In all such cases consumers do so not independently, because the activities of experts/critics and intermediary producers, like commercial-galleries and record companies, also steer consumers and their choices [64].

To study exclusion in the arts it is important to realize that a financial barrier not only follows from price exclusion. Instead it is the overall cost of acquiring works or participating in art events that stops people from buying works or tickets. There always are a*dditional costs*. These are, among others, the cost of not being able to earn money during the time spent on the visit, the cost of transport and the cost of proper clothing, clothing that is necessary not too feel uncomfortable. In the case of technically reproduced art, sometimes cost of equipment matters. The additional cost of the record player may prevent that people buy records and listen to (serious) music at home. During the period of serious art, financial barriers are often insurmountable for working-class people. Given the additional cost, this may even apply to visits to free museums.

The *say* of certain social groups in the kind of artworks that are offered in various art markets, depends on their *collective purchasing power*. In markets with few consumers the say of a small group is decisive. In deep-pocket market this is usually an elite of rich people. In mass low-budget markets this is usually a group of lower-class people without much money. Therefore, in spite of having little money in large low-budget markets, lower-class people usually have a larger say in the kinds of art offered than higher-class people. Their collective purchasing power is higher and their preferences are most important for producers who want to earn money. Presently in the market of, so-called, art prints—the kind that is sold by IKEA and the internet seller AllPoster.com—the say of not well-to-do people is higher than that of well-to-do art-lovers.

Prices have symbolic meanings. They "talk".[8] Many examples can be given of prices and pricing having meaning(s). Very important for the analysis of the social economy of art is the phenomenon that for art consumers prices may stand for the quality of artworks. The higher the price the better the artwork must be. As we shall see, many artists and art-lovers think that in general in the arts, price and quality do not correspond and that art-lovers should not believe they do [66].

But in various situations art-lovers apparently believe that price stands for quality. As a consequence, when a dealer raises the price of the works of a certain artist, he may make the work attractive for people with more money and earn more. "Look at the price. The artist must be well-known. His work must be really good". In such cases raising prices is also a deliberate form of price exclusion. The higher price makes works more exclusive. This also applies when concert-organizers raise the price of already expensive performances in order to let them appeal to rich consumers who prefer to be among themselves.

Aside: In such cases economists call works a *Veblen good*. In the case of Veblen goods, higher prices are accompanied by higher demand and lower prices with less demand. (This goes against the economic *Law of supply and demand* in economics.)

Often, independent of people's ability to pay, a price can tell about the intended group of buyers or visitors. A high or low price may tell "this is not for us" or "it is not for our people". Or the opposite: "This is for us". When prices are so high that people cannot pay them, a "this is not for us" does not increase actual exclusion. But among people who can afford to pay a certain price and are interested in the offered art, a price can still stop them. It forms a barrier.

Price differentiation can also serve deliberate exclusion. Exclusivity is important for art-lovers. *An illuminating example of prices having meanings, bringing along symbolic barriers and serving inner-art-world exclusion is that of price and product differentiation in the case of the Victorian theater. In the theaters, there are different spaces with higher and lower ticket prices. They are well separated and it is hard or impossible to move from one to the other, that is, there is a literal barrier which is hard to cross. (Often the spaces have different entrances at street level and different stairs, as Anna, to her amazement, discovered when in 1965 she visited The New Theatre in London./*10*) Some people who can afford the more expensive tickets giving access to the more elite areas with better views nevertheless buy cheaper tickets. They can be said to be excluded or to exclude themselves; not because the price is too high but because the prices and consequent price differences signal where they belong and will feel comfortable and where not. In the different areas, especially the expensive areas, people can stay among their own group and this is attractive and as art-setting it is another quality of the artwork they "buy". In this case there is inner-art-world exclusion. The people feeling obliged to go for the inferior-artwork—a performance with a lower visual and/or sound quality—are excluded from the superior artwork.*

(49) During the period of serious art: OVER TIME ART EVENTS WITH TICKETS REPLACE ART EVENTS ONLY FOR INVITEES. PRICES PLUS ADDITIONAL COST EXCLUDE LOW INCOME GROUPS. Before the serious art period, to participate in art events people seldom had to pay, but during this period and after, having to buy tickets is most common. Nowadays, most often one also has to pay for museums. This is not to say that earlier all events were free or that artists did not earn money.

The rich employed artists commissioned art and at times paid traveling artists for their services. Common people sometimes also paid for shows, but more often they donated to performing artists. Wandering minstrels, musicians, music ensembles and theater groups often financed their activity by soliciting and receiving donations from their audience, not unlike today's buskers do. Artists could make a living because the average production cost of their performances was low. Also, in palaces minstrels and ensembles often performed at own risk. They received a donation if their host and his invitees were pleased. For common people there is also art for free in public space and semi-public spaces like churches and taverns. Music performers were paid by the church. (In Europe monarchs sometimes decreed that certain art was only allowed at the courts, with, as a result, an enforced formal exclusion from certain art. But this is exceptional.)

Among the rich sharing performances and exhibitions for free was common. By invitation they granted one another access in their palaces and mansions. There was a formal barrier but no price exclusion. Aristocrats, bishops and merchants could stop people at the door and directly or indirectly they had the power to determine the choice of the people who they allowed to enter. Exclusion was therefore based on personal characteristics and not on ability and willingness to pay. For instance, certain friends or officials or diplomats could enter and not others. The habit of inviting people to art events continues to the present day, but now the events are usually small, like in the case of music performance by one or more family member singing or playing the piano. The tableau vivant, which is popular in the nineteenth century, is another example. Also today the phenomenon of a host inviting a large group continues: examples are royal banquets, performances during diplomatic missions and so forth.

Relevant for the social economy of art is that during the period of serious art, prosperity increases and the demand for performances and exhibitions grows much. In the nineteenth century increasing numbers of bourgeois are interested in art, want to go to exhibitions and be present at performances. This requires and brings along new and supplementary forms of art provision. At first academies and local councils as well as associations of well-to-do citizens organize performances and exhibitions for larger but still select audiences. Especially the activities of associations represent an important step toward modern forms of provision with price exclusion. Usually one has to be a member to be present during performances. One can become member by invitation. Sometimes members donate money, sometimes there are membership fees; sometimes members and their invitees pay an additional fee at the door for performances. The latter implies that an additional formal barrier is introduced: price exclusion. This is, however, not yet the kind of exclusion economists have in mind. There is no price exclusion irrespective of persons. But during the period of serious art, provision of art for a price altogether irrespective of persons gradually becomes the common way of provision.

The provision of art by associations to somewhat larger and more anonymous audiences represents an intermediate phase between the aristocratic time of altogether regulated provision of performances and exhibitions and that of the later public provision with price exclusion irrespective of persons. Aside: In the USA this period lasts much longer than in Europe. After a while there is price exclusion irrespective of persons except for non-white people. Even when the latter are willing to pay, they are not admitted or are only admitted to segregated areas in halls and theaters.[9] (The straightforward exclusion of Negroes in the USA is, of course, not limited to the arts. It, moreover, also occurs in, a smaller part, of the provision of popular art.)

Apart from race discrimination—which in the USA continues well into the second half of the twentieth century—in the course of the serious art period the common form of art distribution is based on the asking of prices by professional providers, foremost nonprofits. In principle they admit anybody willing to pay the price. Sometimes there is, however, still exclusion of lower-class people on the basis of the characteristic of clothing. Wearing working men's clothing, they are stopped at the entrance of halls and theaters. (Often, because they know they will not be let in, they do not even try.) Museums—many of whom do not charge prices—are more liberal, but in rare cases people are refused because of "improper" clothing.[10] The difference between admittance policies of museums and performance venues can be explained from the phenomena that, at the time and up to the present day, museums attach more value to their educational function, and to the phenomenon that in halls and theaters people are closer to one another. It is harder to literally distance oneself from "others".

The text so far is likely to raise two questions. First, would, during the period of serious art, overall lower prices of serious art have increased the participation of lower-class people? Usually also lower prices are too high. There, moreover, are other phenomena to be discussed in the following sections that keep them from participating. The answer is therefore "not or hardly" [57]. Secondly, are high prices used to deliberately exclude "others". During the period of serious art, the majority of art-lovers do not approve of high prices as an instrument for a general exclusion of lower-class people. On the contrary, they often plead for public and private support to allow lower prices and less exclusion of poor people [57]. Nevertheless, a love of exclusivity may still be a motor behind indeliberate exclusion through unaffordable prices.

In the twenty-first century, despite increased prosperity, relatively high prices continue to contribute to the exclusion of people with relatively little money, including some art-lovers. In the arts prices have risen more than corresponds with inflation and continue to do so. In the performing arts and especially in serious music, this is partly caused by a continuing cost disease [34]. And in both the performing and visual arts it is also caused by an increased willingness of a rich elite to pay high prices.—An increasing unequal distribution of income contributes to the latter phenomenon.—The resistance against the development of lower-cost performances also continues to contribute to exclusion.

All in all, as far as price exclusion is concerned, the exclusion of people due to high prices has increased rather than decreased. The increase now foremost affects not that well-to-do art-lovers, with, as a consequence, more *inner-art-world exclusion*. Financially under-resourced groups are anyway excluded.

(50) During the period of serious art and after: EXCLUSION IS OFTEN INFORMAL. IN ART-BUILDINGS, "OTHERS" MISS SOCIAL AND CULTURAL COMPETENCES AND ARE INFORMALLY EXCLUDED. In the serious art period next to formal exclusion there is *informal exclusion*. Most of the time the exclusion is not deliberate. Common is that an art-setting or art environment has been created that is unattractive for outsiders who otherwise would have wanted to participate. An important part of a prohibitive art-setting is the audience itself and its behavior.

Before proceeding, reading this and the following sections, one has to keep in mind that it is not always just informal exclusion that causes "others" not to participate in art events. It can also be the nature of the art offered. For reasons to be discussed in section 85, some art in art-buildings is unlikely to ever become attractive for "others"; the same as groups of "others" have own art, which in the existing form will never become attractive for art-lovers. (After civilization and appropriation, it may, however, become attractive [52].)

In various sections I described the typical serious art-setting in art-buildings. The setting is opulent. Part of the setting in halls and theaters is the absence of physical and behavioral distractions during performances. During the performance they are taboo. Up to the present day, given the common art-setting in concert halls, theaters and many museums, for lower-class people almost everything is unusual and strange. Both physical aspects, from exterior and interior to clothing, and behavior, from that of the regular visitors and attendants to ritualistic behavior on the stage, contribute to informal exclusion. Lower-class people do not understand the setting. They are in this respect *under-resourced* and informally excluded.

Aside: Unlike formal exclusion *informal exclusion* has no legal basis. It does not rest on a legal right as in the case of price exclusion, but it is also not forbidden by law. "Others" who want to enter and are able and willing to pay the ticket price are not stopped. Instead it is the art-setting and, in particular, the presence of people in art-buildings who are "among themselves" that makes visits for "others" unattractive./11

Aside: whether or not a person or social group is socially and culturally under-resourced (or rather wrongly resourced) depends on the situation. When higher-class or well-educated people were to participate in certain popular/inferior art events, for instance, a house party in the 1970s, many will not like it because they are wrongly resourced. They cannot understand the music and the behavior of the audience.

In serious art-settings others miss necessary *social and cultural competences* and do not feel comfortable among the existing crowd of art-lovers. In this respect they are, indeed, *under-resourced*, even when they are not financially under-resourced and can pay for the ticket and for the additional cost of, among others, proper clothing.

In this context the verb "to understand" is appropriate. An important part of understanding art and artworks is the understanding of their setting. For instance, in the serious music hall, the "necessity" must be understood of subdued behavior, stillness, no applause between the parts, the conductor shaking hands with the first violinist, the tone of the conversations during the break, the luxurious interior, proper clothing and so forth. The visitor must understand—be it not necessarily consciously—that such characteristics are essential and a part of the artwork in a broad sense. This even applies to the absence of price-tags in clearly commercial-galleries. (In the remainder of this section I ignore that they may miss competences necessary for "understanding art itself", that is, in the way artists want people to understand their work. This is a topic in later sections.)

During the period of serious art, lower-class people usually respect and admire art and look up to the people who consume it. They therefore also respect the barrier. Participation in art events is beyond their reach. And, given their socialization and consequent social and cultural competences, they are right. Their social network does not extend to the people present. And even though their knowledge of the art-setting may be stereotypical, it is not incorrect. They know, for instance, that art in art-buildings is almost exclusively consumed by people in higher positions, and that these people are white and highly educated. They not only form a dominating majority; they are the only people present, and they behave in unfamiliar ways. Lower-class people rightly think that they will feel uncomfortable among them. Even if they could afford a visit, it is likely to be disappointing and frustrating. The appearance and *reputation* of art-buildings form a short-cut for all such knowledge. (Together the buildings represent a brand—be it without a single brand name.)

Aside: A serious art-setting is not limited to art-buildings; it often is also present in churches in which ensembles perform serious music and spaces exhibiting visual art. In a lesser degree this also applies to the art-spaces or "shops", like commercial-galleries, and shops specialized in serious literature, serious music records and classical sheet music. The serious setting is attractive for some and unattractive for others.

In the 1960s during four successive summer holidays, Anna stayed with a working-class couple in Evesham, England. At the time Juliette was a waitress and Dave a day laborer.—Anna picked fruit in Dave's gang.—Anna noticed that in the evenings they listened to records of both classical and popular music, and that they watched ballet on television.—At the time still much ballet was broadcasted.—Anna, who is an enthusiastic lover of serious music and dance, proposed to go to the real thing: a live ballet performance. They were hesitant. They nevertheless saved some money and, the next summer, they, together with Anna, went to a performance of Tchaikovsky's Swan Lake *by The Royal Ballet in Birmingham.*[11] *Dave had rented a proper suit and Anna and Juliette wore inconspicuous dresses. Nevertheless, once in the hall they were immediately "found out" by the regular visitors who glanced at them, not unfriendly, but nevertheless causing them to feel uncomfortable and embarrassed. Afterward Dave and Juliette told Anna that they had very much liked the performance but would not go again.*

In the local pub they told friends about the wonderful event, but they also spread the message that, although live ballet is great, visits are not recommendable. Anna next noticed that after having been "punished" in the hall for being there, they were punished again. In the pub they overheard a conversation in which friends said that they were getting "above themselves".

Informal exclusion in live serious art performances applies to lower-class people, but not only. In practice, it is foremost little-cultured higher bourgeois, parvenus and social risers wanting to join the family of art, who are made to feel uncomfortable. In their case exclusion can well be deliberate. When visiting for the first time, their experience is the same as in that of lower-class people, even though they may not feel that intimidated. Some, however, come again. In their imagination the expected long-term benefits of becoming a cultured person and a member of the family of art exceed the anticipated further mental cost. Becoming a participant in one or more art-worlds can serve, among others, as a vehicle for a higher position in society.

Even though their arrears are less than of lower-class people, in the halls and rooms they as well are "found out" and continue to be found out by regular art-lovers. They may well be treated in humiliating ways, unlike Anna's friends who were treated in a predominantly friendly way. This is understandable: Anna's friends were no threat to the family members, while they could be. Because they are believed to never properly understand art, that is, the "sacred object" of the regulars, and because they could potentially become the majority of visitors, they are indeed a threat for the art-lovers' "sacred object".

And it is true that the parvenus and other social risers are likely to never altogether learn the proper ways. Due to their earlier "wrong" socialization, their behavior may change, but the new behavior will never come naturally, and others continue to notice this. (As Bourdieu would say: they do not develop a "sense de jeux"; a "feel for the game".[12]) With time some nevertheless become accepted as art-lovers.—This is certainly likely to happen when they also become important donors.—But they will never enter the inner circle of true art-lovers; they remain extraordinary. (As said, also within art-world's symbolic boundaries and social barriers exist separating people.)

In her enthusiasm Anna liked to bring friends to serious performances. On another occasion in London, she accompanied a rich but not very "cultured" friend of her to a theater performance. Her friend's behavior was over the top; it was too civilized and too courteous. Also her clothing was not okay. She noticed that she was found out and treated in a cruel way. They together overheard a conversation—which was clearly intended to be overheard—in which in a disdainful voice another woman said to her companion: "Look at that woman wearing that ridiculous hat". Later on her friend was addressed over-friendly by someone else: "Oh, it's so nice that you are here". This was just as painful.

Since informalization has become important, socialization has gradually changed, as has overall culture [38]. As a consequence, first well-educated young people and, later, most well-educated people start to find it hard to understand and enjoy the typical art-setting. By now they as well can be said to be wrongly resourced. They miss the competences to enjoy the common serious art-setting. This has contributed to the decline of the established arts. Since the 1960s demand for established art has gone down.

Over the last decades, with the exception of classical-serious music, the decline has halted. In the new more user-oriented direction in the arts, the de facto informal exclusion of uncultured higher middle-class people and social risers, and in museums of old art also of lower-middle-class people, has not disappeared but has become less intense. This applies, indeed, most to art museums and least to opera and serious music performances. Partly due to market forces, art organizations do their best to cater for a larger group of relatively well-educated people. The result is an increased accessibility for this group. In this respect the arts have become less exclusive. The development is also a much belated reaction to the overall process of informalization in society. But the de facto exclusion of low-class people continues. It corresponds with a social barrier that runs all through society but is still stronger in the arts than in other important areas of collective consumption.

(51) During the period of serious art and after: IN THE ESTABLISHED ARTS, A MONOCULTURE EXISTS. THE UNWILLINGNESS TO OFFER SERIOUS ART IN DIFFERENT SETTINGS WITH DIFFERENT ATMOSPHERES CONTRIBUTES TO THE EXCLUSION OF OTHERS. In this section I tell last section's story again, but from a different perspective: that of majorities and their culture(s). I compare those in the live serious arts with those in the live popular arts. In the popular arts there is far more variety in atmospheres.

Where people are together a *majority rule* exists. The same as in cafés and restaurants, in art-buildings and popular art venues, consumers are relatively close together and majorities create own settings, own atmospheres and own artworks. This applies to the serious arts as well as the popular arts. A difference is that in the arts in art-buildings, majorities tend to create cultures which differ little, while in the popular arts many parallel cultures exist. The differences in the serious arts are so small that one may well argue that a world-wide monoculture exists. *This is what Anna noted, when she was present at a classical concert in Sao Paulo. The atmosphere and behavior in the hall did not differ from that in the Concertgebouw in Amsterdam.* In popular art there are many parallel cultures, but none which takes over and turns into a forceful long-lasting dominant *culture* as exists in serious art events.

Given different cultures the phenomenon of informal exclusion can also apply to live popular art. The "sacred object", that is, the own atmosphere, must be protected against outsiders.[13] But with some exceptions there is more tolerance./12 Certain subcultural conventions rapidly change, but this does not apply to broader social (sub)groups. In the popular arts such groups may "take over" buildings. The building attains a certain imago. This is a self-perpetuating phenomenon; only after one or another external intervention another group can start to form the majority. In the serious art the imago is largely fixed.

The exterior of the art-buildings is such that people know what kind of audience will be inside. In the popular arts venues differ much. On average, just looking at them does not tell much about a possible audience. Some serve very different audiences on different nights. Others host foremost one type of audience, but uninformed people cannot tell this by looking at the buildings. One has to know. Usually such buildings have a certain imago people know of.

The imago prevents a short-term possible takeover. Nevertheless, over time the audience composition may change, the same as the imago. If unwanted, managements usually have means to prevent such change./13 It is also possible that managements deliberately try to change the composition and imago. Sometimes whole-heartedly, sometimes with regret. *Over the last decades* in some countries local governments demand from subsidized venues that at least a certain percentage of their yearly visitors belongs to an ethnic minority, a percentage that is higher than the existing percentage. When management try, they usually fail. The existing imago of the building is too strong, can not be changed and ethnic groups continue to be largely excluded.

In the serious arts there can be complaints about relatively influential minorities, which are experienced as threat. *Not that long-ago Anna overheard a conversation in the foyer of The Concertgebouw of visitors complaining about the growing number of nouveau riche among the audience. They were said to spoil the atmosphere by their too conspicuous and supposedly uncivilized behavior.* But the same as in similar occasions in earlier decades, such situations do not last long. The majority of serious visitors is so large and the overall setting so imposing that before too long the newcomers start to hold back and sometimes, more or less, learn the proper ways.

In spite of an existing imago managements are not powerless. Increasingly venues manage to offer slightly different atmospheres on different nights. More importantly, the management of well-known venues now opens new venues with different atmospheres. (Or they do part of the programming of other venues.)

The managements of large halls offering popular art events in various art forms, like music, theater and cabaret, as well as entertainment events, usually design their interior in a relatively neutral way, to be able to cater to different social groups. Some offer only theater, and this makes a comparison with prestigious art-buildings, the municipal theaters, possible. *In Amsterdam Anna regularly visits two theaters that are positioned exactly opposite of one another with a narrow street in between: the subsidized Stadsschouwburg (the municipal theater) with a long-term serious art reputation and the newer for-profit the Delamar theater. In the first the interior is pompous, luxurious and old fashioned. In the other it is slightly posh but not imposing; more social groups feel comfortable. In conversations with her theater-loving friends, most much prefer the interior of the Stadsschouwburg. Some even felt disgust for the interior of the for-profit theater. But other friends said that they, the same as Anna, preferred the more neutral interior of the for-profit theater. There they felt more comfortable.*

In popular music there is not only more choice in art-settings and atmospheres, but also in the number of (sub)genres that are offered. There are accessible events for almost all social groups. A more commercial attitude (or market ethos) among art-companies, including non-profits, contributes to it. The unwillingness to offer serious art in different settings with different atmospheres contributes to the exclusion of others. It is, partly, thanks to private and later public subsidies that, during the period of serious art, the non-profits offering serious art can maintain a monoculture.

The typical *monoculture* in the serious arts is still omnipresent in the Western world as well as in rising new economies. If somebody now visits a contemporary-art gallery in Helsinki and one in Bombay, he would find that there are hardly any differences. Both are white cubes and behavior is subdued. Or if he goes to a classical concert in Rio de Janeiro, he will feel comfortable because the art-setting and atmosphere are the same as in Helsinki. The family of art is still one family, a family that is at home in art-buildings all-over the world.

Nevertheless, *over the last decades* some art providers have now started to offer art in different settings with different atmospheres, for instance, at different nights. Often, they do so in newly built venues, in which they attempt to create a more anonymous setting. These developments are strongest in the present more user-oriented domain in the museums./14

Deliberate interventions in older art-buildings also occur. An example is the mentioned *Stadsschouwburg* in Amsterdam. By changing part of its interior, it now attempts to change its imago of being traditional and interesting for an old-fashioned clientele. Recently a second, more neutral, smaller entrance hall has been created, which is used when plays are particularly interesting for a cultured young and cool crowd of visitors.

The existing imago of buildings, nevertheless, continues to limit the possibility to attract new audiences. It is therefore understandable that those who at present try to revive classical music in the Netherlands by attracting a younger audience have chosen to present the music in a venue with a popular music reputation: the famous Amsterdam Paradiso instead of the world-famous Concertgebouw. Not accidentally the music is performed by a chamber orchestra and not a symphony orchestra. There are other ways to get round limiting brand names connected with art-buildings. Sometimes organizations manage to run other buildings while successfully creating new and different reputations for the buildings.

The shops with a serious atmosphere which earlier sold only classical recordings and classical sheet music, and only serious literature and poetry have by now largely disappeared. In most serious art galleries run by profit-oriented dealers, the atmosphere is still unattractive for others than higher-class art-lovers. *Over the last five years* in big cities a new kind of visual art "shops" emerges with a more neutral atmosphere, an atmosphere that is attractive for young and "cool" people from various social groups, but they sell foremost poster art and reproductions and not exclusively serious art.

(52) During the period of serious art: BOUNDARIES BETWEEN SERIOUS AND POPULAR ART ARE OCCASIONALLY REDRAWN. THIS WAY THEY CONTINUE TO BE IN LINE WITH CLASS BOUNDARIES. When popular art genres or subgenres become meaningful, attractive and popular among art-lovers, art-worlds sometimes "intervene" by redrawing boundaries. The art is upgraded, civilized and appropriated, making it more exclusive.

Serious art is not "popular". When popular art becomes also successful among art-lovers, an intervention is necessary. In the twentieth century, attempts to discourage consumption by putting down the popular art that is becoming popular among art-lovers are no longer successful. Instead the popular art genres or certain (sub) genres are appropriated and "civilized".

The works become more refined and sometimes more complex. They are, or appear to be, more singular. There is intellectualization as shows from the discourse surrounding consumption. In other words, existing works "change" due to the discourse. They become "enriched" in ways that appeal to a larger group of art-lovers. Moreover, departing from existing works, new more sophisticated works are created. Thanks to this, the appropriated part is no longer popular art, for which just "more of the same" is thought to be typical. Thanks to appropriation, the line between what is serious art and what popular art is redrawn with the consequence that the symbolic boundary between art and no art stays in line with the social boundary between social classes.

Aside: appropriation in the opposite direction is, as far as I can tell, non-existing./15 In Western culture the overall trend is bottom up. This also applies to the assimilation of the art of non-Western cultures. In the process it is destructed, but the overall effect can be "creative destruction./16

Jazz represents an example of civilization and appropriation of subgenres. In the twentieth century, some classical composers become interested in Jazz, which brings along influences of Jazz on their work. More importantly, an increasing group of serious music consumers start to consume certain kinds of Jazz. It is meaningful for them. The genres are appropriated. One part becomes more difficult, and another more civilized and "sweet". It is a bottom-up movement because Jazz has been created by lower-class people. In Europe this leads to de facto exclusion: uncivilized Jazz has no chance of success.

This is not how it began. In the 1950s, after the import of, not yet civilized, Jazz from the USA, better-educated youngsters are enthusiastic, too enthusiastic./17 During a concert of Herbie Hancock in The Hague, they stand on chairs, with the consequence that the press cries shame and a moral panic arises in society. But other than in the USA, in Europe, and especially in continental Europe, the answer to art causing *moral panic* is not suppression or a "letting be" as is common in the USA, but a "constructive" control by authorities; a control that next contributes to a civilization of consumption practices and appropriation. (After the import from Jazz from the USA and its civilization and intellectualization, civilized jazz is exported to the USA.)

Aside: The appropriation of Jazz is half-hearted. The new Jazz subgenres start to be taught at the conservatories, but they are not promoted by the conservative serious music establishment. It is hardly ever performed in the traditional concert halls, though some art-buildings for jazz performances are created./18 The lack of resources and attention partly explains that by now the civilized subgenres of Jazz are reconnecting with popular music as shows from the programming of traditional Jazz festivals like the North See and Montreux Jazz festivals. (In this long web-note there is more about developments in Jazz./19)

Another example is film. In the 1950s and 1960s, part of film gradually becomes legitimized as serious art.[14] All film had been regarded as entertainment. Therefore, part of film becoming serious art can be said to be a form of appropriation. But it is no bottom-up movement and there is no moral panic. Here increased demand, pressure of film artists, together with intellectualization of the discourse, lay at the basis of the redrawing of the line between art and entertainment. However, due to its late inclusion and even more to the fact that film, the same as literature, is only consumed in technically produced relatively large series, never a clear boundary between serious film and popular film is established [15]./20

Aside: Ever since the 1950s there is also appropriation by higher educated groups within popular art: that is, "within" because the appropriated genres remain in the domain of popular art; the line between serious and popular art is not redrawn. This applies to certain popular music genres that are first developed by and are popular among lower-educated groups, ethnic groups and minority groups. It often is a form of bottom-up appropriation. Examples are, among others, Rock (black and lower class), part of Dance (gays and blacks) and part of Hip-hop (colored and lower class). In all these cases there is some moral panic, which increases attention and consumption. And, the same as in the case of jazz, in the latter two cases Europe comes again first in the civilization and institutionalization process. There is a degree of intellectualization: among others serious reviews written by experts/critics appear. This neutralizes the initial protest aspect of the genres and contributes to consumption by higher educated groups. (After having been "imported" from the USA and been civilized in Europe, certain civilized Dance genres—and the way to properly organize large Dance parties—are exported again to the USA.) A difference with appropriation by the established arts is that the boundary between the appropriated and not appropriated parts remains weak.

When, in the aftermath of the serious art period, many well-educated youngsters start to consume popular music, the answer of the serious music art-world is no longer appropriation of part of the genres which are becoming popular. Instead it is an emphasis on the superiority of the own music and a putting down of popular music. Youngster are discouraged, and sometimes forbidden to listen to the new music. There is moral panic, and the same as in other cases, this indirectly stimulates the new genres. They also become slightly more civilized but not in a way that makes them unattractive for lower social groups. Certainly not as far as broadcasts and records are concerned. They are somewhat underrepresented in popular music concerts but far less than in serious music concerts.

In the twenty-first century, however, along with the weakening boundary between serious and popular art, appropriation becomes rare. A recent example of a bottom-up movement without appropriation is that of break dance. Moreover, break dancers did not attempt to first intellectualize their genre. Intellectualization, however, remains the common mechanism for letting popular art become serious. For instance, presently, within the electronic music genre, there are attempts of musicians, producers and critics to upgrade part of it and let it become serious art. The initiatives come from the popular art side, but since the demand for the own music is going down, they are now sometimes welcomed by the serious music world.

Only the powerful visual art-world, with its financially attractive monolithic art market bringing income and reputation to former popular artists, continues to "suck". This hinders or slows down developments in popular visual art genres, like street art; but less so than 30 years ago.

(53) During the period of serious art: THE DISCOURAGEMENT OF THE PRODUCTION AND PURCHASE OF LESS EXPENSIVE POSTER REPRODUCTIONS CONTRIBUTE TO EXCLUSION. REPRODUCTIONS ON THE WALLS OF MUSEUMS ARE TABOO. THE AUTHENTICITY DEMAND SERVES AS JUSTIFICATION. As noted, high prices lead to exclusion. Visual art prices are very high. But during the period of serious art the prices of reproductions are affordable. In the twentieth century, their production and sale is, nevertheless, discouraged. This contributes to exclusion.

Before the art period, the production of copies was common. Ever since the Renaissance, along with a growing demand for visual artworks, "artists used various techniques and technologies to quickly reproduce their art to increase distribution of their original style...".[15] In workshops, like that of the Bruegel family, artists and students painted copies and created copper engravings and etchings that reproduced the original. Also "illegal" copying was common. Sometimes the copies were so cheap that also less-well-to-do people could afford them. Most people did not care much about authenticity.

Thanks to new technologies in the nineteenth century, it becomes possible to produce series of copies, foremost chromolithographs. They are produced by for-profit companies. At first mainly small series are produced. Common boys are employed to manually "re-paint" originals; using a different woodblock or stone for each color. Other techniques are developed requiring less manual labor and allowing larger series. Costs are lower, but the quality is lower than that of the early chromolithographs. Again, nobody cares much about authenticity. Especially when photographs of paintings start to be mechanically transferred to the stones, large series start to be produced but the quality is low. When the reproductions are not large—usually much smaller than that of the original works—cost and prices are so low that also relatively poor people buy them. They are not excluded from consumption.

Larger size reproductions are more expensive. And their cost and prices rise when, thanks to technical improvements, reproductions of higher quality start to be produced. Examples are black and white reproductions of etchings of Rembrandt and of paintings of Rubens and Gainsborough. Prices are now so high that lower-class people cannot afford them anymore. Even though at the time this is not the intention, they are de facto excluded from the consumption of large and life-size reproductions. The same does not apply to the well-to-do bourgeois. They are not excluded.

Earlier, in spite of their still relative low quality in the nineteenth century and the early twentieth century, there is enthusiasm about reproductions in larger editions. They are enjoyable and are also thought to assist in learning to understand art. Representatives of the Enlightenment commend the copy as a means of aesthetic appreciation and education.[16] There is much demand for technical reproductions of famous artworks. They can be found on the walls of the homes of both higher and lower bourgeois. There is little exclusion.

In the course of the twentieth century, the low quality of reproductions is increasingly emphasized.—This is remarkable because in the same period, the quality of reproductions increases much.—Among smaller groups the habit of putting down replicas and reproductions starts earlier. Already in the nineteenth century, there are so-called aesthetes who turn away in disgust from the chromos they see on the walls of higher-class people. Reproductions are said to be impure, vulgar and *inauthentic* art.[17] "They give people false hope of becoming cultured". They are said to be part of a pseudo-culture". The lack of aura is also emphasized as shows from expressions like: "There is no more art in producing 'machine-made pictures' than there is in producing 'machine-made shirts and carpets'".[18] With the new technologies, also reproductions can, in principle, be produced in unlimited editions and therefore have little aura in the eyes of the aesthetes. In this they are not alone. Each time new and more perfect reproduction techniques become available, there are serious art-lovers who warn against them.

With time ever-more art-lovers agree; and putting down large and even smaller size reproductions of paintings, most of all because of their supposedly low quality, becomes a widely shared practice. The offensive against reproductions is successful. With time on the walls of progressive serious art-lovers no more reproductions of well-known paintings can be found. (The same does not in the same degree apply to reproductions of etchings and drawings. Till the present day they can be found on the walls of mainly an old-fashioned and rich elite of art-lovers.)

After circa 1920 the demand for reproductions starts to go down, and with some ups and downs, it continues to go down. The same does not apply to art books; they are in demand. Demand mainly comes from art-lovers somewhat reducing inner-art-world exclusion. Also some less-cultured bourgeois buy the books, but for low-class people they are too expensive.

With time it is not in the first place the demand for reproductions that is going down, but the supply. For financial reasons producers of reproductions, graphics and later on also photos deliberately limit production. In the second half of the twentieth century, living artists are advised not to have posters made of their work and to limit the edition size of graphics and photos, also when large editions are possible. (In the case of photos and lithographs, very large editions are possible.) Various justifications are given, but the goal of these practices and their explanation rest in a wish to keep visual art exclusive. As we shall see [57], exclusivity in the arts is profitable.

Aside: There are indeed waves in the demand and supply of large reproductions and for serious poster art: especially around 1960, there are more reproductions on the walls, especially in the rooms of students. It is also important to note that not all artists agree. As we shall see [57], there are decades in the twentieth century that groups of visual artists stimulate the creation of affordable (re)productions. They want art to be less exclusive and are in favor of larger series of reproductions.

Reproductions in museums, museums that are free or low-priced, can in principle diminish the exclusion of not that well-to-do bourgeois, because the same works can be present in many places at the same time. Moreover, if a low or zero price comes together with an atmosphere in museums that is also attractive for low-class people, their exclusion as well can be less severe. But in the twentieth century, with a few exceptions, there are no reproductions and few authorized replicas in museums. And the atmosphere is such that also with low or zero prices, lower-class people are much underrepresented. They are de facto excluded.

The rejection of reproductions and replicas in museums is relatively new. It is significant that around the turn of the nineteenth and twentieth centuries, many historical art museums become established who acquire plaster replicas of ancient models for their collections, such as the Venus de Milo. Some museums are entirely founded on plaster copies. But apart from such museums, with time, regular art museums stop exhibiting plaster copies and reproductions. They disappear the same as in many homes. Even in education institutes educating prospective artists, plaster replicas of old statues are destroyed or disappear in attics to be next forgotten.

Aside: Especially in the case of museums, the emphasis on the low quality of reproductions in the second half of the twentieth century is strange. The quality of reproductions has become so high that, in the case of thinly painted works, it is already impossible to note a difference from a distance of one meter, and in the case of less thinly painted work from three meters. (Only in the case of extremely pasty works, as were popular around the 1970, a longer distance would be required.) Moreover, the quality of originals with a very high estimated value that are exhibited behind glass is almost always lower than that of high-quality reproductions of the works. (It is true that the art-setting and maybe even the mentioned three centimeters thick glass of the *Mona Lisa* in the Paris' Louvre adds to an experience of aura and singularity, but that does not alter the fact that the glass gives the painting an ugly greenish glow. A replacement by a high-quality reproduction not behind glass would offer a more adequate impression of the real painting.)

Finally, the overall exclusion in the visual arts is less dramatic than the previous text may suggest. Already for several decades many people, also those who do not buy art books or glossy magazines, have seen images of famous visual art on television, in daily papers, in class rooms and on social media. *Nowadays*, even some museums, not only show reproductions on their websites but also on social media. But showing reproductions in the art-buildings is still rare. Given that one original can only be present at one spot in the world, exclusion continues.

Significant is that in the case of well-recognized artists, also *over the last decades*, their income/profit-orientation continues to restrain the offering of affordable reproductions and poster art. This shows when one checks well-known poster websites.[19] If they sell copies of work of these artists, prices are over $1000. Exclusivity is important. As it says on the English ModernPrints site: "Eye-catching original signed prints by bankable modern British artists. Why choose mass-produced high street art when you can own an iconic original?"

In the twentieth century, there is also disdain for music recordings. But because the sale of recordings is, until recently, very profitable, a taboo never existed. I say more about this in web-text wt-32.

(54) IN THE ARTS AN UNWILLINGNESS TO LOWER COST EXISTS. THIS ADDS TO THE EXCLUSION OF OTHERS. UP TO CIRCA 1980, BY GENEROUS SUBSIDIZATION, GOVERNMENTS HAVE ENHANCED EXCLUSION. THE COST OF HIGH-END PERFORMANCES RISES MOST. "FOR ARTISTIC QUALITY NO COST IS TOO HIGH". THIS LEADS TO INNER-ART-WORLD EXCLUSION. In section 34 we have seen that the cost of the production of art performances rises faster than the cost of production in other sectors. If authenticity would not be such a great good, and if obvious cost-saving techniques—as can be found in the popular arts—would not be rejected, high-quality, lower-cost performances could have been developed. Instead, art-companies demand ever more support and receive more support, be it that in Europe, in most countries governments stopped increasing subsidies after circa 1980.

Since European governments have become less willing to cover deficits, entrance prices—corrected for inflation—rise. They rise even more because with time standards of quality rise, making high-end performances even more costly. Therefore, exclusion of others continues to increase, and now also less well-to-do art-lovers are excluded.

Aside: First, an unwillingness to search for lower-cost techniques applies foremost to the performing arts, especially music. This is not to say that there is no very expensive visual art in the top of the markets, with artists not caring much about cost. But here it is foremost other factors than just cost that cause high prices.

Second, creative artists are sometimes more willing to lower cost than companies.—In an interview, John Adams said that he chose to compose a piece for only one singer, also to keep cost down.[20]—Third, insofar as technical (re)productions are concerned, including recordings, efforts to lower cost are usually as strong as in other sectors of production. This applies to film and literature, as well as to most recordings of music and other performing art and visual art reproductions. This is what can be expected given the fact that in these areas, commercial companies play an important role in production.

Given the extreme goodness of serious art, high quality and, increasingly, the highest possible quality has priority, while the lowering of prices has not. This explains that there has never been much attention for the possibility of developing lower-cost performances. There is also no attention for the phenomenon that with high priced but nevertheless much subsidized prices, it is only a small well-to-do elite that profits from the subsidies. Around 1980 in Europe, on every opera ticket that is sold by main opera companies, taxpayers add around 1000% in the form of subsidies. To cover cost without subsidy, a ticket of $100 would have to be $1000. For excellence, no cost is too high.

Aside: in popular art increasingly also very exclusive performances with high ticket prices are offered. The difference is that there is much diversity. Often the same ensembles also or foremost offer low-cost and low-priced live performances to usually larger audiences. Significant is that all pop musicians who at present offer performances accompanied by large orchestras—some of whom desperately need extra income—still perform mostly without the orchestras and offer also or foremost low-cost performances./21

By generously subsidizing the performing arts, governments have indirectly contributed much to rising cost, as well as the absence of major efforts to seek ways to develop high-quality less costly performances. Contrary to official policy goals, the subsidies have indirectly contributed to exclusion. This is not to say that it has been the intention of politicians to give performing art-worlds a free hand. Politicians also believe in the goodness of art and the importance of great art and they trust art-worlds. Nevertheless, expressed goals of art policies change over time [19]. For a while now, excellence in art comes first. It is much stimulated. Certain creative artists are thought to make excellent artworks and performances, and are praised, and some receive honorable state prices of many thousands of dollars. In a small country, like the Netherlands, this strange practice certainly not only serves excellent art; it also aims to stimulate a stronger Dutch presence on the international cultural and economic stage./22

In the twenty-first century, in opera, supposedly high artistic quality bringing national and international prestige rests ever more in very costly stage settings and so-called props. *Recently in London, Anna saw a performance of Wagner's Ring cycle by the Royal Opera House. The performance did not touch her as much as the other two did. But unlike Anna, critics were enthusiastic. All mentioned the exorbitant and costly stage setting and the many props as if these were the things par excellence that made the performance so very good. The props were indeed numerous and outrageous. As Anna noticed, humans had been transformed to aliens. The head of the singer, Brindley Sherratt, had been prolonged with some 30 centimeters—the sort of thing, Anna thought, one would expect in a second-rate comic book.* No wonder that in spite of very high prices and increased sponsorship and donations, subsidies per visitor remain some tenfold of the entrance price. A strive for nternational cultural prestige can explain part of the subsidies. At the same time, it is well possible that the exclusivity for a very small well-to-do art elite for this kind of performances, in combination with much public attention, could be a more important explanatory factor. This is a topic in section 59.

Efforts to develop persistent formats of lower-cost operas, ballets and classical/serious music performed by professional performers, are largely absent. If they would be developed in the decade to come, given the reputation of the existing performances, the new formats will need much promotion. Probably a (brand) name would be required, like for instance "single A" instead of "triple A" performances. The same as in the case of B movies or, earlier the B-side of pop singles, this could be a derogatory term, but audiences would soon find out that such performances would, apart from being lower priced, have attractive qualities, while some consumers, and later on also experts, may well judge overall artistic quality to be higher than in many "excellent highest quality" performances. *(The two opera performances that let Anna have a very intense artistic experience and touched her most, were low-cost student performances with a small ensemble and a simple but effective stage setting.)*

Over the last decades the boundary between those who are de facto excluded and those who have access to the highest quality "live" art is shifting. Now there the boundary is straightforwardly in line with income and wealth differences and not so much with sociocultural differences. Over the last decade, however, this is not altogether true anymore. Probably as a means to continue to be able to offer the best possible performances in halls with a very good acoustics, as noted, some top orchestras now also perform for very large audiences in the open air and stadiums, while using amplification. Whether or not one can call this a real "willingness" to lower cost, it is likely that in the decade to come, more lower-cost live art will be offered. (In the section on the cost disease, more examples have been presented [34].)

(55) THE SERIOUSNESS OF ART BRINGS ALONG INTELLECTUALIZATION, ARTISTIC DISTANCING AND SCIENTIFICATION. THIS CAUSES INNER-ART-WORLD EXCLUSION. In the serious art period, there is a gradual process of intellectualization in the arts. The "proper" understanding of serious art not only requires social competences but also ever higher cognitive competences. In the times of contemporary-art, this not only leads to exclusion of little educated people but increasingly also of art-lovers.

These are the topics in the extensive web-text wt-55. While simplifying much, here I briefly summarize the web-section.

I argue that since the nineteenth century, the way of art consumption that is supposed to be proper and that is demanded from art-lovers is a, at least partly, contemplative way. Others are made to believe or they believe that the art-lover's intellectual way is and must be the only way. More than anything else, it is the discourse surrounding art consumption that over time becomes first more serious, and next more intellectual and analytical. Part of art-lovers become expert-consumers, they become connoisseurs.

Since the late nineteenth century, in successive phases, each time a new cultural elite start to prescribe a new and more intellectual discourse. This only partly corresponds with a rising education level of art-lovers in general. Pierre Bourdieu studied a transition around the 1960s. He uses the terms "aesthetic distancing" and "aesthetic disposition".[21] Because at that time, not only lower-class people but also conservative art-lovers miss this disposition, they are de facto excluded from the innovative art in the restricted domain of art production.

Though the origin of conceptual and contemporary-art go further back, it is around the 1980s that a new cultural elite introduces again a more intellectual and difficult discourse. The discourse moreover becomes an integral part of the artworks. (Some conceptual and contemporary-artworks are like puzzles.)

It is articulation and conversation that turn contemporary-art into art.[22] The works must be talked about, analyzed, theorized and not only be experienced in unmediated form. Relatively few people, including art-lovers, have sufficient art consumption space, that is, have enough time and energy, to learn the additional cognitive competences that are needed to decipher contemporary-art and so be able to participate in the discourse. Given their limited time, many art-lovers therefore continue to go for less demanding and, for them, more satisfying art. They are de facto excluded from the new art, with, as a consequence, *inner-art-world exclusion*.

As said, *over the last decades* two domains are developing in the arts. On the one hand, there is a small more studious domain which is foremost a continuation of the earlier domain of long-term restricted production in the arts. The main difference with before rests in, what I call, scientification in art: art being treated and organized the same as a scientific discipline. Students in art schools are now said to do research.

However, over the last *two* decades, in the new and much larger user-oriented domain—also in that of classical-serious music—there is now less very "intellectual" art and an increasing number of artists involved in the production of contemporary-art that is more focused on accessibility. The artwork may be layered, but should also be "understandable" without much preliminary knowledge. It is also significant that experts/critics now sometimes call works "beautiful", a term whose use was earlier taboo. For art-lovers unmediated enjoyment of art is no longer taboo.

(56) MOST TALENTED PROSPECTIVE ARTISTS WITH A LOWER-MIDDLE AND LOWER-CLASS BACKGROUND HAVE A HARD TIME BECOMING RECOGNIZED. THEY ARE, DE FACTO, EXCLUDED FROM OFFICIAL ART EDUCATION AND MOST ART CIRCLES. A so-called *class ceiling* exists in the arts, even though exceptions suggest the opposite.—The

exceptions are much emphasized in art circles [46].—A privileged background enables prospective artists to profit from the cultural and social capital they earlier obtained. It follows that wrongly resourced social groups are not only excluded from consumption of serious art but also from its production. In practice, without government support their means to develop, produce and distribute own art are also limited.

The mechanism of exclusion resembles that of concert halls and museums with their monoculture. In the art profession—the same as in a large company—going from one level of success to the other culture may differ a little, but privileged artists can go with the flow and so acquire additional cultural means. For others, however, the main barrier is the one at the bottom. Already at the lowest level, their arrears are such that for them it is impossible to "follow the flow". Unlike what art-world people (and art experts) tend to believe, there is no true meritocracy of artists. Or in other words, "merits" rest in behavioral and not in artistic qualities.

The "others" are wrongly resourced. They have not and cannot develop the mentioned "feel for the game". Next to insufficient or rather unsuitable or wrong cultural and social capital or means, also a lack of financial means limits the possibilities of many "others". The effect is stronger in the art profession than in many other professions. First, much art education—also private art education—is relatively expensive. Sometimes grants exist for applicants with parents with few means, but usually their portfolio or performance must be much better than of the average applicant. Second, becoming professional artist is risky. Financial prospects are low. Most wrongly or under-resourced, but artistically talented, lower-educated and non-white or migrant youngsters do not even consider becoming artists and otherwise seldom apply for official art education. Moreover, given low financial prospects, parents in migrant families, families in which children are supposed to later on support parents, will advise sons and daughters against becoming artists.

Truly racist motives can also lead to exclusion of non-whites, higher educated or not. Longer ago, the same as in the case of consumers, exclusion was substantial. The same applied and sometimes still applies to women wanting to become creative art professionals. They are no longer excluded from schools, but being female, it is harder for them to move from one level to the next, and to sell their works, including performances to consumers. It is not accidental that in the visual arts and literature, women chose and sometimes still choose male aliases and pen names.

Mutatis mutandis, what applies to artists with a lower-middle class and low-class background also applies to art-producers with a similar background. Anna noticed that the class background of the owners of commercial-galleries is on average high and higher than that of some artists they represent.

Finally, in practice, given their limited financial capital and relevant social capital, and without government support, lower-class people often also have a hard time to develop, produce and distribute *own art*, that is, art which is appreciated by the own social group [85].

Although underrepresentation and de facto exclusion are usually ignored in art circles, when questioned, art-lovers occasionally attempt to justify them. The common justification is sought in the primacy of quality in the arts. "Quality may be less important in popular art, in the arts it comes first. If this implies that there are relatively few women artists or non-white artists this is regrettable, but inevitable". The possibility of prejudices and discrimination is not considered. The quality argument is widely shared in society; otherwise it is hard to explain that art-worlds are less criticized for their whiteness than the worlds of popular art are, even though in the latter non-white artists are far more present.

Presently in the USA, 60% of professional artists are graduates, but only 16% are arts graduates.[23] A majority of artists are well-educated, while the percentage of those with well-educated parents is even higher. An official form of higher education clearly helps in becoming a professional artist. Official art education, however, appears to be unimportant. But as said [14], having followed some years of official art education and having graduated can help to become a recognized and more or less successful artist with a lasting career.

In 1985 when she was part-time teacher at the Rietveld Academie of visual art, she was part of a committee deciding on the admittance to the academy. Aspiring artists show portfolios and on the basis of the portfolio they are admitted or not. One of the applicants clearly had a lower-middle-class background. He showed work in an inferior-art style, but as Anna thought could easily develop his work in a direction that would be acceptable. Another applicant was an immigrant from an Arabic country and everybody agreed that his work was fine. Both were rejected. They would not fit in. Anna was furious and the following years refused to be part of the committee. Only much later she realized that the committee members were right in saying that they would not fit in. Being admitted, they would have felt comfortable in the school environment, would become disappointed and most likely would have quit. (She later came again across the former migrant student and she and Mohammed became friends. With considerable effort, he had become educated without following accredited art education. He had, after all, become an art-world-recognized artist who occasionally exhibited in contemporary art galleries.)

Attempts at Inclusion

(57) During the period of serious art: GROUPS OF ART-LOVERS WANT TO BRING ART TO THE PROLETARIAT. THEY ATTEMPT TO ELEVATE THE WORKERS OR PURSUE ECONOMIC GOALS. THE ATTEMPTS ARE PATERNALISTIC AND UNSUCCESSFUL. So far, I discussed mechanisms of exclusion, which make participation in live events in art-buildings and visits to museums unattractive for lower-class people. This is not the whole story. All through the serious art period, there are art-lovers who want to bring serious art to them. Till the present day—be it less outspoken—a belief that it is important to let "others" get acquainted with serious art, remains important among art-lovers. Governments often agree. Earlier the term "dissemination" is used; art must be disseminated. Attempts were little successful. Now the use of the term "participation" is common; others must also participate.

Although in the early stage of the serious art period art-lovers appreciate not to have to share their art events anymore with frivolous and "uncivilized" aristocrats and higher bourgeois, they nevertheless also worry about their absence. They adhere to an educational or civilizing ideal and want to elevate them, or they want to assist them in self-education. A *"Bildungsideal"* is important./23 The art-lovers, moreover, need them, because, given their own limited number, they have a hard time funding their art events. They therefore encourage well-to-do, but in their eyes little-cultured bourgeois to develop an interest in serious art and to start visiting the serious art events and accept the subdued behavior and still consumption practice. Often the encouragement is successful—be it sometimes only in the case of the sons and daughters. Therefore, with respect to higher middle-class people, next to *short-term exclusion*, there is *long-term inclusion.*

The latter is a form of *horizontal dissemination*. There is horizontal dissemination of serious art when bourgeois or middle-class people who do not yet consume art in art-buildings start to do so. *Over the last decades*, the group of people participating in the arts becomes larger. A special form of horizontal dissemination is *geographic dissemination*: more people participate thanks to provision of art in smaller cities further away from the metropoles. *Vertical dissemination* refers to bringing art to lower-class groups. They must become acquainted with serious art and start to consume it on a regular basis. In theory vertical dissemination could be bottom up, but in practice the term is only used to refer to top-down dissemination. Sometimes there is *limited vertical dissemination*. People, a bit lower on the social ladder start to participate, but low-class people still do not.

Early in the serious art period, vertical dissemination has no priority. Not many art-lovers worry about the de facto exclusion of lower-class people. This is not extraordinary. In all areas of luxury consumption, wrongly and thus under-resourced workers have no access. This is experienced as natural, the same as the barrier between higher and lower classes is natural. But with time groups of bourgeois begin to realize that the overall barrier between the classes is not altogether natural, that the barrier is possibly bad for society and that a barrier is extra unfair in the case of art consumption, because art consumption could elevate the poor. Their education and civilization through art is a good thing. The ultimate goal is to share art with lower-class people, that is, long-term inclusion.

This certainly is the aim of socialists. At the time of the industrial revolution in the rapidly growing towns, the living conditions of most people are appalling. Socialists want to improve working and living conditions. Some, like William Morris, think in terms of, sometimes drastic, social reforms (without being true revolutionaries), while others, like John Ruskin, propagate a moral *reveille* among all social groups. All point to art consumption as a means to elevate the poor. For some bringing art to lower-class people is a form of charity. But, within the labor movement the access to art is regarded as a right. Moreover, several leaders also think that art can empower people and thus can indirectly contribute to the emancipation and possibly even the victory of the proletariat.

The groups around Ruskin and Morris emphasize the aesthetic dimension of socialism. Socialism implies not only equality for the poor, but also another way of life, a life in a more aesthetic environment and with more participation of the common man in, not only the use but also, the production of art. These socialists, and also some progressive liberals, believe in the possibility of a social as well as spiritual improvement./24

In 1891 the Metropolitan Museum of Art in New York—whose entrance is free all through the week—decided to also be open on Sundays to give lower-class people who work six days a week a chance to visit. This leads to more inclusion. On Sundays there are more blue-collar workers in the museum. Together they create a different atmosphere and thus a slightly different product.[24]

An example of an attempt to disseminate art in the early twentieth century is that of the "Kunst für Alle" (Art for Everybody) movement in Germany. People within the movement attach much value to the educational role of art. They successfully promote the production and distribution of large size black and white reproductions of famous paintings and etchings, like those of Rubens and Rembrandt. During the twentieth century, the educational role of art continues to be emphasized. In the second half of the twentieth century, there are, for instance, many popular radio and television programs in which visual art is shown and explained./25 The result of these and similar activities is, however, foremost horizontal and with little vertical dissemination.

At times also groups or movements of artists strive for democratization of art. For instance, in the "long 1960s", there are several movements among artists, who explicitly want to produce a new kind of art; art is interesting for everybody. The content is often political. In all art forms such movements exist and some cross the borders of art forms, as in the case of Cobra and Fluxus. There are groups who not only produce art with critical content but also strive for low-priced artworks and performances. Moreover, in the visual arts, taking position against the general inclination to look down on larger series of (re)productions, a few well-known and more little-known artists produce larger scale multiples, foremost silkscreen prints which are relatively cheap./26 They also "illustrate" magazines and pamphlets. But also in the case of these movements: if successful the success foremost rests in horizontal dissemination of art.

Aside: At the time in Western countries there is more poster art than before and after, and not only in the communist countries where poster art is much promoted by the regimes. The phenomenon of certain artists making graphics with a political message is of all times, but in this period it clearly runs counter to the longer-term developments in the visual arts [20 and 55].

The efforts of good-willing art-lovers and subsidizing governments to disseminate art among lower social groups are paternalistic: "others do not know how good art can be for them".—In terms economist use, art is a "merit good" [19].—The goodness of art is such that the bourgeois want to disseminate art. But what they want to disseminate is their own serious art. This also applies to prominent socialists, like William Morris and John Ruskin. (Aside: during the period of serious art, higher-class paternalism is an integral part of a hierarchical society. Paternalism is strong in the arts but not limited to the arts.)

The goodness of art calls forward opposite inclinations among art-lovers. There are art-lovers who want to protect art against uncouth outsiders and others who want to share and disseminate art. There is also a group who want both: short-term exclusion in the situations in which they themselves consume art together and so stay among their own group, and the realization of longer-term inclusion by other ways. The same well-to-do person, who within the walls of the theater or concert hall, deliberately or not, shows disdain for an outsider, may in other situations sincerely plead for the civilization and elevation of the proletariat through art. He may, for instance, propose to establish museums in poor neighborhoods or promote separate serious music performances for lower-class people.

A good example of mixed behavior can be found in Amsterdam in the beginning of the twentieth century, when white collar workers are invited to visit free "popular concerts" (volksconcerten) *in a bandstand next to the luxurious Concertgebouw. There is insulation and exclusion because* lower-class people *who do not belong in the Concertgebouw do not enter the building but only visit the bandstand. Art-lovers can stay among their own kind, while others can create their own atmosphere. But the latter clearly is not the intention. Instead the aim is to educate others and next share art with them. (Sometimes others are attracted by also offering some "light music".) It is significant that during the concerts, workers are not only "taught art" but also civilized consumption practices. Not that many show up. Usually those who participate are members of workers' unions who are eager to be educated in manners as well as in a proper understanding of serious music.*

The establishment of museums in poor neighborhoods represents a combination of sharing and insulation. *An example is the founding in 1901 of the Whitechapel Gallery in London. One aim is to bring great art to the very poor lower-class people who at the time live in the Whitechapel district of East London—the classic "Dickensian" part of London. Art is supposed to be good for them. The intention is indeed sharing with poor people, but* de facto *exclusion is not unimportant because a crude physical separation of social groups is maintained./27 Well-to-do people would certainly continue to visit the National Gallery at Trafalgar Square, while for others visits are unattractive due to cost of transport and informal exclusion. For them there is now a separate space. (By now the Whitechapel Gallery is a highbrow gallery exhibiting contemporary-art.)*

Motives for vertical dissemination are not always just noble. The elevation of the proletariat is thought to promote the nation state, social cohesion and the prevention of unruly behavior, social unrest and even a revolution.[25] Such goals are supposed to be in everybody's interest. This shows, among others, from discussions in parliament. Another goal of dissemination is often emphasized: it serves the economy.

To serve the economy the dissemination of a feel for artistically pleasing applied art is thought to be important. Among others due to the pressure of international competition in many countries, lower level art-and-craft schools are established. Pupils do not only learn artistic skills but are also brought in contact with classic master pieces. (During *The Great Exhibition* of 1851 in *The Crystal Palace* in

London, people criticize the disappointing artistic quality of the exhibited industrial products made in England in comparison to those of other countries and blamed the low quality of general and art education in England.)

Courses are thought to serve the economic betterment of society and of the pupils but also their cultural betterment. As said, the twentieth-century socialists who are interested in social reform and averse from an altogether profit-oriented capitalism, emphasize the aesthetic dimension of socialism and favor the realization of artistically pleasing architecture in housing projects for lower-class people.

The vertical dissemination of serious art among lower-class people is largely unsuccessful, as research done in the late 1950s shows and as is confirmed in later research: they do not start to participate in art events.[26] In the 1980s in many European countries the conviction that vertical dissemination has failed has become generally accepted.[27] Since then and until recently, not only in public policy, but also among art organizations and artists the wish to share with lower social groups has lost momentum./28

Given the analysis in this book, the fact that vertical dissemination is unsuccessful is what can be expected. The forces in art-worlds that keep art exclusive are strong and cannot easily be undone. Art-lovers want to protect their "sacred object" against others. As social scientists have noted, for at least some art-lovers, the failure of top-down vertical dissemination is not unwelcome. They feel that they have done their best to vertically disseminate art. They can now stay among their own kind of people without having to feel bad about it. Moreover, for quite a few, the failure demonstrates once again that in practice lower-class people are not fit or ready for true art. For them the failure indirectly contributes to distinction and the positive feelings connected with art consumption: art is clearly not for everybody.[28]

That, unlike vertical dissemination and inclusion, horizontal dissemination and inclusion is successful can foremost be explained from an upward social mobility in society, which runs parallel with an increase in the average level of education. Each decade there is a considerable group of newcomers in the higher echelons in society; and at least part of them is interested in art. In spite of short-term attempts in art-buildings to exclude groups of newcomers who draw attention [50], many newcomers, step by step become art-lovers without drawing much attention.

Nevertheless, as late as the 1960s, many well-established art-companies also resist horizontal dissemination. Among others, they did so for financial reasons. For instance, in 1966, the Ford Foundation was prepared to donate several millions to the Philadelphia Orchestra on the condition that it would open its board and make it more representative, and to start a matching fund raise among the population at large, hoping that the orchestra would start to serve a larger part of the population. The existing board did not want this: "We don't need Negroes, educators, or musicians on the Board because they don't swing any financial weight".[29]

A means of attracting lower-class people which has not been discussed in this section could be the lowering of prices and the provision of free live art with the help of government subsidies. But in spite of generous subsidization in the performing arts, prices only rise in the second half of the twentieth century and after.

However, gradually schemes have been developed—foremost that of price discrimination—which make performances more accessible to people with small pockets. These are topics I discuss in section 91.

Over the last decades there is limited vertical dissemination. More middle-class people now participate in live art events. Moreover, inclusion of lower social groups is back on the agenda of art organizations and (local) governments. I discuss this in section 90.

A Love of Art and a Love of Exclusivity

(58) THROUGH ART CONSUMPTION, PERSONS AND SOCIAL GROUPS DISTINGUISH THEMSELVES AND SOMETIMES DOMINATE OTHERS. ART CAN STAND FOR POWER. IT CAN ALSO EMPOWER. Art bringing distinction implies that others look up to the distinguished person or group. This way art contributes to the authority and power of a person who owns art or visits art events, or to a group who symbolically owns art. The association of serious art with an expression of power and the domination of others is painful for art-lovers. They want to believe that art has goodness and this does not rhyme with a strife for distinction, power and domination. (The latter three are emphasized by Bourdieu in his book *Distinction*.[30] It is no accident that after its publication in 1979, many informed art-lovers are shocked and that they are happy when in the 2000s some social scientists start to criticize Bourdieu's work.)

Aside: First, the mechanism of "art giving distinction and power", exists at all levels, from a monarch to a simple art-lover impressing others. Second, other means than art can be more effective in bringing authority and power. If the monarch had spent more money on his army or the citizen on a prestigious car this may have been more effective. And third, the mechanism can apply vertically or horizontally or both. The businessman horizontally impresses other businessmen and he vertically impresses employees. Talking about groups, higher educated people may attempt to horizontally impress other higher educated people and vertically little educated people.

Before the serious art period, the display of magnificent art is common and altogether acceptable. Art stands for wealth and power and it indirectly contributes to power. It, indeed, impresses other monarchs, bishops, nobles, rich merchants, and it impresses lower groups. In the serious art period, expressions of wealth and power through art are not as acceptable as before. In the second half of the twentieth century, expressions of superiority through art are anyway subtler, but probably still effective. Along with informalization, an open display of superiority in the relation of higher groups with lower groups becomes somewhat taboo. But horizontal distinction through art consumption continues.[31]

Aside: During the major part of the serious art period, consumption and what it stands for always played a role in the struggle between lower and higher groups *within* the overall elite. There is competition, and the consumption and display of art indirectly serves as a weapon. When Bourdieu discusses distinction and domination in his book *Distinction*, he has this kind of vertical distinction in mind.[32] Bourdieu discusses developments in society and art in the 1950s, 1960s and 1970s. In this period—using Bourdieu's terminology—a dominated faction within the dominant class of the overall elite is becoming more powerful and attempts to take the place of the existing dominant faction. A new better-educated cultural elite consuming modern-art struggles with the at-first still-dominant financially successful elite and gradually takes over power. A similar process occurred in the early period of serious art, when the creation of serious art helped the emancipation of a new group of educated but not yet very rich bourgeois in their struggle to escape the domination by aristocrats and financially successful, but less civilized bourgeois.

How important art has been in the domination of lower social groups is hard to tell.—Lower groups are anyway inferior.—Art, nevertheless, certainly plays a role in the maintenance of the status quo. The magnificent art-buildings are intimidating. They inspire reverence and awe. Higher bourgeois looked down on the populace from the (still existing) balconies. (The 1956 musical *My Fair Lady,* based on Bernard Shaw's 1913 theater play, *Pygmalion,* indirectly testifies of reverence and awe. Cheeky Eliza Doolittle is an exception to the rule.)

Also *over the last decades* for lower groups of people art-buildings and their assumed rich interiors can still be intimidating, but, arguably, I think it unlikely that the art consumption of the elite and its display still impresses excluded under- and wrongly resourced groups in such degree that it adds much to general existing domination. Causes are manifold. One is that the symbolic boundary between serious art and popular art has weakened. Higher groups now freely consume popular music. This corresponds with a decreasing respect for serious art. It is less suitable for group distinction and domination.

This does not necessarily imply that exclusivity in the arts in the case of individuals and small groups has become less important and profitable. The opposite is the case. Exclusivity and exclusion now befit a meritocracy in which individuals are often more important than social groups. Successful people distinguish themselves also by means of their art. *Over the last decades* an open display and expression of power through art has become more common again, especially among the rich—and not only among business tycoons buying and possessing art.[33]/29 For the rich and very rich art consumption is increasingly an effective means to show off wealth and power, while suggesting that they are deserved. The effect can also be a form of white-washing: bad business practices are compensated and sooner forgotten. Consuming very expensive art may not add much to the possibilities to execute power vertically, but resulting prestige is evidently very enjoyable. Otherwise top prices of visual art would not be so high and still increasing.

At lower levels rich people buy expensive art and participate in very expensive performances specially designed for them. It allows them to distinguish themselves. The distinction-benefits of this kind of art consumption foremost occur horizontally, that is, within a social group. Small differences in wealth can correspond with larger differences in a "being cultured"./30

Top-down vertical empowerment through art—high-up people becoming more powerful—is not absent, but it is rather the opposite that matters most in society or is best noticeable. Relatively underprivileged groups empower themselves horizontally but every now and then also bottom up. This occurred during the period of punk and at a larger scale in the period of hip-hop, which last to the present day.

(59) ART-LOVERS ARE WILLING TO PAY FOR EXCLUSIVITY. THEY BUY MEMBERSHIP IN GROUPS. Last section's story can also be told in more economic terms. There is supply and demand of distinction; buyers of art buy (also) distinction. The attraction of exclusivity can explain all sorts of behavior, which otherwise are hard to explain. For a proper understanding of the social economy of art, an understanding of exclusivity in the arts is important. Exclusivity is a cornerstone of art-worlds. The belief in the goodness of an "art for the sake of art only" and therefore implicitly in the badness of "art for the sake of exclusivity and distinction" led in the time of Bourdieu to denial, but presently, given ever higher prices, art-lovers and artists start to notice that, at least in the top of art markets, exclusivity is very important for buyers. This causes anger.

A love of art can accompany a love of exclusivity, or a love of exclusivity can accompany a love of art. When deciding to purchase artworks, people imagine experiences, with one or the other or both figures highly and is rewarding. Both can therefore motivate purchases of works and tickets. In practice separating the two is difficult, and determining their relative weight is impossible. But phenomena exist that prove that exclusivity matters much for many art-lovers or that this is highly plausible. The exclusivity of art is a cornerstone of art-worlds.

The fact that many visual artists limit the edition size of graphics, photos and poster art is, indeed, proof of the fact that many art-lovers are interested in exclusivity. They are willing to pay for exclusivity, even though the artwork itself would not have been different if more copies would have been made and sold./31 Aside: this proves as well that many visual artists are (also) income/profit-oriented; more than people are inclined to think.

As said, prices have meanings. High prices and a high reputation may not only signal quality but also exclusivity or both. In the case of a single artist, it is unlikely that over time the quality of his works increases much from one work to the next and can explain a price which is each time higher. This suggests that the reputation of artists in combination with the exclusivity of his works matters much for buyers. The fact that, when earlier works are later auctioned, prices are much higher than before makes the thesis only more likely.

Other phenomena exist which we already came across, that also suggest that exclusivity matters. The rejection of popularity—and especially popularity among common people, the "populace"—which was discussed in section [52]—must, at least partly, follow from a wish to let art be exclusive and only consumed by an exclusive higher social group.

Looking at the history of photography, it is particularly clear that art-worlds and artists embrace exclusivity. Photos becoming more exclusive appears to have been a condition for photography to become real art. This shows from the phenomenon that art photographers started to produce much smaller editions of their photos. If they had continued to produce large editions, the establishment of a recognized photography art-world would have been impossible. Indirectly governments also promote this kind of exclusivity (and the delineation of art and no-art) by subsidizing artists who make small editions. This is the case in countries where a lower VAT rate for photos applies if the edition size is less than a certain small number—in the Netherlands this is seven copies.

Artworks are what economists call *positional goods*. They tell about characteristics of the buyer, for instance that he belongs to a group of very rich people. Showing this position is rewarding for him. In the arts one characteristic is particularly rewarding: this is being a member of a real or imagined group that stands out by literally or figuratively owning exclusive art.

It implies both sharing and exclusion. Humans are social beings: in order to enjoy art's exclusivity, a person must relate to others, that is, to others he does not share art with, but, just as important, also to others he shares art with. Buyers of artworks and art tickets share one or more art-related positional characteristics with other buyers. Their purchases and possible love of art make the group members stand out. They, the same as the artworks, have one or more characteristics others have not. In this respect they have exclusivity and may well be admired by others, who do not have the characteristic.

When Leonardo DiCaprio in 2011 buys Salvador Dali's "Chevaliers en Parade" for $1.2, he cannot but have had some self-constructed groups in mind with whom he shares one or another characteristic that is related to the artwork. He may well feel connected with the group of collectors who buy and own Dali paintings or important symbolist paintings. Or he may think of yet a set of people who collect very expensive paintings including very expensive paintings. He may also picture groups with whom he does not share related characteristics, like the many jet-set people, which he knows and who do not collect art. Maybe DiCaprio pictured more groups or other groups, but it is impossible that he has not occasionally thought of any such group.

Sharing art in groups of people who are together in person while informally excluding others has been discussed in section 50. Also mentioned above is the phenomenon that people share art with an imagined community, while in their imagination they exclude others. Imagined groups can be small or large; from an imagined group owning an etching in a small edition and three thousand people present in a concert to the overall imagined "family of art". People in such groups celebrate their "sacred object", feel superior and want to exclude others.

Memberships have a price. To be a member of the exclusive circle present in the concert hall, one must have paid for the ticket. Sometimes the cost of membership in such art-related groups can be very high. This applies for instance to membership in the group of people who own Picasso paintings. And becoming a member of the imagined group of five persons who own one of Koons' series of five *Balloon Dog* sculptures in different colors must be extremely rich. But it evidently is worth it. The same as DiCaprio, the initially not very-cultured tycoon also buys membership in various other groups, probably most importantly in the imagined group of rich as well as cultured people and/or the overall group of cultured people. (In 2013 one of the sculptures was sold for $58.4 million, making the sculpture the most expensive by a living artist at that time.) Not only does he imagine group members and benefits. In practice he is bound to come across people in such circles and notice that he is being accepted as a cultured person. The more so if he also makes very generous gifts. Now there are people who are prepared to "donate" $10 million, at least partly, to become a member of the real, and not imagined, board of directors of the Metropolitan Museum of Art.

Buying very expensive art is particularly effective and rewarding for raising prestige not only in small but also very large circles, because the purchase and ownership draws the attention of people in general. The higher the price the easier the display of one's ownership and the communication with people, possibly all-over the world. Journals, glossy magazines and other media do most of the work. (There are exceptions. Not all buyers appreciate this mechanism and they buy expensive works altogether anonymously.) (In this web-note, I present two appealing examples. One of Anna buying distinction./32 And in this web-note, I mention the lack of choice and freedom rich people have and the diminishing marginal return in the case of expensive things referring to Justin Bieber and DiCaprio./33)

Aside: So far in market-research on visual art, there has been much attention for the collecting of visual art as a form of investment. It is acknowledged that next to a love of art, longer-term financial considerations may play a role for collectors. There is far less or no attention for purchasing art to gain various forms of membership, which is somewhat amazing, because especially in the case of newcomers, the simultaneous purchase of memberships may also explain their behavior and possibly better. In practice it is a combination. Economists figured out that in the very long run, art is not a better and probably a worse investment than investments in other assets, and some expect that in spite of presently strongly rising art prices this will continue to be the case. The possible development in the worth of artworks is indeed on the buyers mind, at present especially on that of the youngest generation of collectors.[34] But buying art in the top of the market is very risky. (The chance that the value of the Balloon Dogs and similar works goes down in the next four decades is large.) It follows that, forgetting about short-term speculation, other than just investment considerations, must explain behavior. And if memberships matter in the top of the market, they will also matter further down.

Art-companies "enrich" artworks in many ways [77]. One important goal is creating an experience of exclusivity. Many art experts/critics contribute to this. Deliberately or not, they help raise the income of art-companies and collectors.

Over the last decades, along with an increase in income inequality, the willingness of rich individuals to pay for exclusivity and membership has increased. It contributes to the present hype among billionaires to establish and open own art museums—which does not mean that an intense love of art may not motivate them as well. Moreover, with a further noticeable commercialization of the visual art-world, art-companies and experts/critics have become keener and better in exploiting this willingness. They "enrich" and "improve" the works, making them appear even more singular and exclusive, and therefore more attractive for rich people. Along with globalization, the winner-take-all mechanism has become much stronger, and this as well may go at the cost of art offered at intermediate levels of the art markets. Only at the bottom of the visual art market, where for relatively low prices the largest quantity of visual artworks is sold and bought, developments point in another direction. It appears that at that level groups of buyers do not care much about exclusivity anymore. If they can distinguish themselves in the own small circles of family and friends, this suffices.

Notes

[1](Adams, Kräussl, Navone, & Verwijmeren, 2017).

[2](Susan Jahoda & a.o., 2014).

[3](Bryson, 1996). She uses 1993 data. I think it highly plausible that her conclusions also apply to an earlier period.

[4]Cf. (Bourdieu, 1984) 31 and 390 and (Heinich, 2005) (in French) 181–182.

[5]Both examples: (Levine, 1988) 136.

[6]Cf. (Wouters, 2007).

[7]Cf. (Weber & Owen, 2004). (Elias, 1994) discusses the emergence of a, so-called, monopoly of violence.

[8]Cf. (Velthuis, 2005).

[9](Dimaggio & Useem, 1978).

[10]In 1918 a not properly dressed blue-collar worker is refused entrance to the museum in New York, but this was criticized in the press. (Levine, 1988) 185.

[11]At the time its base was the Royal Opera House in London. Later it became the Birmingham Royal Ballet.

[12](Bourdieu, 1984).

[13](Collins, 2005).

[14]Cf. (Baumann, 2001).

[15]("Original, Copy, Fake, On the significance of the object in History and Archaeology Museums," 2010).

[16]("Original, Copy, Fake, On the significance of the object in History and Archaeology Museums," 2010).

[17]Clapper, M. (2002).

[18](Levine, 1988) 160–165.

[19]Presently the largest are allposter.com and art.com (by now part of the same company).

[20]If I remember well, Adams was interviewed in the context of the performance in 2015 in Amsterdam of his Scheherazade 2.

[21](Bourdieu, 1984) and (Bourdieu, 1993).

[22]Danto may have said that it is (an atmosphere of) art theory that turns anything into art. Cf. (Danto, 1986).

[23](Susan Jahoda & a.o., 2014).

[24](Levine, 1988) 182.

[25]Cf. (Taylor, 1991).

[26]Cf. (Veld-Langeveld, 1961) and (Dulken, 1988) (both in Dutch).

[27]Cf. (Dulken, 1988) (in Dutch).

[28]Cf. (Swaan, 1986) (in Dutch).

[29](Arian, 1971) 57 and 70.

[30](Bourdieu, 1984).

[31](Collins, 2005) distinguishes horizontal and vertical distinction and domination.

[32](Bourdieu, 1984).

[33]Cf. (Wouters, 2007).

[34]According to U.S. Trust 2018 Insights on Wealth and Worth survey—with a Spotlight on Art Collecting.

Literature

Adams, R. B., Kräussl, R., Navone, M. A., & Verwijmeren, P. (2017). *Is Gender in the Eye of the Beholder? Identifying Cultural Attitudes with Art Auction Prices* (SSRN Scholarly Paper No. ID 3083500). Retrieved from Social Science Research Network Website: https://papers.ssrn.com/abstract=3083500

Appadurai, A. (1996). *Modernity at Large: Cultural Dimensions of Globalization*. Minneapolis/London: University of Minnesota Press.

Arian, E. (1971). *Bach, Beethoven, and Bureaucracy: The Case of the Philadelphia Orchestra* (1st ed.). Alabama: The University of Alabama Press.

Baumann, S. (2001). Intellectualization and Art World Development: Film in the United States. *American Sociological Review, 66*(3), 404–426. https://doi.org/10.2307/3088886.

Bourdieu, P. (1984). *Distinction. A Social Critique of the Judgement of Taste*. London: Routledge and Kegan Paul.

Bourdieu, P. (1993). *The Field of Cultural Production : Essays on Art and Literature*. Cambridge: Polity.

Bryson, B. (1996). 'Anything But Heavy Metal': Symbolic Exclusion and Musical Dislikes. *American Sociological Review, 61*, 884–899.

Clapper, M. (2002). "I Was Once a Barefoot Boy!": Cultural Tensions in a Popular Chromo. *American Art, 16*, 16–39.

Collins, R. (2005). *Interaction Ritual Chains*. Princeton/Oxford: Princeton University Press.

Cowen, T. (2002). *Creative Destruction: How Globalization Is Changing the World's Cultures*. Princeton: Princeton University Press.

Danto, A. C. (1986). *The Philosophical Disenfranchisement of Works of Art*. New York: Colombia University Press.

Dimaggio, P., & Useem, M. (1978). Social Class and Arts Consumption: The Origins and Consequences of Class Differences in Exposure to the Arts in America. *Theory and Society, 5*, 141–161.

Dulken, H. v. (1988). *In Ons Diaconale Land*. Amsterdam: Boekmanstichting/Van Gennep.

Elias, N. (1994). *The Civilizing Process* (p. 1993). Oxford: Blackwell.

Frank, R. H., & Cook, P. J. (1995). *The Winner-Take-all Society*. New York etc.: The Free Press.

Heinich, N. (2005). *L'Élite Artiste, Excellence et Singularité en Régime Démocratique*. Paris: Gallimard.

Jahoda, S. (2014). *Artists Report Back, A National Study on the Lives of Arts Graduates and Working Artists*. Retrieved from BFAMFAPhD Website: http://bfamfaphd.com/

Levine, L. W. (1988). *Highbrow/Lowbrow: The Emergence of Cultural Hierarchy in America*. Cambridge, MA: Harvard University Press.

Original, Copy, Fake, On the Significance of the Object in History and Archaeology Museums. (2010). *22nd ICOM General Conference*. Presented at the Shanghai, Shanghai.

Schumpeter, J. A. (1934). *The Theory of Economic Development*. Retrieved from http://www.hup.harvard.edu/catalog.php?isbn=9780674879904
Swaan, A. d. (1986). *Kwaliteit is Klasse. De Sociale Wording en Werking van het Cultureel Smaakverschil*. Amsterdam: Bert Bakker.
Taylor, C. (1991). *The Malaise of Modernity*. Cambridge: Harvard University Press. In 1192 the book was reprinted under the title The Ethics of Authenticity.
Veld-Langeveld, H. M. (1961). De sociale cultuurspreiding. In A. H. J. den Hollander, E. Hofstee, & J. A. A. van Doorn (Eds.), *Drift en Koers*. Assen: Van Gorcum.
Velthuis, O. (2005). *Talking Prices. Symbolic Meanings of Prices on the Market for Contemporary Art*. Princeton: Princeton University Press.
Weber, M., & Owen, D. S. (2004). *The Vocation Lectures*. Indianapolis: Hackett Publishing.
Wouters, C. (2007). *Informalization, Manners and Emotions Since 1890*. London: Sage.

Distrust of Commerce and Commercialism

Before the period of serious art, artists were well aware that market income could increase their freedom and they had no problem with commerce, commercialism, self-branding and the enrichment of their work, to make it more attractive. As we would say now: they were willing to compromise. But during this period such activities are taboo, and artists who compromise are blamed. Artists must be as autonomous as possible.

Around 1980, along with developments in capitalism, attitudes and practices change again. First, marketing and next cultural entrepreneurship by art-companies become common. Not much later many artists follow. Often without being aware of this, artworks and the art products of art-companies also change in content, with higher sales as the outcome. Moreover, some artists start to worry less about artistic autonomy and develop hybrid art practices.

Not all art-lovers agree. They resist that art-companies and artist are becoming cultural entrepreneurs. And leftist critics warn against a commercialism in the arts that is becoming as common and intense as in the commercial popular arts. An orientation on sponsors and donors is thought to lead to a loss of autonomy and compromise.

Over the last decades, artworks and art products are increasingly enriched; their "wrapping" looks more attractive. This contributes to another phenomenon. Along with commercialization and other developments in society, a winner-take-all mechanism has become more important in the arts. This leads to extremely high incomes among a small group of artists and to a small number of very successful ensembles and venues.

In the following sections I present and discuss many situations in which artists and art organizations attempt to make artistically autonomous art or follow an own mission in offering art, while in practice they often create relatively other- or user-oriented art, art that can be called market-, supporter- and art-world-oriented art. During the period of serious art, when artists are thought to do so, and even more when they are thought to deliberately do so, they are blamed for compromising.

H. Abbing, *The Changing Social Economy of Art*,
https://doi.org/10.1007/978-3-030-21668-9_5

This still happens, even though over the last decades blaming artists becomes less intense. But as I notice many artists still feel guilty when they do not make "own work" but compromise, I discuss the phenomenon in detail in the following sections.

Lines on either side of the text indicate that recurring concepts are defined or described. This chapter is accompanied by web-notes and web-texts, which are available on the website: *www.hansabbing.com*. Numbers between brackets refer to other sections, including web-texts. Numbers at the end of a sentence preceded by a forward slash refer to web-notes. Holding a pc, tablet or phone next to this text, it is easy to "scan" the web-notes and web-texts. (Quantitative data I most often present in web-notes.)

Hostile Spheres

(60) Introduction: THE TERMS COMMERCE, COMMERCIAL, COMMERCIALISM AND MARKET ARE USED IN MORE THAN ONE SENSE. SOMETIMES THEY ARE USED IN A METAPHORIC SENSE. In this part of the book I discuss various convictions and opinions in the arts that are related to *"commerce", commercialism*, and *"the market"* or *"markets"*. To be able to do so, in this intermezzo I explain these and related concepts. They are sometimes used in confusing ways. General readers—but not students—can scan or skip the section, and, if necessary, later have a better look at some paragraphs.

In this text I use the term *commerce*, that is, commerce without inverted commas, the way economists do. *Commerce* refers to trade in goods and services. Artworks are usually, but not always, traded while money is used as currency.

But when artists and art-lovers reject commerce, they often do not just have trade in mind. They use the term commerce, the same as *the* market, markets, and sometimes also money in a metaphorical sense. For instance, when somebody says, "Art and money do not go together", he has far more in mind than the currency money.

"Commerce", "the market", "markets" and *"money"* stand for various combinations of different but related things, like the *pursuit of profit*, *compromise*, *economic values*, the *world of commerce,* a *commercialized world*; and sometimes, "*trade in general*" and "*a market economy*". To prevent misunderstanding, I put the terms between inverted commas when used in a metaphorical sense. (Note that whereas Europeans more often use the collective noun *"the market"*, in the USA people more often speak of *"markets"*. The intended meanings are usually the same.)

In this text *profit* and *income* refer to financial gain./1 The terms income and profit are often used in an imprecise way. A private collector can be said to make a profit when he sells an artwork, but he generates income and not profit. The opposite applies to independent artists. We talk about their income and not their profit, but in a legal sense they are for-profits, companies which generate profits. As said, to stress the relativity of the distinction and not to have to explain each time why I use income and not profit and vice versa, I regularly use the term *income/profit* to refer to the one or the other or to both.

In this text the terms "*commerce*", *commercial* and *commercialism* refer to a being much oriented on users in a broad sense, that is, including sponsors, donors and governments, in order to have (more) income or gain or rewards. Artists and art-companies are *oriented on users* and *entrepreneurial*. There is a clear *user-orientation*. This may imply an intense promotion or marketing of the own product and a pursuit of personal "gain" or income/profit but not necessarily. Income may serve art or all sorts of good courses. There does not have to be an orientation on profit-for-the-sake-of-profit. (In principle, the income, gain or reward can be altogether "altruistic", as at present in the case of an artist who by means of an artwork intensely tries to let people participate in Extinction Rebellion protests, directed at measures to contain climate change.)

In practice, when people talk about a commercial artist and commercial art, they associate this with a pursuit of profit-for-the-sake-of-profit. In my approach, this association is often not correct.

In this text when I speak of a *strong profit-orientation* as in a strongly profit-oriented artist or art-company, I have an artist or company in mind who pursues profit-for-the-sake-of-profit and not foremost for other goals. (This explication is useful, because the term profit is also used in a far more general sense, like in the case of an artist making a profit on the sale of an artwork, implying that he can more than cover its cost.)

Commercialization in the arts refers to the phenomenon that with time artists and art-companies become more commercial, that is, they become more user-oriented and entrepreneurial. Although in the period of serious art there is much commerce in the arts, commercialism is probably less than before and after. It follows that there can be *decommercialization* and *recommercialization*.

Many art-lovers do not agree with the recommercialization after 1980. This applies strongest to conservative art-lovers and the leftist, whom I call, *new critics of "commerce"*. Both groups oppose that artists are becoming cultural entrepreneurs. The leftist critics, moreover, criticize a possibly emerging strongly profit-oriented commercial culture industry in the new more user-oriented domain in the arts.

Aside: Sometimes the popular arts are called the commercial arts and, as such, oppose the serious arts.[1] This also shows from the fact that in the UK, courses of "commercial music" are given—some at BA level. Checking the programs all music except serious music is included. But the way I use the term commercial, the provision of classical/serious by nonprofits is sometimes very commercial. There can only be a relative difference between the two domains.

For economists a thing—a good or service—is a *commodity* if it is sold—or offered as a service for payment—and bought on a regular basis. A commodity is usually thought to be a *homogeneous* or *standardized product*, but it can also be relatively *heterogeneous*. There can be *(re)commodification* or *marketization* and *decommodification*.

An example of commodification is that of selling tickets for concerts in parcs, while earlier these concerts were free. As a consequence, there is *price exclusion* [48]. If the opposite happens, it is an example of *de-commodification*. The term commodification can also be used in a metaphoric sense, referring, among others, to homogenization and standardization.

Aside: Nowadays, one regularly comes across a very broad notion of "commodification". People may, for instance, refer to the "commodification of culture". But culture is not something that can possibly be bought and sold. It is no commodity in the normal sense. What they may have in mind is usually not clear. The association(s) is anyway negative. They may think of a collection of previously free cultural products being sold in markets, and/or of increasing commercialism in the world of art and culture and/or of increasing homogenization and less diversity and/or of art and culture becoming part of an industry-produced-culture and/or of the possible phenomenon that cultural products are increasingly used instrumentally and foremost to serve economic goals. Whether used in a literal sense or instead in a narrow or broad metaphorical sense, for artists and art theorists the term commodification tends to have a negative connotation. It is associated with popular art and popular culture.

If there is homogenization, the *substitutability* of artworks increases. One can more easily replace another. Commodification can come together with *standardization* and *homogenization* but not necessarily. Free concerts in parcs may be relatively heterogeneous, and due to commodification become more homogeneous. The opposite is also possible.

I use the term *market* the way it is used in economics. Simplifying a little: in economics a *market* refers to allover trade in a specific commodity in a certain region. (A market is therefore not a specific space where products are sold and bought.) Markets can be small or large. The commodities (or goods and services) that are traded in small markets are also traded in large markets together with related goods and services. For instance, paintings are goods in the market of paintings, while impressionist paintings are goods in the market (or submarket) of impressionist paintings, and a certain kind of impressionist paintings in a sub-submarket, possibly a very small market or *niche market*. It follows that the possible goodness or badness of markets has nothing to do with the size of a market.

In section 48 I distinguished *deep-pocket, medium-pocket and shallow-pocket, as well as niche and mass markets*. I also mentioned the concept of *purchasing power* and the say of various social groups in different markets. Readers may like to have another look at the section.

I occasionally use the concept *imagined market*.[2] People construct in their mind markets which do not really exist, or they organize behavior as if a market existed. The first matters in the arts. For instance, people may negotiate about the payment for a commission. While doing so they have in mind payments in the case of similar commissions and imagine a nonexistent "market"./2

Finally, the way economic terms are used and their importance changes over time. A general trend *over the last decades* is that economic terms are more often used, also in art circles.

(61) "ART AND MONEY DO NOT GO TOGETHER". IN ART-WORLDS THE SHARED ETHOS IS ANTI-COMMERCIAL. THE CULTURE INDUSTRY IS THOUGHT TO BE HARMFUL. Artists, art-lovers and art theorists—especially those on the left side of the political spectrum—are inclined to blame everything or much that is wrong in the arts on "commerce", "the market", neo-liberalism and capitalism. Not all art-lovers and art theorists agree with such convictions, but the notion that the world of art and the world of "commerce" are hostile spheres is widely shared. Each using different terms, famous scholars agree, like Georg Simmel, Max Weber, Arnold Hauser, Theodor Adorno, Max Horkheimer, Luc Boltanski and Eve Chapello.[3] Famous critics like Peter Bürger and Robert Hughes also agree.[4] Some economists as well, like Arjo Klamer, adhere to the notion of hostile spheres.[5]

That many art-lovers regard art and "commerce" as hostile spheres shows, among others, from the phenomenon that an open denunciation of commercialism and commercialization is an important symbol of membership in art circles. "Money corrupts art". Putting "commerce" down can add to a positive mood and feelings of solidarity among artists in a local pub, among art-lovers during an opening reception in a gallery, and so forth. Non-art-lovers often agree. Construction workers during their lunch hour may as well say that money and art do not go together. Art officials, like directors of non-profits, can raise their status by putting down "commerce" in the arts, for instance, in their new year's address/speech, and often more so if they manage to combine it with an anti-capitalist stance. (Presently, this way some directors of large non-profits may well attempt to cover up, or launder, the very commercial activities of the own organization.)

An indirect expression of hostile spheres is that artists sometimes think that money (and not just "money") is the source of much evil. Ever since the beginning of the twentieth century, artists come up with proposals that serve the goal of getting rid of money. And presently some put much energy in the development and small-scale application of systems of exchange in which no ordinary money is used—often forms of barter are involved.[6] Applied at a small scale, this can have advantages, but it is no alternative for money in general. Or more recently they go for crowd-funding (which makes sense), while emphasizing that this is a form of non-monetary exchange (which is not true).[7] Artists anyway can be said to have a problem with money and "money". It is not accidental that over the last hundred years many visual artists have made artworks that involve money.[8]

In spite of commerce, in the sense of buying and selling, and considerable commercialism in the serious arts, during the period of serious art, the shared ethos is anti-commercial. In the prelude to the period, commercialism becomes less strong and/or is more covered up. It is supposed to be less strong than in other sectors of production and in particular the popular arts. But as we have seen and will note again in the next sections, in practice the difference with other sectors is not as large as art-lovers tend to believe.

The main difference with other sectors is a matter of principle: in principle, commercialism in the arts is wrong. The art ethos is indeed *anti-commercial* (or a-commercial).—It can be said to oppose a commercial ethos or "market ethos"./3— What is important in the art ethos is the goodness of autonomy and the badness of compromise. Autonomy and commercialism are thought to be incompatible. The art ethos anyway promotes a less intense commercialism and more "decent" forms of self-promotion and marketing than exist in other sectors, including popular art. But it also contributes to a covering up of commercial activities [67], among others, by gift-giving [68]. An important difference is that in the popular arts, the presence of commerce and commercialism is well-acknowledged, while art-lovers and other participants in art-worlds tend to deny or prefer to overlook their presence.

For many art-lovers, what distinguishes serious artists from popular artists is foremost an anti-commercial attitude. Serious artists are not after money, while popular artists are. The first are therefore more autonomous than the latter. But the differences are relative. In the trajectories of new genres toward mainstream popular art, the artists are increasingly oriented on markets and in that sense become more commercial [23]. But, looking more carefully, an anti-commercial ethos is also widely shared among popular artists; probably mostly so among the huge number of, not very successful, popular music musicians. Moreover, serious artists also depend on market income, but often less so. Some receive subsidies. More can afford to be less oriented on consumer markets because they receive money from non-profits who are oriented on not only subsidies but also money from donors and sponsors. But if this allows them to be more autonomous remains to be seen.

I already presented many examples and proof that art consumers are influenced by others, including companies, and more will follow. They, the same as artists, are little autonomous. It is foremost, so-called, critical theorists who argue that powerful companies directly or indirectly influence the choices and opinions of consumers. Well-known is the text from 1944 of Adorno and Horkheimer and Max Horkheimer *The Culture Industry: Enlightenment as Mass Deception.*[9] The title is telling. As far as art is concerned, they blame foremost the commercial popular art industry./4 When after the 1960 critical students notice that the popular music industry offered interesting and very diverse music, the attention for the body of thought of Adorno and the Frankfurter Schule somewhat diminished.

But *over the last decades* and especially after 2000, the criticism revived along with commercialization in the arts and neo-liberalism. The belief that the commercial popular art industries promote homogeneity and further homogenization in popular art and produce trivial artworks has now also become more important. Art-lovers, moreover, belief that the commercialization of the serious arts will have similar effects. It is questionable if these beliefs are justified. But some marketization of art, that is, art in public space and the public domain certainly occurs and could be worrisome.

The main criticism of art theorists is now not only directed at a possible influence of a culture industry on tastes in popular art, but at the media influencing public opinion and promoting neo-liberalism with its emphasis on the goodness of markets, also markets in the arts. The media leave people little choice and so also reduce their "voice".[10] Moreover, some art theorists argue that given the content of some serious art, this art, the same as some popular art, promotes a neo-liberal mindset.

(62) AT FIRST ARTISTS APPRECIATE THAT EXPANDING MARKETS CONTRIBUTE TO THEIR INCOME AND AUTONOMY. LATER ARTISTS ARE BLAMED FOR MAKING COMMERCIAL ART, ALSO WHEN THE EXTRA INCOME SERVES THE MAKING OF RELATIVELY AUTONOMOUS ART. Before the period of serious art, artists and art-companies did not reject commerce and commercialism. Especially in the seventeenth and eighteenth centuries, there was an orientation on emerging markets and a, sometimes intense, pursuit of income/profit. Market income increased the overall *autonomous space* of artists. Many artists openly embraced commerce and commercialism. This changes during the period of serious art.

In the eighteenth century and even earlier, the autonomous space of those who we now call artist was clearly limited. Many composers but also painters were employees, among others, at the courts of princes and bishops. Most had to take strict orders. Independent master craftsmen in painters' and other guilds produced what was demanded by commissioners and what conformed with the standard of the guild. Within the limits set by the commission, they took pride in qualitative good work. Maecenases gave outstanding independent artists some freedom in the execution of works. Independent creative artists, visual artists, poets, composers and others chose the commissions, which brought most income/profit; and if they were free to travel, they sold their labor to Maecenases like bishops, and princes or cities that offered most income. Their freedom in the execution of their paintings, musical compositions, plays, poems and performances was very limited as well./5 If they had some autonomous space—successful artists had more autonomous space—they reduced it again by attempting to please their commissioner in order to raise their reputation and longer-term income. The artists can be said to have adhered to a commercial logic.

Sometimes the bond between lord and artist was more like a feudal bond. Employers, that is, the Patrons, gave artists along with a considerable reputation more artistic freedom, but their overall autonomy was limited. Many artists, like Bach (1685–1750), had to ask permission for traveling. Or they were still regarded as minor servants. *When in the service of the Esterházy family, Haydn (1732–1809) wore livery and had to sit with the servants. (At the time Haydn already had quite a reputation and he complained about it, but unsuccessfully.*[11]*)*

But the dependence of artists on others must not be exaggerated.

Visual artists belonged to painters' guilds, which limited their freedom, but they usually had more autonomous space than composers. Peter Paul Rubens (1547–1640) successfully had run a large studio and business. In contemporary terms Rubens was a good "cultural entrepreneur". He, for instance, looked for and developed a niche market for his work. He also pursued, acquired and executed privileges, like the privilege that prevented others from copying his works without payment. Rubens is no exception: he is representative for many artists running an own business. Evidently running a business is not incompatible with being innovative in art.

Artists not only took commissions, they also produced for stock and sold works from their stock. *Production for stock* refers to the phenomenon that entrepreneurs produce work without knowing for sure if they will be able to sell the products. Up to the present day, this is *the* business model in the visual arts, and, to a lesser degree, also in other art forms./6

Maybe not Rubens, but the Bruegel family and many other artists not only took commissions but also "produced for stock". They sold works in their studios. Some painters had a real shop with works displayed in front of the shop or in the shop window, comparable with the way art is now sold in open-air markets.

Working for stock is indeed still the business model in the visual arts, but selling immediately to consumers has become less common. The phenomenon of selling works with the use of an intermediate art-company, that is, a dealer, increases much in the eighteenth and nineteenth centuries, and this contributes to some commercialization and internationalization of the visual art trade.[12] In the case of music and dance performances, the same phenomenon occurs in the twentieth century. Commercialization in publishing and the consequent selling of technically (re)produced artworks, in particular, books and sheet music, starts earlier. In the eighteenth century, publishers sold copies of large series in large markets using sophisticated marketing techniques. This way, most of all in England, music publishers contributed much to the growth of the overall market of music, including that of live performances.[13]

At first composers mainly earned money in markets from the sale of sheet music. So-called Hausmusik—often simplified versions of own compositions—represented an important source of income for composers. For more income from commissioned work and live performances, they had to wait for the emergence and liberation of markets. In the course of the eighteenth century, along with the growing importance of a market economy in society at large, their financial situation improves and more importantly their autonomy increases. They operate in a growing "market" for commissioned performances and compositions.

The case of Mozart is interesting. He stood at the crossroads of a non-market economy, a rather regulated market economy and a largely unregulated market economy. In 1781 he left his position at the court of the prince-bishop in Salzburg and established himself as an independent artist, that is, a self-employed artist. He first went to Paris, but within the centrally controlled music scene in France, and therefore in a de facto *regulated market, he had no success. Next, he tried his luck in Vienna. There he successfully provided music in a local largely free "market" for commissions of compositions and subscription concerts and operas. The concerts were frequented by noblemen, aristocrats and an increasing number of patricians. He also offered his services in a market for piano lessons. (For a while Mozart could make a living from these activities, but not for long. But the consumers in these local art markets were still very sensitive to the artistic judgment of the emperor. When they noticed that Mozart's music was not appreciated by the emperor, the local society let him down. Mozart faced financial problems and was disappointed. He died as an embittered person.)*

This takes us again to the issue of the open pursuit of income/profit and commercialism. As said [13], in an intermediate period between the traditional old-style worlds of art and the emergence of new-style art-worlds, markets are relatively free and there is considerable commercialism in the arts. In the new market economy, composers are indeed not ashamed of pursuing (more) income, and not just income for the sake of art. *Mozart (1756–1791) wrote to his father: "Believe me, my sole purpose is to make as much money as possible; for after good health it is the best thing to have".*[14] *But around that time, already a modern art ethos is developing. Beethoven (1770–1827) expresses himself differently. "I am not out to be a musical usurer as you think, who writes only to become rich, by no means! Yet, I love an independent life, and this I cannot have without a small income".*[15] *—As an independent artist and entrepreneur, Beethoven can be said to have pursued and realized "income/profit for a reasonable standard of living".—*

In the nineteenth century, when impressionist painters and composers of romantic music offer their works in art markets or otherwise in imagined markets of commissions, they clearly have an intention to pursue predominantly artistic goals when making art, but markets remain their friends rather than enemies. Markets enable them to be more autonomous. Income/profit serves art; it is income/profit for art. But compromising is evidently not yet taboo. Even the later paragon of the selfless (and supposedly poor) artist Van Gogh (1853–1890) is eager to sell and is willing to make other work, if this other work, unlike his "own" work, would sell, as he mentions in the letters he writes to his brother.[16]

In the middle of the nineteenth century, Dickens (1812–1870), whose works have successfully been turned into classics and who is regarded by many as the greatest novelist of the Victorian era, combined a clear social message with evident attempts to please his well-to-do readership./7—If he had written his texts a century later, he would have been disqualified by diehards in the literary art-world as a non-serious writer, not only for offering entertainment, but also for openly inserting a political message in his works.—

All in all, in the course of the seventeenth till nineteenth centuries, the dependency of artists on Patron and Maecenas is replaced by a dependency on markets. As said, art markets expanded along with increased prosperity and with a somewhat less skewed distribution of wealth and income as well as some democratization in the higher echelons of society. They are not experienced as a burden but as a benefit. It is true that earlier a good-willing Maecenas and Patron sometimes offered the more talented artists a limited "dependent independency", but in the case of markets, the overall dependent independence of artists is much larger.[17] It follows that *the notion that the creation of relatively autonomous art and an orientation on markets are incompatible is a fallacy.* Art and money can go well together, and do not necessarily represent hostile spheres. New markets allow artists to make relatively autonomous work. At the time most artists did not distinguish between relatively autonomous or own art and art for a market. They perceive all their art as own art. This changes in the course of the period of serious art.

During this period the contribution of markets to the relative autonomy of artists becomes routine and the awareness that markets often increase the relative autonomy of artists disappears. In the twentieth century, offering their art in markets, artists start to focus on their dependence rather than independence. They increasingly stress the importance of being autonomous and of not compromising. That income/profit from both relatively autonomous and relatively market-oriented art, and that an intense pursuit of income/profit, that is, commercialism, can increase the artist's overall artistic autonomous space, is altogether forgotten.

As noted, during the period of serious art, bourgeois spend money increasingly on art in general, and on serious art. An important trademark of serious art is that, unlike popular/inferior art, it is supposed to be not commercial. As said, the pursuit of profit/income is thought to be unimportant. Its market, moreover, is not formally regulated but it is indirectly controlled by gatekeeping art-worlds [14]. Only artists who believe in the anti-commercial art ethos as promoted by art-worlds have, in principle, access to the market. And given the grandeur of art and the art ethos, compromising is the worst thing serious artists can do [70]./8 Art is good; profit is bad. This goes so far that in the twentieth century, consumers are often regarded as enemies of art and artists. Consumers are thought to keep artists from making relatively autonomous or own art.

Presently, in the more user-oriented domain in the established arts, major nonprofit art-companies no longer see consumers as enemies of art and artists. Serious artists, moreover, have broadened the group of consumers they trust and are happy to offer their art to them.

(63) ALSO DURING THE PERIOD OF SERIOUS ART, THERE IS CONSIDERABLE BUYING AND SELLING AND COMMERCIALISM IN THE ARTS. BUT THE ETHOS IS ANTI-COMMERCIAL. Art objects and tickets are sold and bought. Some artists resent this [65], but most do not. More artists have a problem, not with commerce in an economic sense, but with consumers and their insufficient demand for good serious art, and with, more or less, commercial art-companies which force or persuade them to make commercial choices. For most artists, for most expert/critics and for many art-lovers, commercialism and a fanatic pursuit of profit which go at the cost of artistic autonomy are taboo.

The shared art ethos is anti-commercial. In the beginning of the period of serious art, there is, indeed, decommercialization: commercialism and the pursuit of profit become less intense and more covered up. But all through this period, the two are far from absent. After circa 1980, they become more intense again. There is recommercialization.

First, it is important to keep in mind that, in spite of sometimes much support, serious art-companies, artists, dealers, impresarios and publishers, de facto, compete with one another and with other providers of luxury goods. They cannot escape *market forces*; they are always influenced by the demands of others—be it in different degrees. In spite of nonprofits, many art-world participants pursue profit and often consumer demand affects supply.—This is what economists expect.—

The most convincing proof of, supposedly selfless, artists being (also) commercial and after money is the phenomenon of visual artists and art photographers maximizing profit by choosing a small edition size bringing most profit (and reputational benefits). Consumers are also not "innocent": when they have sufficient money they are willing to pay for exclusivity. The phenomenon occurs at all levels of the market and can therefore not be explained from low incomes and a wish to survive as artist./9

For-profit art-companies can be expected to represent the most commercial group of art-world participants. This certainly applies to the majority of dealers in the Paris art-world in the 1920s and 1930s. There was a "cutthroat commercialism".[18] Such commercialism does not apply to all periods and to all for-profit art-companies—let alone to all creative artists. In the mentioned field of restricted production in the arts, small publishers and many dealers are not (very) commercial. They do not fanatically promote their activities. And in as far as they are after gain, they are foremost interested in a good reputation and profit in the long run.—In this respect an anti-commercial stance can be profitable.—Thanks to the not-orchestrated, but nevertheless attuned behavior of art-world participants, this also applies to whole art-worlds. The anti-commercial stance of art-worlds brings prestige to the participants in a society in which everything appears to be about "money".

Through the book I gave many examples of influence which I will not repeat here. Given the fact that there is considerable, but covered up commercialism during the period of serious art, commercialization after circa 1980, that is, *over the last decades*, must not be exaggerated. But there is recommercialization. The process has maybe accelerated over the last two decades. Up to the present day, the expressed shared ethos in the arts is anti-commercial, but the ethos has weakened and its impact on actual behavior has become less strong. Instrumental decision-making, commercialism and the pursuit of profit become more intense and are less covered up. This shows from a stronger orientation on not only consumers, but also sponsors, donors and governments. It also shows from more intense enrichment practices and marketing by art-companies, which accompanies a stronger winner-take-all mechanism. Higher up in the markets, the activities of "taste makers" in the media certainly contribute to commercialization.[19]

(64) Excurse. SOME ECONOMISTS ARGUE THAT MARKETS ARE GOOD; ALSO GOOD IN THE ARTS. MARKETS ARE THOUGHT TO PROMOTE CONSUMER SOVEREIGNTY. CRITICAL THEORISTS DO NOT AGREE. Many economists depart from the notion that markets are in principle good, but also acknowledge that they can "fail". The notion of market failure stems from welfare economics, a well-known branch in economics, which I briefly explain in web-text 19. Because some art policy makers still refer and base recommendations on welfare economic findings, students in cultural economics are advised to read the web-text.

In the web-text concepts, like public good, external effect and merit good are explained Their existence make markets "fail"; markets cannot properly handle them. Sometimes there is also attention for an unwanted unequal distribution of income. Or for monopolies. They also make markets fail and prevent that markets can properly function./10 It is significant that in this context economists speak of market "failures".

The use of the term "failure" suggests that many economists depart from the goodness of markets and of the goodness of a free market economy. Subsidies and regulations may be required to correct markets, but these interventions in the working of markets should be as limited as possible. Talking with economists it is good to keep in mind that many depart from the notion that markets are, in principle, good.

Aside: This is not to say that all economists interested in the welfare economic approach believe in the overall goodness of markets. Earlier some saw everywhere market failures and pleaded for a centrally led economy./11 Around 1970 more economists—at the time I was one of them—emphasized the shortcomings of markets and subsequently the need for generous (art)subsidies. (This was not accidental because at the time, other economists proposed to reduce subsidies, because they foremost ended up in the pockets of well-to-do people. As noted: they had a point.)

There are many economists who are aware that demand does not always determine supply. Supply can create demand and must create demand when products are new. Innovative artists have to develop a (niche) market for their work, or otherwise the nonprofits must develop niche markets for them. But these economists nevertheless argue that in the end consumers have the final say. Given the possibilities and impossibilities of producers, in the long run they determine the outcome of market interaction and are therefore sovereign. Demand determines supply.

But as I will show, in art-worlds demand influences supply, but it certainly does not determine supply. Several parties, including consumers and producers, depend on one another. There is *interdependence*. Given a shared art ethos, within the overall network, preferences become attuned. No single party has a final say. Experts, consumers, nonprofits, art schools, dealers, impresarios and so forth, all depend on one another, and the say of each of them is always limited. Artists or nonprofits are never altogether sovereign or autonomous.

Finally, it must be noted that the belief that "consumer wishes must come first" and consumers must be sovereign is important for the justification of *neo-liberalism*, which from the 1980s onward becomes an important force in society. The goodness of markets is emphasized and often *deregulation* and *marketization* are promoted, also in the arts.

Disapproval and Covering Up of Commerce

(65) ART IS SOMETIMES THOUGHT TO BE TOO PRECIOUS AND PERSONAL TO BE SOLD. In practice art is always *alienable*, but for many artists it should not be. And if it is sold and bought, works must be unique and not substitutable, while prices must certainly not stand for quality. In practice, in spite of much goodness, art is not treated like certain other precious goods, like children (or women), whose buying and selling in most countries is taboo and even forbidden by law.[20] For artists their art may be very precious, its buying and selling is not taboo. Nevertheless, artists sometimes resent having to sell their work. They rather keep it or give it away, instead of exchanging it for money.

Many creative artists, visual artists, composers, writers and so forth, look at their work as being their children. They feel that they put their soul in the work, and often dealers, directors and publishers as well as consumers agree [27]. As said, the artist is "in the work". Therefore, selling art is selling part of oneself./12 *The American painter Mark Rothko indeed stated that his artworks were his children and that he experienced selling them as painful.*[21] *(But opinions differ. Exactly because she regards her drawings as very valuable children, Anna does not want them to stay in her chest of drawers. They must go out into the world and she is happy to sell her drawing. Her children give her "voice".)*

If works are sold, their final destination can also make a difference. What is hard for many artists is a mere rational and business-like exchange with consumers, dealers or publishers. Moreover, some destinations of works are more impersonal and alienating than others. For some artists knowing the buyer and liking him makes selling easier. But if artworks end up in the storage room of collectors and museums or on the shelves of publishers, and are never shown or performed or printed and published, this certainly is hard for artists.

Anna often prefers to sell her works through her commercial-gallery to people she does not know and probably will never know. But sometimes her dealer sends potential buyers to her studio to meet up with "the artist". And it is true that there were occasions that she enjoyed getting to know them. They became friends. But two regular buyers of her work she hates. She would much rather have that they bought her work only in the gallery or not at all. Evidently also for Anna parting of her "children" is a personal affair. /13)

Even though artworks are alienable, they are, indeed, a class apart, also in society at large. This shows from the fact that artists do not have to give up their authorship and thus their symbolic ownership. Symbolically the work continues to "belong" to the artist. Society acknowledges this. In some countries this leads to the phenomenon that in the case of certain types of artworks, the legal rights of the owner of an artwork are limited: the owner may not change or destroy a work. In other countries, like England, destroying a work is not punishable, but the person who destroys a major work is shamed. *When in England it turned out that the late wife of Churchill had destroyed a portrait of her husband painted by Graham Sutherland, a portrait which Churchill hated, there was much indignation.*

Nowadays many artists have started selling their works through the internet. There is no enjoyable relationship with a caring dealer and usually also no personal relation with buyers. It, nevertheless, appears that even on the internet, buyers and artists often communicate and that this is satisfying. But on average selling and buying is undoubtedly going to be more anonymous.

(66) MANY ARTISTS AND ART-LOVERS RESENT THAT THE SELLING AND BUYING OF ARTWORKS MAKES THE WORKS COMPARABLE AND LESS UNIQUE. THEY ALSO RESENT THAT MARKET SUCCESS MAY STAND FOR ARTISTIC QUALITY. Most art is not given but sold and bought (or commissioned). It is exchanged for money and it has a price. Visual artworks can have lower or higher prices. Prices of other art, like records or books, do not differ

that much, but being priced more or less can be sold. In either case market success can stand for artistic quality.

When artworks are traded, there is *commensurability*. Given a common denominator, that is, the currency money, their value in terms of money is comparable. Prices paid are comparable. The financial value of this painting is twice the price of a holiday in Greece; and it is four times as high as the price of this other painting. Or the ticket price of this concert is as high as that of a meal in a restaurant and twice as high as that of another performance.

That buyers and sellers in this respect compare artworks with holidays or with other artworks is inevitable. Artists as well as art-lovers nevertheless experience this as painful or wrong. The economists Arjo Klamer argues: "…the monetary measurement of value may corrode the art experience".[22] Oscar Wilde is more outspoken in his famous and much quoted remark: "Nowadays people know the price of everything and the value of nothing".[23] More interesting is that Arnold Hauser, points at imagined standardization. He writes: "People get used to buying what they find in stock at the art dealer's and begin to regard the work of art as just as standardized and impersonal commodity as any other".[24]

What artists and art-lovers resent is indeed that, given trade in art, artworks are *substitutable*. What is detested is that when art is for sale it has a price and this may cause people to forget about the "true value" of art. Commerce is rejected. Ideally art should not be for sale. But even if artworks would be free, this will not stop people from making financial comparisons./14

In 2010 Anna saw the huge sculpture The Virgin Mother by Damien Hirst in public space—and thus for free—in front of Aby Rosen's Lever House in New York. She much liked the sculpture, but she also knew what the sculpture had cost—$5 million in 2008—and she could not stop herself from wondering if the artistic value of the work deserved such a high price. She believes that in this respect, the price is ridiculously high. She also thinks about the possibility that Aby Rosen could have spent the money on more and cheaper artworks or donated it to a foundation funding the education of disadvantaged kids. In short, she makes comparisons, most of which involve financial value.

As noted [48], prices have symbolic meanings. Prices "talk".[25] For the buyer of one of the five *Balloon Dogs* of Jeff Koons, its high price stands for artistic value, as well as exclusivity, as well as the possibility of becoming member of a very select group and more of such things. Prices not only have such symbolic meanings in the top of art markets. They talk at all levels and in all markets. (*When Anna is about to buy new headphones and sees that the price of one is much higher than that of another, she almost automatically assumes that the higher priced headphone is better.*)

Most artists do not like it when for consumers, price or market success stands for quality. They prefer that people judge their work for artistic qualities and hate that sometimes non-artistic factors come first. This can be the price but also other non-artistic factors. (*This is what Anna experienced in the illustration. She, however, also experienced that for herself non-artistic factors mattered as well.*/15) Other non-artistic factors, indeed, matter for judgments on artistic quality. For instance, the sex of the artist matters. The artistic value of works made by women artists is systematically judged to be lower than those of comparable works made by male artists [46].

For the analysis of the social economy of art, the phenomenon that for art consumers price often stands for artistic quality of artworks is most important. *Market success* often stands for quality. "The prices of Anna's portraits are so much higher than those of her colleague. Her work must be better". Or in the 1960s or 1970s, someone may have said: "More recordings of Von Karajan conducting Beethoven symphonies are being sold than of any other conductor. His must be really good". An inverse relationship is also possible. "Because Justin Bieber's work sells so extremely well, his work must be super mainstream and really bad". (*This is not what Anna says.*)

It is indeed market performance or sales that matters and not necessarily the height of prices. The prices of the Von Karajan records may well have been the same as those of his colleagues. Nevertheless, in the case of art objects, it is usually prices that are significant for consumers, while in the case of recordings, books, posters, performance tickets and cinema tickets this is foremost sales in terms of money or (more often) in terms of numbers sold. Sales are sometimes presented in charts. Evidently such charts as well are significant for consumers.

Other than one may expect, not only art-companies but also artists and even experts sometimes, opportunistically or not, go along with the conviction that a higher price or more sales correspond with a higher artistic value. They are at least double minded. They may not straightforwardly say that high prices or sales stand for quality, but when a work is sold for a high price or concerts are expensive and sold out, there are always experts who point at the extraordinary good qualities of the works and performances—and so, de facto, justify commercial success. (Recently this happened when Hockney's Pool with Two Figures was sold for a ridiculous high price.)

The developments in prices can be significant as well. If the prices of the artworks of an artist rise rapidly, this indicates that his reputation goes up, that his work must be very good and that prices may rise further. Dealers will certainly mention this to potential buyers. For the same reason, they would not like customers to note that prices go down. This is the reason why they discourage or forbid artists to lower their price even though this in the short run may generate more income. This is a problem which many older artists face.[26]

Worth mentioning in the context of this section is the ongoing discussion among art theorists on the relation between artistic value and economic value. Do they correspond or do they not correspond? The idea is that expert/critics determine artistic value and commercial producers determine economic value, in terms of prices or sales. Most art-lovers and artists believe or hope that the two are unrelated and that therefore there is no correspondence. Neo-classical economists on the other hand expect that there is much correspondence.

Experts and commercial producers are not independent. All major groups within art-worlds—experts/critics, official art education organizations, consumers and the producers: artists, non-profit art-companies and for-profit art-companies—depend on one another and are influenced by one another. *Over the last decades*, interdependence increases [88]. Given interdependence, no or almost no correspondence is unlikely, but also a maximum of correspondence is unlikely. Moreover, with increasing interdependence, correspondence between artistic and economic value may well increase.

The neo-classical economist William Grampp is well-known for his research in which he finds much correspondence. His research is criticized by other social scientists who also did research. In most research an indicator of institutional or art-world-recognition of artists, which stands for artistic quality, is compared with prices (or sales) standing for economic value.[27]/16

The results are inconclusive and also little significant. This is because in the researches the position of only a small group of most successful visual artists (around 100) is examined. This group is unlikely to be representative of all visual artists. The large majority operates at the bottom of the market. I expect that at that level correspondence is not very low. However, slightly higher up, in the realm of recognized, but little recognized artists, correspondence could be somewhat higher. At this level there is more interdependence between expert critics and commercial dealers. But this is uncertain, because as far as I know, no research exists on a representative group of visual artists or creative artists in other disciplines.—It would also be more difficult.—

Even though people do not "know the price of everything and the value of nothing", it is possible that (*over the last decades*) in times of finance capitalism more people know the prices of more artworks—Anna does—or otherwise wonders about prices or asks for them. It is therefore likely that in people's self-constructed artworks, financial value is more often present. It colors the overall work. Finance capitalism in a broad sense is not "innocent". In many spheres, including that of the arts, it "infiltrates" our thinking.

(67) REJECTION OF COMMERCE LEADS TO ITS CONCEALMENT. SPONSORS WHO PURCHASE ART-RELATED PRODUCTS OFTEN PRETEND THIS IS PHILANTHROPY. SPONSORS AND DONORS SOMETIMES USE ART TO LAUNDER AND COVER UP OWN BLAMEWORTHY ACTIVITIES. Commerce in the arts is supposed to be a necessary evil. It does not befit the sacredness of art. Therefore, using various means, market participants try to conceal and cover up commerce; or they pretend that what is commerce is gift-giving and not really commerce. The goodness of art calls forward such behavior. Art is for art's sake and not for the sake of money. Personal interests are disavowed. But in practice, techniques for covering up interests often serve commerce.

Because market participants expect from one another that they go along with the apparent disavowal of interests and appreciate this, the person who in the arts is open about having a financial interest in buying and selling is at a disadvantage. His profit is less than the profit of those who pretend that it is all about art and not about money. It follows that in the arts, it can be "commercial to be non-commercial" or, as Bourdieu says: "the economic world is reversed".[28]

Because commerce, that is, buying and selling, is much more pronounced in the case of unique visual artworks than in the case of books and performance tickets with fixed prices, the need to cover up commerce is strongest in the visual arts. I give a few examples. The first is very straightforward. Unlike in other shops, in serious commercial art galleries, there are no price tags next to the artworks which are for sale. Sacred objects are "priceless". (As noted, there is art and not-really art. The absence and presence of price tags is a good indicator of art being real art or instead inferior-art.)

Also without tags, works must be sold and bought; money must pass hands or—preferably because less notable—a bill is offered which is paid later. But the trade aspect can still be mitigated by a separation in time and/or space of commercial and non-commercial activities. At one moment and/or in one space, there is commerce and commercialism, while at other moments and/or in another space there is only attention for art.

When Anna welcomes the collector Mr. de Bruin in her studio, the conversation is almost exclusively about art, about the importance of art for people and about the high quality of Anna's work. Only during a short intermezzo De Bruin asks Anna for the price of a drawing and they negotiate. The atmosphere during the intermezzo differs from before and after: the conversation is efficient and down to earth. De Bruin tells about a comparable work he recently bought which was cheaper than Anna's. Anna offers a rebate and De Bruin buys the drawing. Next the earlier pleasant and civilized conversation is resumed, as if nothing happened in between.

In commercial-galleries sometimes not only a temporal but also a spatial separation is created. There is a spacious front room, often a cube with white walls, which is totally dedicated to art. The atmosphere is relaxed and serious. And there is a backroom, which serves the administration and commerce. Here are shelves with files, a desk with one or more monitors, a telephone and sometimes also a busy assistant.[29] The visitor who wants to buy a work is led into this space where the acts necessary for selling and buying are realized.

Artists and art-companies often sell non-art products as well. This can be coffee to consumers. Or, in the case of sponsors, it is advertisement space. Selling coffee is okay, but in the period of serious art, selling advertisement space to sponsors is suspect. It brings art down. And even today many art-lovers have more problems with sponsoring than with donations. They are right in being suspicious. Major sponsor contracts may well influence the overall art product of art-companies. But in practice, the influence of large donations is often larger [75]. However, due to a rejection of "commerce" in the arts, they are glad to hear about donations, while they are suspicious when noticing that the name of the art-company is used for advertisement by a commercial non-art-company. But along with a degree of re-commercialization, the group who is suspicious is becoming smaller.

An indirect proof of covering up is that sponsors and art-companies have started to, sometimes, call sponsors donors and donors sponsors. Both are good for art and art-companies. For the general public, the terms are now often interchangeable. This is extra welcome for sponsors, who want to cover up not only the commercial aspect of the exchange with the art-company but also their own detrimental activities. They want to launder the latter by being good for art; that is, art with its high prestige in society.

Donors are, indeed, no sponsors, but if they wish they receive goods, services and, in the case of large donors, sometimes influence in the management of art-companies "in return" for their gift. There is an exchange aspect, which especially in the case of large donations is covered up. The donation is emphasized and the return is not. As we shall see [75], major donors, sometimes donate millions and "buy" exposure, membership and influence.

Aside: Also in the case of small donations, returns are a form of exchange. The donation is a condition for receiving more or less "goodies". It is a special form of commerce. Not all donors are interested in the "goodies". But for others, it can be the extra which just persuades them to donate. However, the aspect of covering up is limited. There is some covering up because the donation is not just a donation but less so because the returns are well advertised; otherwise less people would donate.

The "laundering" by a buyer, sponsor or donor of own "bad" activities by associating their name with art, art that has goodness, is also a form of covering up of commerce. Ever since the middle of the twentieth century, tobacco companies with their worsening reputation "bought" a better reputation. By collecting visual art and sponsoring art museums and performing art organizations they attempted to launder an unhealthy product. They collect more visual art and sponsor more than other companies who collect and sponsor. Although the product of banks is not necessarily bad, for many people, their reputation is not good and they as well have large collection. Later tobacco companies and banks are joined by oil companies, who foremost sponsor art-companies. They also attempt to launder activities, which are increasingly judged to be detrimental.

Over the last decades there are still no price tags next to works of art in commercial serious art commercial-galleries and there may never be. This is understandable, since with ever more art fairs and sales through internet platforms, the remaining galleries have to distinguish themselves. Having no price tags probably helps.

The schemes for smaller donors have become more elaborate and calculated and better advertised [75]. This also applies to the possible returns. Covering up has become less important.

At the same time, however, the new critics of "commerce" become more critical of certain well-advertised large donations and sponsorship by commercial companies, which evidently serve the covering up of bad behavior. If the core business of the donor or sponsor is detrimental, there are now more often protests. An example is that of artists openly protesting against the support of British Petrol of Tate Modern./17 The support, the same as that of the Edinburgh festival, was terminated. So far, the trustees of the National Portrait Gallery in London do not consider to seek another sponsor for the famous yearly BP Portrait Reward. (But they may listen to Nan Golding, who in February 2019 threatened to boycott the gallery because of a planned donation of £1 million from a fund of the pharmaceutical family with a link to the addictive painkiller OxyContin./18)

Aside: Banks still advertise their art collections, but less so than 30 years ago. Instead the departments of banks, which earlier were only responsible for the management of the own collection, now foremost use their expertise to advise rich people and smaller companies on investing in art and/or setting up a collection. It is a profitable activity.

Several explanations have already been given for the phenomenon that the new very rich increasingly spend money on the purchase of visual art. In the background an aspect of whitewashing is almost always present. Being extremely rich in times of financial crises and an ever more extreme and unfair distribution of income calls forward resentment. Diverting attention to good deeds can make a difference.

(68) IN THE ARTS A CULTURE OF GENEROSITY EXISTS, WHICH MASKS AS WELL AS FACILITATES COMMERCE. IT ADDS TO THE EXPLOITATION OF ARTISTS. In the previous section certain kinds of gifts serve the covering up of commerce. There are many other kinds of gifts. Together they are part of a "culture of generosity", a culture that is stronger in the arts than in most other sectors of production. This culture covers up commerce, but, just as important: it facilitates and serves commerce. This is not acknowledged. Instead people think that gift-giving and commerce are opposites, opposites that can replace one another. But they are not. Therefore, as said, there undoubtedly is decommercialization in the period of serious art, but, again, less than one may think.

In trade a quid pro quo exists "you can have this, if I can have that". This does not apply to *gift-giving*. Nevertheless, in almost all gift-giving there is an exchange aspect as well. An expectation of counter gifts exists.—These can be tangible and/or intangible.—This is why social scientists sometimes use the term *gift exchange*. Moreover, because gift-giving by various partners in a sector of production is usually interrelated, they also speak of a *gift economy*.[30] It is an economy that supplements the *market economy* based on quid pro quo exchanges. A market economy can probably not exist without a parallel gift economy.

Buying and selling is often accompanied by gifts—from friendly conversations to rebates. The phenomenon of gift-giving exists in all sectors of production, even at the floor of the stock exchange, but in the arts a "culture of generosity" exists that is particularly strong. Gift-giving is normal and expected.[31] The culture is promoted by a shared art ethos in which the conviction that art is good and commerce and commercialism are bad is strong. An "everything for art" calls for gift-giving and not for commerce. And if commerce is inevitable, gift-giving can take its edge off. But it is more than an inner-art-world laundering of commerce; due to the association with the goodness of art, it facilitates commerce: and probably more than in other sectors of production.

When there is a clear expectation of possible future gain, gift-giving tends to be more or less calculated. But when, for instance, a warm relationship between partners has developed, like between a visual artist and a dealer, or a writer and a publisher, gift-giving is less calculated and often automatic.—The warm relationship is by itself already a form of gift-exchange. Unless something unexpected happens, the financial transactions are accompanied by a stream of intangible gifts. (Nevertheless, often power differences exist, which are somewhat covered up by gift-giving.)

In the relationship between producers and customers, interests are clearer and gift-giving better noticeable. The buyer has an interest in a lower price and the seller in a higher price. They may negotiate, but most sellers are not prepared to do so. Instead, dealers and visual artists often give discounts, discounts that are higher for certain buyers and lower or absent in the case of others. The price difference is a tangible gift. Intangible gifts also matter in the relationship with customers. These can run from short term flattery to a long-term friendship.

The return to flattery is an immediate return but, whether or not the people involved are aware of this, many gift exchanges are a longer-term "investment"; an investment in possible later tangible and/or intangible returns. The dealer (or publisher or impresario) hopes to continue his relationship with an artist who may well become more successful. Or he and an artist hope that the collector comes again. The collector hopes that the dealer will inform him earlier than others about a forthcoming sale of a work the collector likes. The artist hopes that the dealer (or impresario or publisher) will help him with his further career. And so forth.

Aside: Because all such future returns are ultimately uncertain, partners who trade and exchange gifts, in various degrees, trust one another. No trade and no gift-giving without trust. Will the buyer who took the painting with him transfer the agreed upon price. Will the visitor who paid for a ticket be enabled to listen to the promised concert? Returns are uncertain and this applies strongest to longer-term returns. By now most economists emphasize that trust is essential in trade. This runs counter to the common notion of commerce. Commerce is associated with a simple quid pro quo and not with uncertainty and returns to gifts. But a market economy can only exist when there is also gift-giving and trust.

The exchange of gifts and the presence of trust do, indeed, not imply that no power differences exist. It can be the opposite. Given the culture of generosity, people are nice and friendly toward one another, but often, given power differences, one party must be more thankful for the other's gift than the other party. In giving commissions or employing artists Maecenas and Patron of old appeared to be generous; they supported artists, while the artist offered a counter gift by being thankful. But they may well have exploited artists. At present the same often occurs in the relationship between non-profits and artists. The latter offer artists work and chances but underpay artists who are supposed to be thankful.

Handling gift relations in the arts requires skills. This is what Anna experienced. *In the 1980s Anna had a dealer who treated her and colleagues badly because he was always late in paying them; otherwise he was friendly and supportive. At one time the dealer owed Anna and her colleague and friend Eric each an extraordinary large sum of money. (He evidently had cash flow problems.) After a long time, he paid Anna but not her friend. At first Anna found this hard to understand, but later she realized the cause. She had mastered the "generosity game" in the arts and her friend had not. They both had complained about the clearly overdue debts, but Anna had in a theatrical way called for the dealer's sympathy by telling him that she could no longer pay the rent of her studio and that the paint she used turned viscose from cold, because she could not pay for gas. None of this was true, and her dealer probably knew this. But she gave him a gift: the chance to play the role of a benevolent "maecenas" who could now help her, a "poor and miserable" artist. The dealer wholeheartedly paid her, as if this was not a payment but a gift, and Anna told him how thankful she was. Her proud colleague Eric on the other hand, had complained in a business-like and unemotional fashion. He had threatened to involve a collecting agent. Evidently, given his earlier socialization—he had a lower-class background—he had not been schooled in the ways of the art-world. In the end the dealer paid him but no longer wanted to represent him and his work. Though in Anna's view Eric was a good artist, after more disappointments he left the arts and joined an advertisement company.*

By taking so much time to pay, the dealer exploited the weaker party: his artists. That is, artists, who moreover are obliged to be thankful in return. Not very successful artists—the majority—regularly come in situations in which due to their low income there is an imbalance in power and they must be thankful, while they are de facto being exploited, and not only by commercial producers but also by non-profits. There is inner-art-world exploitation of artists [45].

If a contract had been drafted in which rights and obligations are made before artist and dealer start to work with one another, problems as those of Anna and her friend Eric may not arise, but in the case of not very successful artists, this is not done. It would signal distrust and not friendship. Having no contracts "softens" commerce while enabling exploitation of little successful artists.

All this is not to say that exploitation is deliberate. Not only artists but also dealers, impresarios, managers and publishers compete with one another. Some of the latter also have low incomes, be it generally not as low as those of the artists they work with. Most of the time they as well have no choice but to go along with "market forces".

That trust relations can work out badly applies to the majority of artists (and nowadays also to most interns). It usually does not apply to other workers in the arts who earn normal or above normal incomes. For them the benefits of trust in the buying and selling of goods and services usually well-exceeds possible costs. This includes the selling and buying of people's labor, in the case of employees and employers of art-companies. In the relationship of bookers, programmers, impresarios and dealers with larger companies, trust is very important and usually beneficial for all parties.

Because performing artists in larger ensembles are employees, who as a group have more power than individual artists and can negotiate, their incomes are low but not very low incomes. Or employers must at least pay the minimum wage. But *over the last decades*, their bargaining power has gone down, while employers have found ways to employ them without offering longer-term contracts. The same as most creative artists, they have become independent workers. In our gig economy, they are no exception. Now many more "independent" workers depend on trust relations with incomes that resemble gifts or gratuities. They as well have to be thankful. In a neo-liberal environment commercialization in the form of a fanatic pursuit of profit—or income in the case of nonprofits—by lowering labor cost of the weakest parties has contributed to this development.

Thanks to technological developments, in the case of an increasing number of visual artists, an opposite trend occurs. Thanks to the internet, now sales directly to customers or indirectly with the help of platforms are realized without a need for trust relations. In their case a larger independence may well reduce exploitation. People offering the specialized platform services possibly earn high incomes, but the cost of running a platform is low, as are fees or commissions for artists. At the moment many visual artists already earn an income by using the general platform of Instagram for free.

For other creative artists like composers and writers, thanks to the internet, new opportunities will undoubtedly develop, but benefits will probably be lower. Many performers/composers of popular music already use social media to advertise their work on social platforms. They would not do this if there were no benefits in the form of a somewhat higher income.

Commercialism and Dependence of Artists and Art-Companies on Demand, Sponsorship and Support

(69) Introduction: IN DIFFERENT DEGREES, ARTISTS AND ART-COMPANIES PRODUCE ART THAT IS ORIENTED ON VISITORS, BUYERS, SUPPORTERS, SPONSORS AND ART-WORLDS. *Over the last decades*, ART-COMPANIES AND ARTISTS BECOME MORE OTHER- OR USER-ORIENTED. In the following sections I present and discuss many situations in which artists and art organizations attempt to make artistically autonomous art or follow an own mission in offering art, while in practice they often create relatively other- or user-oriented art, art that can be called market-, supporter- and art-world-oriented art. During the period of serious art, when artists are thought to do so, and even more when they are thought to deliberately do so, they are blamed for compromising. This still happens, even though over the last decades blaming artists becomes less intense. But as I notice many artists still feel guilty when they do not make "own work" but compromise, I discuss the phenomenon in detail in the following sections. In preparation of these sections, I explain some concepts I use in the following sections. I advise students to read the text. If they wish, general readers can just scan the text.

Artistic compromise refers to the phenomenon of not solely pursuing own artistic goals and make truly *own art*. Instead the artworks or the art product is adapted to "please" others. This is a matter of degree. Artists can foremost or hardly pursue own artistic goals. They can unwillingly or willingly do so. Or they may not be aware of doing so. Judgments are anyway subjective. (When I use the term compromise without explication, I refer to artistic compromise. Not all compromise in the arts is artistic compromise./19)

Other-oriented art or *user-oriented art* refers to artworks and art products in which artists and art-companies have, intentionally or not, made adaptations to attune them to wishes or assumed "needs" of others, that is, buyers, donors, governments and art-worlds. Adaptations can be small, major, and anything in between. (Other-oriented art is no applied art.)

If artists and art-companies are buyer-oriented (or consumer-oriented), they can also be said to be *market-oriented*. Artists can make *market art*. Buyers can be visitors, who purchase tickets, individuals and companies, commissioners, governments and art-companies. They purchase or order artworks. Sponsors are also buyers. They buy advertisement space as a sideline product. It follows that some art-companies can be *sponsor-oriented*. Moreover, market-oriented performing art-companies can be *visitor-oriented*. Further distinctions in market art are possible. For instance, at the moment in visual art circles, the term *art-fair art* is used.

Next to being market-oriented, artists and art-companies can be oriented on donors and governments who financially support them, that is, they can be *donor-* and *government-oriented*. They can therefore make *donor art* and *government art*. (Donors are no sponsors and sponsors no donors [19]. In theory subsidizing governments could be categorized as donors, but in practice this is unusual.)

Finally, the user- or other-oriented art and art products of artists and art-companies can be *art-world oriented* and artists can make *art-world art*.

Artists often think in terms of *own art* or *own work*. The largest part of own art is *artistically autonomous work*. This is work in which artists believe that they have *only* pursued own artistic goals, goals which have not been influenced by other people. Ultimately such work does not exist. There is always *(inter) dependence*. As we shall see [88], especially over the last decades—in the times of network capitalism—artists inevitably operate in large network of many art-people as well as non-art people. Artistic goals cannot but be influenced by others: experts/critics, government administrators, art-companies and many others. It follows that no artist or artwork is altogether artistically autonomous. As said autonomy is always relative [26]. Due to effective attunement, own art is often, but not always, *art-world art*.

Another smaller part of own art is not or not only artistically autonomous work. Instead in his work, the artist pursued (also) own non-artistic goals. An example is political art. This work kind of work can also be only relatively autonomous.

If the artist adapts his work for personal gain, he not only artistically compromises, but his work is also commercial and he may be called a commercial artist. However, if he is not after personal gain, for instance, when he makes political own art, it is not commercial work, also not when he fanatically tries to bring his message across.

On a scale from more to less other-oriented art, there are two extremes. The one is the *artistic autonomous extreme* or the *autonomy extreme*. The art produced is altogether artistically autonomous. The other extreme is the *other-oriented extreme*. Artworks exclusively serve wishes or assumed needs of others. Between the two extremes, different degrees of being other-oriented or being artistically autonomous exist. Different artists hold different positions on the scale, running from one to the other extreme.

As said, given complicated (inter)dependences, in practice, no artist is altogether artistically autonomous. Or in a more limited network, figuratively speaking, there are always people looking over their shoulder and this influences their work.[32]/20 Therefore, the autonomy extreme is empty. Probably some artist can be positioned in the user-oriented extreme. But their relative number is small.

(70) ARTISTS OFTEN HAVE NO CHOICE BUT TO (ALSO) MAKE RELATIVELY MARKET-ORIENTED ART AND "COMPROMISE". SOME DO SO FROM CONVICTION. ARTISTS ARE EASILY BLAMED FOR COMPROMISING. Many artists are noticeably other-oriented and after money. Because a majority of creative artists cannot make a living from their art, this is understandable. Most artists have little means and therefore also little artistic autonomous space. They must (also) make relatively other-oriented art, bringing in income to sustain themselves.

In the case of commissioned art, they have freedom within the boundaries they agreed on with the commissioner, but their overall autonomous space can still be very limited. In a lesser degree, the same applies in the case artists receive subsidies and private support with strings attached. It increases as well as decreases their autonomous space.

If artists have sufficient own means, for instance, from a heritage or stemming from income of earlier sales, commissions and support, they have a choice in the degree they want to go along with "demands" of others. Often, they decide to "censor" themselves and make relatively other-oriented art. They deliberately reduce their own negative freedom and thus their own overall autonomous space to increase their chances of selling or receiving commissions and support. But they may also do so without being much aware of their self-censorship.

The terms commercial and commercialism refer to an intense pursuit of personal "gain" (usually in combination with an intense promotion or marketing of the own product) [60]. Other-oriented artists who are after money—as said artists can be other-oriented without being after money—may intensely pursue profit and can therefore be said to be commercial and make commercial work. The term commercial has a negative connotation. But money can serve many purposes, from helping a friend, subsidizing own relatively autonomous work, being able to continue working as a professional artist, somewhat raising a low standard of living to showing off wealth. Since the majority of artists are poor, somewhat raising one's standard of living by having more money is common.

Nevertheless, many poor artists still use the extra money which they earn with selling more commercial work to subsidize their less or hardly market-oriented work, and to increase their overall artistic autonomous space. Such artists only compromise much in their "commercial" work. Also, people running small intermediate companies, in particular dealers, are poor and internally subsidize their preferred art activity.

Next to *self-subsidization*, a different kind of "noble" purpose exists. Some artists make market-oriented art from conviction. They honestly want to serve audiences. This is not uncommon among the many visual artists—the majority of visual artists—who make inferior-art. It is certainly common among popular artists. Other artists may pursue causes, which at least some people will sooner acknowledge as noble, like the pursuit of the mentioned political and religious goals. With their art artists may intend to promote a revolution or persuade people to worship God./21 If artists do so in a moderate fashion, they are not that exceptional. The same as there are probably no artists who never consider artistic goals, it is unlikely that artists never have any social goal in mind. Even artists who attempt to exclusively pursue own artist goals and want to make altogether autonomous own art cannot stop themselves from every now and then thinking of art that is meaningful and "good" for potential consumers.

Aside: It is good to keep in mind that artists who are commercial in the sense that they intensely market their work—and possibly also are foremost interested in money—may not compromise. They may make (relatively) autonomous work "that sells". It is nevertheless likely that in little noticed ways, marketing affects the content of their works. For this reason as well, their work cannot be positioned in the autonomy extreme.

During the period of serious art and, to a lesser degree, till the present day, artists are easily blamed for compromising. Although from an outsider perspective, artists and artworks can hold many different positions between the two extremes of altogether other-oriented and not at all other-oriented, this is not what most art-world participants are aware of. They think black and white. Even when positions are closer to the autonomy extreme than to the other-oriented extreme, works and artists are often judged to be commercial and artists are judged to compromise. The artist is said to have renounced artistic principles and to "sell out". Artists are blamed also when they care about artistic or altruistic goals. This causes distress among many, usually poor and not very successful, artists, but also some successful artists. The fate of artists making art with a message can be worse. Some are "expelled" from their art-world. Their art is, almost automatically, thought to be inferior-art [20]. (I have the impression that in the second half of the twentieth century, artists are often unjustly blamed for compromising and being commercial.)

It can indeed be success and popularity that raises suspicion. Successful artists whose works are popular are easily thought to make concessions to please consumers, at least in part of their work. Sometimes they are also judged to be commercial. Even the works of composers, like Philip Glass and John Adams, who make works that have become very popular, is, within certain music circles, judged to be easy and said to please listeners. With retro-active effect, this even applies to work by Eric Satie. These composers are generally not accused of being commercial. But, for instance, a painter like Corneille has been blamed for compromising as well as—at high age—having been after money. Some also accuse the visual artists Koons and Damien Hirst for compromising as well as being after money.

Lower in the market, artists who quickly become successful are often blamed for making commercial art. In the case of some the judgment is clearly unjustified. This makes one wonder if jealousy may play a role./22

By now, when artists, soon after graduating from a well-recognized art school, become successful, this is no longer looked at with suspicion. It is rather the opposite. This could be a sign of a (further) recommercialization in art-worlds. Moreover, that successful artists, like Hirst and Koons, now sometimes show off how commercial they are is certainly a sign of recommercialization or at least a less covered up form of commercialism. (Visual artists are good in making ironic comments which they turn into artworks. When it comes to money and commercialism, they have done so for many decades.)

Some artists *now* openly look for *niche markets* for their own art. It is likely that artists on average become more market-oriented in their works, that is, move away from the autonomy extreme. Also the number of artists increases, who make consumer-oriented art from conviction, and not because they are after money or need money to sustain their practice.

A *recent development* is that certain artists emphasize that making consumer-oriented art is an autonomous choice. They make clearly consumer-oriented art, which they regard as own art. A smaller group goes a step further and qualifies certain activities, which others would judge to be not art work but art-related work, as true art work. Increasingly these, what I call, *hybrid artists* perform these artistic activities in cooperation with others, including non-artists.[33] They may even do so while being employed by a firm. Or they themselves start firms in which artists and others work together. For them the distinction between own art, art-for-others and art-related products is not important anymore. What matters are "good" goals and missions. (Whereas the leftist new critics of "commerce" oppose commercialization, most do not oppose this development.)

(71) ARTISTS DISTINGUISH OWN WORK AND WORK FOR OTHERS. ARTISTS NEGOTIATE WITH THEMSELVES AND OTHERS. Some artists say that in part of their work—but only part—they pursue other than own artistic goals. They make a distinction between *own work* (or "autonomous work") and not-own work. Sometimes they are secretive about it. The work for others is often commercial, but not always. It can, for instance also be political work. (Artists not only use the term own work but also "autonomous work". As said, this work is "relatively autonomous".)

Often not-own work is work that brings more income and can therefore be judged to be commercial, but this is not always the case. If it is commercial work, artists run the risk of being blamed. To a degree, they can prevent this by openly declaring that they make own as well as commercial work. In the visual arts, many artists who create inferior-art sold in shops and open-air markets, do so. Their clientele understands this and appreciate it.—When art-world people see the works they invariably think that in creating the works the artists have compromised and made art that sells, that is, commercial art. This contributes to the disgust they experience when seeing the works. The possibility that the artists also make other work (*as Anna found out on several occasions*) does not occur to them.

For many of these artists making own work is important. But there is a group that says that they are not interested in making own work. They just create what consumers may buy and are not ashamed of this. They are therefore maximally market-oriented. I have the impression that this is a relatively small group. A much larger group says that all their work is own work. They are proud of this. I think they are honest.—*I spoke with Dutch artists painting tulips and the heads of cows. The works sold well, but they maintained that they pursued artistic goals. I think they were honest. Their works certainly had a personal streak.*—

Art-lovers are less tolerant and more averse of commerce and commercialism than the clientele of artists making inferior-art. This explains why many recognized artists are secretive about making a distinction. They are afraid of being blamed and in the worst case stop being an art-world-recognized artist. But among friends they may be more open. *Not long after graduating Anna regularly met up with Margaret and Peter, two ex-classmates, to discuss each other's work. At the time they distinguished three categories: own work, work for the market and art-world work (or government work). Own work did not sell well. Market work and art-world work served to try and make a living from sales and subsidies to have some extra money for making own work.*

There are also artists who say that next to their commercial art they make own art. These artists make a clear distinction. The own art they usually sell from their studio. (I visited some of them in their studios and noticed that the own work indeed differs from the work they sell in the open-air markets and shops.) (It therefore appears that the adherence to the art ethos is not limited to the group of serious artists but is also important among artists who make inferior-art, the same as among many popular artists.)

Artists who are art-world-recognized, but whose work is little recognized or appreciated, can be in a difficult situation, especially when they make works in earlier styles. Given their education, they would like to be well-recognized within their art-world. They want to "belong" to the art-world family. Although most are not banished from the art-world, well-recognized colleagues and experts/critics argue that they cannot be better recognized because their art is not sufficiently autonomous. They do not pursue the "proper" artistic goals, the goals of the art-world.—Evidently the critics think that art is autonomous art if it befits the dominant contemporary rules of the art-world.—

At some stage Anna was member of an association of portraitists. Most members made portraits in impressionistic and earlier nineteenth-century expressionistic styles. There was demand for their portraits, more than for Anna's portraits. Although her own work was more "up to date", she admired the artistic quality of the other's work. She thought that, although the works were clearly market-oriented, the artists compromised little. Well-recognized artists, however, thought that the work was inferior and that the artists were too market-oriented. Sometimes their work was laughed at. She noticed that most of these artists suffered under the negative judgments. Anna thought that this was altogether unjustified. (Nevertheless, after a while, she terminated her membership: it could harm her career.)

Maybe because portraitists accept commissions, they are sometime better aware of being market-oriented and making concessions than other artists. They are involved in a *balancing act*. They wonder how far they shall go in the direction of doing their "own thing" and how far in that of pleasing the commissioner. In their imagination, they *negotiate* with the commissioner. (Usually they do not go for an easy "compromise". Instead the outcome is often creative and interesting.)

Imagined negotiation is important in the arts. It probably much enhances creativity. (The notion that much artistic autonomy always corresponds with much creativity and that therefore artists must be autonomous is unfounded.) *Based on conversations with little- as well as well-recognized artists—visual artists, composers and writers—I noticed that, in different degrees, all artists in their imagination negotiate with others, who look over their shoulder: expert/critics, members of committees deciding on grants, consumers, people who commission art and other market participants, like dealers, impresarios and publishers. Art-world-recognized artists as well are often involved in a balancing act.*

Sometimes artists openly negotiate. For instance, in the case of a commission for an artwork: a visual artwork, a composition, a performance and so forth.

Aside: In this context the situation of poor as well as rich artists accepting commissions is interesting. The commissioner provides them with money and, at the same time, sets constraints which limit their artistic freedom. By negotiating the price and the demands, artists can sometimes increase their autonomous space. They may do the same in the process of creating the work, while in the imagination continuing to negotiate with the commissioner: they can make a work that either pleases the commissioner more or instead pleases themselves more, because it is the kind of relatively autonomous work they would like to make. If given all the constraints, artists can no longer take responsibility for the work and cannot say "this is also my own work", they return the commission or compromise.[34] And if the outcome of all such negotiations is such that the autonomous space of the artist is still very small, others may, indeed, blame the artist for accepting and executing the commission and making inferior work.

Most of the time, however, artists are not aware of communicating and negotiating with others. That many artists are de facto involved in a balancing act with respect to the "choice" of positions between the autonomy extreme and the other-oriented extreme in which artworks are maximally adjusted, does therefore not imply that most of them are very conscious of the fact that they have something to choose or that their choices influence their position. They do not seek an optimal position. Finding a more or less satisfying position is a matter of, de facto, trial and error; of expectations of "demands" of groups of others, of learning from past experiences, and so forth. It is probably best to say that they "go with the flow".

(72) ARTISTS USE VARIOUS SOURCES OF INCOME TO INTERNALLY SUBSIDIZE THEIR OWN ART AND INCREASE THEIR AUTONOMOUS SPACE. AN IMPORTANT SOURCE IS INCOME FROM SECOND

JOBS. SOMETIMES ARTISTS HAVE A WORK PREFERENCE. The artistic autonomous space of artists is always limited. Poor artists have less autonomous space than not-poor artists. Because in the twentieth century the large majority of creative artists have a hard time making a living from their art, many make also commercial art and/or they use non-art sources of income, foremost that of second jobs, to *internally subsidize* their true art job. This way they increase their limited artistic autonomous space. (As we shall see further down, art-companies as well are often engaged in commercial art activities in order to internally subsidize their core art activity, their mission.)

Any artist has limited artistic autonomous space. This is space in terms of time and other means and in terms of the (negative) freedom they have [26]. Usually other means can be bought with money. The situation of artists in terms of time and money differ, some have more time, others more money. Whereas maximum time is the same for rich and poor, the rich have far more financial means than the poor. Rich artists have plenty of money which they can, if they wish, spend on their art production. *(Most artists have little money, but may have time. As the pop musician Paolo Nutini sings: "I am short on money but long on time".)* An artist who is a millionaire can afford to make very expensive works, even when the chance of selling or covering the cost is low. For instance, some very successful film directors, film actors and pop stars use part of their wealth to create such artworks. Presently also some visual artists do so. An example is Hirst. In 2017 he spent a fortune on his work in the Vienna Biennale./23

Most artists have very low incomes [41]. In terms of money, their autonomous space is very limited. Often, they have so little money that their art cannot but be low-cost art. The autonomous/own art they want to make may well be too costly. In that case their small autonomous space clearly limits their artistic freedom. A poor visual artist may have plenty of time but not enough money to buy the expensive paints he needs; or a composer cannot afford a (grand) piano—or, nowadays, a high-end computer—to develop his works. Also, in the case that their low-cost art is no commercial art, such artists may be blamed for continuing to work as artist and making relatively inferior works. They could be amateurs. (Maybe there is a chance of later recovering the cost of costly works, but for a poor artist this is too risky. He is anyway not able to pay in advance for the cost.)

Most artists are poor [41]. Many poor artists earn so little from making own art that they are unable to sustain themselves as a person and as an artist. When their income per hour from making (low-cost) own art is very low or negative, having other sources of income is necessary to be able to maintain a professional artist. Working fewer hours also increases income. And as noted, a third way is making and selling much other-oriented (or commercial) art.

Various sources of additional income exist. Important is income from second jobs. Another is subsidies and grants. Several other sources of additional income exist, which are sometimes used for the art job, like money from a heritage, from family members and from a partner. In the nineteenth century, support by family members was important. And up to the present day, many artists are supported by partners. Nevertheless, in the twentieth century, income from second jobs is *the* source of complementary income.

Artists with low, zero or negative income from their art work, *internally subsidize* their artwork with income from other sources. Income from second jobs is particularly important. Most artists are so-called *multiple jobholders*. (For data on incomes and multiple job-holding see web-text wt-41.) Second jobs can be *non-art jobs* and *art-related jobs*. Many different kinds of non-art jobs exist; from working in a café to writing academic texts. Examples of art-related jobs are: giving music- or painting lessons to amateurs, teaching art students in professional art education, sitting on a committee distributing grants and so forth. Artists with art jobs as well as art-related jobs have a *plural art practice*. Especially when they earlier chose to be educated in other disciplines as well, and later have an art job in combination with one or more better paid art-related and non-art jobs, they can be said to have developed an attractive *portfolio of jobs*.[35]/24 (The commercial activities of artists could be said to be a second (art-related) job, but this is unusual.)

Economists have noticed that in some cases relatively poor but dedicated artists have, what they call, a *work preference*.[36]/25 Certain groups of artists are sometimes "abnormal". They spend, at least, part of the additional money from a pay rise in a second job to increase the hours spend on the art job. (They are "abnormal", because in standard economics this kind of behavior is unexpected.)

When "normal" people get a pay rise, they spend the extra money on all sorts of consumption activities. They raise their standard of living, buy a car, go on holiday and so forth. Or they spend the money on apparently altruistic causes like helping a friend or family members. They may also start to work fewer hours and have more free time. But certain groups of artists spend part of it to increase the number of hours working in the art job. This is indeed "part", because the research shows that when there is a work preference it is weak. Most additional money serves to raise the standard of living, which is not amazing, given the low incomes of artists.

The work preference theory has romantic appeal: poor artists being so dedicated that they spend a bit of extra money on their art. The theory suggests that artists are selfless. But no artist is selfless nor only intrinsically motivated, and this also applies to no artist with a proven work preference. Because of the appeal, also within cultural economics, and because the work preference theory runs counter to what standard economists expect, I have inserted a long web-note to explain the theory in more detail. In the web-note I start with an experience of Anna which general readers may find interesting. The remainder should be interesting for students./26

Aside: First, that some artists like their art job so much that they have a work preference does not imply that they and other artists are compensated for their low incomes by non-monetary rewards [44]. Second, also for poor artists spending additional money on making autonomous/own art can represent a rational investment, which in the long run may lead to more monetary and/or non-monetary income. Third, as noted, artists with a work preference can also spend the extra income on material means, which allow them to make better art, but this has not been researched. Fourth, some social scientists engaged in related research assume that artists have a work preference, without having done any research on its existence and relative importance. They assume it exists and is important and even think that they confirm its existence, for instance, by showing that artists have more job-satisfaction than other professionals [44].

Research on the causes that artists use money from other sources is limited, but it is reasonable to assume that artists who can hardly make a living or only just make a decent living spend additional money on a higher standard of living.—This is what I noticed in my contacts with artists in various art forms over a period of 50 years.—They buy a car, go on holiday, have children and so forth. (And when they are not that poor, alternative spending may well serve noble causes like offering children a proper education.)

Aside: As noted, some artists who are successful and rich sometimes spend their extra money from creating art on more or more expensive own art "for the sake of art" but often they also do so to invest in future success. Others spend it on a higher standard of living and are not ashamed of it. Picasso and the German painter Markus Lüpertz bought a castle. Lüpertz, moreover, bought a Mercedes SE class and Von Karajan, the same as Justin Bieber, bought several fast cars, and unlike Bieber, bought a private Jet.

Artists who spend much time on their second job(s) usually have no other choice. They survive but at the same time have less autonomous space in terms of time, while they already had little autonomous space in terms of money. Most poor artists miss the qualifications to have better paid second jobs. And even when they manage to make some interesting "true" art, they are blamed for working so few hours and making so little own art. Sometimes they are judged to be no professional, while they ought to admit that they are not, that they are amateurs. The same applies a fortiori to artists with well-paid second jobs who work few hours in their art job. But differences exist between art forms. A poet creating art only a few hours a week will not be criticized, while a visual artist who does so will be. (I know several well-recognized poets who have a full-time academic job.)

Aside: Mutatis mutandis what is said in this section about artists can also apply to art-companies. Non-profit and for-profit art-companies can have a true artwork preference as well.—Most are also "multiple jobholders".—But their definitions of "true artwork" or mission will differ much.

Over the last decade, the part of aspiring artists, who let themselves be educated in an art discipline and simultaneously in one or more non-art disciplines, has increased much. This way they have a plan B. But it also serves later second jobs that are well paid. It is possible that with time this will lead to a rise in average income; and maybe even to a higher average hourly income from creating art if more people, on second thought, chose to execute their plan B.

(73) OFTEN, IN LITTLE NOTICED WAYS, MARKET DEMAND AND ART-WORLD DEMAND AFFECT THE OWN/AUTONOMOUS WORKS OF ARTISTS. COST DEVELOPMENTS ALSO HAVE AN IMPACT. As noted, in different degrees artists make work that is other oriented, but most of them prefer to believe that their work is altogether artistically autonomous. In this section I present examples of consumer demand and art-world demands as well as cost developments

influencing the artistic choices of artists. In as far as artists are little or not aware of it, they cannot be said to compromise, let alone be commercial. But for a proper understanding of the social economy of art, acknowledging the influences is important. It can also be insightful for artists.

During the period of serious art, pleasing governments, donors and art-world participants contribute to a gain in the form of institutional recognition, especially in the case of starting artists. Because of the large say people in art-world establishments have in the distribution of subsidies and sometimes also donations, a "pleasing governments" is de facto a "pleasing the own art-world". The same applies, in a lesser degree, to donors and donations. It follows that "pleasing consumers" has a counterpart in "pleasing one's art-world".

Sometimes artists are little aware of pleasing others. Often artists are secretive about somewhat pleasing others, and with time awareness disappears. In little noticed ways, works change. *As said, not long after graduating, Anna regularly met up with Margaret and Peter, two ex-classmates, to discuss each other's work. They distinguished three categories: own work, work for the market and art-world work (or government work). Own work did not sell well. The other two served obtaining market income and income from subsidies, that is, income they needed. After first losing contact, they met up again ten years later. Margaret had become successful with her art-world-work; she had become a well-recognized artist. The committees granting subsidies liked her work. Peter was now successful with his market work and could make a decent living from his sales. Anna was a bit successful. She had received subsidies, but only twice, and she sold some market work. But all three of them maintained that they no longer made three kinds of work; all their work was own/autonomous work, and they were proud of this. However, looking closely at their work, Anna noticed that Margaret's and Peter's work were not in line with their earlier work. It had developed, but in the case of Margaret's work, it was in line with her earlier art-world work and Peter's work, the same as her own, in line with his earlier market work.* Going with the flow, these three artists adjusted their "own" work. Their work had become more other-oriented.

Over time art-world demands change. Anna's earlier success with committees granting subsidies and her later lack of success could be explained from changing demands of the committees. Developments and influences can also be more concrete. Examples are the demand for sizes of paintings and the length of manuscripts, plays, scores, choreographies and films. Changes in demand influence artists, but they will usually give artistic reasons for their changed works. Many examples can be given. It is easiest to demonstrate influences of a changing demand for sizes of paintings and length of manuscripts, scores and choreographies.

Around 1980—at the time Anna had a part time job at the Rietveld Academy in Amsterdam—teaching live drawing, many students made very large paintings and drawings and this was stimulated by the teachers. However, she noticed that after graduating, most students started to make much smaller works. Moreover, not much later also, teachers started to advise students to make small rather than large works. All of them gave artistic reasons for the new and different choice. But in hindsight

Anna is sure that economic reasons offered a better explanation for the change. Around 1980 museums—the customer par excellence, bringing young artists prestige—as well as companies and important collectors bought large works, and several teachers sold large works to them. But within a few years the preference of the museums and other buyers changed, and the demand for large works went down. The market for large works had never been large, but was now so small that even successful ex-students rarely could sell large works. Less successful postgraduates who wanted to make a living from their art work had little choice but to make small work. But, as Anna noticed again and again, most of them—not all—said, and honestly believed, that they had decided to do so only for artistic reasons./27

Not that much later a similar process occurred: museums got very interested in installations and teachers at academies started to promote such works. And again, after leaving art school only very few students who had got into making installations could sell such works. For artistic reasons they started to make flat work.

Cost developments can also influence choices without artists, ensembles and art-companies being much aware of it. An example is that of playwrights and choreographers writing pieces with fewer performers on the stage. Another is the adaptations of older plays to let them be performed with fewer actors. Cost went down and the cost disease became less intense. In this case changing artistic goals are certainly important, but rising cost must have been a catalyst.

Aside: material changes in the form of the size of works or the length of pieces and books cannot but affect the content of works. Content change makes it easier for artists to believe and say that their artistic choices have changed. (An artist who was well aware of changes in content was Henry Moore. He created the "same" sculptures in different sizes and noticed that he had to make changes to create a more or less similar art experience. He was also aware that a work's settings changed a work. He wanted his large works to be shown in open spaces, like meadows, and not in the sculpture gardens of museums.)

Most likely, *also today* many artists believe that their work is only or foremost own work, work that is not influenced by market developments or developments in art-world preferences. But, as said, the relative number of artists who chose to be more market-oriented and deliberately take wishes of consumers into account has almost certainly increased. This applies a fortiori for the new hybrid artists [43]. In either case there will also be unnoticed influences—it would be strange if there were none. It is, nevertheless, likely that, along with a weakening of art-worlds and less autonomy of overall art-worlds, and no longer a need to make art-world art, the relative autonomy of these artists increases.

(74) THE CHOICES OF LARGE ART-COMPANIES ARE INCREASINGLY AFFECTED BY DEMANDS OF CONSUMERS. THEY TEND TO HAVE FOREMOST THE DEMAND OF ELITE AUDIENCES AND DONORS IN MIND. Art-companies, like museums, halls, theaters and large ensembles are, the same as artists, other-oriented as well and an influence is almost inevitable. Others are consumers, small donors, sponsors, large donors and governments. Modern cultural entrepreneurship has enhanced the phenomenon that art-companies are oriented on

others. Their choice of products not only rests on artistic considerations. As far as consumers and small donors are concerned, they are more oriented on art-lovers and not on lower-middle- and low-class people, and also not on non-white people. This orientation certainly affects their mission or overall art product.

Aside: First, although part of the text in this section also applies to sponsors, large donors and governments, in this section I focus on consumers and small donors and in the next on the others. Second, a strong orientation on consumer wishes and consequent adaptations is less common among small art-companies, like art-spaces and small music venues, minor dealers, impresarios and labels as well as small film producers and some small publishers. The wishes of a relatively small group of consumers or "fans" matter, but thanks to self-organization and an opportunistic orientation on broader markets, donors and governments, their autonomy is relatively high. This is why in this and the following two sections I focus foremost on larger non-profit art-companies.

The same as in the case of certain artists, an orientation on others does not always imply that the overall art product is adapted. Sometimes it sufficiently appeals to consumer to sustain the company. But, the same as in the case of artists, it is also possible that as part of the overall art product, art activities are produced that are artistically less interesting but sell better, while the extra income is used for internal subsidization or growth. Both for-profit and non-profit art-companies almost always want to grow or expand and need extra income to do so. In this case art-companies may be blamed for compromising and being commercial, but not as easily as in the case of artists. (Instead of using the term internal subsidization, economists may use the term "*cross-financing*".) People understand that art-companies want to continue their activities.[37]/28

It is likely that, sometimes being hardly aware of this, not only managements of art-companies but also curators, programmers and people working in serious publishing houses have consumers at the back of their minds—as well as possible sponsors and supporters. In practice, it is rare that art-companies, in the choice of their overall art product, only go for artistic goals. In the best case they, de facto, chose positions close to the extreme of an "art for art's sake only" or of "autonomy" and further away from the extreme of "anything goes as long as others are interested" [69]. Art-companies were never autonomous and their autonomy decreases.

Over the last decades in the more user-oriented domain in the arts, an orientation on users and in particular consumers becomes ever more important. This cannot but affect the choice of artworks. More "appealing" visual artworks are exhibited, and more appealing performances are programmed. This can indirectly affect the work of living artists. By adapting one's work, the chances of the work being selected by art-companies increases.

Adjustments do not have to be deliberate—also not in the case of support by sponsors, major donors and subsidizing governments. Sometimes adjustments are the consequence of unnoticed or hardly noticed self-censorship. Although the inclusion of certain artworks, compositions, plays and ensembles would better befit the mission of the institution, they are not included because consumers buying tickets may be less interested in the overall art product. The possibility of self-censorship is seldom considered by curators, programmers, conductors in charge of a choice of artworks as part of the art product of an art-company. They believe that they only think in terms of artistic quality. If self-censorship exists, it usually has been internalized. (The personnel in small or large commercial art-companies who offer (re) produced artworks in larger series, like publishers and record companies are better aware of being market-oriented.)

As can be expected art-companies are more oriented on the wishes of art-lovers and not on those of middle- and low-class people, and also not on those of non-white people. This orientation certainly affects their mission or overall art product. But because this orientation does not have to imply adaptation of the serious art product, it is less important in the present context. More relevant is the possibility that art-companies orient themselves on the wishes of the part of their clientele that is relatively rich and less on that of the part that is not that rich. Often art-companies can raise their overall income by orienting themselves on the former group.

Part of the visitors of art museums and of the performances of art-companies are not only consumers but also donors. They regularly donate some money. And because the financially most interesting group of regular donors are also more well to do than the average visitor, the donation schemes may well enhance the mentioned possible influence of the more well-to-do consumers. (In this long web-note, I say more about donation schemes, which over time have become more elaborate and calculated./29)

Aside: A related and probably much stronger effect occurs in the case of museums. The preference of the extremely rich people who buy works in the top of the visual art market, very likely have an impact on the overall art product offered by major museums. More than in the case of the performing arts, the importance of the impact depends on the power distribution and relationships of experts, artists, art-companies and rich consumers [88].

Most art venues offer non-art services to consumers, from coffee and art books to merchandize. The income is usually higher than the cost, and the surplus is used to internally subsidize the art activities. But expertise in these areas is limited; therefore, art venues increasingly license such activities to specialized firms. This is more profitable. If these activities do influence the overall art product is hard to tell. It may do so indirectly. Offering expensive drinks and food may enhance the attraction of venues which are oriented on rich consumers.

Aside: By now, most popular art venues have lowered their overall cost by letting a firm which works for several venues, take care of ticket sales./30 It is predictable that soon more serious art venues will start to do the same—and probably make use of the same largest internationally operating firm, that is, Ticketmaster, which is owned by the concert organizer Live Nation.

(75) IMPLICIT OR EXPLICIT DEMANDS OF SPONSORS, MAJOR DONORS AND GOVERNMENTS INCREASINGLY AFFECT THE OVERALL ART PRODUCT OF ART-COMPANIES. MAJOR DONORS SOMETIMES “BUY” INFLUENCE. Along with further commercialization in the arts, attempts of art-companies to sell advertisement space to sponsors and to obtain subsidies and donations have become more intense and calculated. It is inevitable that in decisions on the core product, managements, curators, programmers and publishers have sponsors, donors and subsidizing governments in the back of their mind, even though some may hardly be aware of this.

Aside: In practice, the terms earned income, interest and endowment income, philanthropy, support, public and private support, subsidy, grant, donor and donation, sponsor and sponsoring, and related terms are often used in multiple and sometimes confusing ways. I expect that most of the time the meaning in this text of the other terms will be sufficiently clear. I, nevertheless, explain some of the terms in the web-text wt-2.

The contribution of sales to sponsors to, so-called, *earned income* of art-companies is considerable, but it is small compared with overall *support* (i.e. “not-earned” income). Some influence from sponsors, and even more than that of supporters, is likely. It is likely but not certain that the kind of influence of the various groups of donors differs. Especially the influence of governments could differ from that of other supporters. (Earned income is income from all sales, i.e. tickets—and extras like coffee—to visitors and advertisement space to sponsors. Usually regular small donations from visitors are also counted as earned income.)

Overall support is indeed large. Both in the USA and Europe, on average more than half of the overall income of non-profit performing art-companies and art museums stems from public and private support. Earned income, that is, income from visitors and sponsors is less than 50%. In the USA, private support is far more important than public support, that is, if indirect public support is included in private support. In the context of this section treating influence, the latter makes sense, because in the case of indirect public support, influence comes from others than governments. In Europe direct public support is larger than private support, but the difference is becoming smaller. (In section 19, I presented data on the importance of indirect support in the USA and briefly discussed its underlying ideology.)

Private support comes from foundations, corporations, individuals and indirectly from interest on and expenditure of earlier endowments. In the USA, support of rich individuals is circa 30% of all private support and in Europe this kind of support is less but growing. Its importance shows from the phenomenon that highly qualified personnel, including the artistic director, in art-companies spends a large part of its time on the acquisition of donations of individuals. It follows that there is much personal contact between very rich people and the artistic management of art-companies. It would therefore be strange if artistic preferences of the very rich would not have an impact on the content of the overall art product.

During the period of serious art in Europe, the major part of overall income—sometimes up to 90% and in the case of free art museum almost 100%—comes from direct public support, that is, from local and central governments./31. Government influence is likely. During the period of serious art, many art-buildings and large ensembles are legally owned by governments. The personnel are civil servants. In Germany, Austria and other south and eastern European countries, this is still common. Even when an "arm's length principle" applies, some straightforward influence is likely. (The *arm's length principle* refers to governments deciding on the overall size of an art budget, but the actual distribution is done (at arm's length) by independent foundations financed by governments./32)

Over the last decades, due to increased sponsoring, major donations and sometimes government support, most art-companies become more other-oriented and/or become oriented on different "others", with the consequence that the art product changes. In as far as the successful acquisition of large sums of money from rich private donors is concerned, the effect is usually, indeed, a richer audience than before—an audience with relatively deep pockets. This is likely to lead to, little noticed, adjustments of the art product. They make the choice of artworks more interesting for this group. It also makes art more exclusive and increases the exclusion of others. The latter most often also applies to government subsidies. The largest part of government support allows companies to remain oriented on relatively rich people. Without the subsidies, due to market forces, the companies would possibly have become more oriented on a broader group of middle class people, including middle class immigrants.

What matters for sponsors is the publicized connection of the own name with the name of the, often prestigious, art-company which offers "great art". This way the own name becomes associated with the world of art. For sponsors this is profitable, while major donors become a member of a select small company of people within the larger family of art-lovers. This is attractive and rewarding, and the more so if many people know about the gift and the "membership".

But the opposite, the name of the art-company becoming associated with that of major sponsors and donors occurs as well. One imago meets another and both change, be it sometimes only very little. It is not accidental that managements put more effort in approaching certain donors or sponsors and not others.

Most individual donors including corporations "buy" things. They "buy", among others, public exposure and attention, if not immortality, a better imago in society, a clear conscience (laundering), a membership in elite art circles, and/or influence in the art-company. The phenomenon of donors "buying" membership does not differ from that of rich people who purchase very expensive visual artworks. The latter often also buy exposure.

But exposure in the case of large donations resulting in names become attached to buildings is larger and also more lasting. An example is that of the concert hall of the New York Philharmonic being rechristened as David Geffen Hall. In 2015 the mogul David Geffen had made a "gift" of 100 million dollars serving the renovation of the existing hall. (There certainly must have been drawn a contract stipulating the rights and duties of both Geffen and the Philharmonic.) *Over the last decades* many rooms in art-buildings are called after a donor. The "sale" of room names brings much additional income. Although art consumers quickly get used to new names and the association of the offered art activities with those of the sponsor or donor fades, little noticed self-censorship and adjustments in the overall art product may well set in motion a train of changes.

Art-companies are likely to deny a (possible) influence or emphasize that large gifts foremost serve internal subsidization or are necessary for the continuation of their organization, which is so important for art and artists. At the same time staff knows that many large donations serve forms of covering up and laundering. Stakes are high. Especially when artists start to protest—as is now happening more and more often [67]—, this puts them in a difficult position.

Many donors "buy" not only membership and exposure, but also influence. They are willing to pay much for influence. Wanting to join the board of directors of the Metropolitan Museum of Art, one has to pay at least $10 million. Recently Ann Ziff made a $30 million gift to the Metropolitan Opera. Simultaneously it was announced that she was to become the next chairwoman. In the case of slightly less prestigious art-companies, "fees" are lower, but amounts of $250,000 on a yearly basis are not uncommon. By now this is a hardly covered up form of commerce. Recently the director of the Lincoln Center said in an interview that art-companies in conversations with major potential donors wanting to become board members mentioned the "price" of membership. De facto a market of "donations with influence" exists.[38]

Nevertheless, some, mainly local, governments¸ sponsors, donating foundations and a rare important individual donor are particularly interested in an art product that (also) appeals to not well-to-do art-lovers and immigrants. And when art-companies go along and move into an opposite direction, by also orienting themselves on not that well-to-do customers and immigrants, this may raise own income as well. But this is rare. When activities are sold out, raising prices is more profitable.

Some foundations are indeed interested in promoting a more democratic art product, and in different degrees, they succeed by making demands. (But they do not succeed always. As noted [57], in 1966, the Ford Foundation offered the Philadelphia Symphonic Orchestra a grant of two million dollars, demanding that it would make its board more representative of the Philadelphia community and would make a four million fund drive among a large part of the population.[39] The orchestra did not do so and the money was nevertheless given.) (For the demands of supporting foundations, their history and the origin of their money can make a difference./33)

Certain sponsors are clearly interested in a large audience with a not too elite taste. For instance, the brewery Heineken is interested in a large audience with a taste for beer rather than champagne. Whether such sponsors indirectly influence the art product is hard to tell, but some art-lovers certainly fear this. This kind of sponsor tends to sponsor festivals with many visitors, usually popular art festivals, but nowadays increasingly also (open-air) serious or crossover art festivals.

In all cases the nature of the sponsor offers some information to audiences; usually information the art-company does not mind or even appreciate. For instance, if a serious music concert or festival is sponsored by Heineken, a potential visitor will probably expect that the atmosphere will be less elitist than if it is sponsored by Rolex (watches) and this may suit the organizer well.

Often not only purchases of sponsors but also support from major donors and central and local governments have explicit strings attached—the same as in the case of the Ford foundation. Such strings diminish the artistic autonomous space of art-companies in terms of negative freedom, while, due to the extra money, they increase their positive freedom.—The strings may affect the choice of art products by the art-company; sometimes making the art product more exclusive and sometimes less.

Also without official conditions, donors and supporting governments may steer the art product that is offered by an art-company (or artist). This is because they always make a certain choice of the companies (and artists) they subsidize and not others, and because they decide on a higher or lower donation or subsidy. This can lead to self-censorship. It can also lead to making promises in the application forms which are in line with the policies of donating foundations and governments. At present (2018) many art-companies promise to become more consumer-oriented, sometimes explicitly mentioning other ethnic groups.

But demands are not always met; or only partially. It regularly happens that after art-companies receive support, they do not fulfill the conditions or do not keep their promises, while this has no consequences.—They sometimes cheat in their reports./34—Internally art-companies motivate their behavior by emphasizing the need to maintain an own/autonomous product. They anyway argue that artistic quality must come first, and that given their skills they know best what in their case is the best product. They only use the money to subsidize that true art product. The end justifies the means.

(76) SINCE CIRCA 1980, CULTURAL ENTREPRENEURSHIP AND INSTRUMENTAL REASON BECOME COMMON AMONG ART-COMPANIES. SINCE CIRCA 2000, CULTURAL ENTREPRENEURSHIP BECOMES ACCEPTABLE AMONG ARTISTS. CULTURAL ENTREPRENEURSHIP ALWAYS AFFECTS ARTWORKS AND ART PRODUCTS. Whereas forms of cultural entrepreneurship have always existed, before the 1980s' commercial turn, no art-company or artist would be and wanted to be called cultural entrepreneur. Not much later, cultural entrepreneurship becomes acceptable in the case of art-companies. But it is only over the last two decades that this also starts to apply to artists. Up to the present day, there are conservative art-lovers and new (leftist) critics of "commerce" who reject cultural entrepreneurship in the case of artists.

Implicitly in the previous and following sections, much is said about activities that are part of cultural entrepreneurship. This section may nevertheless interest readers and in particular students of cultural entrepreneurship. Among others I show that the promise of some economists that cultural entrepreneurship will not interfere with the art product, and thus with art, is a false promise.

An organization that pursues income/profit is an *enterprise*. Income/profit can serve various goals and not only profit-for-the-sake-of-profit. An *entrepreneur* is a person who organizes and manages an enterprise, innovates, and usually takes initiative and risk.[40] Economists emphasize the latter. An enterprise is usually a business with personnel, like an art-company, but not necessarily. Most creative artists also run an enterprise and are entrepreneurs. Most artists are *independent artists*, also called *self-employed artists*. (The latter term is a commonly used but unfortunate term: a person cannot employ himself.)

In the case of *cultural entrepreneurship* in the arts, cultural economists have a restrained form of entrepreneurship in mind. Only if the entrepreneur pursues own artistic goals is he a proper cultural entrepreneur. He may develop new artworks—and new overall art products in the case of art-companies—and develop niche markets and intensely market his work, but he does not compromise. Up to around 1980, cultural economists much emphasize that in cultural entrepreneurship, the existing artworks and art products are given and inviolable. Later on, the interpretation of cultural entrepreneurship of most cultural economists broadens. Cultural entrepreneurs can pursue more than just artistic goals.

For cultural economists cultural entrepreneurs are, the same as other entrepreneurs, innovative. In the case of artists being innovative is not special: in the second half of the twentieth century, artists are expected to be innovative. By becoming and remaining an innovative artist, artists take considerable risks. (This also applies to many small art-companies, like "marginal" dealers, impresarios and publishers.)

Typical for a good *entrepreneur* is that he organizes and manages his business in an efficient way. This also applies to the cultural entrepreneur. As said, even though they may deny this and pretend that they have no business skills, part of artists, already for a long time, take initiatives in markets; they are alert on chances in markets and develop niche markets./35 They are also alert and take initiatives in obtaining subsidies and donations from foundations, companies and individuals. Though nobody says so, ultimately, their behavior is calculated. Instrumental rationality is important.

Instrumental rationality or *instrumental reason* refers to a specific form of rationality—or use of reason—focusing on the most efficient or cost-effective means to achieve a specific end, but not in itself reflecting on the value of that end.

Instrumental reasoning does not necessarily imply that entrepreneurs never consider missions. But the former may easily take over the latter. They may forget about possible missions, while means turn into ends. By now instrumental thinking is typical for the managements of most larger art-companies, and if thinking in economic terms and financial profit is normal and a choice of mission no longer on the agenda, criticism of art-lovers is understandable.

There is anyway a fear among artists and art-lovers that entrepreneurship leads to artworks and art products that sell better, and thus to artists and art-companies compromising. It is therefore no accident that at first cultural economists much emphasize that, the same as in the case of marketing, the artwork or the art product is given. As late as 1999, the well-known economist Frederick van der Ploeg states (as politician) that the cultural entrepreneur sticks to the realization of existing artistic goals. Several cultural economists still do. The artwork and art product and the artistic autonomy of an artist or artistic director come first.

Nevertheless, since then some cultural economists develop a broader notion of cultural entrepreneurship. The cultural entrepreneur can choose another overall product than only one that is artistically interesting. He is more flexible. Given his skills he looks for new opportunities: opportunities that are profitable (in a broad sense).

Aside: First, Arjo Klamer expects the cultural entrepreneur to think about and choose one or more *missions* and to so realize what he calls *cultural values*. In the case of art-companies, artistic values come first.[41]/36 Second, the own overall product is comparable with the own/autonomous art of artists. Using terms comparable with those I used in the case of artists, the art-company is now "allowed" to choose positions on a scale running from, what I called, an "*art for art's sake only*" to "*anything goes as long as others are interested*" —the others usually being consumers and sponsors.

Aside: The demand that cultural entrepreneurs must only pursue artistic goals has contributed to dual leadership in art-companies. Whereas at first a single director decided on the nature of the art product while also taking care of business, in the dual leadership situation, an artistic director together with a management director runs the art-company. This is thought to prevent artistic compromise. Only the artistic director defines the art product or the artistic mission of the organization. The manager helps, realizing the artistic mission in an efficient and entrepreneurial way. (Often the dual leadership gave rise to controversies and was little efficient. This, together with a broader interpretation of cultural entrepreneurship—led in many art-companies to the discontinuation of dual leadership.)

Main recent developments have been mentioned in the text. Overall cultural entrepreneurship has indeed become accepted, be it not by everybody. The resistance against cultural entrepreneurship among artists has gone down. This shows among others from ever more courses in cultural entrepreneurship. Such courses are now an integral part of the curriculum of many professional art education institutes. The behavior of the typical artist is more entrepreneurial, and it is more openly entrepreneurial than it was around 1980 or just 10 years ago.

Nevertheless, most artists, also those who followed the courses and behave in more entrepreneurial ways, still resist being called cultural entrepreneurs. And resistance among some art-lovers is still considerable. The other day I read a blog in which an indignant art-lover complains: "There are no artists anymore but only creative cultural entrepreneurs".

Up to the present day the behavior of larger art-companies becomes more entrepreneurial and calculated. It is entrepreneurial in a new sense. Increasingly there is little or no attention for an own art mission.

Aside: Arjo Klamer has observed that, in practice most art-companies do not really consider their possible mission(s), while he argues that discussing and choosing a mission—I would rather say missions—is or should be an integral part of cultural entrepreneurship.[42]/37 Presently this is often not the case. In our more commercial times, more than before, companies go with the flow, that is, a flow that serves instrumental goals, while means may well become ends.

Enrichment and Marketing

(77) COMMERCIAL ENRICHMENT PRACTICES IN THE ARTS ENHANCE A WINNER-TAKE-ALL MECHANISM. *Over the last decades*, PRICES, RETURNS AND INCOMES IN THE TOP OF ART MARKETS HAVE INCREASED MUCH, LEADING TO (EVEN MORE) INEQUALITY. So far, I paid most attention to consumer demand and demands of others influencing the art of artists and art-companies. That in the economy at large producers listen to consumers is what economists expect. Producers need to make a profit and have to compete with other producers. They better listen to consumers. However, economists are also aware that supply can and sometimes must influence demand. New innovative products require the development of, at least, a niche market. This also applies to the innovative art of avant-garde circles, in the arts and even more in popular art. But it also applies to small and large art-companies wanting to sustain their business in competition with others, that is, other art-companies or other companies offering products for luxury consumption. Or they want to sell to be able to internally subsidize own activities. For this marketing is an important tool. Sometimes producers can be said to manipulate consumers. (The notion of consumer sovereignty anyway makes little sense [64].)

In this context some sociologists started to think in terms of "enrichment", that is, an enrichment that has become more important and more calculated *over the last decades*. Producers, including artists and art-companies, pay more attention and spend more money on the "wrapping" of their artworks and art products or the "appeal" of the works and products themselves. In the more prosperous countries, enrichment activities are leading to an aestheticized world. This gives artists more opportunities, but it also comes with costs. Enrichment also enhances a so-called winner-take-all mechanism, which economists already earlier analyzed. It leads to huge income differences, also in the arts.

Enrichment in the case of art refers to the phenomenon that people—foremost experts/critics, art-producers and artists—add extras to artworks (and sometimes œuvres and genres) in the form of information, narratives and labels with the consequence that they become more interesting and/or appealing for consumers.[43] There can be, but does not have to be, a commercial incentive; due to enrichment there is reputational and/or financial gain. Two forms of enrichment exist. In one the artworks and art products themselves are not affected, but their wrapping is enriched. The other form affects the artwork or art product. They get extras and change. The extras are incorporated. The changes serve other than artistic goals. All enrichment influences consumer choice.

Examples of the former can be the introduction of appealing program notes in concerts and more intense and "creative" advertisement of concerts. In the arts extras in the artwork itself tend to be subtle and difference of opinion can exist if they serve or do not serve artistic goals. Therefore, a related example is more illuminating. Apple laptops have a lighted apple on their covers. This is an extra that does not serve any computing related goal. But it is appealing and serves commercial interests. Additional profit apparently is higher than additional cost.

When in program notes and books or during lectures and interviews in the media, more detailed information and narratives are presented, this affects the nature of the art experience of the consumer. The information can refer to actual characteristics of artworks and their creators. "The skull in the foreground symbolizes the mortality of the portrayed person." "Beethoven composed the piece when he was deaf".

Narratives can also refer to characteristics that have little to do with the actual work. "The price is high; this shows how valuable the work is". The latter could result in artistic impoverishment: the price may make people forget about the artistic qualities of the work. (As said [66]: "price must not stand for artistic quality.") Or art-producers may categorize and label works. "This is our literature series of books made by Moroccan writers". It makes the works more singular in one aspect and less in other respects. Evidently many intermediate cases exist.

Aside: The informative extras can also have a physical form. The chandeliers in the halls and the frame of a painting, as part of the overall art-setting, inform people that the performed works and the paintings are art and are important—even though they may be distracting.

Usually enrichment enhances experiences of singularity and aura [37]. Attention for artistic quality can increase but also go down. In the latter case enrichment leads to *artistic impoverishment*. In either case motives can rest in the pursuit of financial or reputational gain, but not necessarily.

Enrichment practices play an important role in so-called winner-take-all markets. A *winner-take-all market* is a market in which large differences in *income* (or return) exist, while differences correspond with small differences in quality or content. Part of art is offered in such markets.[44] The winner-take-all mechanism is strong in the top of art markets. It is absent in the lowest level of the market, where most artists are active. In intermediate levels and in various submarkets, its intensity varies. (Aside: Because, winners hardly ever "take all", the expression "winners-take-much" would have been more adequate.)

Several factors explain the existence of the winner-take-all mechanism A general explanatory factor is that of a limited, so-called, mental shelf-space of a consumer. A related factor is the limited luxury art consumption space [8]. It is attractive for consumers to foremost mentally "store" a few very successful artists and their works. Another factor is a possible wish to be able to communicate with many different people about artistic preferences. It is rewarding to be able to communicate with many others, possibly world-wide, about artworks and artists. This is enabled by storing knowledge of successful artists and works in a broad range of art rather than storing many names in a narrow art domain. Other factors explain an increasing impact of the mechanism. Winners now win more than some decades ago. One is globalization in the top of the markets. Another is the more intense enrichment practices of art-world participants, often in combination with media activities. Winners stand out more. Another rests in the media which have become ever more present and also operate worldwide. (That some artists are not just successful but extremely successful may contribute to the attraction of the art profession among youngsters.[45])

Tennis can serve as example of both a winner-take-all phenomenon and enrichment. Players are ordered in terms of performance success and can be ordered in terms of their income and net worth in the market of professional tennis. These two rankings largely correspond. Moreover, the yearly income of the first tennis player in the world is much higher than that of the 10th and certainly much higher than that of the 100th best player, but in the case of the top 10, the quality of the play differs little and in the case of the top 100 differences are still not large when compared with the top 1000th best player. It follows that for income winning and losing matches matter much, but this can only be the case because of enrichment activities of others. Managers, media and players must blow up the differences in performance in order to make them large in the mind of consumers and so raise the income of the top player(s)./38 (Players, like McEnroe, sometimes do so by striking behavior, not unlike Damien Hirst does.)

The added narratives are based on "real" differences, for instance, in ways of playing, but also on phenomena that are only indirectly, or not at all related to tennis. For instance, media may add narratives about the personal life of a player (or artist) which draw much attention. A manager or player will have told them. Some narratives may well be fake.

In the arts, the same as in tennis, for enrichment to be successful, narratives and their distribution and amplification by media is essential, both at local and global levels. "Van Gogh was poor and selfless". "The Glyndebourne Opera House and Festival have no equal in the world". These are appealing narratives. They do not have to be true. Given the willingness of his brother to support him, Van Gogh was not really poor. In enrichment, a "make-believe" is important. Making people believe is in the financial and reputational interest of those involved in enrichment practices.

The winner-take-all mechanism in combination with enrichment practices—supported by (worldwide) media activity—has contributed to a disproportional increase in the incomes and net worth of top artists. In 2018 the estimated net worth of the most successful artists are very high. That of the writer J.K. Rowling and of the visual artist Damien Hirst is $1 billion, of the actor Shah Rukh Khan $ 500 million, of the tenor and conductor Placido Domingo $230 million, and of popular musician Sean Combs (Diddy) (only) $ 130 million.

Aside: First, when questioned, most people expect pop-singers backed up by *the* music industry to earn most, but this is not true. Second, some artists do almost as well as athletes. Third, the winner-take-all mechanism is indeed already very strong among the top ten of artists in various art forms. The tenth artist's worth is around one-fourth that of the first.

Aside: The high income of top-selling visual artists like Hirst suggests that there is a so-called financialization in the visual arts: art serving foremost as investment. As mentioned, it is unlikely that art is a good investment. This can anyway not explain a winner-take-all mechanism./39

Over the last decades the winner-take-all mechanism has become stronger. When corrected for inflation 20 or 50 years ago, top incomes were less high. (Differences were large but not always very large. As said, the conductor Von Karajan earned so much that he could afford a private jet and several fast cars.) Corrected for inflation, the average (median) income of all artists has gone down; much over the last 50 years and a little over the last 20 years [41]. The income of the majority is now (still) around the, so-called, poverty threshold. *Over the last decades* the income distribution in the arts has become far more skewed. Taking into account that annual income is lower than net worth, the income of the top five artists is now easily eight thousand times as high as that of the average artist. (Artists are aware of the large differences and this has contributed to their protest against the overall precarity in the arts [45].)

A comparable, increasingly intense winner-take all mechanism also applies to major ensembles—be it not as strong as in the case of some football teams. In spite of declining markets, the returns of major opera ensembles and symphony orchestras, like The Metropolitan Opera, The Royal Opera House, The Royal Concertgebouw and The Berlin Philharmonic, have risen relatively much, that is, when the returns are compared with those of minor ensembles. They are, more than before, winners in terms of returns as well as attention.—Along with the termination of many ensembles, they also stand out more.—(But although incomes of conductors and soloists are high, most "ordinary" performing artists earn amazingly little.)

Unlike in sports, in the arts, no generally accepted measures of quality exist. Quality judgments are subjective and relative. It is impossible to tell if, the same as in tennis, differences in levels of "objective" quality at various levels in art markets are large. Nevertheless, experts and art-producers blow up real or imagined quality differences. Doing so they indirectly impoverish the works which minor artists and minor companies offer. Their artistic quality appears to be lower. (In classical/serious music, some more or less objective criteria exist for measuring performances of individual performers. Positive results are, the same as in sport, extensively used by managements but, of course, do not cover overall quality.)

Finally, because enrichment practices are common and intertwined, it makes sense to speak of an *enrichment economy* and/or an aesthetic economy. Although enrichment practices are not new, they are common and altogether normal in so-called *aesthetic capitalism*. This is a topic in a following section.

(78) IN MOST ARTFORMS, ENRICHMENT PRACTICES NOW LEAD TO EXTREME WINNERS AMONG TWENTIETH- AND TWENTY-FIRST-CENTURY ARTISTS AND ENSEMBLES. EXPERTS AND ART-PRODUCERS OFTEN WORK TOGETHER. THE ENRICHMENT HARMS LESS SUCCESSFUL ARTISTS AND CONSUMERS. FOR ARTISTS THE AESTHETICIZATION OF SOCIETY COMES WITH BENEFITS AS WELL AS COST. During the period of serious art and up to the present day, classic artworks have always been winners. *Over the last decades* the enrichment of old as well as new works by art producers and experts have become more important and sometimes more calculated, contributing much to the winner-take-all mechanism. As far as new artworks are concerned, differences exist between art forms.

Enrichment of twentieth and twenty-first-century work is intense in theater and dance and very intense in the visual arts. Significant is that, along with more contemporaneity, at auctions, prices of works by living visual artists now sometimes exceed the prices of very famous works of old. In literature and the new art-world of film, it is also more intense when twenty-first-century works are compared with twentieth-century work. However, in the classical/serious music, it is the enrichment of the classics of old that is still very intense, while that of earlier twentieth-century work is limited and of later work very limited.

Enriching is part of the job of employees of museums, halls and publishing houses as well as that of larger dealers and impresarios. It certainly is part of the job of the marketeers they employ./40 But expert/critics and artists are often, deliberate or not, also involved in the enrichment practices. In interviews, Damien Hirst adds many narratives about his character and lifestyle, and experts/critics add much to the mystique surrounding him. (Recently Hirst told on Instagram that he likes sausages.) Experts are more serious in their contributions, but not or no longer independent.

In enrichment activities, experts and profit-oriented art-companies often work together. Just now (2018) the Dutch dealer Jan Six claims to have found a new Rembrandt, *Let the Children Come to Me*. This is disputed by some experts, but he found other experts who have examined the painting and support his claim. It is likely that, even with other experts not believing that it is a true Rembrandt, the work may be sold for more than €40 million. Non-profit museums, whether strongly profit oriented or not, also have directly or indirectly high financial and reputational stakes in right or wrong attribution, and they as well work together with experts, some of whom they employ.

To justify high prices in the top of the market of performances and even more in the visual art market, enrichment is necessary. Differences between the most expensive paintings and those of somewhat less expensive paintings or between the real thing and an (almost) perfect copy must be emphasized and explained. Also the special qualities of the expensive performances of a world famous orchestra need to be emphasized and explained with various narratives; the more so because most non-expert-consumers are not able to hear differences. But thanks to enrichment, they "hear" differences. (Of course, some really "learn" and after a while not only imagine differences. In a blind test they may hear differences between one recording and another.)

With ever higher prices of paintings in the top of the market, the prices have become incomprehensible and cause anger—also among artists. As a consequence, art-world experts increasingly use enrichment narratives to justify the high prices of extreme winners. I give two recent examples. In November 2018, David Hockney's painting *Portrait of an Artist (Pool with Two Figures)* was sold at an auction for $90.3 m—at that moment, the highest price ever paid for a work by a living artist. Probably not aware that they also whitewashed the activities of very commercial dealers, art experts worked their guts out to tell on television and in (internet) newspapers, to emphasize how exceptional the painting is, while also adding all sorts of additional narratives like the picture dating back to the year that Hockney's great love affair with Peter ended and that the swimmer in the picture must be the new lover of Peter—something Hockney never said. The work is enriched, another testimony is added to the works aura or emphasized, an experience of aura is stimulated, and the high price appears to be justified.

In the case governments, after having listened to art-world experts, financially support the purchase of very expensive works with taxpayer money, justification is extra important, and certainly nowadays with diminishing respect for art. Recently, the Dutch government subsidized the purchase of two Rembrandt paintings from the wealthy Rothschild banking family, with €80 million.—As mentioned, the decision was taken behind closed doors.—In the media art-world experts enriched the paintings with all sorts of narratives; and to such a degree that one might start to think that they are really worth €180 million./41

Motives of those involved in enrichment practices differ. Usually they are mixed. Art-related motives can accompany a pursuit of financial profit or reputational gain. Extras can add to a better "understanding" of artists and their works. Knowing that later in life Beethoven was deaf can, indeed, make a difference. And the publication of a photograph of the extremely messy studio of Francis Bacon adds a relevant narrative. Also the exhibition by the Van Gogh museum of the original pistol that Van Gogh used to kill himself, can make a relevant difference, even though the motivation of the museum probably foremost rests in a love of income/profit and of more consumers. That Leonardo DiCaprio—after spotting the work on Instagram—bought a painting by the, at the time little-known artist Jean-Pierre Roy adds to the aura of the œuvre of the artist and the latter's income, but if it adds to the focus on and understanding of his works is questionable. Nevertheless, in all such cases, thanks to the narratives in the imagination of people, one or more aspects become more special, while the focus on the works may well become stronger. (Enrichment influences people's self-constructed artworks [24].)

Winners breed winners. For instance, presently famous major museums become more famous and attractive by connecting themselves with very famous living artists and celebrities and vice versa. Already for decades, museums do so by organizing solo exhibitions of the work of major classic artists. (Recently Tate Modern took over the first place from the British Museum in the number of yearly visitors, thanks to a major Picasso exhibition: *Picasso 1932: Love, Fame, Tragedy*.)

New is that art museums boost their attendance by connecting to living celebrities. This applies, among others, to the Louvre, at present displaying Apeshit, a music video of Beyoncé and Jay Z, and the Smithsonian's National Portrait Gallery in Washington that exhibited a striking pair of portraits of the Obamas, bringing in a million more visitors.

Aside: A noteworthy difference exists between winning artists who earn ever more without making additional efforts, that is, without personally enriching their work, and artists who further increase their income, also after they become very successful, by continuing to enrich and promote their work. Examples of the first are writers, like Rowlings, and little-known music producers and text writers, like Dave Cobb—a producer of country music. Thanks to copyrights, money just continues to pour in. Examples of the latter are visual artists, like Koons and Hirst. They cleverly run enterprises and market their work. Most other artists in serious and popular music hold intermediate positions.

Ever higher prices in the top of the visual art market limit the possibilities of museums to collect and exhibit art. In the serious music art-world, a continuous enrichment of classics reduces the chances of contemporary works and artists. And, as we shall see in section 81, it is possible that enrichment leads to less diversity in art as well as more triviality.

In all art forms more intense enrichment practices in the top of the market in combination with a winner-take-all mechanism worsen the financial situation, and chances for creative artists and ensembles lower in markets. They have less "voice" and ensembles sometimes have to discontinue. Several examples were presented in previous sections. One is the case of high prices in the top of the visual art market going at the cost of the chances of artworks and their artists in the sub-top. When, for instance, museums from their own available budget—including subsidies and money from donors, governments and sponsors—buy modern and classic paintings that cost tens of millions, that amount and the higher insurance premiums cannot be spend on not one but several works which are offered at a lower level of the market. Aside: Taking into account that "masterpieces" make museums stand out while this may lead to higher returns from ticket sales, sponsorship and/or donations and subsidies, the net savings are lower but still considerable.

What applies to major museums also applies to collecting corporations and some rich collectors. *Over the years Anna has seen the collections of many important modern art museums as well as of major corporations. In 1992, while visiting Fort Worth and Dallas in the USA, she went to see the exhibited modern art collections of two museums and two corporations. She noticed that they all showed work of the same group of very successful artists, that is, extreme winners.*/42 Aside: in the visual arts some states somewhat regulate the market of expensive art by forbidding export of expensive pieces with the consequence that prices are not as high as they otherwise would have been./43

Due to the continuing and over time accumulating enrichment of composers of old and their works, the chances for twenty-first-century composers are very limited. The contemporaneity in popular music and the increasing contemporaneity in other serious artforms is absent in classical/serious music. No twentieth-century composer is as successful as top composers of old, like Beethoven, Mozart, Brahms, Wagner, Tchaikovsky, Bach and Brahms.

And in comparison, twenty-first-century composers are unimportant. There is much recent contemporary work in the long tail of recorded music, but numbers of sold recordings per composer is low, as is the number of their live performances. Aside: It is significant that some decades ago, starting composers still compose works for symphony orchestra. But since most of them have stopped composing such works, which is understandable, because most works are never performed or otherwise only once. (Only the works of "outsiders", like the composers of film music, John Williams and Hans Zimmer, draw attention, are now increasingly live performed and are, somewhat reluctantly, promoted. Part of the present enrichment of their works follows from an emphasis on the connection with overall blockbusters.)

The lack of promotion of new work clearly shows from the low percentage of performances of symphony music composed by living composers. Many of their works are never performed, and if they are performed the large majority is only performed once./44 But for popularity and the possibility to compete with the classics, repeated performance or, otherwise broadcast and streaming, is essential. Most Billboard-charting popular music tracks have become successful through repeated plays on Spotify, the radio, and at clubs by DJs. The more often they are played and heard, the more familiar they become and the greater the chance they become successful.

Consumers are harmed in more than one respect. By lack of the enrichment of new work, consumers have less access to this work. They also miss out on new work that could have existed if the lack of enrichment had not gone at the cost of innovation leading to attractive new work.

Most importantly, the ongoing "over-enrichment" of the classical music heritage goes at the cost of an attractive and lively heritage, a heritage that is attractive for larger audiences [18]. By lack of new work and a heritage that is hardly alive, consumers lose interest also in the heritage.—The art-world, de facto, "digs its own grave"./45—Consumers miss out on heritage music, which they otherwise may have appreciated. Moreover, when only top ensembles survive with very high ticket prices, this leads to more exclusion also of many art-lovers from live performances. The winner-take-all mechanism enhances inner-art-world exclusion. (The new and successful real time broadcasts of opera and ballet in cinemas are an affordable but inferior substitute. The performances are real time but not live.)

The winner-take-all mechanism is very strong in the arts. More than before the amplification of differences between artists by enrichment contributes to a *meritocracy of art and artists*. The artistic quality of works offered by top artists appears to be much higher than that of artists in the sub-top, and this applies a fortiori in a comparison of high and low levels in the market. This is painful for many artists. Aside: This is especially painful, because the high incomes in the top of the art markets—the same as elsewhere in society—cannot possibly be deserved. If one agrees, given the unfairness of high incomes and the dangerous consequences of an ever-increasing inequality in income and wealth, more regulation and a drastic tax reform is called for./46

The increased enrichment activities also follow from more interdependence in and around art-worlds. Whether they are aware of it or not: expert/critics and commercial art-companies increasingly join forces, and in larger networks, governments both depend on them and influence them. The consequences of increased interdependence for art-worlds and their uncertain future are profound. This is the topic of section 88.

(79) ARTISTS AND ART-COMPANIES PARTICIPATE IN AN AESTHETIC ECONOMY. THIS HAS ADVANTAGES AND DISADVANTAGE FOR ARTISTS. The aestheticization of society, which by now penetrates all areas of consumption in prosperous countries, cannot exist without intense enrichment activities. In the arts they affect the work of artists. So-called aesthetic capitalism

brings groups of artists opportunities and benefits, but may well harm the average artist.

As noted [38], depending on what is singled out, different terms are used for the present phase of capitalism. Aesthetic capitalism is one of them. It refers to an aesthetic economy in prosperous societies in which basic needs are met and commodities are continuously enriched. The enriched works create an atmosphere and helps people in staging their lives.[46] The mentioned Apple laptop is indeed a good example. There is no need for a lighted apple on the cover. It only adds to cost. But the work is enriched and more appealing, while it "stages" the life of the owners. They stand out among the users of laptops.—This certainly applies to the first waves of users.—However, with time the laptops become less rich. It is therefore predictable that before too long Apple will re-design the apple, to let the laptop and its users stand out again. Such behavior is typical for enrichment economies. In the long run consumers are dissatisfied, and they are kept dissatisfied by industries. (Depending on one's point of view, strong enrichment economies are wasteful—and may well indirectly contribute much to climate change. From clothing to kitchens, everything must regularly be replaced, even when they are still useful.)

The aestheticization of society is advantageous for artists. There is much need for designers who design wrappings and enriched products. There is also need for an intermediate form of the latter two. This can be clear utility art, like music in advertisement. But composed music can also enrich films, and as such be said not just to accompany music but be part of the artwork, also when the director has the final say. Spectacular is not so much the growth of such added art, but the growth of well-designed things, from suspension bridges to toothbrushes. An ever-larger part of GDP goes into design.

In most art schools there are design departments. The number of students has increased, but not very much. The graduates do not call themselves artists or call their design products art. Design is foremost taught in other education institutes, often at university level, with strong links with industry. This makes graduates better prepared for their design work. It is, however, significant that increasing numbers of graduated and other artists do not start to work as artists but become designers or later decide to do only or also design work. They are evidently welcome. This implies that they have skills which work well in an enrichment economy. It offers artists work; and artists who go partly or altogether along usually find the work satisfying and enjoy the work. Many enjoy it better than not art-related work. In other words, the labor market for people with artistic skills has become much larger.

But the enrichment economy also has disadvantages for those artists who continue to make not-applied art. Well-designed products are attractive and can partly replace artworks. It causes art markets to grow less than corresponds with increasing prosperity. This applies to serious visual art, and, to a lesser degree, also to serious and popular performing art. Moreover, art becomes less special and this goes at the cost of the prestige of art and the respect for art. This in turn contributes to subsidy cuts. At the same time, the art profession remains extraordinarily attractive. Even though the attraction of alternative creative professions increases, the attraction of the art profession remains high. In combination with less demand for not-applied art and fewer subsidies, this leads to even more artists with very low incomes.

(80) During the period of serious art: MARKETING BY ART-COMPANIES AND ARTISTS IS TABOO. THIS ALSO APPLIES TO (SELF) BRANDING. AFTER CIRCA 1980, MARKETING BY ART-COMPANIES BECOMES ACCEPTABLE. MARKETING ALWAYS AFFECTS THE OVERALL ART PRODUCT. After the discussion of the important phenomenon of enrichment, I now take a step backward to look at marketing and branding and the changing attitudes in the arts toward them. Marketing and branding inevitably lead to enrichment, but their main goal is promotion and not enrichment. Marketeers in the arts attempt to increase sales and are usually not aware of the fact that they give artworks "extras", which necessarily have an impact on the art experience of consumers.

In business economics, *marketing* is defined as making the public aware of a product by using advertising and other methods. A special form of marketing is branding. *Branding* refers to the process of creating a unique name and image for a product in the consumers' mind. Successful branding causes products (or the person who makes them or the institution which offers them) to stand out. They are not like others.

Even though marketing can be very moderate, but in art-worlds, the term marketing is associated with an intense promotion by use of advertisement and other techniques. It is commercial, and in the period of serious art, it is taboo. Nevertheless, to sell art objects and tickets, some form of marketing is always necessary. Without marketing, people would not know that artworks exist, that is, works that significantly differ from other works. They would not buy objects and tickets.

As noted, in the seventeenth and eighteenth centuries in parts of the arts, and foremost in publishing, there is intense and even elaborate marketing. Moreover, in the eighteenth and the first half of the nineteenth centuries, several artists clearly marketed their work by "marketing" their personality, that is, by forms of self-branding. *For instance, Paganini (1782–1840) used his showmanship and sex appeal as selling points.* But since music has become serious, such behavior is taboo./47

During the period of serious art, there is marketing but usually no intense marketing. This is associated with commercialism and taboo. Given its association, the term marketing is not used. But in the 1970s, some good-willing economists start to propagate the use of marketing techniques in the arts, and several managing directors of art-companies are interested. Others, however, are suspicious and resist the idea. The economists try to convince them that proper marketing will not affect the nature of the marketed art products. But they are not believed. Around this time, the term marketing becomes a "dirty" word in art circles—while for some art-lovers it still is a dirty word. Marketing is not compatible with the extreme goodness of art. At least up to 2000, information about the product qualities of serious art is given in a discrete and chic way. Marketing belongs to the domain of vulgar popular art and other entertainment products.

In 1985 Anna was shocked when she heard the business director of a museum in his public new year's speech use the term marketing in a positive sense. Later in 2005, no longer shocked but with amazement, Anna noticed that at the facades of the prestigious Concertgebouw and the Municipal Theatre, there were huge banners advertising the forthcoming concerts and plays./48

Artists and art companies who do not (or did not) believe economists, who say that marketing does not need to affect the nature of artworks and art experiences, are right. Marketing always enriches and changes works and experiences.

Artists and art-companies, deliberate or not, create an image of who they are and what they have to offer. This takes us to the topics of branding and labeling. When branding is successful, the brand name is a profitable asset. Even though the term was at first not used, already for several decades now, art-companies and large ensembles are clearly involved in deliberately branding their art product. And, although the term is not used, over the last decade, self-branding has become acceptable and normal among large groups of artists. Nevertheless, for many conservative art-lovers and leftist art theorists, branding has remained something bad and, for some, increasingly so. It is associated with capitalism and commercial popular art.

Brand names can be valuable assets. Presently, on the website of the Van Gogh Museum it says: "Collaborate with the Van Gogh Museum to develop branded products and reach a wide and varied audience".[47] Within limits the brand name is licensed. A specific form of generating profits from the investment in a brand name follows from the establishment of auxiliaries with the same name. Examples are the Guggenheim in Bilbao and the Louvre in Abu Dhabi. Unlike in sport and popular music, so far most famous serious artists do not license their names or appear in advertisements, but it is likely that not only more art-companies but also more artists will start to do so in the next decades.

Because capitalism is based on private ownership, the exploitation of the ownership of names is what can be expected in capitalism. Also, a more calculated use of brand names is what can be expected in the present phase of capitalism.—Branding and the exploitation of copyrights often come together./49—Whether one likes it or not, it is "natural" that art-companies and artists who want to have voice go along. Branding can increase voice, which may not be a bad thing. It can also speed up careers and so contribute to the winner-take-all mechanism, which as noted has drawbacks in the arts (and elsewhere). The presence of new media and its use for personal branding probably increases the effect. At the moment some young and previously altogether unknown makeup "artists" without income from their work are becoming extremely successful and earn much money. It would be strange if unknown and poor serious artists would not try to achieve the same. Aside: Self-branding in the case of art is not that extraordinary. It connects with the discussed notion of the artist-in-the-work [27].

The additional characteristics marketeers emphasize are part of the overall art-setting, which consumers experience [24]. They enrich the wrapping of the artworks and of the artist and so change the art-product.—This may improve works. But, as said, it can also be a matter of gold plating with as result impoverishment.—When in a marketing campaign the Van Gogh museum much advertises that Van Gogh cut off his ear, or when it shows the pistol, such qualities enter Van Gogh's works as experienced by the visitors of the museum. Or art-lovers can not simply erase the face and facial expression of Vladimir Ashkenazy on the poster they have seen when they—from a distance and without video amplification—listen to him playing live. The same applies to well-branded names like the Royal Dutch Orchestra. The same music—for instance on a CD—sounds different, when the listener knows it is this orchestra performing and not another.

Artist and art-companies cannot do without a name and with a reputation which is connected with the name. People must know that their artworks or art products exist and differ from those of other artists and art-companies. Names are therefore labels that categorize work. In principle, categorizations can be very refined, but in the case of marketing and branding they usually are not. The brand name Berliner Symphoniker (or Berliner Philharmonic) tells that the seat of the Orchestra is in Berlin, that it is a symphony orchestra and most important that the performances are excellent. Because a brand name corresponds with a reputation and imago, it can also limit possibilities. Even if they wish to, it is very hard for traditional serious art venues to reach out to new and different audiences. (That branding can be very successful shows from the fact that there is no need to add New York to the name Metropolitan Museum of Art.)

One may well argue that not only artworks and the names of artists, but that, due to intense marketing, also the person of the artist becomes "commodified, that is commodified in a metaphorical sense. Critics of marketing in the arts (and of capitalism) resent this. They also resent that certain simple aspects of artworks are emphasized and so "commodified". Conservative art-lovers and the new critics of "commerce" on the left resent such "commodification". Simplification is especially bad, because artworks are relatively singular; they are works in which many properties are unique and matter for consumers, or ought to matter for them.

Resentment is understandable. Marketing and branding activities change the artwork or rather the self-constructed artwork of consumers [24]. They do not literally change the actual artworks, but they affect works of art as perceived and processed by consumers.—A dollar sign in the self-constructed work of an expensive artwork certainly affects the work.—This way, by "enriching" works, the marketeer impoverishes them. The same applies to the above-mentioned case of ethnic labeling. But labeling can also be desirable; not only because it gives relevant information to consumers but also because it can give voice to "underprivileged" artists; give them chances they would otherwise not have. (Ethnic labeling and categorizing can also have positive effects.)

Given what has been said above about adaptations by artists, it is likely that marketing by artists, including finding niche markets, can over time lead to the production of different actual artworks, whether being aware of it or not. And given what will be said over art-companies being influenced by demand of consumers and donors, it is even more likely that they adapt their overall actual art product as well. And this is what art-lovers fear. Compromise is a major "sin" in the arts, and marketing is associated with adjustments and compromise; and often rightly so. It is therefore no accident that at first cultural economists and marketeers much emphasized that in marketing the artwork or art product is given. But they are wrong. In little noticed ways, the produced artworks and art products change.

Branding can also more straightforwardly change artworks. Brand names change the art environment or setting, and along with this, the content (in a broad sense) of the work of art, and often, this follows from a combination of brand names. The same as the brand Rieu has become linked to the Strauss brand, the brand Bernard Haitink has become connected to the Mahler brand. Knowing of Rieu or having listened to (recorded) Haitink performances of Mahler one hears other music than without this. But (until recently) Rieu is criticized by many. Haitink is only criticized by some, even though also in the case of Haitink, various art-companies undoubtedly profited from the combination of brand names.

Main recent developments have been mentioned in the text. Here I just mention that in spite of continuing criticism *over the last decades*, artists increasingly use more and also new marketing techniques. For instance, since the 1990s, many visual artists have informative websites. Over time many have become far more elaborate and good-looking. Sometimes it is possible to order works on the website. Now many performing artists and especially musicians have own websites. Artists write blogs and advertise works on internet platforms. Or they send newsletters by email to a large group of loyal customers and possibly interested people. Over the last years the presence of artists on social media, foremost Instagram, has increased much. Video-artists and musicians, moreover, publish works on YouTube, Vimeo and Soundcloud, hoping to attract larger audiences and increase their income. Younger artists do not associate these activities with compromise. And if they do, they do not feel bad about it.—"Millennials are totally cool with selling out".—Sometimes in branding, the branding of the own person becomes more important than the branding of the own work. Or, the personal performance is the art performance and vice versa.

Over the last decades blaming art-companies for intensely marketing their art product is, other than among the new critics of "commerce", no longer common. Nevertheless, it is well possible that within a serious art culture industry marketing can indirectly promote the homogenization and standardization of artworks. This is a topic in the next section.

Finally, it would be strange to argue that artists who are active on social media altogether "commodify" themselves and their work, even though the activity may sometimes (not always) lead to extra income. But they anyway also offer free access to works and in this respect add to the commons. (It, however, indirectly also contributes to the income of the owners of the privately-owned media platforms.)

(81) CRITICS BLAME A COMMERCIAL CULTURE INDUSTRY FOR A LACK OF DIVERSITY AND TRIVIALITY IN THE POPULAR ARTS. THEY THINK THAT ALONG WITH COMMERCIALIZATION THIS COULD ALSO BE THE FUTURE OF A MORE COMMERCIAL WORLD OF SERIOUS ART. Enrichment and marketing of serious art by a culture industry certainly affects the choices of consumers. Indirectly it could lead to less diversity and

homogenization, but not necessarily. It is significant that already for a long time more diversity exists in the commercial world of popular music than in the less commercial art-world of classical and serious music, an art-world that is supported by governments and donors. But arguing that a culture industry, and especially the commercial media, manipulates consumers' tastes is probably correct.

Critics of commerce blame the culture industry for all sorts of wrongdoing including little diversity in poplar art. But often statements are general and lack precision. It is seldom clear what kind of diversity one has in mind. Is it diversity in artistic content, on meaningful content or in just any content? Is it diversity in styles and genres? Is it diversity in live or in not-live art? Is it diversity among best-sellers, in the sub-top or in the long tail? Or, in the case of live events, is it diversity in atmospheres and in types of venues? Or is it diversity in the social groups and age groups that are served. Or is it diversity in geographical areas served? As has been proven or made plausible in the text so far, in all these areas the commercial popular music industry has realized more diversity than the classical/serious music art-worlds. The same is likely to apply to the other performing arts and, to a lesser degree, to the other art forms.

Diversity in content is a different matter. In this case changes in diversity over time are particularly interesting. There could be homogenization, or diversification. Sociologists have measured diversity in artistic content in the case of popular music over time, be it only for the top of the charts.[48] Around 1950 there was less diversity than around 1940 and also less than around 1960 and after. This has been explained by some sociologists from a temporary decrease in concentration in the industry, that is, main producers becoming less powerful.—This is in line with a common theory in economics.—But diversity did not go down when around 1960 concentration increased again. Later this was explained by another sociologist from the phenomenon of a more decentralized form of production by the majors.[49] They bought smaller labels and developed subdivisions.

The outcome is interesting because in the criticism of the culture industry, all sorts of negative effects and above all a lack of diversity and of homogeneity are attributed to the existence of a small number of mega commercial companies. It is indeed possible that with less concentration, there would be even more diversity, but this is not certain. When compared with the lower diversity in the established arts, the effect on diversity must be limited. Evidently in most art-worlds, the "mental concentration", enabled by a not-orchestrated attunement, and the need for unity brings along more homogeneity. Exceptions are the (weak) art-worlds of serious literature and film. Technical reproduction makes diversification attractive. More generally, in aesthetic capitalism, with its emphasis on design, diversity is essential—be it not necessarily meaningful diversity. Things must stand out and be different.

In this context the question arises if the present concentration in the distribution of music streams will lead to less diversity. The market of streamed music (with and without videoclips) is now larger than that of DVDs, and its share of the overall recorded music market is still increasing. It certainly leads to a stronger winner-take-all outcome. But although content diversity in the top is relatively low, it is not necessarily lower than

10 or 20 years ago, while in the very long tail, diversity is probably larger. But then the next question is: which groups are served by the large variety in the long tail. Maybe only for small groups of well-educated people? A parallel development is likely to occur in the distribution of films with Netflix taking care of the streaming of more successful films, and minor platforms and YouTube also taking care of works in the long tail, including masterpieces of old.

This takes us to the issue of meaningful diversity instead of triviality./50 The commercial industry is by many people blamed for producing trivial popular art. Only yesterday I read a blog of a serious music critic in which he refers to popular music as "mass-media glut of factory-produced tripe". But, as noted, no general accepted measures of artistic quality exist and certainly none of relevance or triviality. Judgments are subjective. Most important: the art that one social group judges to be relevant, at least for the own group, may be judged to be irrelevant by another. The last group may even judge it to be unhealthy for the group who thinks it is relevant. Or the former may believe that their art is healthy for the others. As noted, the latter is a common belief among the elites attempting to disseminate their art among others. Given their common belief in universal artistic quality, the notion that social groups may have own art that is important for the own group and not necessarily for other groups hardly occurs [85].

Aside: Artistic diversity in mainstream popular art is limited. The art is meaningful for almost anybody. Meanings are general and sometimes of all times. (The same applies to many operas.) In overall mainstream, imitation comes first [23]. There are formulas. Hit-movies, hit-songs and hit-literature. Nevertheless, periodically, there are changes in common artistic qualities and in popular themes, that is, the opposite of homogenization. Otherwise people would lose interest.

Aside: Another common belief among critics of the culture industry as well as many artists is that large corporations always strive for best-sellers and that a selection of works and artists in the bottom of the market are only supported for scouting potential best sellers. This clearly does not apply to Spotify and i-Tunes, but it never applied. In the arts, and not only music and film, there always have been subdivisions and smaller companies providing small-scale productions or representing not-well-known artists with high return on investment. (Moreover, risks in the top of the market are very large. Long-term return on investment can well be lower than at lower levels in the market. Expensive blockbusters are regularly box office flops. United Artists, for instance, almost collapsed after the *Heaven's Gate* flop in 1980./51)

Finally, consumers are sometimes thought to be influenced by, manipulated by and dumbed by a culture industry. The media, and in particular the popular art industries, are thought to manipulate consumers; they leave them little choice and take away their voice.[50] They also manipulate popular artists who are thought to have far less autonomy than serious artists.

Critics fear that along with commercialization, this will also be the fate of serious art; that is, consumers having little say, artists giving in to the wishes of art-companies and of consumers, homogenization and little diversity. The development of a more user-oriented domain in the arts would be in line with this. But as said, there probably is more overall diversity in popular art than in serious art—and certainly more than in new serious music.

Moreover, in the serious arts as well consumers and artist depend on other parties. There is interdependence and, thanks to the shared art ethos, preferences of the various groups of participants become attuned. As I will argue in section 88, it is likely that *over the last decades*, the overall interdependence within art-worlds increases, and that, within the balance of power of the various groups of art-world participants, the groups of expert/critics and of artists lose some of their earlier power. But this does not have to imply less diversity and homogenization. The opposite is more likely. These are topics in the next chapter.

Notes

[1](Negus, 1999).

[2]Cf. (Zuidhof, 2003).

[3]According to (Boltanski & Chiapello, 2005), 472 artists can only live an authentic life if they reject a pursuit of income/profit.

[4](Velthuis, 2005b) 24–25.

[5](Arjo Klamer, 1996). Several economists, like Tyler Cowen, disagree. "In Praise of Commercial Culture" is the title of a book he wrote: (Cowen, 1998).

[6]Cf. (Arjo Klamer, Langeveld, & Teule, n.d.) (in Dutch).

[7](Beech, 2015) presents an interesting analysis of crowd funding from a Marxist economic perspective.

[8]Cf. (Velthuis, 2005a).

[9](Adorno & Horkheimer, 1991).

[10]A lack of voice of ordinary people in neo-liberal times is emphasized by (Couldry, 2010).

[11](Blanning, 2008).

[12](Arora & Vermeylen, 2013) 205.

[13](Finkelstein & MacCleery, 2005).

[14](Steptoe, 1988) 63.

[15]Cited in (Thayer, 1964). Also cited by (Cowen, 1998) 16.

[16](Gogh, 2003).

[17]Cf. (Wuggenig & Rudolph, 2013) 147/148.

[18]The dealer and publisher, Alfred Stieglitz, attempted to stay away from it (Haines, 1982).

[19](Velthuis, 2016) 19.

[20]Cf. (Zelizer, 1994).

[21]Cited by (Velthuis, 2005b) 43.

[22](Arjo Klamer, 1996).

[23]This sentence is from Oscar Wilde's novel *The Picture of Dorian Gray.*

[24](Hauser 1999) 467, also cited by Velthuis.

[25]Cf. (Velthuis, 2005b).

[26](Abbing, 2002) and (Velthuis, 2002).

[27](Wuggenig & Rudolph, 2013) refer to research for the early period by (Grampp, 1989) and Kleine and, for the first decade of the twenty-first century, by Buchholz and by (Wuggenig & Rudolph, 2013).

[28] (Bourdieu, 1983) 311–356.

[29] (Velthuis, 2005b).

[30] In this context, (Velthuis, 2005b) argues that the visual art market relies on a dense fabric of mutual gifts and favors.

[31] Cf. (Abbing, 2002).

[32] (Abbing, 2002).

[33] I derive the term "hybrid artist" from (Winkel, Gielen, & Zwaan, 2012) (in Dutch).

[34] (Laermans, 2009) did research among choreographers and found that, for them being able to take responsibility for the work in spite of constraints is important.

[35] Cf. (Menger, 2001).

[36] The cultural economist (Throsby, 1994) coined the term "work preference" in economics.

[37] Cf. (Cyert & March, 2013).

[38] Robin Pogrebin: https://www.nytimes.com/2010/04/03/arts/03center.html?mtrref=www.google.com (accessed 18-10-2018).

[39] (Arian, 1971).

[40] This description is in line with the way in which (Schumpeter, 1934) uses the term in 2011.

[41] (A. Klamer, 2011) and (A. Klamer, 2016).

[42] (A. Klamer, 2016).

[43] (Boltanski & Esquerre, 2016) coined the term.

[44] (Frank & Cook, 1995) coined the term and extensively discussed the phenomenon. Earlier the phenomenon was analyzed by (Rosen, 1981) and (Adler, 1985), while having the arts in mind.

[45] Cf. (Abbing, 2002).

[46] (Bohme, 2017).

[47] See: https://www.vangoghmuseum.nl/en/business/van-gogh-museum-brand-licenses?v=1—accessed 12-09-2018.

[48] (Peterson & Berger, 1975).

[49] (Dowd, 2004).

[50] Cf. (Couldry, 2010).

Literature

Abbing, H. (2002). *Why Are Artists Poor? The Exceptional Economy of the Arts*. Amsterdam: Amsterdam University Press.

Adler, M. (1985). Stardom and Talent. *American Economic Review, 75*, 208–212.

Adorno, T. W., & Horkheimer, M. (1991). The Culture Industry: Enlightenment as Mass Deception. In T. W. Adorno & J. M. Bernstein (Eds.), *The Culture Industry. Selected Essays on Mass Culture*. London: Routledge.

Arian, E. (1971). *Bach, Beethoven, and Bureaucracy: The Case of the Philadelphia Orchestra* (1st ed.). Tuscaloosa: The University of Alabama Press.

Arora, P., & Vermeylen, F. (2013). The End of the Art Connoisseur? Experts and Knowledge Production in the Visual Arts in the Digital Age. *Information, Communication & Society, 16*(2), 194–214. https://doi.org/10.1080/1369118X.2012.687392.

Beech, D. (2015). *Art and Value: Art's Economic Exceptionalism in Classical, Neoclassical and Marxist Economics*. Boston: Brill.

Blanning, T. C. W. (2008). *The Triumph of Music. The Rise of Composers, Musicians and Their Art*. Cambridge, MA: Belknap Press of Harvard University Press.

Bohme, G. (2017). *Critique of Aesthetic Capitalism*. Milano/Udine: Mimesis International.

Boltanski, L., & Chiapello, E. (2005). *The New Spirit of Capitalism*. London/New York: Verso.
Boltanski, L., & Esquerre, A. (2016). The Economic Life of Things. *New Left Review, 98*, 31–54.
Boltanski, L., & Thévenot, L. (1991). *On Justification. Economies of Worth*. Princeton/Oxford: Princeton University Press.
Bourdieu, P. (1983). The Field of Cultural Production, or: The Economic World Reversed. *Poetics, 25*, 311–356.
Couldry, N. (2010). *Why Voice Matters: Culture and Politics After Neoliberalism*. Los Angeles: Sage.
Cowen, T. (1998). *In Praise of Commercial Culture*. Cambridge, MA: Harvard University Press.
Cyert, R. M., & March, J. G. (2013). *A Behavioral Theory of the Firm (1963)*. Mansfield Centre: Martino Fine Books.
Dekker, E. (2015). Two Approaches to Study the Value of Art and Culture, and the Emergence of a Third. *Journal of Cultural Economics, 39*, 309–326.
Dowd, T. J. (2004). Musical Diversity and the U.S. Mainstream Recording Market, 1955–1990. *ResearchGate, 82*(4), 1411–1455.
Finkelstein, D., & MacCleery, A. (2005). *An Introduction to Book History*. New York etc.: Routledge.
Frank, R. H., & Cook, P. J. (1995). *The Winner-Take-All Society*. New York etc.: The Free Press.
Gogh, V. V. (2003). *The Letters of Vincent Van Gogh*. London: Penguin.
Grampp, W. D. (1989). *Pricing the Priceless. Art, Artists and Economics*. New York: Basic Books.
Hafferty, F. W., & Castellani, B. (2011). Two Ships: The Rise of a Professionalism Movement Within Modern Medicine and Medical Sociology's Disappearance from the Professionalism Debate. In *Handbook of the Sociology of Health, Illness, and Healing* (pp. 201–219). New York: Springer.
Haines, R. E. (1982). *The Inner Eye of Alfred Stieglitz*. Lanham: University Press of America, Incorporated.
Hauser, A. (1999). *The Social History of Art* (1st ed.). London; New York: Routledge.
Klamer, A. (1996). The Value of Culture. In A. Klamer (Ed.), *The Value of Culture*. Amsterdam: Amsterdam University Press.
Klamer, A. (2011). Cultural Entrepreneurship. *Review of Austrian Economics, 24*, 121–156.
Klamer, A. (2016). *Doing the Right Thing. A Value Based Economy*. London: Ubiquity Press.
Klamer, A., Langeveld, C., & Teule, P. (n.d.). *Pak aan*. Retrieved from http://www.klamer.nl/book/pak-aan/
Laermans, R. (2009). Artistic Autonomy as Value and Practice. In P. Gielen & P. de Bruyne (Eds.), *Being an Artist in Post-Fordist Times* (pp. 125–137). Rotterdam: NAi Publishers.
Menger, P.-M. (2001). Artists as Workers: Theoretical and Methodological Challenges. *Poetics, 28*(4), 241–254. https://doi.org/10.1016/S0304-422X(01)80002-4.
Negus, K. (1999). *Music Genres and Corporate Cultures*. London/New York: Routledge.
Peterson, R., & Berger, D. (1975). Cycles in Symbol Production: The Case of Popular Music. *American Sociological Review, 40*(6), 158.
Rengers, M. (2002). *Economic Lives of Artists. Economic Lives of Artists: Studies into Careers and the Labour Market in the Cultural Sector*. Doctoral Thesis, Utrecht University.
Rosen, S. (1981). The Economics of Superstars. *American Economic Review, 71*, 845–858.
Schumpeter, J. A. (1934). *The Theory of Economic Development*. Retrieved from http://www.hup.harvard.edu/catalog.php?isbn=9780674879904
Steptoe, A. (1988). *The Mozart-DaPonte Operas*. Oxford: Clarendon Press.
Stigler, G. J. (1945). Review of *Review of The Economics of Control: Principles of Welfare Economics*, by A. P. Lerner. *Political Science Quarterly, 60*(1), 113–115. https://doi.org/10.2307/2144462.
Thayer, A. W. (1964). *Thayer's Life of Beethoven* (New ed.). Princeton: Princeton University Press.
Throsby, D. (1994). A Work-Preference Model of Artist Behaviour. In A. Peacock & I. Rizzo (Eds.), *Cultural Economics and Cultural Policies*. Dordrecht etc.: Kluwer Academic Publishers.
Velthuis, O. (2002). *Talking Prices. Contemporary Art on the Market in Amsterdam and New York*. Unpublished Dissertation, Erasmus University Rotterdam.

Velthuis, O. (2005a). *Imaginary Economics. Contemporary Artists and the World of Big Money*. Rotterdam: NAi Uitgevers.
Velthuis, O. (2005b). *Talking Prices. Symbolic Meanings of Prices on the Market for Contemporary Art*. Princeton: Princeton University Press.
Velthuis, O. (2012). Introduction. The Contemporary Art Market Between Stasis and Flux. In *Contemporary Art and Its Commercial Markets: A Report on Current Conditions and Future Scenarios*. Berlin: Sternberg Press.
Velthuis, O. (2016). Are We in a New Era of the Art Market? In *Art in the Periphery of the Center* (pp. 456–465). Berlin: Sternberg Press.
Winkel, C. V., Gielen, P. J. D., & Zwaan, K. (2012). *De hybride kunstenaar. De organisatie van de artistieke praktijk in het postindustriële tijdperk*. Retrieved from https://www.rug.nl/research/portal/publications/de-hybride-kunstenaar-de-organisatie-van-de-artistieke-praktijk-in-het-postindustriele-tijdperk(e173c13d-c532-415c-89fb-710088a86f8d)/export.html
Wuggenig, U., & Rudolph, S. (2013). Valuation Beyond the Market. On Symbolic Value and Economic Value in Contemporary Art. In *Art Production Beyond the Art Market* (pp. 100–149). Retrieved from http://www.sternberg-press.com/?pageId=1465
Zelizer, V. A. (1994). *The Social Meaning of Money*. New York: Basic.
Zuidhof, P.-W. (2003). *Beyond the Polemics on the Market*. Presented at the Paper Presented at the Eastern Sociological Society Conference.

Sharing Art

All through the art period outside art-buildings (including art-spaces), much more art, serious art as well as popular/inferior art, is shared by higher and lower social groups than we are inclined to think. This foremost applies to not-live art. Serious live performing art is not accessible for the latter. It follows that people are omnivorous. They "eat" from both racks. The symbolic boundary between serious and popular art is strong, but as far as consumers—rather than artists—are concerned, the social boundary is less strong.

Most shared art is understood differently by different social groups. Some art is not shared. A part is difficult and interesting only for expert-consumers. Another part is "own art". Social groups have self-developed art that is especially meaningful for them. At least for a while they can keep it for themselves.

Over the last two decades the overlap in the reproduced art social groups consume is becoming larger. A weakening of the symbolic boundary between serious and popular art contributes to this, as do the (commercial) media. Moreover, in a new user-oriented domain in the established arts, there are now many attempts to interest more middle-class people in the art they offer. Sometimes serious and popular art is again offered in the same events.

The attempts of local governments to let more people participate in art events have increased. Important for the sharing of art is the emergence of ever more parallel channels of scouting and gatekeeping. The traditional media and nowadays also the social media contribute to this development. It much increases the chances of all social groups to produce art and have their art noticed.

Lines on either side of the text indicate that recurring concepts are defined or described. This chapter is accompanied by web-notes and web-texts, which are available on the website: *www.hansabbing.com*. Numbers between brackets refer to other sections, including web-texts. Numbers at the end of a sentence preceded by a forward slash refer to web-notes. Holding a pc, tablet or phone next to this text, it is easy to "scan" the web-notes and web-texts. (Quantitative data I most often present in web-notes.)

H. Abbing, *The Changing Social Economy of Art*,
https://doi.org/10.1007/978-3-030-21668-9_6

Increased Sharing

(82) AFTER CIRCA 1960, THE PARTICIPATION IN LIVE POPULAR ART EVENTS INCREASES MUCH. PARTICIPATION IN LIVE SERIOUS ART EVENTS GOES DOWN TO RECOVER A LITTLE IN THE TWENTIETH CENTURY. In web-text wt-82, which accompanies this section, I present data.[1] Here I just mention some general developments.

The demand for popular art and especially so-called pop music grows in every decade since 1950. (Around 1950 the term pop music starts to be used.) The gradual spread of television among the population much enhances the success of popular art—and so does the transistor radio in the case of pop music.[2] The absence of an imposing art-setting and the informal atmosphere in situations in which people consume popular art together, explain part of the success, also the success among higher-educated people, including the children of art-lovers. Taking into account the growth of the population, in the period 1950–2000 the relative number of visits to organized popular art events in venues increases much. It remains high till the present day. From the start of the increase higher-educated people are overrepresented—be it less overrepresented than in the case of established art events. Data, corrected for the growth of the population, confirm these conclusions. In most Western countries, the growth of visits to popular music concerts is spectacular.

From circa 1960 onward in the established arts the absolute number of visits to live art events, including visits to art museums, goes down. Taking into account the growth of the population the decrease is large. Significant is that the percentage of higher educated people among the population increases in this period but that the percentage of them participating in live events decreases. That art museums suffer less is in line with a gradually more informal atmosphere in the museums. (I ignore visits of foreigners to museums. Part of the recent success of art museums is caused by more visits by foreigners./1)

(83) During the period of serious art and up to the present day: OUTSIDE ART-BUILDINGS, LOWER-CLASS AND HIGHER-CLASS PEOPLE ARE EXPOSED TO POPULAR AS WELL AS SERIOUS ART. THEY ALSO INTENTIONALLY CONSUME EACH OTHER'S ART. THEY ARE OMNIVOROUS. Art-worlds create, maintain and sometimes adjust the symbolic boundary between art and no-art by deciding that certain art-in-a-broad-sense can or cannot enter art-buildings. Almost everybody is aware of their choice. There is a symbolic boundary. Nevertheless, outside art-buildings in (semi) public space and at home, the social boundary is less strong. Lower-class people deliberately or casually consume serious art and higher-class people popular/inferior art. Part of serious and popular/inferior art is shared. There is a considerable overlap.

In web-text wt-83, which may interest all readers, I discuss the various ways in which higher social people in the period of serious art come across the art of low-class people and often enjoy the art. I also discuss how low-class people come across serious art in semi-public space, and consume reproductions and recordings at home. There is far more serious art in their homes than people tend to think. I give many examples.

The continuing presence of each other's art in (semi-) public space and in people's homes indicates that people somewhat know and like the other group's art; otherwise it would not be present. People anyway are or become familiar with the most widely shared works that "belong" to the other group. This is interesting because "learning" of art begins with exposure. This is the topic of the next section.

(84) "LEARNING ART" IS FOREMOST A SOCIAL AFFAIR. EMBODIED LEARNING, ENTHUSIASTIC OTHERS AND LIVELY ART SCENES FACILITATE THE UNDERSTANDING OF ART. In order to better understand the sharing of art, its limitations and the importance of having own art, in web-text wt-84, which may interest all readers, I look at the way many people "learn art". I also pay attention to worries about art education disappearing from the curricula in primary and secondary schools.

Here I only note that "learning art" starts with exposure, as may occur in the situations described in the previous section. But especially for a learning to "understand" art, enthusiastic others are indispensable. Moreover, different groups will usually learn art in different ways, which leads to different kinds of understanding. This is the topic of the next section.

(85) SOCIAL GROUPS UNDERSTAND THE SAME ART DIFFERENTLY. GROUPS HAVE OWN ART, WHICH THEY ARE PROUD OF. ART SOMETIMES "TRAVELS" FROM ONE GROUP TO ANOTHER. Given different ways of "learning art", it can be expected that when different social groups share art, they may well understand the same art differently. The art is meaningful but in different ways. Sometimes groups have own art that is not shared. Others think that the art is meaningless for them, or they are deliberately or de facto excluded.

A similar or different understanding of the same art already starts at the level of individuals. Even though they "learn art" in the company of friends, an own private history and identity is reflected in an own choice of art. The same applies to social groups. They have shared histories, problems and challenges. Not only do choices resemble within the group, but the group also has favorite art genres and styles. Sometimes this is *own art*, art that is developed within the group and not shared with other groups, at least not in the short run. Given different backgrounds such art could not have been developed by another social group. Moreover, like individuals, social groups have *own ways of understanding* the same art. The conventions of social groups in experiencing art and in constructing meaningful narratives differ [24].

Avant-garde innovative art circles usually form a subgroup within a larger social group, which in turn can be part of an even larger social group. The artists who develop House music in Detroit and Chicago belong to local groups of gays and blacks—sometimes gay as well as black. But the subsequent scenes and corresponding social groups are larger; from low-class youngsters to youngsters in general.

The same as earlier in the case of Jazz, movement from one social group to the next is often an upward movement. At present part of Dance enters the realm of classical/serious music, where a young crowd of music lovers is interested. Sometimes a change of setting is—at least at first—sufficient to get an upward movement going. At present black Rap music creators perform in Europe for very young and very enthusiastic white audiences. Partly for the money, the black rappers are happy to perform in Europe, even though they know that in the halls their social critical Raps are inaudible or misunderstood./2 (Especially the self-created own art of immigrants "travels". With some modification it starts to appeal to ever-larger social groups. Examples are RAP of North-African immigrants living in the South of France and Beats of Antillean immigrants living in an Amsterdam suburb.)

New art is at first "owned" by the group who developed it. It belongs to them, and they are proud of it. If possible, they monopolize the own art. They anyway believe that their understanding of the own art is superior, when compared to the possible understanding by other groups. They therefore create, emphasize and attempt to maintain a symbolic boundary around the own art. This applies to groups developing new popular art as well as groups developing new serious art.

Top-down movement of new serious art is rare, even though some serious art clearly influences popular art [52].—As mentioned [57], the earlier attempts of groups of art-lovers to vertically disseminate the own art among lower social groups were unsuccessful.—In this respect economic reasons are significant. Partly thanks to government and donor support, the relative well-to-do art-lovers can afford to monopolize and not share the own art. They can reserve it for the own group. But this is only partly possible: it does not apply to serious art in reproduced form. As noted [57], it has been (and is) shared and this is possible, thanks to low prices.

As said, a bottom-up movement of popular art is common. Often, before too long, lower-educated groups stop monopolizing the own art and start to share it. This follows from enthusiasm and taking pride. There may also be a wish to let other groups, possibly higher-educated groups, acknowledge the quality of the own work. But most important are economic reasons. The artists in a group must make a living. One possible consequence is, however, that the own art is not only modified but also gets lost in a process of appropriation [52].

Since the 1960s, not all new and innovative popular music is at first developed by low-class social groups, but it is shared, be it mostly in recorded form. As said, live concerts are sometimes too expensive. Nevertheless, part of all popular art starts to be "owned" by certain higher groups. It is their art, which may or may not be interesting and meaningful for others.

The overall picture is one of own art next to shared art, that is, shared art which is usually understood differently by different social groups. Lower and higher groups share part of their serious and their popular/inferior art. In the case of serious art, this is almost exclusively technically reproduced art. In the case of popular art, both live and not-live popular/inferior art is shared between groups of lower-educated people, while a large and growing amount is shared with higher-educated people and shared between groups of higher-educated people.

Some art, however, is not at all shared. It is the own art of a social group. "Ownership" is usually temporary, but "temporary" can be a matter of decades if not centuries. (If one were to argue that serious live art differs fundamentally from serious not-live art, then the first kind of art has not or hardly been shared with lower-middle- and low-class groups for a period of more than 150 years.)

All this is not to say that all art is and can be very meaningful for all groups, that is, groups with different histories and different positions in society. First, it cannot be meaningful simply because it is unnoticed. Second, it is anyway too difficult also for many art-lovers. Third, it could become meaningful but only in the long run and after modifications. Fourth, the own art of a group can be too meaningless for another, especially when groups hold positions on the social ladder that are further away, or when their background is very different. When a little-educated young immigrant listens to Mozart's music, he is likely to be little interested. For him the music is meaningless; and more meaningless than much Hip-hop music. For serious art-lovers, on the other hand, if they were to listen to Hip-hop the music can also be (almost) meaningless. Nevertheless, in the long run, social groups change as does much art. Hip-hop certainly changes and Mozart can become meaningful for others, who discover or construct new and other meanings.

Often it is prejudices which make art meaningless for other groups. Many higher-educated people assume beforehand that inferior visual art is trivial and irrelevant for them, while it could be meaningful. The opposite also applies. Youngsters, who think that classical/serious music is boring, may not allow Mozart's music to become meaningful for them.

Sometimes specific art just cannot be shared, because it is too difficult. It can only be appreciated and owned by a group of expert-consumers. Only by joining the group and being taught intensively, the art becomes comprehensible and meaningful. This, for instance applies to serial music, like that of Henri Pousseur, and some IDM (Intelligent Dance Music) like that of Autechre. (This kind of art, however, influences more comprehensible art.)

Given the context of this section two questions present themselves. Is it important that groups have own art? And second, can and must groups have a right not to share own art? The answers cannot but be very subjective. Is it important for the group, for art, for society at large? That it is important for groups is what can be expected. Otherwise there would not be attempts at monopolization, be it in the case of lower groups, often only in the short run. Own art empowers. Higher groups are powerful, lower groups are not or less powerful. Depending on one's political view, one may argue that their empowerment is a good thing.

The answer to the second question can follow from the first. "Lower groups have or must have a right to have art of their own." But the reasoning can also be very different and follow from the supposed goodness of private property. This applies to a commonly heard argument for the right of an elite on own art. "We pay for it. And if governments also subsidize our art, this is fair because we pay higher taxes."

For the period of serious art, the notion of an elite "owning" part of serious art—it is their "own art"—certainly makes sense, but not anymore. Over the last decades, whether due to market forces or changing attitudes, most live serious art starts to be shared with other groups, be it with well-educated middle-class rather than little-educated people.

(86) HIGHER-EDUCATED PEOPLE HAVE BECOME MORE OMNIVOROUS. THEY INCREASINGLY CONSUME BOTH SERIOUS ART AND POPULAR ART. Since the 1980s commercial turn and especially over the last two decades, the *symbolic boundary between serious art and popular art* is indeed becoming less important. The same does not in the same degree apply to the *social boundary between serious and popular art.* Nevertheless, outside art-buildings, well-educated people consume more popular art. They have become more omnivorous.

As noted [83], all through the period of serious art, higher bourgeois listen to some popular/inferior music. For instance, in England the "gentlefolks", enjoyed listening to and singing lower-class drinking songs, that is, folk popular music, in the private bar—the part of the pub that is reserved for higher-class people. At home, they listen to a repertoire that has been around for a while, like Gospel and early R&B. This changes in the 1960s. At the time there is much innovation in popular music and middle-class youngsters eagerly start to listen to bands, like The Beatles, The Rolling Stones and The Who. They offer meaningful music, music that for this group is more meaningful than classical/serious music and also more than the earlier popular ballad and popular song.

At the time well-educated parents still attempt to stop their children from listening to popular music, which is supposed to be inferior music, but this becomes ever harder. *In 1961 at age 15 Anna, the same as numerous other children, listened secretly under the bedcovers to a small transistor radio playing music broadcasted from a pirate ship, Radio Caroline. Moreover, in the breaks between classes, she started to visit a local café frequented by pupils of secondary schools, where popular music was played, taking care not to be noticed by friends of the family. She also started to secretly visit pop-concerts in small venues by, usually lower-class, pop bands.*

In those days youngsters start to cross the social barriers between serious and pop. In the 1970s, most educated people who also listen to popular music are no longer afraid of telling others about it. They now consume both types of music. With respect to serious-music and popular music, they have become omnivores.

Aside: Gradually the process is reversed. The majority of higher-educated people become again univores, with the difference that they now only listen to popular music./3 But it is quite possible that in the decades to come, along with major changes in the world of classical/serious music, more people will become omnivores again. It is also possible that with a less important boundary crossover, music will become most important. In that case the distinction of omnivores and univores will be unimportant, at least as far as these two broad categories of music are concerned.

With time higher-educated people not only listen to popular music at home and in concerts, they also start to consume recorded and live cabaret, musicals and popular film, and they no longer apologize for this. Already earlier they watched dance movies, like those of Astaire and Rogers, comedies, like those of the Marx Brothers, or blockbusters, like *Spartacus* and *Exodus*. But now much more time is spent on watching popular movies—most often at home. A large variety of comedies, thrillers and blockbuster science fiction and fantasy movies is consumed, like *Star Wars, Lord of the Rings* and the *Game of Thrones* series.

Very important for a weakening boundary is the phenomenon of *crossover art*, which is produced by artists in the established arts, by popular artists and a new kind of hybrid artist who no longer lets himself be categorized. Significant is that in 2017, a graphic novel was included in the Booker prize longlist./4 Serious critics indeed go along. They discuss and review not only popular music but also cabaret, musicals and popular film. They reflect on quality differences, which may matter for some higher-educated people, while they don't mind that others are not interested.

It also appears that the symbolic boundary between art and popular art is no longer connected with a major hierarchical difference. As said [7], in quality papers, serious and popular art events are reviewed on the same page. Earlier people would have protested. It would have put superior serious art down.

In the USA there are now prestigious buildings for popular art that can compete with prestigious art-buildings. One of the first is the Rock and Roll Hall of Fame in Cleveland, Ohio. The number of such buildings is, however, still low. The increased combining of serious and popular art in live events outside art-buildings is another sign of the symbolic boundary becoming less important. More significant is that in some of the prestigious art-buildings, now also typical popular performance art is performed [87].

Especially higher-educated people have become more omnivorous. They care less about the distinction serious-popular. Because omnivorousness is an important topic in the sociological literature of the last decades and because students should learn about it in the following four paragraphs, I say more about.[3] In a metaphoric sense, people can indeed be said to be omnivores, if they consume serious art as well as popular art. They may eat from both racks and maybe increasingly. Are both higher and lower social groups omnivores and in which degree? Does the kind of art make a difference?

As noted, during the period of serious art, both groups are omnivores in the case of technically reproduced art rather than live art. But as also noted, not all art is shared. Although there is a considerable overlap, some art is not interesting for the one or the other group. It remains unnoticed, or it is thought to be not meaningful enough or too difficult. For the last decades surveys and data exist on expressed preferences for what sociologists call high-brow and low-brow arts. They found an increased omnivorousness in tastes for the two among foremost higher-educated people. Aside: Though research and data on actual behavior would be more interesting, such research is, as said, difficult and largely absent.

Sociologists often have a broader notion of omnivorousness in mind. They research now not only tastes with respect to high-brow and low-brow art but also with respect to different genres in serious and especially popular music. For them omnivorous consumers have a broad cultural taste and are willing to cross established hierarchical genre boundaries. They found that tastes with respect to music genres broadened, at least up to the beginning of the twentieth century.

Nevertheless, the inclination to construct hierarchies in art in a broad sense by both high and low social groups has not disappeared. This is in line with Pierre

Bourdieu's findings with respect to the 1950s and 1960s. What is however different is that hierarchies are constructed within genres of popular art, like genres in music (and games)./5

It is important to stress that although by now the symbolic and social boundary between serious and popular art is less significant, the boundary has not disappeared. Popular art still has little access to the traditional art-buildings. And in Europe, for decisions on art subsidies—as well as value added tax—the distinction can be decisive. Moreover, even though lower social groups now more often participate in live popular art events, they continue to be absent in live serious art events in art-buildings. In their case the social boundary, a too-high price barrier, is important.

Thinking about art people still distinguish the two and this is significant. Over the last ten years, I asked groups of university students in different disciplines and in several countries, to quickly write down first associations with terms and, quasi-accidentally among them, the term art. The names of prestigious local art museums, concert halls and theaters were mentioned, the same as the names of classical artists like Mozart, Rembrandt and Picasso. Also, terms referring to characteristics of art and art events were mentioned, like "important", "boring" and "serious". Terms never referred to popular art; no mention of The Beatles, Michael Jackson or Prince; no well-known popular art venues like the Music Hall of Williamsburg, and so forth.

Sometimes in the conversations of certain groups, negative connotations with art and the arts, implying real or serious art and not popular art, are openly expressed. Art is associated with little interesting and boring art events. Evidently for them, popular art is still no art. It is significant that art-lovers also still use the term art while assuming that everybody understands that they mention real or serious art and not popular art. (In this respect telling differences exist between countries./6.) Moreover, popular musicians are still seldom called artists; and they do not call themselves artists.—Only very recently this is somewhat changing.—They still tend to think it presumptuous to call themselves artists.

The continuing symbolic boundary between art and popular art cannot but influence the social boundary. Choices of donors, sponsors and central and local governments on the distribution of their art budgets are certainly affected. Another example is that in many countries, a lower VAT rate exists for art and not for popular art. The former, therefore, receives an indirect subsidy. The latter does not. For the tax authority, popular art falls in the category of entertainment and not of art.

(87) THE MEDIA INCREASINGLY COMBINE SERIOUS AND POPULAR ART. ALSO THE NUMBER OF LIVE EVENTS WITH COMBINATIONS INCREASES. In movies and television and on social media, that is, in not-live events, the provision of combinations of serious and popular art is not exceptional anymore. All social groups are interested. The media activities much contribute to the weakening of the symbolic and social boundary between established art and popular art. Also, in live events, more often combinations of serious and popular art are offered, sometimes together with other forms of entertainment. The offering of

such events was common before the period of serious art. Presently they are still exceptional, but this is bound to change in the 2020s.

Already for quite some time, both serious and popular music are included in the same soundtrack of movies. Special is that now in several movies, television programs and series the recorded performances of established and popular art are combined. Combinations of ballet, modern dance and popular dance—break dance and urban-dance—are most common. They are watched by young audiences from all social classes. Examples of series are the *Dance Academy* and *The Next Step*; two very popular series which since 2010 and 2013 in ever new episodes are broadcasted all over the world. In the depicted academies, the teaching of various popular and serious dance styles to a group of dancers with different dance backgrounds is normal. Interesting crossovers are developed and performed. (*These series are sometimes called teen dramas. But Anna, as well as probably many other adults, watches them.*)

What is normal in the series is not normal in the movies. Here the combining is usually problematized. A common theme is that a typical non-ballet kid who is a gifted urban or break dance dancer manages to get admitted to an established ballet school and next let the ballet students try out popular dance styles. To their amazement the students notice that they like doing so. In the movies there still is a social boundary, but it is crossed.

In this context it is significant that in several feature length dance movies directed at youngsters, not only the social boundary between established ballet/dance and popular dance is bridged but simultaneously the boundary between higher and lower social groups and ethnic groups. Common is that a lower-class black or Hispanic male urban-dance dancer and a privileged white female ballet dancer find one another and start to respect each other's style of dancing. They get intimate and start to form a successful dance duo. The combination of three types of inequalities in a single movie suggests that established art is still experienced as higher and popular art as lower but also that this is unjustified in the eyes of a younger generation.

There appears to be an eagerness among all youngsters to bring high- and low-class art together and among low-class youngsters to gain more respect for the own supposedly inferior-art. This phenomenon is not new but that it is supported by (commercial) mass media and given shape is new and significant.

Combinations also occur in at present very popular television competitions like *The Voice*, *We can Dance* and so forth.

Interesting is a real live case of a professional dancer crossing social boundaries in art. In a popular video clip, the successful young Ukrainian ballet dancer Sergei Polunin dances on a very popular pop song *Take Me to Church* of Hozier in a half ballet half contemporary-dance style. It was a public demonstration of "I don't care about boundaries in music and dance". (This is remarkable, because Polunin was not just any ballet dancer. He had been principal dancer of *The Royal Ballet* but left the company because he was fed up with traditional ballet and its nineteenth-century extreme discipline and demands on dancers.)

On YouTube and Vimeo with only a few clicks, users can move from very serious short clips and movies and feature-length movies to very popular videos, and evidently many users do, as shows from the lists of suggested videos./7 Although much perception of serious and popular/inferior visual art on the internet is accidental and casual, an increasing part is now also consumed deliberately. Combining serious art, popular art and inferior-art is anyway common. Scrolling on social media, like Tumblr, Pinterest and above all Instagram, one almost inevitably comes across both. On poster sites, images of serious, popular and inferior visual art are often shown on the same page. And if they are categorized, it is in categories like abstract, botanical, dance and figurative and not according to the seriousness of the artists. People also deliberately visit new "cool" visual art platforms; platforms that often also mediate in buying and selling, like the platforms of Saatchi Art and Lumas. All of these sites show both serious and "better" popular/inferior art. The traditional boundary between real art and not really art is altogether absent.

Interesting are also the free magazines that nowadays can be found in many cafés for middle-class young people. Pictures are entertaining as well as serious. (Some of the best are those which simultaneously advertise fashion clothes. What probably makes them more serious is the low quality paper.)

Already for a long time we live in a so-called visual culture. In a (semi) public space, we are surrounded by digitally produced artworks as well as technically reproduced artworks. Moreover, over the last decades, people increasingly watch artworks in magazines and even more on the internet; that is, at the moment especially on Facebook, Tumblr, Pinterest and most of all Instagram. They are getting used to interesting, technically (re)produced visual art, serious as well as inferior visual art and anything in between. Most images do not have an original. People have learned to live with all sorts of mixtures of original and copy, authentic and fake.[4] This causes that most people now care less about unique originals. Together with fading boundaries between serious visual art and popular visual art, this development is bound to lead to more sharing of art and less exclusion. Even some well-known artists now create art, which they only publish on Instagram. (Examples are in 2018/2019 Cindy Sherman, Nan Golding and Wolfgang Tillmans.)

Now in major cities there are cool shops, like the physical outlets of Lumas—in 40 major cities all over the world—which sell all sorts of (re)productions, popular as well as serious. Even though they do not sell originals, they are comparable with the serious art commercial-galleries, with the difference that the offering is mixed, while the visitors are not typical art-lovers but middle-class social and cultural risers. Naturally also in more prestigious bookshops—and earlier in the shops selling CDs and DVDs—serious and popular are or were close together.

Combinations of live serious and popular performances are still rare but, as we shall see [89], they occur in festivals. Interesting are combinations in a single performance, as was common before the period of serious art [9]. The example par excellence is that of the open-air concerts of André Rieu. He offers a combination of traditional classical/serious music with orchestrated traditional popular song and other entertainment, from musicians in eighteenth-century dresses to carriages appearing. And apart from being an excellent violinist, he is also a good comedian.

The grandeur of the orchestra—with fewer players than would have been the case in concert halls—an interest in the grand musical heritage and open entertainment makes the concerts attractive for everybody. Some of the concerts are free, most are not and prices are not low, but people with all size pockets watch the television registrations which are broadcasted at prime time.

Though less "serious" than the dance series and movies, now also a comedy series has been produced in which classical music is mixed with entertainment: the successful Amazon's television series *Mozart in the Jungle*.[5]

Finally, a special and significant new form of sharing of various forms of live music by all social groups follows from the recent placing of pianos in the halls of railway stations, airports and shopping malls. Both amateurs and professionals play Classical, Jazz and Pop music. In passing by people evidently appreciate the performances and some stop to listen.

The increasing presence of combinations in almost all spheres of live art makes the serious arts less special and less exclusive. As far as recorded and reproduced art is concerned, this probably applies to all social groups. Moreover, increasingly established art venues and ensembles become involved. This is a topic in the next sections.

Less Exclusive

(88) IN LARGER NETWORKS, INTERDEPENDENCES INCREASE. ART-WORLDS WEAKEN. As mentioned in section [3], in art-worlds, various interrelated groups of participants exist who interact with one another and depend on one another. They are connected in an art-world network with many smaller subnetworks. In that section I distinguish five groups. These are experts/critics, official art education institutions, art-loving consumers, artists, non-profit art-companies and for-profit art-companies. Within the overall art-world network, there is a power balance. It is possible that one or more groups have a larger say than others, and this can change. Overall can be higher or lower. The overall art-world network has links with outside networks; foremost, networks of governments, donors and sponsors.

It is possible that during the period of serious art, within the always shifting balance of power, artists and expert/critics have relatively much power. Artists are not independent but have more power than before this period, when many of them, in simple networks, directly depended on others. Moreover, in this period the number of expert/critics increases and they as well are relatively powerful.

Over the last decades, within the so-called network economy everywhere in society, interdependence increases./8 This also applies to the overall art-world network and the larger network in which art-worlds participate. The latter shows most clearly from the increasing dependence of art-world groups on governments, donors and sponsors [75].

Some government officials and donors are fanatic art-lovers. Thanks to attunement and much respect for art and artists, during the period of serious art, there is interdependence, but the interference of governments, donors and sponsors in art-world affairs is limited. Governments buy and order art and use it for all sorts of purposes—art is useful for them [11]—but unlike before the period of serious art, during this period, an overall steering and controlling of artists and other art-world parties is no goal. The autonomy of art and artists is highly valued. Within the larger networks, art-worlds are relatively powerful. Over the last decades, steering and controlling is still no goal. Nevertheless, art-worlds become more dependent on others and lose autonomy. This is understandable. Interdependence grows in increasingly complicated networks, which cross the traditional boundaries of art-worlds. Art-worlds and each of the five groups of art-world participants become more dependent and less powerful.

By now it is no longer art-worlds that define true art and draw a line between art and popular/inferior art. The symbolic and social boundaries are quickly becoming weaker and more flexible than they were before. The position of the boundaries has become the outcome of the not-orchestrated cooperation of many groups. Some are art groups: more are non-art groups. Art groups often no longer exist of only people active in the established arts but also in the popular arts. Art often is not serious art but art in a broad sense. For many people, including administrators, there are now only *worlds of art*. The established art institutions continue to play a significant role, but are more dependent and less powerful than before. Art-worlds do not stop to exist, but become much weaker given increasing interdependence.

In the worlds of art, the art ethos is less intense. It still influences decisions, but a market ethos is often more important. Art is no longer grand, and art-world-unity no longer a major goal. Instead there is fragmentation; a fragmentation that occurs not only in art-worlds but also in society at large. Interdependence also shows from the fact that each of the five art-world groups participates in the networks of the new creative industry, that is, an industry in which interdependence also grows. For- and non-profit art companies certainly participate, and so do artists.—Now many artists, willingly or not, *also* work in non-art creative companies.—

In aesthetic capitalism, in an urban environment there is an aestheticizing of public space going on in which numerous artists and designers play a role. They cooperate and sometimes become indistinguishable./9 Many groups are also involved in urban policy decisions, which involve both serious and popular/inferior art. For instance, at a local level, the encouragement of "decent" graffiti and street art can be an as important matter of discussion as plans for extensions of the traditional art-buildings of opera, theater and concert hall. The extensions with catering facilities are accessible for everybody and not only visitors. Both street art and extensions juice up the urban environment. That dependencies increase and boundaries are taken less seriously also shows from the rapidly increasing number of events in an urban environment in which there is a combination offered of serious and popular art, sometimes rounded up with other forms of entertainment.

This is not to say that, fragmented as the new worlds of art may be, established art and art establishments no longer exist. For instance, art-world groups still manage the established traditional art-buildings and the official art education institutes. But by now management is only possible with continuous negotiation with several other groups. For instance, in continental Europe, it is usually due to pressure of other groups—and market pressure—that over the last decades conservatoires establish departments for popular music education. (In most major cities the managements of the schools situate them in separate and little prestigious buildings allowing an, evidently still attractive, degree of insulation of serious art.)

The role of art-worlds and their establishments at high levels in the art markets remains important. There continues to be much personal contact and attunement in small powerful networks. For instance, there exists a small network of directors of top-museums and they regularly meet in person.

Personal contact also matters at the highest levels of power in society. But negotiation is necessary. Administrations, for instance, no longer automatically choose for serious art to "decorate" the celebrations it organizes. Organized combinations of serious art and popular art in national events have become common. They change over time. When in 2005 the silver jubilee of the office accession to the crown of the Dutch queen Beatrix was celebrated, there were two major events in a large tent in the center of Amsterdam: one night for invited dignitaries with classical music, and the next for "ordinary" Dutchmen with popular music and other entertainment. Organizers judged both to be important, and offered both, but still held on to an insulation of serious art. But when eight years later, in 2013, Willem-Alexander was crowned king in Amsterdam, a (unhappy) Royal Dutch Concertgebouw Orchestra was demanded to perform, together with the world-famous Dutch DJ, Armin van Buuren.

Aside: Weakening of art-worlds also shows from the nature of some recurring national celebrations. In France in 2017, during the anniversary celebration of *Quatorze Juillet*, in the presence of the new president Emmanuel Macron, a military band played a mash-up of compositions of the pop group Daft Punk.—In the media it was described as "a surprise" and "unconventional".—In the USA and England, there are far more large public events in which popular art sets the dominant tone, from the inauguration events of the new US presidents, to the funeral event of Princess Diana.

Several established art institutions respond "proactively" to the new, far more fragmented, situation. This shows from more user-orientation within what I call a user-oriented domain. In this domain the companies and their networks function better within the larger and broader networks with more intense interdependence than the earlier rather closed, much respected and relatively autonomous art-worlds.

Given increased interdependence the overall autonomy of the new, much weakened, art-worlds is less than that of the former art-worlds. It is nevertheless possible that individual artists and small companies have more freedom than before. Gatekeeping by art-worlds has become harder and being recognized by one's art-world is less important. Art-world-art still exists, but creating it brings less rewards than before. More than before autonomy is not given but gained by individual artists, small groups of artists and other small art groups, in negotiation with one another and with outsider groups.

Finally, it would be incorrect to assume that in the new situation, there is much homogenization and less diversity. It is the opposite. Now also established art institutions start to offer more diverse art and more diverse art-settings.

(89) IN THE ESTABLISHED ARTS, NEXT TO A SMALL STUDIOUS DOMAIN, A LARGE USER-ORIENTED DOMAIN DEVELOPS. SOME ART INSTITUTIONS BECOME ORIENTED ON RICH VISITORS, OTHERS ON MIDDLE-CLASS VISITORS. THE NET EFFECT IS LESS EXCLUSIVITY. Over the last decades two poles have developed in the established arts. This is, on the one hand, an extreme of serious, studious and supposedly autonomous art, directed at artists and expert-consumers, who discuss art using a specialist's discourse. On the other there is an extreme of user-oriented and even entertaining art for a large audience. Between the two extremes, two domains exist, with a broad gray zone in between: a small *studious domain* closer to the studious extreme and an ever-larger *user-oriented domain* closer to the user-oriented extreme. In the latter two subdomains exist: a small *deep-pocket user-oriented domain* and a much larger *medium-pocket user-oriented domain.* It is the emergence over the last decades and the present extension of the latter domain that makes the established arts less exclusive.

In the studious domain there is scientification: art education is increasingly treated and organized the same as a scientific discipline. Students in art schools in this domain do not make art; they are involved in "projects" and do "research". Curators in art-spaces explain works in texts that are incomprehensible for laymen. (Looking at the texts accompanying exhibitions and concerts in art-spaces, the "worst" now is over, but many texts remain unnecessarily difficult.) Consumers are artists and expert-consumers. Advanced students in all artforms can write practice-based dissertations.

This domain is much smaller than what was covered by the earlier art-worlds and covered by the new user-oriented domain. Rich consumers are not particularly interested and prices are relatively low. Most income comes from subsidies. People in the domain seek a stable income and find "refuge" in an academic surrounding. Where this was not yet the case, art education becomes part of universities. Governments are happy to go along; they have to worry less about subsidies. Gatekeeping is now officially a matter of art schools under the umbrella of universities, which are partly state funded. Because the dependences are organized in limited networks, autonomy in this domain could be larger than before, but it is not. For artists and ensembles, the studious domain is not a sanctuary. Leadership of the art institutions has a large say in what is good and bad art. Additionally, over the last decades, the autonomy of workers and departments within the larger universities has been diminishing, and this affects this domain as well. If the arts are becoming less exclusive, it is not in this domain. (Or it must be in some initiated social critical art projects, but their effect in society is usually limited.)

In the context of this book, the much larger user-oriented domain is more interesting. In this domain of established art, many art-companies and artists are now focused on accessibility. Artworks may be layered, but they are also "understandable" without much preliminary knowledge. It is significant that in this domain, experts/critics now sometimes call works "beautiful", a term whose use was earlier taboo. For art-lovers unmediated enjoyment of art is no longer taboo.

To earn an income in the user-oriented domain, entrepreneurship of artists and companies is important. And in the medium-pocket user-oriented domain, with far more interdependence than earlier and with fragmentation, to be successful, flexibility and entrepreneurship are a sine qua non. This is, flexibility and entrepreneurship in the development and use of innovations in art products and art-settings, as well as in ways to promote the own product. By now many companies understand this. Museums are ahead.[6]

Art museums cooperating in various networks with municipalities and other "stakeholders" were probably the first in creating a free and exciting public space next to their buildings. These spaces are user-friendly. Much happens for free. An example is the Museums Quartier in Vienna, created around 2000. Buskers perform and are encouraged to perform. Free activities for children and old people are offered. On terraces and in indoor catering, prices are affordable. And thanks to commercial and profitable licensing, overall maintenance cost for the municipality and the museums and exhibition spaces is low. By now many more comparable spaces have been created in towns all over the world. Everywhere the insulation of serious art is reduced, and outside the buildings links with entertainment activities and the presence of entertainment-art are no longer avoided and, in fact, increasingly promoted.

In the text so far, I have given several examples of changes in the provision of live art inside art-buildings, including museums, which occurred over the last decades and which made them accessible and attractive for broader social groups. I do not repeat these examples here.—In web-text wt-83, I give more examples.—Anyway important are changes in "tolerated" audience behavior, different behavior of personnel, and, very important, more neutral and less posh interiors. This allows more social groups for which art is not that grand to be comfortable and participate.

Of course, also changed established art venues are sometimes more attractive for one middle-class social group, and others for another group, that is, including various age groups.—The same applies to popular art venues.—But because there is more choice in atmospheres, on average, live established art has become less exclusive, and with a growing and more intense visitor-orientation, it will continue to become less exclusive.

Entrepreneurial artists and small ensembles came first in promoting their artworks and art products by means of websites and next by use of social media. Not much later, following a trend in overall business, most art-companies, including the largest and most famous, now use social media to promote the own art product as well as own donor schemes.

Promotion and artistic use of social media sometimes coincide. At the initiative of the Van Gogh museum and in cooperation with Facebook, recently, five famous museums of which each owns a sunflower painting by Van Gogh, brought them together in a well-advertised online virtual 360° exhibition. (As noted, the commercial non-profit Van Gogh museum initiates more innovations, including the Relievo reproduction technique.)

By now social media have completely reshaped the world and will continue to do so in the decades to come. Much is unpredictable. Some art museums and music ensembles have started to use them to let people participate in projects. Such participatory art has artistic value, and cannot but promote interest in the "real thing". This is bound to become more common and take unpredictable forms in the 2020s. In many foremost virtual projects, the presence of consumers in the traditional as well as new art-buildings, art will no longer be required. Also, people who feel uncomfortable in the buildings will start to participate. Consumers, artists and managements will learn from the experiences. In a self-enforcing circular process, the interest of nonvisiting participants is raised, managements make the building visitor-friendly for broader social groups, the atmosphere changes, both real and digital visits increase and so forth.

Another significant development is that art-companies, in the user-oriented domain, are now sometimes involved in the offering of combinations of own serious art, popular art and other entertainment. In the performing arts there are sometimes after-parties, with DJs playing Dance music. And, for a while, the well-known *Residentie Orkest* in The Hague had a comedian perform during the break. Or established companies initiate quasi-crossovers, as in the case of orchestras accompanying pop musicians or DJ-producers.

Another form of a deliberate "combination" is that of art-companies giving up insulation. Now each year a Dutch symphonic orchestra—the first was again the *Residentie Orkest*—performs in a tent in the famous popular music festival *Lowlands*. During the performance, there are pop performances in other tents and the open air. (The sphere in the tent is informal. Visitors move in and out.)

The managements of some important art-buildings already gave up all over insulation earlier. In the Anglo-Saxon countries, the practice of allowing popular art and entertainment events to enter art-buildings is by now common. The continental European countries are catching up./10

Market forces play an important role in these developments. With less consumer demand, orchestras and other companies attempt to survive. They also follow from entrepreneurship within larger networks.

Nevertheless, in spite of all such developments, a limiting factor is that, especially in the performing arts, there is no or little willingness to lower cost. A second limiting factor in reaching out to lower-educated people with small pockets are the relatively high average prices, prices that have risen more than corresponds with inflation. In the case of art museums, they have risen much more.—That is on average; part of museums are still cheap or free.—And a third factor is that many middle-class people with medium-sized pockets are willing to pay for exclusivity. Therefore, raising prices can lead to more overall income, income which can be used for all sorts of "good" art causes. It does not go at the cost of the number of middle-class visitors to the own institution. (But looking at the longer-term interests of the sector, it is probably short-sighted.) Being oriented on users in the medium-pocket-users-oriented domain can lead to longer-term democratization, but not necessarily. Government interventions can however help, letting developments in this domain promote inclusion or promote inclusion more than it already does.

In the deep-pocket-user-oriented domain, very high prices, as presently asked by major orchestras and opera companies, do not stop audiences from coming. Rich people are able and willing to pay for assumed high quality performances and even more for exclusivity. The companies can choose prices and numbers of performances, which lead to the highest income from ticket sales or rather of so-called earned income because a considerable part of their income stems from sponsors, donors and governments. Taking the willingness to pay, donate and, to a lesser degree, subsidize earned income may well be higher when performances are almost always sold out and therefore higher ticket prices could lead to higher income from ticket sales. It raises the already high reputation of top ensembles and venues.

Aside: This is what can be expected in a winner-take-all-society [77]. Whether one judges that the phenomenon of winners taking so much is more undesirable in the arts than in other sectors of production, like sports and finance, is a subjective matter. One circumstance that could lead one to say it is not necessarily worse is that the same choice of art offered at the highest level is also offered by other companies for lower prices somewhat lower in the market, while the quality is almost the same. (As noted [77], higher up, in winner-take-all markets, income and price differences are large, while quality differences are small.) The same as some other social groups, the rich have "own art", but unlike other groups this is not because of style, genre and meanings, but because of more perfection and especially a richer ambience or richer buildings. Some traditional buildings can be said to be owned by the rich. But if governments and not only consumers, sponsors and donors pay for the maintenance of such buildings and for the presence of very expensive performances, people may well disagree with this.

(90) Over the last decades: IN THE USER-ORIENTED DOMAIN, UNDERPRIVILEGED GROUPS REMAIN MUCH UNDERREPRESENTED IN CONSUMPTION AND PRODUCTION OF SERIOUS ART. THE ATTENTION FOR THEIR UNDERREPRESENTATION IN BOTH SERIOUS AND POPULAR ART EVENTS INCREASES. Over the last decades, the underrepresentation of lower-class people and non-whites among *art consumers* in art-buildings has hardly decreased. They continue to be absent. Actions to increase their presence are very limited. The difference with live popular art remains large. But underprivileged groups are also underrepresented in popular art events and among artists producing popular art—be it in a much lesser degree. Attention for these phenomena among artists as well as among civil servants at local levels who are responsible for art subsidies increases, and sometimes this results in conditions attached to subsidies.

The overall difference between serious and popular art is still large. Nevertheless, a decline in numbers of visitors and an awareness of the changing composition of the population—in some Western countries, the percentage of non-white people in the population is now more than 50%—make some established art-companies reconsider the product they offer.[7] Financial worries and market forces contribute to this.

In this context it is interesting to note that in early 2019, the American Alliance of Museums (AAM) launched an initiative including a $4 million program to let the museums diversify its directorships. A survey by the AAM found that half of all museum boards are white. (In 2017, the Walton Family Foundation and the Ford Foundation developed another, similar project that pledged $6 million that would go toward diversifying 22 institutions.) One can be assured that in Europe, this percentage is much higher than 50% and that in both the USA and Europe, the percentage in the case of established performing art-companies and venues is also higher. In most European countries, the percentage of "whites" among the population is not higher than in the USA. In 2016 in Amsterdam, half of the population is migrant or has at least one migrant parent. (If colored people who immigrated longer ago would be included, the percentage would be larger.)

Given the rapidly changing composition of the population, art-companies in Europe have much reason to worry about their future, but most do not. It is significant that representatives of not only underprivileged but also of middle-class non-white groups say that they have given up on the established arts./11 They have put pressure on local governments to set as a condition for subsidization, that at least one member in the board of directors must be non-white, but so far unsuccessfully.

This is not to say that local governments are inactive. Popular art venues—and not established art venues—are told that they will face subsidy cuts if they do not manage to increase the percentage of non-whites among their audiences. This affects the nature of subsidy proposals and the imago of companies but only to a lesser degree real policies aimed at including more colored and underprivileged groups. Evaluation is indeed difficult.

Finally, over the last two decades, there are again more subsidized educational activities aimed at low-class people, in particular youngsters. There still is much paternalism. In many schools pupils learn about established art, while their interest in popular art and its new genres, like Hip-hop, is ignored. But in part of the schools, this is changing and there is more attention for popular art. Nevertheless the ideal of top-down vertical dissemination has not disappeared.

Next, I look again at the underrepresentation not among consumers but among *creative* artists./12 In the established arts the underrepresentation of women and non-white people has become somewhat less strong, but least in classical music [46]. The relative difference in presence with popular music continues to be large. As noted, in all established art-worlds, women continue to earn less than men, but the difference now corresponds with the difference in many other sectors of production. (In as far as creative artists in popular film are concerned, the underrepresentation of women among directors remains very large./13)

The increase in the relative number of non-white artists is probably largest among the group of successful artists. Criticism and own worries about underrepresentation induces high-end art education institutes to accept more non-white applicants and to promote their careers. When Asians and non-white people come from other countries, this sometimes raises the prestige of the schools. This phenomenon is strongest in the visual arts. Moreover, at present in well-known art fairs and in exhibitions in museums of modern-art, non-white artists are sometimes overrepresented. However, at lower levels of success, underrepresentation persists, while at higher levels of success, ethnic labeling of non-white artists is still common practice.

Earlier in the visual arts, creative artists from exotic ethnic groups came and went, and this practice is likely to continue. For instance, in the 1980s, the much praised aboriginal creative artists are now altogether absent again. However, due to a general process of undoing of the remainders of colonialism, I expect that Blacks in the USA will not only at present but also in the future be less underrepresented among successful as well as less successful creative artists. But non-white immigrants are still much underrepresented in the average US and European art schools. Therefore, underrepresentation is likely to continue for many years to come.

Aside: It is significant that presently, since new waves of protests about the still inferior position of women and blacks have reoccurred in the Western world, curators suddenly start to recover pieces of art by long dead black (and female) artists, which they now judge to be of high quality, while earlier, they or their predecessors did not.

Up to the present-day, non-white actors, singers and dancers are underrepresented in the established arts. In major roles they draw much attention, but this is the consequence of underrepresentation. Underrepresentation is largest in the established art performances by top ensembles, that is, companies that receive by far most public and private support. Even nowadays, when a script refers to a non-white person, the role may well be performed by a white actor or singer. (This is comparable with women being played by men; a practice that lasted well into the seventeenth century.)

A significant example is that of Otello in Shakespeare's play with the same name, and in Verdi's opera based on this play. In England, in theater, it is only from 1990 onward that the role of Otello starts to be played by black actors. Continental Europe is later and major theater companies still let "blackface" white actors play Otello./14 *With one or two exceptions so far, no major opera ensemble has staged a black Otello. In guarded terms it is argued that quality comes first and that, for top performances, no non-white performer is already good enough for playing the difficult role. Recently in an Otello case, it turned out that not good enough meant "not loud enough"*./15

Unlike in popular art, there are still no annual reports showing the development or lack of development on the representation of non-white people and women among artists. In the film industry in the USA, and in other branches of popular art production there are. The major Hollywood companies finance research and together publish an annual report.

As can be expected, given the growing number of female students in professional art education, *over the last decades*, the relative presence of creative women artists has increased in most art professions even though their chances to become successful are still lower. Forgetting about the top of the markets, earnings are almost certainly lower than those of male artists, be it by now not necessarily lower than in other sectors of production./16 Among both successful and little-successful conductors and composers, the underrepresentation remains high. A difference is that the serious music world is now sometimes publicly blamed for the absence of women conductors. (In this conservative art-world, this has led to weird and sexist justifications by well-known male conductors./17)

(91) Excurse. SUBSIDIES HAVE BEEN MOTIVATED AND USED TO LOWER PRICES IN ORDER TO ENABLE LESS-WELL-TO-DO GROUPS TO PARTICIPATE IN SERIOUS ART EVENTS. EXISTING VISITORS PROFIT MOST. ALTERNATIVE MORE EFFECTIVE SUBSIDIZED PRICING SYSTEMS EXIST, ARE SOMETIMES APPLIED AND COULD BE APPLIED MORE. FAR MORE ART COULD BE FREE. In the second half of the twentieth century, low prices thanks to subsidies—rather than thanks to the lowering of cost—are used to attract "others" with the effect that art in theory could have become less exclusive. Because regular visitors profit most from lower prices, it is sometimes hard to tell what comes first: self-interest or the assumed interests of others. Over time more effective pricing systems start to be used. By now they could be used very effectively.

Next to other goals, a common goal of financial public support is the vertical dissemination of art. But in practice money for art is altogether or almost altogether spend on keeping deficits down and not on lowering prices. Due to the cost disease, in the course of the twentieth century, the deficits of art-companies increase. It follows that given the unwillingness to develop and offer lower-cost performances, the art-companies cannot afford to lower prices and often have to raise prices. As a consequence, exclusion increases, and existing support goes almost altogether to the upholding of existing practices. Moreover, if part of support goes to lower prices, the difference is so small that underresourced groups can still not afford to visit performances in art-buildings, let alone visit them regularly.

Aside: Sometimes governments not only attempt to promote performing art visits by enabling lower prices but also the sale of visual art by enabling art-world-recognized commercial-galleries to lower prices for all buyers./18

Three alternatives exist for the lowering of prices for everybody. The first is price discrimination and the second price differentiation. *Price discrimination* refers to giving a discount to specific groups of consumers, like giving a discount for serious music concerts to people under 18. *Price differentiation* refers to the charging of higher and lower prices for (almost) the same product, like asking in a theater a higher price for the seats on the ground floor and a lower price for seats in the third balcony./19

A third important alternative exists: *product differentiation.* It refers to the process of distinguishing a product or service from others, to make it more attractive to a particular target market. A target market can be a market for a specific not well-to-do group. It involves differentiating the own product (or let it stand out more in comparison with similar more expensive goods of competitors). An example of clear *product differentiation* is offering serious music in different venues with different atmospheres for different prices./20 Governments could employ subsidies to stimulate art-companies to differentiate more.

For the purpose of inclusion of financially underresourced groups, positive price discrimination represents a pricing policy that is less costly than that of an overall lowering of prices. It, moreover, has the advantage that in the case of subsidies, the taxpayer does not pay for the lower ticket prices of well-to-do visitors. Not everybody in art-worlds is aware of the latter possibility or is willing to acknowledge it, but economists are. From circa 1980 onward, they openly and persistently pleaded for price discrimination and vouchers. This has three reasons. First, after that time, members of underresourced groups can ever better be identified and the possibility of fraud can be limited. Second, since that time, economists more than before condemn subsidies, resulting in lower prices for everybody and a possible consequent redistribution of income from poor to rich, and art-companies find it harder to reject the argument. Third, earlier, economists did not speak out, because many are art-lovers and were afraid of being shamed. But since that time, respect for art is going down and economists dare to speak out.

Another reason for the application by art-companies of price discrimination—usually in combination with price differentiation—is that they can be profitable, both in the short and the long run. In the short run they can be profitable, because giving discounts to certain groups for any visit or for a visit to specific seating areas, companies manage to profit more from differences in people's willingness and ability to pay for a visit/21 (The phenomenon of last-minute price reductions also fall in this category.) Not all schemes are profitable in the short run, but they may encourage people to come more often. Educated youngsters, for instance, who get a discount, may "learn" serious art, start to appreciate it and continue coming when they become older and have more money to spend.

Sometimes discounts are given to all people under or over a certain age, for instance, under 18 and over 60. Although identification is easy and fraud is almost impossible, and although their average spending power, income and wealth is lower than that of the others, the price policy is crude: especially part of older people are well-to-do and would have come as often without the discount. Less crude is giving discounts to all underresourced adults. Over the last decades their identification has become easier and therefore ever more local governments hand out cards to these adults, which allow discounts in a number of spending situations. Usually cultural institutions participate in the schemes—they pay for part of the discount, but often only in the case of last-minute tickets.

Finally, worth mentioning are voucher schemes. These are indirect price discrimination systems, which leave recipients more freedom of choice. At present in some countries, local or central governments hand out vouchers to secondary school pupils to be spent on visits to cultural institutions of their own choice, institutions that next let them in for free. Next governments compensate the latter for the foregone income. Given overall changes in society, in the 1990s in some countries, the choice of free cultural events had to be supplemented with visits to popular art venues and cinemas. Next, pupils—also those from the better schools—started to mainly or altogether spend the vouchers on visits to popular art venues and cinemas, while this had not been the intention of the voucher scheme. In several countries, this outcome led to the abolishment of the schemes.

All-in-all these forms of price discrimination and lower prices sometimes work well for people already somewhat interested in art. They also diminish inner-art-world exclusion. But they do not work well for underresourced groups. The price reductions are usually too small and there are informal barriers that keep them from participating.

Over the last decades, the inclination among art-companies has become much stronger to attract youngsters, by giving them discounts and hoping that later in life they will become regular visitors. At present, with the graying of the average visitor of classical symphony concerts, concert organizers evidently have high expectations of the long-term effect of discounts for young people. It could serve the survival of orchestras. Many halls now give young people rebates of 20% and more for visits to symphony concerts. At present (2017) the Amsterdam Concertgebouw regularly gives discounts of 90% to people under age 30.

To be complete, I mention one more pricing system: Pay As You Want (PAYW). The consumer determines and donates an own price, while being asked to donate/pay in advance what he expects the event will be worth for him, or afterward what he experienced the event was worth. Over the last decades, the pricing policy is sometimes tried out by paid-for art museums, but often terminated again because overall returns go down. Done in the right way, it could be or rather could become a powerful means for inclusion./22

The ultimate means for also attracting not that well-to-do groups as well as underprivileged groups is offering art for free in art-buildings, other venues and the open air. This can lead to congestion problems but not if the space is large, if it happens often and if regular visitors are less interested. Governments could buy such performances from established art-companies or enable them by means of earmarked subsidies. It happens—for instance in the context of ceremonies—but it could happen far more often [96].

(92) NEW, ALTERNATIVE, VARIED AND PARALLEL CAREER PATHS AND CHANNELS OF SCOUTING AND GATEKEEPING DEVELOP. New channels and career paths supplement or rather replace the few channels and paths that earlier were monopolized by art-worlds. They exist in the real world, but increasingly also in the virtual world of websites and social media. Writing in the preface that the arts are now in turmoil, one of the main things I had in mind is the emergence of alternative career paths. Now even lower-class people can become well-known and respected artists. Moreover, now turning from an amateur into a successful professional artist can be a matter of years if not months. Education can be altogether self-organized or organized within new channels, which earlier did not exist.

In the user-oriented domain of the established arts, the old-style art-worlds have disintegrated, and conductorless orchestration no longer works. Institutions have own identities, own policies, own ways of scouting and gatekeeping. Sometimes unusual techniques are used. Not long ago The Van Gogh museum hung posters on the walls of cool cafés in Amsterdam, asking young people to make a Van Gogh inspired painting. A selection would be exhibited in the museum. This is advertisement, but it is also a new form of scouting among a very large group—amateurs and not even amateurs—ignoring all existing art education. It is a technique that tells of changing times.

Competitions play an important role in the development of new and especially more parallel channels of recognition, allowing new career paths. Competitions are not new. Concourses already exist for a long time in classical/serious music, but candidates are extremely well-trained. The same as in any other competition, the concourses offer a possibility for scouting and help winners in their future career. But in this case surprises are minimal and the concourses very similar. If a young cellist can win in one cello concourse, he could also win in another. Moreover, the number of parallel concourses is small.

This is different in the new century with an ever-increasing number of festivals with different honorable and monetary prizes: foremost jury prizes but also public choice rewards. In many pop music festivals there are rewards. The same applies to film festivals. Often groups of festivals are comparable, but other than in the traditional concourses, candidates differ more and unexpected choices are made. The festivals offer a new form of scouting among an usually much larger group of candidates. More importantly they offer new career paths. No longer are accredited education institutes or subsidized major art institutions the most important scouts and gatekeepers and organizers of careers.

The competitions that are created by "the media" and broadcasted on television certainly represent a breakaway. Well-known competitions are, among others, the "voice of…" or "I can dance" programs. Similar competitions or battles are organized at different levels by many different institutes. They can be very local or rather national, in the open air or a venue, in a suburb or in the city center, broadcasted or not, and so forth. Organizers also differ: local governments, a shopkeepers' association, a commercial association, like the British Phonographic Industry and British Association of Record Dealers, which organizes the Mercury (Music) Prize. In our new "organized culture", local governments and commercial parties may well work together.[8]

In the major media competitions, next to juries of experts, often also large groups of consumers participate. It is an audience in the hall, or on the phone or internet. (In the European Song Contest, there are no judges; just millions of consumers determine success and failure.) The major media competitions are also interesting for other reasons. First, juries are no ordinary expert/critics. They are well-known artists, who know the profession in and out but are not necessarily schooled. Second, some have, the same as part of the candidates, clear working-class backgrounds, like the miner's son and singer, (Sir) Tom Jones, in The Voice UK.

Third, they motivate their choices *en plein public*. Motivations can be remarkably elaborate. Evidently, always changing standards of quality circulate and are shared within various alternative circuits. Next, sometimes between the successive rounds of a competition, judges or others train the candidates. Several candidates have a lower-class background. They would not have stood a chance in the official art education institutes. Being trained between shows, they get better from one show to the next. (Competitions or shows cannot but be "staged". Juries are not only chosen for expertise, but also for being famous and acting qualities. Also the selection of candidates through preliminary rounds is biased—but not always.)

These channels do not offer a career path to many. The number of candidates is a very small part of all aspiring artists who are as good as they are. But others notice that making a career in the arts, independent from wealth, level of education and ethnic background is a real possibility.—I do not know if this is deliberate, but candidates and winners are representative for the composition of the population, or there is some positive discrimination./23 Given the encouragements of enthusiastic audiences, the main message may well be that one needs a large group of fans to make a career. And creating a large fan base is exactly what entrepreneurial young and starting performance artists now do on the internet.

A social media surrounding offers many new channels and career paths. They are still hard to pin down and this situation will continue for many more years. All the time entrepreneurial youngsters—or their parents—develop new paths; or it is just luck that shows new ways. Aspiring artists learn from one another, but there is no simple guide telling what is best for whom. Ways to success differ, but success itself can be more or less measured by numbers of "likes" and "emojis". They often correspond with differences in income, differences that can be very large. Income has many sources and these as well can be organized in entrepreneurial ways. (The winner-take-all mechanism is strong in the social media.)

Internet activity shows how complicated virtual and real networks have become and how much they overlap. There is much interdependence. In the fragmented new worlds of art, the number of alternative channels has not only grown much, they also come and go. The internet artists anyway cannot do without the real, non-virtual world. They have a foot in both worlds and need to be present in the real world as well to be successful and earn money. Other than in the case of the extreme winners in the real-world arts, like Koons and Rowling, on the internet, success can be short-lived.

It is therefore interesting that there are now, in the real world, professionals who teach youngsters who are successful on the internet, how to continue a possibly short internet career in the real world; not only as comedian but also as performer in theaters, or on television and in movies. So far internet careers in the visual arts are less spectacular. It is nevertheless predictable that before too long here as well coaching will start to be offered to artists who are successful on the internet.

Internet activity stimulates artistic innovation as well as the diffusion of innovation. Artistic innovation occurs at all levels. (Famous artists like Cindy Sherman,

Nan Golding and Wolfgang Tillmans are not the best examples, but they, at least, publish innovative work on social media, which only works well in the virtual surrounding.)

With the internet and social media, several symbolic and social boundaries become ever fuzzier. Where does art performance stop? Is a youngster performing on YouTube and Instagram an actor and artist? Does he create art or applied art? *Is, for instance, the young "makeup artist" and vlogger James Charles a professional artist, an amateur artist or not "really an artist". (He can anyway make a living from his art and cause chaos in the real-world Birmingham streets. He has 16 million subscribers on YouTube and thus much voice and his net worth is around $12 million.*

The boundary between professional artist and amateur artist anyway becomes very unclear. Being artist was always a self-declared state, but it needed confirmation. This still is the case, but sources of confirmation change and become far more varied. Existing conventions change. No institution or art-world controlling numbers of artists still exist. This as well affects the social economy of art.

Even the boundary between artist and consumer may become fuzzier. Artists have always related to consumers and sometimes controlled their behavior, but the separation was clear. But as a student of mine writes in an essay: "The fan culture and the fan economy are prospering to gradually eliminate the binary opposition between the author and the fans, but to some extent make it harder for the new artists to create original works". The addition "it becoming harder to create original work" is interesting. Possibly, as she argues, there is an element of exploitation.[9]

The same as already earlier, the symbolic boundary between serious art and popular art has weakened and has become much fuzzier. So has the boundary between art and applied art and between art and inferior-art. That is also a matter of bad, good and better artists and artworks. A single artistic quality meritocracy created and maintained by art-worlds no longer exists.

This raises the question, who are experts/critics in the new world and how important is their say. Who are the new gatekeepers? Much has been written and is being written about the important topic. Further developments are inevitable. The role of this group has certainly changed. A much broader group of experts is now involved in gatekeeping. They use new means, like blogs, social media, Quora Digest, IMDb, Soundcloud, Medium.com and YouTube. The boundary between expert/critic and consumer is very fuzzy.

All such developments suggest a "democratization" in the arts or of art. Much depends on the interpretation of the term. Some economists argue that, *in principle*, a market economy with its consumer sovereignty can be democratic. True or not, the internet economy is anyway, also or more democratic, be it not necessarily fair. There is no de facto preselection of consumers as, for instance, exists at the entrance of traditional music halls. As far as markets exist, they are differently organized. Willingness to pay by consumers plays no or a very limited role. There usually is no price exclusion. One sometimes pays for not being disturbed by popup advertisement. Or there is pressure to donate, which may or may not be linked to specific music and videos. But in indirect ways artists' success and income depend altogether on consumer choice. Artists as well as consumers are bound to take the choices of many consumers and their numbers seriously.

Due to a limitation of pages in this book, I pay little—insufficient—attention to not only recent developments in the role of experts/critics and gatekeeping, but also to the phenomenon of self-organization and the commons. Self-organization is both a typical outcome of neo-liberalism and the neo-liberal mindset, as well as a counterforce.—The latter is much emphasized by art theorists.[10] One may well argue that many of the new channels and career paths, in particular those on the internet, are the result of self-organization by entrepreneurial individuals and small groups. They organize new and inventive ways between and beyond markets, governments and traditional art-worlds. This area is no art sanctuary; it takes much effort to maintain. But it is well-possibly that entrepreneurial self-organizing artists have more autonomy than those who foremost focus on markets or foremost on governments and donors.

I, indeed, pay too little attention to the notion of the commons and as some now say of "commoning".[11] Many artists, on the internet and elsewhere, offer free art or art with a free impact, and so contribute to art in the commons. The art and/or its effect is usually enabled by forms of self-organization. In the real world, this applies, for instance, to graffiti and other urban art in public space. It also applies to works of artists used in demonstrations. An example of operating in the commons and beyond markets and governments, is that of artists artistically and critically contributing to broad social movements, like Occupy Wall Street or Extinction Revolution.

Another phenomenon that is at least partly caused by the phenomena discussed in this section is that being a hybrid artist is now an acceptable form of being artist. One does not have to be ashamed of combining "proper" art activities with design and other creative activities. Some artists are proud of being a hybrid artist and are increasingly praised for it.

One thing is clear: further developments are hard to predict. Boundaries that have existed for more than a century are not only weakening but also shifting. These are, indeed, exciting times in the arts.

Notes

[1]In (Abbing, 2006) (in English I present Dutch data).

[2]Cf. (Dolfsma, 1999).

[3]The term "omnivore" in art was coined and first defined and operationalized by (Peterson & Simkus, 1992).

[4](Schwartz, 2014).

[5]As stated on the IMDb site: Mozart in the Jungle is about love, money, ambition and music as experienced by a maestro, Rodrigo, of the "New York Symphony" and a young oboist, Hailey, hoping for her big chance.

[6]Cf. (Bakhshi and Throsby, 2012).

[7]See, for instance: http://artsconsulting.com/arts-insights/inclusion-diversity-equity-and-access-why-now-in-the-arts-and-culture-sector/ (accessed 19-10-2018).

[8]Cf. (Bevers, 1990) (in Dutch).

[9] It is the unpublished essay—not a master thesis—of Lin Mingzhu which she wrote in the context of a MA course I give. I can give contact details.

[10] See for instance (Republic et al., 2016).

[11] Cf. (Dockx and Gielen, 2018).

Literature

Abbing, H. (2006). *From High Art to New Art*. Amsterdam: Vossius Pers (Amsterdam University Press).

Abbing, H. (2009). *Van Hoge naar Nieuwe Kunst*. Groningen: Historische Uitgeverij.

Adams, R. B., Kräussl, R., Navone, M. A., & Verwijmeren, P. (2017). *Is Gender in the Eye of the Beholder? Identifying Cultural Attitudes with Art Auction Prices* (SSRN Scholarly Paper No. ID 3083500). Retrieved from Social Science Research Network Website: https://papers.ssrn.com/abstract=3083500

Bakhshi, H., & Throsby, D. (2012). New Technologies in Cultural Institutions: Theory, Evidence and Policy Implications. *International Journal of Cultural Policy, 18*(2), 205–222. https://doi.org/10.1080/10286632.2011.587878.

Bevers, T. (1990). Convergenties tussen Overheid, Markt en Kunstwereld. *Boekmancahier, 2*(3), 79–83.

Bevers, A. M., Colenbrander, B., Heilbron, J., & Wilterdink, N. (2015). *Nederlandse kunst in de wereld: literatuur, architectuur en beeldende kunst, 1980–2013*. Nijmegen: Uitgeverij Vantilt.

Borowiecki, K. J., & Navarrete, T. (2017). Digitization of Heritage Collections as Indicator of Innovation. *Economics of Innovation and New Technology, 26*(3), 227–246. https://doi.org/10.1080/10438599.2016.1164488.

Dockx, N., & Gielen, P. (2018). *Exploring Commonism: A New Aesthetics of the Real*. Amsterdam: Valiz/Antennae Series.

Dolfsma, W. (1999). *Valuing Pop Music. Institutions, Values and Economics*. Delft: Eburon.

Elias, N. (1994). *The Civilizing Process* (p. 1993). Oxford: Blackwell.

Lebrecht, N. (1996). *Who Killed Classical Music (title GB. edition: When the Music Stops)*. Secaucus (London): Carol Publishing Group (Simon & Schuster Ltd.).

Peterson, R. A., & Simkus, A. (1992). How Musical Tastes Mark Occupational Status Groups. In M. Lamont & M. Fournier (Eds.), *Cultivating Differences* (p. 346). Chicago: The University of Chicago Press.

Republic, A. D., Dockx, N., Geys, J., Gielen, P., Hagoort, E., & Hirschhorn, T. (2016). *Mobile Autonomy: Exercises in Artists' Self-Organization*. Amsterdam: Valiz/Antennae Series.

Schwartz, H. (2014). *The Culture of the Copy: Striking Likenesses, Unreasonable Facsimiles*. Cambridge, MA: MIT Press.

Conclusion

Reading the first sentences of the sections in the book, one obtains a fairly adequate summary of the book's findings. In several ways the previous chapter is already a conclusion. Therefore, in this chapter I only present a selection of findings in the book, while adding a few. One important red line in the book is related to the presence of commerce in the arts and the interventions by governments. Therefore, most of the findings in this conclusion are related to this. The findings or theses miss nuance. This is partly deliberate and partly due to the wish to publish a moderately sized book. In the previous chapters most are explained in detail. In the conclusion I implicitly include recommendations.

In principle, a moral perspective in science is not taboo, that is, if it is used carefully. Care implies that—as especially economists are taught—a certain formulation is required: "If you want to achieve x, than you can do y." (Note the term "can", and not "must" or "should".) Therefore, presenting several of the findings and theses in this conclusion, I could each time add, "if one wants the arts to be less exclusive, then one can do the following" and "if one wants underprivileged groups to be able to participate in live art events and develop own art then one can do this". It would become too repetitive, and maybe irritating. Therefore, I will not do so. I assume that several readers of a book with the subtitle "are the arts becoming less exclusive" want to know what "can" be done to make the serious arts (even) more inclusive than they are now, implying that also underprivileged groups are included. It is, nevertheless, important, to keep the formulations in mind, when reading the following text.

This chapter is accompanied by web-notes, which are available on the website: *www.hansabbing.com*. Numbers at the end of a sentence preceded by a forward slash refer to web-notes. Holding a pc, tablet or phone next to the text, it is easy to "scan" the web-notes.

(93) ON THE OWN ART OF SOCIAL GROUPS.

Much popular and serious art is shared. Higher and lower social groups share more art, also established art, than people often think. In the case of lower-class

H. Abbing, *The Changing Social Economy of Art*,
https://doi.org/10.1007/978-3-030-21668-9_7

groups, this is foremost art in (technically) reproduced form, that is, recordings and reproductions. Participation in live serious art events and, to a lesser degree, in popular art events is usually not possible or unattractive. Prices are too high and the atmosphere is unattractive. [50 and 51]

Aside, various higher and lower social groups understand each other's art differently. They also have own art, which they at first do not share and which is not interesting for others. The art is exclusive. With time much of the own art starts to be shared, sometimes unchanged, sometimes in modified form. Some art is annexed by other groups. [52 and 55]

Combinations of popular and serious art become more common. The commercial media play a significant role. Art can be shared; it can also be combined in a live or recorded art event. Interesting are "sandwiches" of lower-class forms of popular art and forms of established art. Because there is demand for combinations, the (commercial) media produce them in the form of movies, television series and competitions on televisions. They, for instance, develop dance movies and television series in which ballet and urban dance meet. Live sandwiches are also becoming more common. André Rieu, for instance, performs popular song together with classical music. Nowadays there are also established art-companies who offer such sandwiches.—A related phenomenon is the development of crossover art as a form of new and sometimes innovative art.—[86 and 87]

Much renewal in art follows an upward trajectory. Renewal of art is essential in a changing society. Much renewal in art is bottom-up renewal. In the popular arts innovators belong to lower-class groups and are supported by an enthusiastic crowd of people in the own group. In various ways the art "moves up". It affects serious art. Or the art moves up in adapted versions. Or the art is annexed. Usually it is a bit of all. [23 and 52]

There is also innovation in the serious or established arts. Much of it is at first not meaningful for larger groups of art-lovers, but with time it becomes meaningful, or it leaves traces in other serious art, or it just disappears. Much innovation in these arts stems from little-known artists working in the margin of art-worlds. They do not operate in the top of the market. If their innovations are successful and become diffused, they move up, be it usually slowly and slower than in the popular arts.

There is some innovation in the top of the markets. One cannot say that the visual art of Damien Hirst and Jeff Koons is not at all innovative. But they copied much of what happened lower in the market. And the Dutch National Opera is innovative, but mainly in the sense of "daring". It dares to enrich—literally and figuratively—innovations, which were developed at lower levels in the opera market.

Finally, it is true that some innovation in the established arts affects popular art, also the art of lower social groups. But it is relatively unimportant. For instance, Techno and House were developed by marginal lower-class groups in Detroit and Chicago. But the later producers of the minimal versions, like Daniel Bell and Jeff Mills, were probably influenced by the minimal music of Steve Reich and Philip Glass.

There is no reason to worry about the art of the rich. First, the rich do not really have own established art, that is art which in style and meanings differs from the art offered at somewhat lower levels in the market where consumers are relatively well-to-do but not rich. If one were to say that the rich "own art", this can at best imply that they "own" the most prestigious art-buildings, at least for most of the time, and "own" certain settings within the art-buildings. Part of their setting is having the most famous artists perform; meeting them in person, and so forth.

As said, it is possible, that very expensive artworks and performances have some innovative qualities that influence (slightly) costly art objects and performances. But because consumers are rich, the somewhat innovative artworks will anyway be created. Rich consumers are willing to pay the high prices of performances and the extremely high prices of visual artworks in the top of the markets. Naturally sponsors are willing to spend much money on the events. And, for various reasons, as discussed in the book, donors, including foundations, donate much. Therefore: no reason to worry. Also, no reason or almost no reason to worry, if governments were to stop their generous subsidies.

Artistic expression of underprivileged groups is important for these groups and probably also for society at large. Depending on one's point of view, worries about the possible under-production of own art within these groups can be justified. More respect for their art would be a first step.

(94) ON MARKETS IN THE ARTS. *Markets do well, but not always.*

In principle, markets are neither good nor bad! Depending on one's goals and the issue at stake, market forces do more or less good or bad. Often market forces work "best" if governments enhance their working by means of subsidies or, instead, restrain their working with regulations./1

Including underprivileged social groups in art production and consumption the commercial markets of popular art have done better than the highly subsidized markets of serious and established art. In the latter highly subsidized art-companies are active; in the former nonsubsidized, small and large, commercial popular art-companies. The difference applies to both live and not-live art. In live popular art, consumers from underprivileged groups are also underrepresented, but less than in the established arts. The same applies to artists. The differences were larger 50 years ago but are still considerable. [46]

In the serious arts, market forces work both ways; they increase as well as decrease exclusivity. First, they contribute to exclusivity. For various reasons non-profits and for-profits attempt to maximize revenues. Because higher social groups are able and willing to pay for live art—performances as well as original art objects—markets contribute to relative high prices with the effect that they are usually too expensive for other social groups. Effects are also indirect. Because in the performing arts, revenues in markets can be increased by creating and maintaining an atmosphere that is most attractive for relatively well-to-do art-lovers and unattractive for others the entrepreneurs go along. At the moment in the top of the markets where the rich purchase art tickets and buy art objects, along with an increasing unequal distribution of income, prices rapidly rise. In the top of the markets, performances are now only accessible for rich art-lovers and art objects only for multimillionaires. This is caused by market forces. (In the visual arts, governments that buy "top" pieces enhance the market forces in the top of the markets.) [19–78]

By now, forgetting about the top of the markets, *broad market forces indirectly start to decrease overall exclusivity in the established arts. Market forces contribute much to their democratization*—be it foremost in the case of middle-class people.— They indirectly cause the largest part of established art-companies to become deliberately more user-oriented. The art-product-in-a-broad sense, that is, including its setting inside and outside the art-buildings, is made more user-friendly, at least for middle-class consumers.

A market mechanism is at work. Managements noticed a waning demand or the graying of audiences; and they started to worry about future demand, the future of the company and the continuation of its core activity. This is the outcome of the working of markets. By way of speech, markets put pressure on the companies and they change their behavior. (Sometimes pressure of local governments enhances the working of markets, and/or moral considerations play an additional role. Board members may, for instance, choose a slightly different mission including a different kind of visitor-friendliness in order to reach out to other social groups.) [57 and 75].

To a degree commercial markets in popular art enable the creation and distribution of critical art that matters in society. They do so more than the subsidized markets in the established arts. This applies to bringing or enhancing ongoing social change. All sorts of critical popular art that matters are created, from Punk music to the music of some super stars, like that of Beyoncé. (Aside, art is only truly critical or political if it moves people and mobilizes them. Much supposedly critical art developed in the studious domain of established art does not mobilize people.)

To a degree commercial markets in the popular arts enable underprivileged groups to develop own art and to express themselves artistically.

(95) ON GOVERNMENT FORCES AND INTERVENTIONS IN THE ARTS. *Often, they contribute to the arts remaining exclusive.* In this respect *governments can "do better".*

In the next paragraphs I discuss government intervention in markets. Governments can be central and/or local governments. The same as applies to governments may also apply to certain foundations and donors. For instance, not only local governments but also certain foundations sometimes donate money to art-companies on the condition that one way or another they increase the number of visitors of other ethnic groups or have colored people on the board of directors.

Subsidizing the art of the rich is a waste of money and gives off a bad signal. It is even more a waste because, not only are rich consumers willing to pay high prices but for commercial and social reasons sponsors are willing to spend large amounts of money on the art events of the rich while donors are willing to donate large amounts. [75]/2

Classical music subsidies enabled the sector to not modernize and so fossilize and "dig its own grave". Therefore, by now, the intangible heritage of classical music is endangered. Generous subsidies also contributed to classical music becoming and remaining the most exclusive of the art forms. The same applies to opera and ballet. Subsidies could be reduced and/or drastically changed. The problem remains that thanks to the sector's high prestige sponsors and donors spend and donate much and it is able to continue without much change—be it slimming down.

Subsidies could serve to promote the enlivening of concerts, the development and application of lower-cost production and more free or low-priced concerts. Also, subsidies could serve the (temporary) promotion of classical music on streaming sites and social media. Such subsidies could be (more) conditional and regularly be evaluated to ensure that the aims are achieved. If they are not achieved, the common leniency is unwanted. (As said, art-companies are fanatic about realizing own artistic quality goals and rather spend extra money on them. At present members of government committees are often similarly inclined.)

Traditional media, in particular television, have already started to offer programs with an informal setting including light-hearted discussions with musicians. By now many musicians are more than willing to enliven classical music. It is mainly an elite audience which is able and willing to pay that believes it "owns" classical music and keeps to it for itself. In this respect short-term market forces do not work well. But all in all, it is likely that the important heritage of Western classical music will revive.

If after all permanent subsidization is necessary to maintain a lively heritage of classical music, theater, dance and opera, this can be justified. It is also justified and happens in the case of the material heritage of old visual art, literature and film. Digitalization helps but is insufficient to maintain a live heritage.

The same as in the case of other immaterial heritage, volunteers and amateurs can and will play an important role. *It is predictable that in the near future, the majority of performances by large orchestras with live and not virtual players will be provided by talented amateur orchestras.* It already happens, but there could be more respect for the orchestras and more prestige in participating as amateur musician and as listener. The market will do its work, but (temporary) subsidies can help.

In all performing arts subsidies can promote the development and use of lower-cost production techniques—from amplification to the use of virtual players in music. *In music temporary subsidies can be offered to much promote and consequently more often perform attractive existing repertoire for small ensembles and the development of new repertoire for small ensembles*—with or without virtual players.

In case of some of these options, altogether earmarked subsidies usually do not work well. But evaluations can be better than they are now.

Over the last decades government demands of local governments have contributed to the arts becoming more user-oriented and less exclusive.

Governments can help underprivileged groups to have artistic "voice". They have the means to offer means, that is, resources, to underprivileged groups to develop and distribute own art. They can, among others, provide resources enabling them to organize and provide own art education. Voice can also be enhanced by more respect for the own art of "others"; for instance, by competitions and honorable prizes organized by local and central governments. To a degree, this already happens in the media, but the prestige and weight of governments can make a difference.

(96) ON FREE AND CHEAP ART. *There could be far more free and cheap art. Far more live art can be provided for free, or offered for low prices.* Governments can start to buy performances and offer them for free, or do this more often. (In various ways congestion problems can be prevented.) Or, with earmarked subsidies and advanced selection techniques—preventing (much) fraud—free or low-priced tickets for visits to museums and performances can be offered to low income groups—and not just in inferior seating areas, or last minute tickets.

So far pay as you want schemes given low-income groups access to live art in art-buildings do not work well. People have to become acquainted with them and realize the overall benefits. Governments could promote them by organizing and temporarily paying for campaigns to promote the schemes.

Increasingly nonprofit art venues now offer reproduced art for free on the internet. Cost of doing so is low. Promotion of the own institution always matters, but sometimes it is also a matter of principle, as in the case of museums of old art, which now not only show their works but also make them downloadable, allowing high-quality prints. In campaigns, possibly enabled by (temporary) earmarked subsidies, printing can be stimulated as well as the purchase of ready-made and framed reproductions from the museums. Temporary subsidized campaigns can stimulate the use of these new possibilities. Prices of reproductions are not very high, and could be lowered by means of earmarked subsidies, enabling more people to have almost-live art on their walls. Again, new unusual but potentially attractive practices do not take off without initial promotion. Temporary subsidies for campaigns can help. Forgetting about the (ever lower) cost of printing, the art is free and semi-live.

As already mentioned above: *If the goal is to support underprivileged groups in order to let them have more artistic "voice", governments can help.*

Critical art can be created and distributed in the government subsidized studious domain in established art production. Especially in the new user-oriented domain, sponsors and donors restrain production. In the studious domain, there is more freedom. However, given the economic position of consumers and their relatively small number, critical art is less mobilizing and therefore matters less than the critical art produced in the commercial popular art domain. It may be noticed by people with much power in society, but they are also the ones who have the most to lose. They do not move easily. However, critical and political installations in public space can make a difference.

In enabling art to be free, governments contribute to the commons. *Many artists offer free art and so contribute to art in the commons.* Part of the mentioned critical art and of socially expressive own art of underprivileged groups is free and developed without market or government support. It belongs to the "commons". In this context I ignore the huge amount of free art on the internet. There is no need to stimulate it. (Governments, however, now increasingly regulate the internet and make it easier for copyright holders to forbid use of existing works and sue offenders.—This is what can be expected in capitalism.—It brings benefits to copyright owning artists and/or their representatives, but it reduces overall art consumption and hinders artistic innovation.)

(97) FINALLY.

The established arts become less exclusive—be it not as much as some would like. In the performing arts, it is foremost somewhat lower middle-class people—usually social and cultural risers—who join the "family of art" or rather the "family of cultured people". (This is a case of limited vertical dissemination of established art.)

A less important symbolic and social boundary between serious or established art and popular art contributes to less exclusivity of established art. Some popular art becomes established, some established art popular. Now some works and artists move freely between the two domains, and certainly many consumers have become omnivores.

For artists there is now more room to move. They can be relatively autonomous beyond and between market, government and the art-world. Weakened art-worlds are artistically less demanding—be it least so in the studious domain. Now it is easier for all artists and small groups of artists to "self-organize" artistic activities in small circles. In the many different and interdependent large as well as small networks, self-organization is easier. Artists are not independent or autonomous, but by negotiating in entrepreneurial ways, they can have considerable freedom. (Being entrepreneurial can sometimes bring freedom, also in neo-liberal societies. This does however not apply to the many people from whom entrepreneurship is demanded even though they have no possibility to be entrepreneurial.)

Entrepreneurial artists more often have a hybrid art practice. Such hybrid artists start to regard work in collaboration with non-art creatives in employment situations not as a second job but as proper art work.

Artists become more active in demanding proper remuneration. The same as non-artist groups, whose economic position earlier was not precarious, groups of artists who depend on non- and for-profit art-companies have started to protest against inner-art-world exploitation and increasingly with success.[1] This does not imply that there are no poor and struggling artists anymore. For the decades to come, the social economy of art will remain such that many youngsters want to become artists and many artists will continue to be willing to work for very low incomes.

It would be good if art that is not-applied keeps a "pedestal" that makes it to stand out. I conclude with this moral statement which is a personal note or rather wish. Art does not have to be grand, but it would be a pity if it were to altogether dissolve and disappear among all sorts of creative activity. Symbolic pedestals can be anywhere: in art-buildings, in community centers, on the internet, in the streets and in people's homes. But in spite of all the relativism in this book, this is my wish.

Given fast technological developments, foremost involving the internet, the opening sentence of the preface of the book certainly applies: "These are exiting times in the arts. the arts are in turmoil." Now more than ever before, the future of art is impossible to predict. Nevertheless, for the time being and paraphrasing Joni Mitchell's *Both Sides*, taking a view of the entire book, my personal opinion is *Something's Lost and More's Gained.*

Note

[1]On inner-art-world exploitation see (Abbing, 2014a) or the somewhat more academic text (Abbing, 2014b).

Literature

Abbing, H. (2014a). *Inner Art World Exploitation of Artists*. Presented at the Yearly Conference of Seoul Foundation for Arts and Culture, Seoul. Retrieved from https://www.academia.edu/9793278/Inner_Art_World_Exploitation_of_Artists

Abbing, H. (2014b). Notes on the Exploitation of Artists. In *Joy Forever: The Political Economy of Social Creativity*. MayFlyBooks (also available as pdf).

Index[1]

[1] Note: Page numbers followed by 'n' refer to notes.

H. Abbing, *The Changing Social Economy of Art*,
https://doi.org/10.1007/978-3-030-21668-9

www.ingramcontent.com/pod-product-compliance
Lightning Source LLC
Chambersburg PA
CBHW050524240926
51846CB00003B/679
* 9 7 8 3 0 3 0 2 1 6 6 7 2 *